The T&T Clark History of Monasticism

The T&T Clark History of Monasticism

The Eastern Tradition

John Binns

LONDON • NEW YORK • OXFORD • NEW DELHI • SYDNEY

T&T CLARK
Bloomsbury Publishing Plc
50 Bedford Square, London, WC1B 3DP, UK
1385 Broadway, New York, NY 10018, USA

BLOOMSBURY, T&T CLARK and the T&T Clark logo are
trademarks of Bloomsbury Publishing Plc

First published in Great Britain in 2020
Paperback edition first published 2021

Copyright © John Binns, 2020

John Binns his asserted her right under the Copyright,
Designs and Patents Act, 1988, to be identified as Author of this work.

Cover design: Terry Woodley
Cover image: Hadâmbu Monastery, Church of the Nativity of Mary.
Ralucahphotography.ro/Getty

All rights reserved. No part of this publication may be reproduced or
transmitted in any form or by any means, electronic or mechanical,
including photocopying, recording, or any information storage or retrieval
system, without prior permission in writing from the publishers.

Bloomsbury Publishing Plc does not have any control over, or responsibility for,
any third-party websites referred to or in this book. All internet addresses given
in this book were correct at the time of going to press. The author and publisher
regret any inconvenience caused if addresses have changed or sites have
ceased to exist, but can accept no responsibility for any such changes.

A catalogue record for this book is available from the British Library.

A catalog record for this book is available from the Library of Congress.

ISBN: HB: 978-1-7883-1761-0
PB: 978-0-5676-9936-7
ePDF: 978-1-7867-3593-5
eBook: 978-1-7867-2593-6

Typeset by Integra Software Services Pvt. Ltd.

To find out more about our authors and books visit
www.bloomsbury.com and sign up for our newsletters.

*Christ is risen from the dead, trampling down death by death
And to those in the tomb he has given life*

remembering

Michael Elliott Binns (1923–2003)

Archpriest John Lee (1938–2014)

Stephen Barton (1950–2016)

Contents

List of Illustrations	ix
Foreword	xi
Introduction	1

Part One Monasticism before Monasticism: Up to 320

1	From Asceticism to Monasticism	11

Part Two The Formation of the Tradition: The Period of the Ecumenical Councils

2	Solitude, Community and the Church: Beginnings in Egypt	33
3	Asceticism and Society: The Holy Men of Syria	57
4	An Experiment in Community Living: The Cities of Asia Minor	69
5	The Holy City of Jerusalem and Its Desert	79
6	The City of Constantinople: Where All Roads Meet	95

Part Three The Forms of Monastic Tradition: After Iconoclasm

7	Going West: Two Benedicts	107
8	East to Asia and South to Africa: The Syriac Tradition	111
9	City and Mountains: The Byzantine Tradition	131
10	Missionaries and Kings: The Balkans	149
11	Monasteries in the North: Russia	157

Part Four The Meaning and Purpose of Monastic Life

12	Hesychasm from Origen to Gregory Palamas	175

Part Five Resistances and Renewals: After 1453

13	Part One: Varieties of Tribulation: Under Islamic Government	197
14	Part One: Revival and Renewal in the Eighteenth and Nineteenth Centuries	203

13	Part Two: Varieties of Tribulation: Genocide and Atheism	213
14	Part Two: Revival and Renewal in the Twentieth Century	223

Conclusion　235

Bibliography　237
Index　245

Illustrations

Maps

1　The Byzantine Empire and surrounding area, showing the location of monasteries　6
2　Russia and Eastern Europe, showing the location of monasteries founded after the end of the Byzantine Empire　7

Figures

1　A Monk of the great schema, wearing the analav, the vestment marked with the instruments of the passion　3
2　Anthony of Egypt is recognized as the first monk. He lived as a hermit in the desert moving to ever more inhospitable places　34
3　The monastery of St Anthony was founded at the foot of the mountain where he lived in a cave　35
4　Pachomius, a younger contemporary of Anthony, was a founder of coenobitic monastic life　43
5　The place of the column of St Symeon Stylites, at the centre of the ruined church at Qal'at Sima'an near Aleppo in Syria　64
6　The monastery of the Great Lavra, or Mar Saba is in the valley of Siloam near Jerusalem. The monks lived in caves and huts along the ravine, where the laurite form of life developed　87
7　The extensive ruins of the church of the Stoudios monastery in Constantinople show the size of this important community　100
8　Deir al-Zafaran, the Saffron Monastery, in the Tur Abdin, was the seat of Syrian Orthodox patriarchs of Antioch from 1293 to 1924　118
9　Monasteries in Ethiopia were often in inaccessible places. At Debre Damo access is only possible when pulled up a sheer rock face by a rope　124
10　Abuna Aregawi, also known as Za-Mikael, was the founder of Debre Damo monastery. He ascended the rock face with the help of a long serpent　125
11　The mountainous peninsula of Athos has been a home for monks for more than a thousand years　142

12	The Great Lavra was the founding monastery on Mount Athos	143
13	The hermitages at Karoulia cling to the precipitous cliff face of Mount Athos	145
14	The monastery of Žiča was founded by St Sava of the royal house of Serbia	154
15	In Russia the monastery of St Sergius to the north east of Moscow has remained a centre of church life. The relics of the saint attract many pilgrims	164
16	The blessing of the troops of Dmitri Donskoi as they set out to battle against the Tartars by St Sergius contributed to his recognition as patron saint of Russia	164
17	Seraphim of Sarov prayed for a thousand days on a rock in the forest	209
18	Mother Maria Skobtsova cared for the poor in Paris and ended her life in Ravensbruck concentration camp	221
19	St Panteleimon monastery was a community of over 1,900 monks by the end of the nineteenth century, when there were slightly more Russian than Greek monks on Mount Athos	224

Foreword

It was just over two years ago when I first learned that John was setting out to write this book about the monastic tradition of the Christian East. Two clear thoughts came to mind then. One, that he was perfectly placed to do so; the other, that when completed, John's book will be a labour of love in the best scholarly tradition one tends to associate with most things coming from Cambridge. So, having eagerly expected a complete manuscript since, I was delighted to see that the book delivers on both accounts.

As an Anglican minister and theologian (and therefore not formally carrying an 'Eastern Orthodox' tag), John may seem, at first blush, a surprise choice for penning a book on this topic. Work of this facture demands the kind of 'insider knowledge' that one tends to associate with ecclesial or denominational affiliation. And yet, *Revd Dr John Binns* is uniquely placed to write this book. His 'insider knowledge' of the Orthodox context runs deep.

For most people, I imagine, the author of this book is either *Revd Binns*, or *Dr Binns*, or a combination of the two, or simply *John*. Fewer people will know that for everyone at the Institute for Orthodox Christian Studies in Cambridge (IOCS), where he is currently a Visiting Professor, he has only ever been known as *Father John*. This typically Orthodox appellation, normally reserved for Orthodox ordained clergy, in John's case affectionately goes back decades. It may have something to do with the fact that Father John was one of the founding figures of the Institute, forever planting an ecumenical streak in the DNA of IOCS. However, to think that John's connection with the origins of IOCS is responsible for this paternal designation would be to conceive of some misplaced indebtedness when that is not the case. There have been other non-Orthodox figures involved in that episode, but the appellative *Father* has only ever been used, to my knowledge, in relation to John. Neither has this anything to do with some kind of 'one-sided Orthodox assimilation'. What it has everything to do with is something more profound, i.e. the orthodox mindset that people recognized in the spirit of *Revd* John Binns. I too have recognized that, and it is something which Father John has continually kept alive through his ministry and research of over 25 years, of both Eastern Orthodoxy and Ethiopian Orthodox Christianity. So, his 'insider knowledge' runs deep indeed.

It is always to the benefit of the reader, whether reading for pleasure or research (ideally both), if the author loved writing their book. In several of my conversations with Father John over these past two years, he would often mention the daunting nature of the task before him, given the breadth and scope of the subject. But he would always express a sense of fascination and joy as he would share bits of the progress he was making. I believe that this positive tension, together with the fine line between attention to detail and broad perspective which Father John has trodden in the writing of this book, and the sheer love for the topic transpire clearly from its pages.

Taking the approach of the 'professional stranger' – to use a term one typically finds in ethnography – Father John has succeeded something that is quite rare: to write with the heart of a 'practitioner' and the mind of an 'explorer'. It will come as no surprise if, before long, this book will become both a landmark title in the field and set a benchmark for years to come.

Fr. Dragos Herescu, Principal of the Institute for
Orthodox Christian Studies, Cambridge

Introduction

The first monk who we meet in the long history of monasticism is an Egyptian called Isaac. His presence is gratefully recorded by Aurelius Isidorius who was travelling along a road near a village called Karanis in Egypt on 6 June 324. Aurelius was attacked by a band of robbers and feared for his life. Fortunately for him, just at that moment two passers-by intervened and drove off the robbers. They were two Christians, a deacon called Antoninus and a monk called Isaac.[1] His identification as a monk is the first time that this way of life has been recognized. It is likely that, since Isaac was in the company of a deacon, whose name is mentioned first in the account, the two were members together of a local church. In that case, Isaac the monk was an ascetic who lived in the village and had a recognized position in the Christian community.

He is called a monk. The word 'monk' is a translation of the Greek *monachos*, which is derived from *monos*, meaning alone or single. The word 'monachos' was used in various ways in the language of the time. For example, the first copy of a set of several copies of a legal document could be called the monachos. Or a garment made out of a single rather than double piece of cloth could be a monachos. It is possible that people like Isaac wore a plain unlined robe and were called monachos by local people because of the simplicity of their clothing.

From New Testament times, both women and men often resolved to follow ascetic disciplines. They lived either alone or in small groups. This record of the roadside event in Egypt is the first time, that we know of, when they were called monks. Before then they had gone by several names. In Syria they were sometimes called *ihidaya*, which also means solitary; in Asia Minor they were often compared to philosophers or athletes; sometimes they were called *apotaktikoi* or renouncers. By the time when Isaac was travelling along the road they were recognized as forming a distinct and recognizable *tagma* or order, with a place within the church.

Soon after this, Athanasius, the archbishop of Alexandria, wrote the life of another ascetic, Antony. The *Life* was written after Antony's death in 356 but recollected events which had taken place earlier. Around 304, Antony had emerged from a long period of seclusion in a deserted fort and began to welcome followers. Athanasius tells us that Antony 'persuaded many to take up the solitary life. So from then on there were many monasteries in the mountains and the desert was made into a city by the monks.'[2]

After that the word monk was used more often. The monks who followed Antony withdrew from the world and separated themselves from it. They went to live in the desert rather than in the city. The places where they live started to be called monasteries. This development is shown in another early use of the word monk. About the same time when Antony was attracting followers, a former solider, Pachomius, attracted a group of disciples at Tabennisi after a divine voice had commanded him to 'stay here and build a monastery for many will come to you to become monks.'[3] Pachomius formed these followers into a disciplined community with a shared style of life in which they encouraged each other in their ascetic struggle. So here we find that a word which suggests someone who is alone or *monos* now starts to refer to those who have chosen to live together. This is a further implication of the word, when monachos can mean single not in the sense of living alone, but single in the sense of being single-minded or undivided in the dedication to a goal.

These three early examples show that monks could live out their chosen vocation in different ways. Jerome, who spent the last thirty years of a long life living as a monk in cave at Bethlehem – in the same cave in which, by tradition, Jesus was born – wrote in a letter that there are three kinds of monks. His three kinds of monks correspond to the three kinds of life referred to in these texts. Some monks, he says, live alone following a solitary life. Some live in communal monasteries, which were known as *coenobia*, or the common life, to show their intention to live in harmony together. Then there are others who live in small household groups. He does not approve of this third kind, people like Isaac who rescued our unfortunate traveller, and calls them Remnuoth. He thinks they are quarrelsome, profiteering and overdressed.[4] Another list of kinds of monks is given in the later *Rule of Benedict*, written for monks in Italy. As well as the hermits and coenobites, Benedict says there are Sarabaites, who live in small houses and do as they like, and *gyrovagi* who are unsettled and move from place to place.[5] He objects to both because they do not follow any rule of life. This censure is taken from his Rule, where he sets out a disciplined way of life which he expects his monks to follow. Those who are not subject to some kind of rule are censured.

The critical comments of both Jerome and Benedict are written in response to a movement which could already be described by the title of monasticism but was still varied and unregulated. Monks were free to live in different ways according to their choice. Many of the holy men and women whose lives will be described in this book could be classified as Sarabaites or, in Jerome's terminology, Remnuoth and as *gyrovagi*. Across most of the Christian world, monasteries devised their own typika or foundation charters and hermits chose their own demanding and individual disciplines.

This freedom has continued. Monastic life is an expression of the Christian life which grew out of the New Testament teachings of Christ and the apostles. It is a way of life which is inspired and guided by the Spirit of God, as the monks experienced and shared in a life of discipleship. Freedom and individuality as well as obedience and discipline were the marks of monastic life.

Today, as in past ages, a woman or man who seeks to enter this way of life first joins a community, in a monastery. She or he approaches the superior of the monastery. After a while as a guest, they are admitted as a novice and start to live in the community. They will then progress through the degrees in the monastic state, and the various parts of the monastic habit are given to mark each stage. After the superior is satisfied of the sincerity of the intention of the novice, they are given the title of rasophore, or one who bears the *riassa* or cassock. The next stage is to be admitted to the degree of *stavrophore* or bearer of the cross, which is marked by the wearing of the *paramandas* or *parama*, a cloth worn on the back symbolizing the cross which the monk now bears. Then finally the monk might become a schema-monk and wear the great schema. This is an honour granted to experienced and wise monks and is marked by the giving of the *analavos* or, in the Slavonic use, *analav*, a cloth worn over the breast and marked with signs of the passion. There are some variations in this progression in different areas. In Egypt, for example, the degrees of rasophore and stavrophore are combined. Furthermore, a monastery may legislate for its own character and interpretation of the monastic life.

The life and witness of the monk cannot be confined within the walls of the monastic building. Monasticism is an integral part of the life of the whole church. Monks provide practical service and spiritual leadership. At ordination, a priest who is unmarried becomes and remains a monk. All bishops are monks. The monastic priest or bishop is a member of a monastic community but may live outside the monastic buildings.

Figure 1 A Monk of the great schema, wearing the analav, the vestment marked with the instruments of the passion.

The history of monasticism can be approached from various standpoints. It could be the history of the development of an institution, identifying the influential monasteries and seeing how they grew and changed. Or, since monks were active in all aspects of church life as bishops, theologians and statesmen, it could be the history of the church showing how monks were influential in shaping and guiding the life of the church. Or, since monasticism is made by the monks who lived it, it could be the biographies – or hagiographies – of holy men and women. Or, since monks are all motivated by the search for God, it could be a theology and anthropology showing the growth of a tradition of spirituality. This study will try to bring together these various themes.

A Western reader is accustomed to think of a monk as a member of a religious order, such as Benedictine, Franciscan, Dominican or Jesuit. These have become familiar names but are a Western development and not found in Eastern Christian monastic life. In the course of this study, we will briefly consider the growth of Western monastic orders as a local development of a wider tradition.

The distribution of monasteries across the Christian world is shown on the maps below, which indicates how and where monastic life spread. In Egypt, Antony set off away from the Nile Valley and finally settled on his mountain about 30 kms from the Red Sea coast. Meanwhile, a more individualistic lifestyle developed in the Nile Delta region near Alexandria while a coenobitic style was set up in the south in Upper Egypt. The cluster of places marked around Constantinople shows the central importance of the imperial capital in the subsequent development of monastic life. There is another cluster of monasteries in the high lands where Syrian culture developed around Edessa, Nisibis, and further east around Seleucia. The city of Jerusalem is not only the place where the church began but is also found at the geographical centre of this Eastern Christian world. The map also shows a few places way to the east as far as China and south into Ethiopia in Africa. These distant monastic centres show the restless longing of the monks to move and settle in ever more inhospitable and distant places, and they found these deserts by travelling across political frontiers as well as exploring islands and mountains nearer to home. Later, monastic life moved north, into the Balkans and Russia, where monks found places suited to ascetical struggle in the Arctic north. The monastic map gives a rough idea of the regional distribution and spread of monastic life, and so of the subject matter of this book.

The monastic tradition has progressed through successive stages, always giving life and leadership to the church. The story is told here within a roughly historical framework but with additions to show later developments of the local traditions. In arranging this material, I've noted a rough chronological framework based on events in the history of Byzantium, with accompanying notes to relate this history to that of other parts of the church. Events from the lives of monks and holy men and women are included throughout since monasticism is nothing else than the lives of those who live it.

It begins in the New Testament. Ascetic disciplines were essential to Christian living and took some definite forms. This is the beginning of monastic life, although the title was not yet used, and is the subject of Part One.

Then monastic life gains a recognizable shape in the period after Christianity became the recognized faith of the Roman and then Byzantine Empire. This was a result of the toleration of the church enacted by the Emperor Constantine. Monastic life took different forms in different areas but there was also a shared set of principles and disciplines which enable us to speak of one monastic tradition. The dating of this period varies between different regions but it more or less corresponds to the period when the Ecumenical Councils of the Church defined Orthodox faith, from the first Council of Nicaea in 325 to the second Council of Nicaea in 787. This is the subject of Part Two.

Then the church divided and with it the monastic traditions. Part Three discusses the different trajectories of monastic life in the West, in the Syriac Churches of the Orient and in the Greek-speaking churches of the Byzantine Empire which then was continued in the Slavonic Churches of Eastern Europe and Russia.

Part Four traces the theology of monastic life, taught by monks, shared between communities and affirmed by councils of the church. This is hesychasm, from the Greek *hesychia* or silence. Hesychasm defines the inner life of the monk and so can be seen as the inner reality of monastic tradition.

Then there is the next stage of the history of monasticism when the church found itself living under hostile regimes. For some, this stage began in the seventh century with the arrival of Arab armies. For some the change happened when the Ottoman Turks entered Constantinople. There were some devastating periods of persecution which can only be described as genocidal which destroyed monastic as well as ecclesiastical life.

Alongside this, there was the continuing life which is passed to new generations by the monks who are faithful to what has gone before. The chapters discussing this period are divided into sections to show the varied experiences of different areas and periods.

There are two warnings. The first is that this study does not attempt to be comprehensive. The eastern monastic tradition is far too widespread and divergent to allow this. There are many gaps, but I hope that the selection of events, anecdotes and personalities will give a sense of this tradition.

The second warning is about names. The monastic tradition is drawn from different cultures and languages. Names appear differently in each. I do not try to be consistent, but instead use whatever form of the name seems most familiar in current writing. So, for example, we will meet Sergius of Radonezh but Sergei Bulgakov, Athanasius the Patriarch of Alexandria but St Athanasios of Mount Athos, Macarius the Desert Father but Makarios of Corinth, since the Greek form is used in the standard English version of the Philokalia. I hope this will make for clarity although not consistency.

This book comes after many years of study and reflection which has been guided by many teachers, colleagues and friends in several Orthodox Churches. Some I am still in regular contact with and others have now died but still live vividly within my memory and affection. I am grateful to those institutions where I have visited, studied and been invited to teach. I am especially grateful to staff and students at the Orthodox Theological Faculty in Belgrade who introduced me to the monasteries of Serbia, among them the monastery of Kaona in Šabac-Valjevo diocese; St George's College Jerusalem where I was visiting professor over an Easter when east and west celebrated the Resurrection on the same day; St Tikhon's Humanities University in Moscow, where

I have visited on visits to Moscow; Sellassie Theological College in Addis Ababa, where I have stayed and visited. In the UK, I have valued my membership of the Fellowship of St Alban and St Sergius and also the support of colleagues at Great St Mary's the University Church. I am especially grateful to the Institute for Orthodox Theological Studies in Cambridge, which has been a source of support and encouragement as I have worked on this project. It was Alex Wright, then editor at I B Tauris, who suggested that I write this book. It has then been guided to publication with meticulous care and attention by Anna Turton, Sarah Blake and the staff at T and T Clark, Bloomsbury. But, as always, my deepest gratitude is to my wife Sue, who has supported me through the long process of writing with patience and generosity, and to my family, William, Sally, Thomas and Joshua.

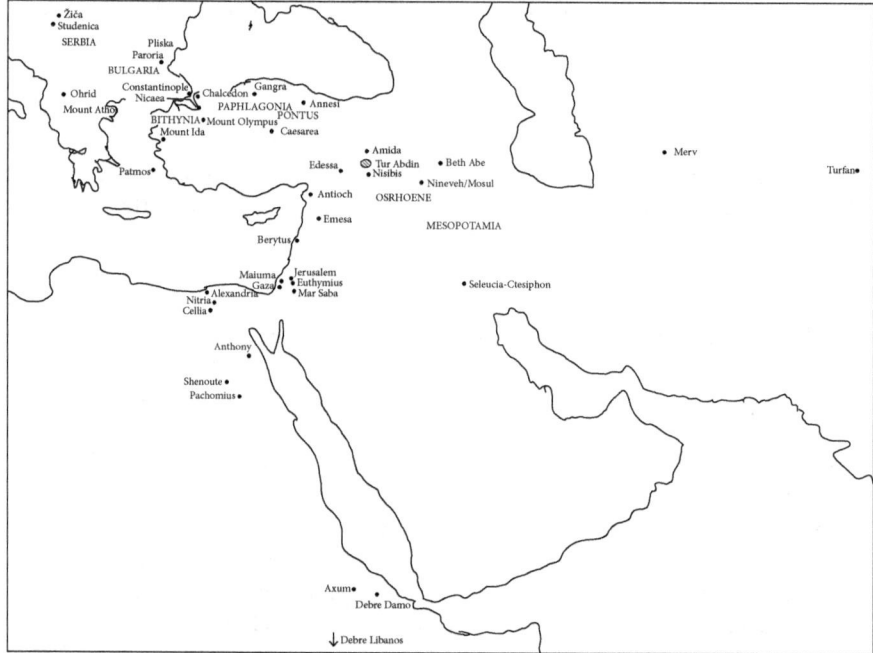

Map 1 The Byzantine Empire and surrounding area, showing the location of monasteries.

Map 2 Russia and Eastern Europe, showing the location of monasteries founded after the end of the Byzantine Empire.

Notes

1. This event is recounted in E. A. Judge, 'The Earliest Use of the Word "Monachos" for Monk (P. Coll. Youtie 77) and the Origins of Monasticism', *Jahrbuch für Antike und Christentum* 20 (1977), pp. 72–89.
2. *Life of Antony* 14, trans. Robert Gregg, *Athanasius, Life of Antony*, Classics of Western Spirituality (London, 1980), pp. 42–3.
3. *Greek Life of Pachomius* 12, trans. Armand de Veilleux, *Pachomian Koinonia*, vol. 1 (Kalamazoo, MI, 1980), p. 305. The monastery was founded in 320 but the Life in which this event was recorded was written some time after 375.
4. Jerome, *Letter* 22.34, CSEL 54.
5. *Rule of Benedict* 1.

Part One

Monasticism before Monasticism: Up to 320

1

From Asceticism to Monasticism

Introduction

The gospels begin with a proclamation of the kingdom of God. 'From that time on Jesus began to proclaim "repent for the Kingdom of Heaven has come near"'.[1] As the gospels continue we are shown that this kingdom is a new way of being, making radical demands and inviting the hearer to a change of life. This change is called repentance.

The call to repentance has been lived out in many different ways through the history of the church. These often involve some form of turning away from a former life and a renunciation of secular values. This is seen in the way that Jesus lived. He left his home and travelled across the region, with 'nowhere to lay his head'. He had reached the age of thirty without being married, as would have been expected of a young Jewish man. His followers were called and 'left everything and followed him'. When they set out to preach the gospel they travelled light, without food or money or a change of clothes, sleeping wherever they were offered a place to stay. They left their possessions behind them or gave them to others. They held money in common with, as the passion narratives relate, one of them – Judas – given the responsibility of acting as steward. The provision of food was erratic and often they did not know where the next meal was coming from. Sometimes this lack of foresight was rewarded by a miraculous provision of food. All these are familiar themes in the gospels and many further references could be added. They will become familiar themes of monastic discipline.[2] They show that the message and call to discipleship make radical demands for a change in lifestyle which challenges the standards and values of the wider society around.

This is not to claim that monasticism, as it developed in later ages, is a precise imitation of the kind of discipleship practised in New Testament times. There were, after all, no monks among the disciples of Jesus. The gospels are rooted in the daily life of the local community and Jesus enjoyed the company of all sorts and conditions of persons.[3] There were meals, conversations and friendships. The stories and parables are drawn from a wide set of circumstances in daily life. The life and teaching of Jesus are rooted in human society, affirmed the goodness of human living and presented by illustrations and images familiar to the audience, often told with imagination and humour. The message has been lived out with an infinitely wide and varied set of responses. No one form of Christian living can claim to be authentic discipleship to the exclusion of others.

Although there was variety within New Testament lifestyles, an ascetic life had a place from the beginning. An approach to faith which has come to be known as ascetic was rooted in the teaching of the gospels. It is an approach also found in other religious traditions of the time and was developed in the early centuries of the history of the church. It belongs within the tradition of faith and was to give to later monasticism some of its ideals and methods. Among this asceticism, there were several forms of discipline which are found in the New Testament and became a regular part of Christian living from where they passed into monastic living. These are, first, the need and longing to withdraw in order to find a deeper experience of God; leading to the formation of communities of people who often resolved to live a celibate life; then the practice of fasting as well as prayer in providing a structure for a shared life style. We will trace the thinking about these in the society of the time; the teaching and practice of the Bible; the development through the early centuries of the history of the church; then the shaping of monasticism. This development demonstrates how monasticism grows out of earlier disciplines and belongs within the ascetic style of Christian discipleship.

First ascetic theme: Withdrawal

Jesus began his public ministry with a forty-day period of withdrawal into the desert. The silence and solitude which is experienced in the desert continued to punctuate Jesus's public engagement. He retreated to the tops of mountains in the early mornings, sought out places of quiet and then, before the crucifixion, he went into a garden to pray.

Deserts and wilderness have a seminal role in the discovery and formation of faith. For Jews, the forty-year wandering through the Sinai desert was the experience which began the covenant relationship of the children of Israel with their God, with the giving of the Ten Commandments to Moses seen as a foundational moment. Some centuries earlier a young Indian prince called Gautama retired to the forests of north India when he was thirty-five years of age and came to his famous enlightenment while sitting under a bodhi tree, which led to the teaching of Buddhism. The prophet Muhammad used to spend periods of prayer in a cave in the mountains where he received his revelations from the angel Gabriel. Each of these deserts was different in character but each provided that physical space where God was found and faith took shape.

In the Palestine of Jesus, the desert was very near, just over the hill. A parable of the New Testament describes a traveller who journeyed from Jerusalem to Jericho was set upon by robbers and helped by a passing Samaritan. He would have left the city and then travelled through a varied landscape in the course of the fifteen-mile stretch of road to Jericho which drew him progressively deeper into desert. He would have passed through distinct and different environments. Once our traveller has left the city and passed over the ridge of the Mount of Olives, he finds himself in a Southern European style *terra rossa* geological landscape, where the red soil is suited to olive and grape cultivation. Then as he descends down the declining gradient to the depression of the Dead Sea, the landscape changes and becomes the pastoral steppe land of Asia, an Irano-Turanian soil type, which supports some vegetation but is more suited to the pastoral life of sheep and goat herding. Then about half way along the road, there is another change and he enters an African desert with a Saharan type of soil. Finally, along the shores of the Red Sea the geological landscape resembles that of the Sudan.[4]

This was the land where John the Baptist and many others retreated and where they made their home. It later enabled the monks of the Judaean desert to develop the practice of leaving their monastery to spend Lent in a more barren and arid part of the desert.[5] The inhabitants of Palestine lived alongside both city and desert, and this ever-present tension shaped the way they approached and understood faith. It was the place where faith was formed and where God was encountered. The attraction of the desert led to the formation of communities of those who were repelled by the materiality of city life and looked for a deeper experience of God and a purer form of faith.

In the Judaism of the Old Testament, this urge for desert living and withdrawal not only was an individual longing for silence but became a form of life followed by communities, who followed special paths of dedication. These practised disciplines of fasting and abstaining from certain foods. In passages of the Old Testament we read of the Nazirites who were consecrated and set apart. The Nazirites vowed to avoid wine and anything made out of grapes and, after a ritual of shaving of the head, not to cut their hair. Samson was a Nazirite, and later the prophet Amos criticizes those who tempt the Nazirites away from their chosen path by offering them wine. This choice of lifestyle set them apart from wider society. It would not necessarily require a physical withdrawal into desert. Another group were the Rechabites, the descendants of Jonadab son of Rechab, who not only avoided wine but chose to settle in desert living in tents rather than houses.[6]

Groups of devout Jews continued to choose to seek a deeper level of purity and dedication in New Testament times. The Roman writer Pliny the Elder (d. 79) described communities of Essenes living near the Dead Sea, 'remarkable among all other tribes in the whole world, as it has no women and has renounced all sexual desire'.[7] The Jewish writers Josephus and Philo of Alexandria also knew about the Essenes, adding further details that they did not use money, ate only bread and water and even then only twice a day. They also shared their property among themselves. Philo said they were 'lovers of the need for little, who turn away from luxury as an illness of body and soul'.[8] There is also evidence for ascetic groups who are described in the Dead Sea Scrolls, a set of documents discovered at Qumran in 1947. These were groups of devout Jews who set up a 'house of perfection and truth in Israel', 'seeking God with a whole heart and soul, and no longer following a sinful heart'. Some members remained celibate, forming a camp of 'perfect holiness'. Excavations in the cemetery at Qumran provide further evidence of these, with the discovery of the bodies of over a thousand men but only eleven women and children. It seems that celibacy was valued and respected, with many male members of the community electing to live celibate lives.[9]

These are communities within communities that showed a longing to draw closer to God and a determination to live a more holy and perfect life. The evidence is fragmentary and the passages have provoked debate. It is unclear whether the Essenes which Pliny, Josephus and Philo were familiar with are the same community as the 'Community of Righteousness' described in the documents found at Qumran.

However, these references make clear that withdrawal into the desert was a way of following the path of perfection sought by many of these ascetic groups.

The life of withdrawal attracted Jews of the diaspora too. In his work *De Vita Contemplativa*, Philo of Alexandria describes the community of Therapeutae, which can be translated as 'worshippers' or alternatively 'those being healed'.[10] These, he says, are numerous and widely scattered, especially in an area just to the south of Alexandria near Lake Mareotis. The Therapeutae long for an immortal and blessed existence and so have left their possessions to various other family members and have fled 'taking up their abode outside of walls and gardens, seeking for a desert place'. They live in small houses carefully placed so as to be neither too near or too far from others. Each house has a shrine or 'monastery' within it, which suggests that prayer was solitary, where they retire to 'perform all the mysteries of a holy life'. These mysteries include prayer in the morning and evening and study of God's law in between. They fast until evening – or, in the case of the most determined, all day – except on the sabbath when there is a common shared meal. In this society there are men and women who live in separate areas and there are no slaves.

The Therapeutae have also been much discussed. Philo describes a way of life and does not say what is the faith of the Therapeutae. Some researchers think that they never actually existed but were described by Philo to give a picture of a community life which existed as an ideal to be admired and emulated. Others have suggested that the Therapeutae were Christians rather than Jews and in that case they could be early experiments in communal Christian living. Or they might be groups of observant Jews, living a similar form of life to the Essenes and others. Philo does not say.

The best way to make sense of Philo's portrait of the ideal community of the Therapeutae – which may or may not have existed as he describes – is to read it alongside another of his ascetic writings, the *Life of Moses*. Philo describes Moses as the philosopher king who excelled in the virtues taught by Greek philosophy. Moses is close to God and has subjected the 'violent affections' of the soul to the governance of reason. These affections are compared to a restive horse, in a reference to a passage in Plato's Phaedrus. Moses controlled his eating, drinking of wine, possession of wealth and sexual impulses through the full range of virtues, excelling in self-control and prudence. He 'never lavished on the stomach anything more than the necessary tribute appointed by nature' and 'ignored the pleasures of the organs below the stomach, except to father legitimate children'. He has amassed neither silver nor gold nor anything else extravagant. His fasts, which he carried out before ascending the mountain to meet with God, purified and prepared him for the encounter. 'He had first to purify his body so that it was attached to no passion, but was pure from everything of mortal nature, from food and drink, and from all relations with women.'[11]

The portrait of Moses as the individual ideal and the Therapeutae as the communal ideal is described in language and understandings drawn from the philosophical traditions shared by the various schools of Greek philosophy. The philosophers belonged within a long tradition which taught the living of a rational and tranquil life. The aims of the philosophers were 'self-control or temperance (the Greek virtue of *sophrosyne*) understood in part as freedom from enslavement to pleasures and as independence from the uncertainties of fortune'.[12]

These examples of Jewish communities show the recognition of the importance of ascetic withdrawal of several authors. There was a widespread longing for holiness and separation among Jews, who had seen the Temple destroyed and were conscious of their insecurity and uncertain about the future of their faith.

Philosophical perfection could be achieved not only by reasoned discussion and contemplation but also by violent and shocking behaviour. This was the method of the Cynic school of philosophy. This school originated in the fifth century BC, with teachers Antisthenes (late fifth century), Diogenes (412–323) and Crates of Thebes (362–285). The word 'Cynic' means dog-like and might have come from the practice of Antisthenes who taught in the Cynosarges, or 'place of the white dog', gymnasium in Athens or from the unpredictability of their lifestyle. One Cynic, Stobaeus, wrote that 'other dogs bite their enemies, but I bite my friends to save them'.[13] The natural life of the dog paradoxically becomes the truly rational and human life because it is free from artificiality of human society. Cynics wanted to live in conformity with nature rather than social convention. They sought out humiliation and discomfort so as to overcome these man-made restrictions on their freedom. 'We have been freed from every evil by Diogenes of Sinope and although we possess nothing we have everything, but you, although you have everything really have nothing, because of your rivalry, jealousy, fear and conceit.'[14] So Cynics ate in places where it was forbidden, masturbated in public, threw their wealth into the sea, slept out in the open without any covering. Diogenes is said to have sat begging before a statue in order to become accustomed to misfortune and failure.

The Cynic philosopher had become a familiar sight, with the cloak which served as both clothing and blanket, his begging sack and a staff. The town of Gadara, which was a day's walk from Nazareth, was recognized as a centre of Cynic philosophy at the time of Christ and so the lifestyle of the Cynic philosopher with his scandalous and riotous behaviour would have been known by people in the Galilee of Jesus's time. This dramatic and startling challenge to society was a part of the background in which the message of Jesus made radical demands and encouraged many to follow an ascetic lifestyle. It will be encountered in later forms of monastic life in those who follow the kenotic way of the fools for Christ.

These ascetics, coming from different places and different backgrounds, all sought out desert of various kinds. Their deserts may have been different but they all had that essential character of being different from the society of the city. The fact of withdrawal and the physical space to which the worshipper withdrew was the experience which formed their faith, and provided the opportunity and occasion for the monastic life. The desert formed the landscape to which the monk went and where monasteries were formed. The monastic deserts had different shapes. In Palestine, it was that varied environment at the meeting point of three continents. In the Egypt, where the fertile valley of the Nile cut through the barren desert, the boundary between cultivated and desert land was sharply drawn. In Syria, the high steppe land of the hills attracted ascetics who found plants to eat and from where they could look down on the inhabited plains below. The mountains of Asia Minor, Greece and the Balkans became home for monks, with a scale of growing harshness of ascetic life corresponding to the ascending levels of the physical mountain. In Russia, the cold forests of the north invited those who sought a solitary way of life.

Sometimes the desert had to be manufactured. If the monastery was in a city or agricultural land then often a wall was built to set the monastery apart from the village or city around. Some monks lived in a city and for them the desert was metaphorical. A monk might choose to separate himself from society by living as an outcast or by behaving in a scandalous way which placed him outside the social life of the city. Some form of desert withdrawal and contrast with the settled life of the city are a recurring theme of monastic life.

The monks loved the desert. For them, it was a place of beauty and wonder. A passage in the Old Testament prophet Hosea says that 'therefore I will now persuade her, and bring her into the wilderness, and speak tenderly to her. From there I will give her vineyards, and make the Vale of Achor a door of hope. There she shall respond as in the days of her youth, as in the time when she came out of Egypt.'[15] Origen wrote that John the Baptist 'left to go into the desert, where the air is purer, the sky is more open, and God is closer'.[16] Athanasius tells us that when Antony came to a mountain where he settled 'he fell in love with the place, for this was the place the one who had spoken to him had designated … he looked on it as his own and stayed in that place.'[17] Later, in Palestine, Euthymius was led to the place where he founded his monastery. 'He fell in love with the spot, because it lies on level ground and is at the same time solitary and airy … he loved the solitude of the place.'[18]

The desert of withdrawal is the homeland of the monk where he suffers temptation and hardship but is also a place of peace and joy, where God is present.

Second ascetic theme: Continence

The communities which retired to the desert, or that chose an ascetic lifestyle, valued continence and celibacy. The decision to live a celibate life encouraged and stimulated the formation of communities where those who had chosen this path met together and supported each other.

The teaching of Jesus as recorded in the gospels suggests alternative approaches to marriage and celibacy. Some of the passages from the gospels uphold a life-long marriage relationship.[19] This teaching is also expressed in the life of the early church where the pastoral epistles portray a church community presided over by respectably monogamously married church leaders.[20] These and other passages teach that divorce is contrary to the laws of God. They uphold the social need for stable relationships and affirm the place of the family as the basis of society. But other passages of the New Testament challenge these social norms and commend the more demanding ascetical lifestyle of abstention from marriage and a celibate lifestyle. This tradition is expressed in Luke's gospel with the teaching that 'those who belong to this age marry and are given in marriage, but those who are considered worthy of a place in that age and in the resurrection from the dead neither marry nor are given in marriage.'[21] This is not just an eschatological description of a future age to come; this way of life can begin now, in this age. 'Not everyone can accept this teaching but only those to whom it is given. For there are those who are eunuchs from birth, and there are those who have been made eunuchs by others, and there are those who have made themselves eunuchs for the sake of the kingdom of heaven.'[22] This mixed message is also present in Paul's epistles. In his letter to the Corinthians, he accepts the value of marriage as part of God's created order, but then he goes on to encourage anybody who can to accept a celibate lifestyle. He summarizes the view of many in the church succinctly. 'He who marries does well, and he who refrains from marriage does better.'[23]

The *Shepherd of Hermas* was written in the mid-second century, probably in Rome. It shows that the early church valued celibacy and also fasting. Sexuality, and the abstention from it, is a recurrent theme in this text. Hermas is a married man, but he is 'continent, who abstains from all evil desires and is filled with simplicity and great innocence'. In his visions, he is given directions on several moral and other matters. He is shown that simplicity and self-restraint are the forces which can renew the church and help it retain its purity. In order to live out the ideal of purity, he decides to live with his wife as though she was his sister. He teaches that if someone is married to an adulterous wife, he should separate from her, but be ready to accept her back if she changes her ways – but from then on to avoid sexual relations with her.[24]

In a colourful section of the visions, he meets a group of young women. They welcome him and when evening comes, he wonders where he will sleep.

> 'Where will I stay?' I said. They said 'you will sleep with us as a brother and not as a husband, because you are our brother and besides we are going to live with you because we love you so much' ... But I was ashamed to remain with them .... The one who seemed most prominent among them began to kiss and embrace me, and when the others saw her embracing me they too began to kiss me and play with me. It was as if I had become young again and I too began to play with them. Some were dancing, some moving rhythmically, some singing. Keeping silence I walked around with them and was very happy with them ... I spent the night with them ... they spread their own linen tunics on the ground and made me lie down in the middle of them, and they did nothing but pray. So I also prayed with them unceasingly and no less than they did.[25]

This last vision may be referring to the practice of *syneisaktism*. This was a common living arrangement which allowed virgins or widows to live with a male priest or ascetic, following a pure and continent lifestyle. It made good sense as it provided support and security for virgins and widows, and domestic care for the widower or priest. It provided a respectable and supportive domestic arrangement for those who had been widowed and had responded to exhortations not to marry again, for younger women who remained as virgins and for men who resolved to abstain from marriage and sexual activity.

Across the world of the early Christians, the avoidance of marriage, the abstaining from sexual activity within marriage and the pressure on widows to remain unmarried resulted in the development of a tradition of celibacy. The pagan writer Galen, writing around 200 AD, observed that Christians showed 'restraint in co-habitation', and there are 'men and also women who refrain from co-habiting all through their lives'.[26]

Susannah Elm, in her study of virgins in the church, has shown that by the early fourth century, which was the time when monasteries were being formed, there was a recognized Christian vocation of virginity. Virgins could be men or women; they declared their commitment to a life of continence by a simple vow taken before the congregation; they were often supported by the church; they were under the protection and guidance of the bishop; and were subject to discipline if they lapsed or offended. This way of life had developed to an extent that the sources refer to virgins as a *tagma* or order. *Tagma* means what has been arranged or ordered and is used in a military context to refer to a brigade or division. From this usage comes its ecclesiastical meaning. There were orders or *tagmata* of clergy and laity. Later a new *tagma* of monks – *tagma ton monazonton* – was added to these. The virgins were protected by the bishop himself who took on the legal right of the father or *patria potestas* and provided both financial support and practical oversight. Within this order of virgins, there was much variety. Virgins of either sex could live alone or in their family, or in communities of brothers or sisters or in a kind of spiritual marriage. This later provided the ascetic virgin with protection and a place in society.[27]

The literature of the early church gives examples of how this practice was lived out. A letter of Basil of Caesarea (330–379) describes the case of Paregorius, an elderly priest somewhere in Cappadocia, who had lived contentedly with a 'little woman' or *gynaiou* in a spiritual marriage. She had no doubt cooked for him and cared for him, and no criticism or suggestion of immorality was directed at them. Now however the chorepiscopus was complaining about their way of life and the case is brought to Basil. He agrees with the chorepiscopus. He instructs Paregorius to find a male servant and arrange for the woman to go to a monastery.[28] Another priest living in a spiritual marriage called Leontius castrated himself so that he could continue living with the woman concerned. This strategy was unsuccessful and he was ejected from the priesthood. His disgrace turned out to be temporary and he was in due course reinstated and rose to become bishop of Antioch.[29] A less edifying story is that of Glycerius, who was ordained deacon by Gregory of Nazianzus. Glycerius made it his responsibility to look after the virgins. He collected a group together and added to their number by coercion, a strategy which included the kidnap of a group of virgins at a local religious festival. He used them to make money, exhibiting them at festivals as a 'chorus of virgins'.[30]

The encouragement of virginity, widowhood and celibacy was considered to be a subversive and counter-cultural movement. Society in the classical world was precarious, a world on the edge, only just maintaining stability. Death threatened, or, as John Chrysostom vividly put it, his was a society 'grazed thin by death'.[31] Average life expectancy was twenty-five years, and only 4 per cent of the male population lived past the age of fifty. In this society, women were inferior beings. Galen wrote that 'the Creator has purposely made one half of the whole human race imperfect and as it were mutilated.'[32] The function of women was to ensure that the population level was sustained and children were produced and nurtured. They had the huge task of maintaining the human race. Peter Brown writes of 'the huge pain that any underdeveloped society places on the bodies of its fertile women'.[33] Both political and religious authorities took their responsibility to support marriage and family life seriously. There were laws and regulations to ensure that women remained in their place in the home. Under the Emperor Constantine, a young couple eloping and leaving the home to get married could be punished by execution. The female servant who cared for the girl would have molten lead poured down her throat for not preventing the misdeed. The church also maintained these standards. Of the eighty-one rulings of the Council of Elvira in Spain, one-quarter were devoted to control of the women of the Christian Church.[34]

In this society, it was regarded as subversive and shocking to encourage and support virgins and widows. For a woman who was required to stay at home and bear children, the prospect of the celibate, virgin life could become a liberation. The growth of communities of virgins gave women a freedom and opportunity. Had this not taken place within Christianity, we can reflect that the alternative was the conventional and conservative social structure familiar in the classical world and continued in modern Islam where women are firmly located in society, with faces covered and behaviour restricted. The celibate life could be seen as liberation rather than enslavement for the women of the ancient world.

The respect given to celibacy resulted in the adoption of double standards. Both monogamous fidelity and virginal continence were taught within the church. The way of virginity and continence was harder and so more highly valued.

Third ascetic theme: Fasting and food

Eating is an essential part of human living. The ascetic discipline of fasting is not so much an abstention from eating, but rather a way of eating, knowingly chosen and with clear aims. Fasting, like desert withdrawal, is an approach to living which was rooted in religious traditions and practised for a variety of reasons. It was accepted that the way to know God is through fasting as a part of prayer.

There are meticulous and detailed guidelines as to how and what to eat which are given in the Old Testament. These make eating into a way to approach God. Leviticus chapter 11 sets out what is and what is not permitted to be eaten. It gives a long and careful list of prohibited foodstuffs which includes rabbit, pig, camel, certain fish and birds, among many other species. These dietary regulations provided an order and a relationship with the environment within which the people lived. It gave them a distinctive place within it and a relationship with other creatures, appointed by God. Mary Douglas showed how this 'holiness was given a physical expression in every encounter with the animal kingdom and at every meal.' She said that following these prescriptions and eating in accordance with these rules are a way of entering into obedience to God and respect for his ordering of the world.[35] These prescriptions defined who the Jews were and their place in the world.

If the dietary laws prescribed what was usual and how people managed their daily diet, then extraordinary events required special measures. A further and more radical abstention helped the disciple towards a closer relationship with God and was a way of managing a personal or national crisis by approaching God in prayer. Fasting was a part of this. This is shown in passages throughout the Old Testament. Fasting had a place in the observation of the day of atonement of the tenth day of the seventh month, along with rest from work. Here the people 'deny themselves' and in the priestly code fasting is part of renunciation.[36] People fasted as part of prayer for God's guidance and for success in battle, as when the Israelites were preparing for battle against enemies.[37] Fasting could be an expression of personal grief and mourning showing the depths of feeling and suffering in the human heart, as when both the inhabitants of the town of Jabesh-Gilead and David and his followers showed their grief at the death of Saul and Jonathan and fasted for seven days. The prophet Jonah preached to the people of Nineveh, who responded with a national fast from food and water, enacted by the royal command. David fasted and prayed after the child which Bathsheba bore to him died, after he had arranged for the death of her husband, Uriah; Ahab fasted after having second thoughts about his murder of Naboth; Nehemiah fasted when he realized how desperate the situation of Jews was at Jerusalem. These are some of the many times when people came before God in times of desperate need with fasting and prayer which went together and opened a way into the presence of God.[38]

Fasting was part of Christian worship from the beginning. As they developed their own disciplines of fasting, they followed practices which were already present within Judaism. For Christians, as for Jews, fasting was part of prayer. It expressed mourning, penitence and humility. It was also a longing for forgiveness, healing or revelation. Christians came to express their difference from Judaism not by whether they fasted but by when and how they fasted. The *Didache*, or *Teaching of the Apostles*, probably written in the late first century, specifies the days on which Christians should fast. 'You must not let your days of fasting be at the same time as the hypocrites. They fast on the second day of the sabbath and on the fifth day of the sabbath (Monday and Thursday) so you should hold your fasts on the fourth day of the sabbath and on the Day of Preparation (Wednesday and Friday).'[39] It is not clear who is meant by 'hypocrites', a word deliberately chosen to echo Matthew 6.16, but the writer is probably thinking of the Jews, rather than another form of Christian sect. The Pharisee in the gospel parable claimed to fast twice a week as part of his practice of worship.[40] This suggests that twice weekly fasting was practised by the Pharisees and so the Didache communities are not only following this practice but also distinguishing themselves by choosing to fast on different days of the week.

Alongside the observance of regular fasting days, the practice of a fast before Easter developed early. The church remembered the words of Jesus in the gospels that his disciples would fast when the bridegroom was taken away from them.[41] They recognized that Lent and Holy Week were the commemoration of the time when Jesus the bridegroom was taken away. Justin Martyr, writing in the second century, says that those preparing for baptism fasted, while the rest of the community also fasted and prayed in their support. It is likely that these baptisms took place on Easter.[42] Later Apocryphal Gospels describe the apostles 'fasting and mourning and weeping day and night until the sabbath (Easter)' and James had sworn that he would not eat bread 'from that hour in which he had drunk the cup of the Lord until he should see him rise from among them that sleep'.[43] These early texts come from different areas and show that the fast in preparation for Easter was widely practised. A critic of the church is reported by the Christian writer Minucius Felix accusing Christians as an unholy conspiracy held together by 'solemn fasts'.[44]

The *Shepherd of Hermas*, as well as commending celibacy, also values fasting. Hermas describes how he prepares for his revelations with fasting. 'As I was fasting and greatly beseeching the Lord, the meaning of these writings was revealed to me' and later 'when I had fasted a great deal and asked the Lord to show me the revelation'. Then in the course of the Revelations the Lady who speaks to Hermas gives a clear statement of the need for fasting. 'Every request requires humility, so fast and you will receive what you ask from the Lord, and so I fasted one day and that very night I saw ... '[45] Later, Hermas is reminded that the point of fasting is to draw close to God and serve those in need.

The passages suggest that there are regulations about what food he can eat on a fast day, and that this is limited to bread and water. 'This is the way you will keep this fast that you are about to do .... After completing what has been written, on the day you fast, taste nothing but bread and water, calculate the price of the food you were going to eat, and give it to a widow or orphan or needy person, and thus you will practice humility.'[46] The connection of fasting with humility and prayer is the origin of the word 'station' which is used in many early texts to refer to fast days, first of all by Tertullian. The word 'station' is derived from the Latin 'statio' or standing and so comes from the standing in prayer before the Lord.[47]

Fasting was not only a method of prayer. In the thinking of classical philosophers, it mattered what kind of food you ate. The nourishing effects of food not only reach the body but also penetrate to the inner person or the soul. Plato, in the Timaeus, says that in order to become perfectly whole a person needed both education and also 'proper nourishment', or *trophe*, a word which includes the physical food which nourishes the body.[48] Later, Galen, the physician, described how both diet and intellectual exercise have beneficial effects on the soul. The mother's milk is especially important, and is thought by Hippocrates to arise out of her blood and to mix with the father's seed to develop intellect and character. Some kinds of food arouse passions, while others can encourage the virtues of the soul. A carefully regulated diet can overcome passions while at the same time promoting and nourishing the virtues.[49] The Neoplatonist philosopher Porphyry(234–c. 305) thought that meat was more material than vegetables and so weighed down the digestion. This made it morally superior to avoid meat since too much weight inhibited clear and deep thinking. While soldiers, craftsmen or athletes may eat meat, the philosopher should eat only vegetables to aid their rational way of life. Vegetarianism had civic advantages too, as it promotes the virtue of justice, since those who are pious and control their appetites will treat their fellows better.[50]

These two approaches to fasting converged as the institution of monasticism developed. The approach to fasting which came from Judaism could be called 'eschatological'. In the monasteries, it was usually a one-day fast, with abstention from all food and drink until the ninth hour of the day. It is the kind of fast practised in many of the Old Testament passages. It is the attitude of a community in this world and yet not of the world, standing or at 'station' before God, looking away from earthly food and drink, with the heart longing for the heavenly banquet. This kind of fasting is 'regarded as a form of festival or solemn celebration' and so is practised as part of, and preceding, the celebration and receiving of holy communion, between the waiting for and being fulfilled by heavenly food. This connection is made clear in the text of the Testament of the Lord. 'The sacrifice (of the eucharist) must be offered on Saturday and Sunday only and on the days of fasting.'[51]

The other strand of tradition is influenced by the Greek philosophical concern to regulate the food taken in by the body. Ascetics noted that Adam's fall had resulted from eating forbidden food and so the regulations over eating restored a freedom which does not depend on indulging in food. A practice of ascetical fasting developed in the monasteries. This is the practice of 'xerophagy', or dry eating, which prescribed what kinds of food could be eaten and when. In fast periods, the consumption of wine, meat and some fruits, and later oil, were prohibited. The church father Tertullian said that these foods stimulated sexual desires, and so should be avoided. He pointed to another advantage of a meagre diet, which was that in a time when persecution was always a possibility, those who fasted would be better prepared for the bread-and-water diet of the prison cell.[52] A further advantage of this kind of fasting was that it was a form of devotion which came naturally to a community which included many poor people for whom food was often in short supply.

As well as these two reasons for fasting, there is a third motivation. Jesus withdrew into the desert and fasted forty days and forty nights and so the ascetic who fasts is identifying himself or herself with Christ. This kind of fasting is shown in the calendar of the Ethiopian Orthodox Church, which along with other Oriental Orthodox Churches, has extensive fasting disciplines. Here the fasting seasons enable the worshipper to live out the events of salvation.

The fasts are as follows:

Every Friday – because that was when Christ died on the cross.
Every Wednesday – because that was when the Jews met Judas and offered to pay him the thirty pieces of silver.
The fast before Easter – because Christ fasted forty days and forty nights, and to this they add the week before Easter because that was when Christ suffered for us, and, with Sundays, that makes a total of fifty-six days.
The fast of the Apostles – because the apostles fasted after receiving the Holy Spirit at Pentecost.
The fast of Mary – which is sixteen days before her falling asleep or Dormition.
The fast of Christmas – another forty days.
The fast of Nineveh – because the people of Nineveh fasted three days after the prophet Jonah preached to them. This three day fast begins three weeks and three days before Lent.

This adds up to a total of around 250 days a year. In Ethiopia, most Christians observe around 180 of these, and usually only monks and the very devout keep all of them. The pattern of fasts follows the events of salvation and so, as the believer shares with others in this, he participates in the actions of salvation. While Christians can identify themselves with Christ by eating – at Holy Communion – in this tradition they can identify with Christ by not eating – through fasting. In Ethiopia, the eucharistic liturgy is celebrated at midday on a fast day, instead of at dawn as on other days. Since food and water are not taken until the liturgy is finished, the midday time of worship ensures that the daily meal is eaten later and the fast until the ninth hour is observed.

The practice of fasting distinguished and identified the early Christian communities. Fasting, especially the practice of xerophagy, became an accepted and essential part of monastic life, and continues to be an identifier of Orthodox groups. Fasting not only mattered as part of a full life of prayer, but it also provided a definition and an identity. Fasting according to the fixed rules shows you to be a member of the Orthodox Church – although different groups produced slightly different versions of what constituted Orthodoxy. Fasting disciplines were especially preserved church within monastic communities, but others were expected to observe them too, even if less rigorously. Fasting imparted a monastic character to the whole church. Peter Brown wrote that 'during certain times of the year, every Christian household was encouraged to become a little monastery.'[53] It is a familiar experience when travelling in Orthodox countries to be asked about your church and one of the first questions is how you fast. Following the same regulation as the questioner establishes your position as a member of the one church community.

Fourth theme: Possessions

There's a fourth theme which has governed the life of the monk and, at least in the Western tradition, become a defining characteristic of monastic life. That is poverty. But while ascetics, whether living alone or in communities, agreed on the need for some sort of withdrawal from society, for a celibate lifestyle and the disciplines of fasting, there was less agreement on how the monk should use possessions. It was clear that wealth and acquisitiveness are harmful for the ascetic. But as the monastic tradition developed monks took different approaches. In a coenobitic monastery, the individual monks handed his possessions to the monastery which could use them to maintain its life or provide care and hospitality. For them, care for the poor was part of the monastic vocation and so a communal ownership of goods was necessary. So some monasteries became wealthy landowners. For the solitary hermit, there was no need to possess. The holy man should be free from all kinds of possession. The Non-Possessing monks of Russia would later argue that almsgiving was not a virtue which the monk should pursue because he should not have anything which he could give as alms. They should own nothing. Then, further, in some communities, monks retained possession of property and wealth, and supported themselves. This practice later became known as idiorrythmia. In the teaching of Christ, true treasure was found in heaven and not on earth. The gospels contain alternative ways to achieve freedom from the need to acquire or own objects.[54] The monks, similarly, agreed on the need to seek only the things of God but were less prescriptive about how this should be lived out.

Asceticism

While the word is not used in the gospels, this lifestyle can be described as ascetic. The word itself only occurs once in the New Testament, where Paul speaks of his struggle, or exercise, to keep a clear conscience. He wrote, 'I struggle (*askeo*) always to have a clear conscience towards God and all people.'⁵⁵ Here, he is speaking of the struggle and determination to follow and to live faithfully. He is describing a deliberate and determined commitment to live in a certain way. Asceticism comes to describe the commitment to live as we decide and choose and to follow our ideals.

The word 'asceticism' suggests the discipline of the gymnasium. Theodoret writes of Julian Saba: 'Many who learnt of this, his consummate philosophy … hastened along to beg to be received into his wrestling school and to live the rest of their lives under him as under some gymnastic master and trainer.'⁵⁶

Asceticism implies more than being just a disciplined struggle. It is a discipline directed towards an end and purpose. It is not a negative withdrawal from society and a denial of the good things of life. Instead it is a positive commitment to a set of ideals and describes the process of shaping life to conform to these. Asceticism is a social and religious process. The ascetic struggle is a determination to live our lives in a specific way so as to pursue our ideals. It is more than a readiness to make sacrifices and accept hardship; it is a choice of a way of life. Those who live an ascetic life are seeking to follow a different and consciously chosen path. In an influential and often quoted article, Richard Valantasis described asceticism. He defines it as

> performances within a dominant social environment intended to inaugurate a new subjectivity, different social relations, and an alternative symbolic universe …. Asceticism does not simply reject other ways of living but rather asceticism rejects precisely in order to embrace another existence, another way of living embodied in a new subjectivity, alternative social relations, and a new imagining of the universe. And this intentionality has power – power to create a new person, power to restructure society, power to revise the understanding of the universe.⁵⁷

It has been suggested that all societies make ascetic demands on their members, which derive from their values and ideals. Even a materialist, capitalist culture such as our own has its own asceticism, directing people to accept prevailing financial and materialistic values, to deny themselves leisure and other forms of relaxation in order to achieve goals set by a success-oriented society, to conform to its requirements and to subordinate personal desires to the demands of the market place. All cultures, suggests another study, need a form of asceticism. As one recent study comments: 'Asceticism is the "cultural" element in culture … the mark of culture is the conviction of the value and necessity of self-denial.'⁵⁸

The ascetic character of monastic life goes beyond the adoption of a set of practices and techniques. It has a wider intention. Commenting on the lifestyle of the early monks, Peter Brown wrote: 'The rhythms of the body and, with the body, its concrete social relations determined the life of the monk, his continued economic dependence on the settled world for food, the hard school of day-to-day collaboration with his fellow ascetics in shared rhythms of labour, and mutual exhortation in the monasteries slowly changed his personality. The material conditions of the monk's life were held capable of altering the consciousness itself.'⁵⁹

From the beginning of the life of the church, these three parts of Christian devotion became rooted in thinking and practice. The ascetic disciplines of withdrawal, fasting and celibacy are the disciplines which have been part of Christian practice from the earliest days of the church. They provided the structure of monasticism, which was a withdrawal from the wider community in order to follow a more radical lifestyle, with a way of eating and living which provided character and identity. The desert became the place where new communities could be experienced and created.

Up to the early fourth century, Christianity was a minority religious movement in Greek and Roman society. This position led them to a new understanding of who they were and how they could live this radical new kind of life within a wider society. The 'church of the second century was a "spiritual republic" that discreetly but radically transforms human relationships … the presence of Christians in society … is that of the soul in the body, a life-giving presence.'[60] The ascetic disciplines helped them to identify and live out this vocation. The life which was later known as monastic was present from the beginnings of the church. It is a culture, by which the believer conforms his life to the demands of the kingdom, and which establishes the kingdom of God in this world.

The disciplines of withdrawal, fasting and celibacy were part of Christian practice from the earliest days of the church. The church has always been monastic. To paraphrase another of Peter Brown's remarks: 'Antony did not start a revolution, he inherited one.'[61]

Notes

1 Matthew 4.17.
2 Among these familiar passages are Matthew 8.20; Luke 5.11, 9.2–3, 9.12–17, 18.22, 18.28; John 13.29.
3 G. R Evans, *The I.B. Tauris History of Monasticism, the Western Tradition* (London, 2016), p. 1. However Sufi authors recognized a monastic character in the life of Jesus, the 'monk of monks', see Philip Jenkins, *The Lost History of Christianity* (New York, 2008), p. 200.
4 This is described in Yizhar Hirschfeld, *The Judean Desert Monasteries of the Byzantine Period* (New Haven, CT, 1992), pp. 6–10.
5 For example, Cyril of Scythopolis, *Life of Sabas* 94.15, trans. Richard Price, *The Lives of the Monks of Palestine* (Kalamazoo, MI, 1991). References are to the edition of E. Schwartz, *Kyrillos von Skythopolis* (Leipzig, 1939).
6 For Nazirites, see Numbers 6.2–21; Judges 13.5; Amos 2.11–12. For Rechabites, see Jeremiah 35.3–11.
7 Pliny, *Natural History* 5.73.
8 Philo, *Hypothetica* 2.11, cited in Richard Finn, *Asceticism in the Graeco-Roman World* (Cambridge, 2009), p. 48.
9 *Community Rule* 1 and 5, in Finn, *Asceticism*, p. 49.
10 The Therapeutae are described in Philo, *On the Contemplative Life* 3.21–34.
11 The 'restive horse' is in Plato's Phaedrus 246 a–b; the extracts from Philo's *Life of Moses* are at 1.6.28; 1.27.154; 2.14.68–9.
12 Finn, *Asceticism*, p. 13.
13 Stobaeus, *Florilegium* 3.13.44.

14 This is cited in Finn, *Asceticism*, p. 19; also Pseudo-Crates, *Letter* 7, in R. Hock and A. Malherbe, *The Cynic Epistles: A Study Edition* (Missoula, MT, 1977), p. 59.
15 Hosea 2.14.
16 Origen, *Homilies on Luke* 11.
17 Athanasius, *Life of Antony* 50, trans. Robert Gregg (London, 1980), p. 68.
18 Cyril of Scythopolis, *Life of Euthymius* 24.1–10.
19 Matthew 5.31–32, 19.3–9.
20 1 Timothy 3.1–13.
21 Luke 20.34–35.
22 Matthew 19.11–12.
23 1 Corinthians 7.38.
24 Shepherd of Hermas, *Vision* 1.2.4; 2.2.3; *Mandate* 4.1.4–8; trans. Robert Joly, *Le Pasteur* (Paris, 1958), pp. 83, 91, 153–5.
25 Shepherd of Hermas, *Similitude* 9.11, p. 315. Also in Carolyn Osiek, *Shepherd of Hermas, A Commentary* (Minneapolis, MN, 1999), pp. 226–7.
26 This passage of Galen is preserved in Arabic in a summary of Plato's Republic, cited in Finn, *Asceticism*, p. 81.
27 Monks are referred to in Canon 24 of the Council of Laodicaea. See Susannah Elm, *Virgins of God, the Making of Asceticism in Late Antiquity* (Oxford, 1994), p. 182. The existence of this group is shown by the regulations made by church councils at Elvira in Spain in 306 which was concerned about virgins who have 'broken their promise and given in to their desire' (Mansi II.8), then at Ancyra in 314 which prohibited men and women virgins living together. There is also discussion in an anonymous text entitled *On Virginity*, and then in Gregory of Nyssa's life of his sister Macrina written in 380–3.
28 Basil, *Letter* 55, to Paregorius in trans. Roy Deferrari, *Saint Basil, The Letters*, vol. I (London, 1926), pp. 347–51. He uses the word 'monastery' to refer to the female community, while a more usual word for a female community is *parthenoon*.
29 Athansasius, *History of the Arians* 28, PG 25.725, cited in Elm, *Virgins of God*, p. 164.
30 Described in Basil, *Letters* 169–71, vol. II, pp. 439–45. In fact this was written by Gregory of Nazianzus.
31 This colourful comment is in John Chrysostom, *On Virginity* 14.1.
32 Galen, *De usu partium* 4.6. See Peter Brown, *The Body and Society* (New York, 1988), p. 10.
33 Ibid., p. 25.
34 Ibid., pp. 204–6.
35 Mary Douglas, *Purity and Danger* (Harmondsworth, 1970), pp. 55, 75, 93.
36 Leviticus 16.29, 16.31; 23.7, see also Finn, *Asceticism*, p. 41, citing J. Muddiman, 'Fast, Fasting', in ed. N. Freedman, *Anchor Bible Dictionary*, vol. II (New York and London, 1992), pp. 773–6.
37 Judges 20.26–28.
38 These examples are at 1 Samuel 31.13; 2 Samuel 1.12; Jonah 3.6–9; 2 Samuel 12.16–21; I Kings 21.27–8; Nehemiah 1.4.
39 *Didache* 8.1, Thomas O'Loughlin, *The Didache* (London, 2010), p. 166.
40 Luke 18.12.
41 Mark 2.19–20; Matthew 9.15; Luke 5.34–35.
42 Justin Martyr, *Apology* 61.2.
43 *Gospel of Peter* 7.27 and *Gospel of the Hebrews* fragment.
44 Cited in Finn, *Asceticism*, p. 61.

45 Shepherd of Hermas, *Visions* 2.1 and 3.1, 3.6–7, in Osiek, *Shepherd of Hermas*, pp. 53, 60.
46 Shepherd of Hermas, *Similitude* 5.3, in Osiek, *Shepherd of Hermas*, p. 173.
47 Tertullian, *On Prayer* 19; *On Fasting* 10.
48 Plato, *Timaeus* 44B–C.
49 The theme of nourishment is explored by John David Penniman in *Raised on Christian Milk* (Yale, CT, 2017).
50 Porphyry expressed these ideas in *Abstinence from Animal Food* written to Castricius Firmus, a friend who had abandoned his vegetarian diet.
51 Alexander Schmemann, *Introduction to Liturgical Theology* (London, 1966), pp. 121–2.
52 Tertullian, *On Fasting* 1.4; 13.3; 15.2.
53 Ibid., p. 255.
54 Compare Luke 6.20, 18.22, 19.8.
55 Acts 24.16, my translation, NRSV says 'I do my best.'
56 Theodoret, *A History of the Monks of Syria*, trans. Richard Price (Kalamazoo, Mi, 1985), p. 24.
57 Richard Valantasis, 'Constructions of Power in Asceticism', *The Journal of the American Academy of Religions* 63 (1995), pp. 795–821 at pp. 797, 799.
58 Geoffrey Harpham, *The Ascetic Impulse in Culture and Criticism* (Chicago, 1987), pp. xi, xii.
59 Brown, *Body and Society*, p. 237.
60 This is the remark of Olivier Clément, *The Roots of Christian Mysticism* (London, 1993), p. 287.
61 In fact, 'Anthony and the monks of the fourth century inherited a revolution, they did not initiate one', in Brown, *Body and Society*, p. 208.

Part Two

The Formation of the Tradition: The Period of the Ecumenical Councils

In the early fourth century the church changed. The persecution by the imperial government ended. This change can be precisely dated to the year 312. At first, persecution had been sporadic and occasional, even if violent and ruthless. An early outburst took place in 63 AD after a fire had raged for several days in Rome and destroyed much of the city. The Emperor Nero may well have been responsible and, probably in order to divert suspicion away from himself, he blamed the Christians.[1] Then there were occasional periods of persecution until this intensified at the accession of the Emperor Decius in 249. In this period, Roman emperors ruled over a huge area with wide diversity of religious faiths and were generally tolerant of diversity. But the later part of the third century was a time of crisis, with economic problems, barbarian invasions and regular assassinations of emperors. In this instability, the performance of cultic sacrifices was considered essential in order to restore stability of the empire through proper religious observance. Since Christians refused to do this, they were accused of destabilizing society and this led to persecution, under Decius (249–51), then Valerian (253–60) and Diocletian (284–305). These emperors defined the accepted religion of the empire and this set up legal boundaries. Those who refused to follow the simple and defined rituals had placed themselves outside Roman society and were forced to conform.[2] We do not know how widely this was enforced but it introduced martyrdom as an expected part of Christian living.

The attitude of the government to the church changed in the early fourth century. There was a dramatic volte face and Christianity, instead of being persecuted and excluded, became the religion of the state which had previously proscribed it. The Emperor Constantine (306–337) brought this about. When he was preparing to go into battle against his rival Maxentius at the Milvian Bridge just outside Rome on 28 October 312, he saw the vision of a cross in the sky. The historian Eusebius described how this happened. 'He saw with his own eyes up in the sky and resting over the sun, a cross-shaped trophy formed from light and a text attached to it which said "by this conquer". He … was gripped by amazement.'³ There are several versions of this vision and there has been debate about what happened and then about the sincerity of Constantine's conversion. He did not immediately seek baptism, and delayed this until he was on his deathbed, although this was not unusual. But whatever Constantine's personal beliefs were, his experience before the battle led to a change of policy towards the church and a new situation for the Christian faith.

It took a while for this newfound tolerance to reach through all parts of the empire. Peter, the patriarch of Alexandria, was martyred after Constantine's vision, on 25 November. Then, later in the century, the last representative of the dynasty founded by Constantine was his nephew, Julian, who has become remembered as Julian the Apostate (361–3). Julian had been educated and brought up within the church, but as an adult changed his views and tried to restore the traditional pagan faith and eliminate Christianity. Clerical privileges were removed and no action was taken against mobs who lynched Christian leaders. Happily for the Christian Church as it sought to find a more secure place in society, Julian reigned for only nineteen months before dying in a battle against the Persians. His successor Theodosius (379–95) was a devout Christian who, soon after coming to the throne, summoned a church council in Constantinople (381) to reject the Arian version of faith. A sentence of a law issued early in his reign states: 'It is our Will that all the peoples who are ruled by the administration of Our Clemency shall practise that religion which the divine Peter transmitted to the Romans.'⁴

From then on Christianity was the faith of the empire. The church gained an accepted place in society. Bishops were recognized and shared in the governance and administration of the cities in various ways. Churches were built. A series of consultations on doctrine and church order took place which defined right belief and practice – called Ecumenical Councils and accepted widely by the church. It was in this period that the asceticism which had been practised by Christians throughout the church became popular and its practitioners grouped themselves in communities which were to become known as monasteries. Monastic life became part of the institutional church.

The sources agree that the first monasteries were set up in Egypt in the fourth century. Antony and Pachomius are recorded as initiating a new form of ascetic life. This brought together two ways of approaching God. The first was the eremitical way of solitary living, seeking silence and struggling against the forces of evil. The second was the communal life, living with others under obedience to the superior. Communities grew up around the holy men in different parts of Egypt. They were given the name of monastery.

Monasticism took other forms in other places. In Syria holy men and women followed a more individual ascetic path but carried this out alongside local communities with which they developed a relationship of support. In the cities of Asia Minor, various kinds of community were formed, often integrated into the church and provided care for those in need. At this stage in these areas, the name of monastery was not yet used, although the widespread respect for ascetic practice and the formation of different kinds of Christian community influenced later monastic life.

The cities of Jerusalem and Constantinople were centres of both political and religious life. They attracted monks from all parts of the empire and also provided a refuge for those who left their homes to escape invaders. In both places, monasteries were established and grew rapidly. They took part in the life of the church and also within the social life of the Byzantine Empire.

These newly formed monasteries had their own distinctive characteristics and lifestyles, caused by the different geographical, economic and cultural influences on them. They exchanged ideas and shared common aims. It was a time of formation of an institution and the articulation of an identity. Monasticism was formed.

Notes

1 For an assessment of Nero's persecution see Bart D. Ehrman, *The Triumph of Christianity* (London, 2018), pp. 198–200.
2 Ibid., pp. 201–6.
3 Eusebius, *Life of Constantine* 1.28.
4 *Theodosian Code* 16.1.2.

2

Solitude, Community and the Church: Beginnings in Egypt

Three pioneers

Theodore, a disciple of Pachomius, wrote how his teacher had reflected on the beginnings of monastic life in Egypt. There were, he remembers Pachomius saying, 'three important things that increase by God's grace for the benefit of those who have understanding', that is the monks. These are 'the bishop Athanasius, the athlete of Christ contending unto death; the holy Abba Antony, the perfect model of anchoritic life; and this community, which is a model for all those who wish to assemble souls in God, to succour them until they be made perfect'.[1] These three elements of the ascetic struggle, the common life lived together and the guidance of the bishop converged in the desert of Egypt to bring about a new stage in the life of the church. This was the growth of the ascetic Christian life of the second and third centuries into the monastic life of the fourth, and later, centuries.

Theodore's three pioneers took steps towards the fulfilment of their vocations in the year 313. One day in that year, the young Athanasius was playing with friends and was acting out the role of a bishop. He was observed by the new Patriarch Alexander, who had succeeded to the martyred Peter. Patriarch Alexander was impressed by the deportment of the boy and took him into his own house to educate him. Athanasius was in due course consecrated patriarch of Alexandria. In the same year, Antony came out of his place of ascetic struggle in a tomb and, at the age of sixty, set out in the company of Arab camel herders and arrived at the mountain where he spent the rest of his life. At that time, there was peace following the victory of Constantine and this led to the discharge of Pachomius from the army. He was baptized, also in 313. And so the changed circumstances of the reign of Constantine gave opportunities to each of these three leaders of monks and led to the formation of the monastic life in the church.[2]

Antony the first monk

Antony was the oldest of the three. He was born to well-off Christian parents living south of Cairo in the central part of Egypt probably in the year 251. By the time he was eighteen, both his parents had died and he was looking after his sister. One day he went to church and heard the gospel read. 'If you would be perfect go sell what you possess and give to the poor, and you will have treasure in heaven.' He went home and sold the family lands and possession, retaining just a few things. But the next time he went to church the gospel was 'Do not be anxious about tomorrow.'[3] So, the rest of the things he owned were disposed of, his sister entrusted to a community of virgins and he started to devote himself to an ascetic life of prayer, fasting and solitude.

Then came his progressive withdrawal from his village and from the life of secular Egypt. He began by living in the village following an ascetic discipline, observing and learning from the lives of other ascetics. After fifteen years of this preparation, he moved into a tomb situated at the edge of the village and asked a friend to wall him up. Here he engaged in long, dramatic and spectacular struggle against the assaults of the devil. Demons broke through the roof and took the form of beasts and reptiles. He was assaulted, wounded and exhausted. After a while the friend broke into the tomb to find Antony prostrate and apparently dead. He carried him back to the village, but Antony revived and insisted on being carried back to his tomb. The next stage of his journey

Figure 2 Anthony of Egypt is recognized as the first monk. He lived as a hermit in the desert moving to ever more inhospitable places.

Figure 3 The monastery of St Anthony was founded at the foot of the mountain where he lived in a cave.

was to go deeper into the desert where he settled in a deserted fort and arranged for a friend to bring him bread twice a year. Here he remained for twenty years. Then the final stage of his long withdrawal came when he was in his sixties and went with the camel herders on a three-day journey into the desert towards the Red Sea. Here at an oasis at the foot of a mountain, which is referred to as the Inner Mountain and now known as Mount Clysma, he spent the rest of his life and died at the age of 105.[4]

It seems an unremarkable life when judged by human standards. Yet his struggle influenced others to follow his example. When he set out on his life of asceticism 'there were not yet many monasteries in Egypt and no monk knew at all the great desert, but each ... disciplined himself in isolation, not far from his own village.' After his first twenty-year period living in the tomb, 'he persuaded many to take up the solitary life. So from then on, there were monasteries in the mountains and the desert was made a city by the monks.'[5] At this point in the narrative of his life, there is a lengthy sermon when Antony begins to teach those who come to him. He has become a leader and teacher of the monastic life.

Athanasius the bishop

Antony's life and teaching are described in various sources. Seven of the letters attributed to Antony are now considered to be written by the saint.[6] Then there are sayings and anecdotes in the *Sayings of the Desert Fathers* and sections in the letters of Amoun and the *Lives of Pachomius*. However, the main source for his life and teaching is the account of his written by the first of Pachomius's three creative influences, the Bishop Athanasius. Athanasius had met Antony at least once when the ascetic went to Alexandria in 338 and visited the monasteries of Nitria, a visit which coincided with one of the times when Athanasius was resident in Alexandria between periods of exile. But he would also have known of him by reputation and he proudly records that Antony asked that his sheepskin and his cloak – which were new when he received them but had become worn and threadbare through being used – should be given to the bishop after his death.[7] Soon after Antony's death in 356, when Athanasius was in exile for the third time, the bishop wrote the life of the Antony, the first monk.

Athanasius shows that the vocation of the monk is continuous with that of the martyr. During Antony's seclusion there was a burst of persecution under the Emperor Maximin. Antony left his cell and went to Alexandria to share their suffering. The judge tried to make the monks leave the city but Antony refused to go. He washed his clothes, stood up in the sight of all and stayed, praying for the gift of martyrdom. But God preserved him so he can teach others the way of discipline. After his struggles against the demons in the tomb, a location which expresses the readiness to accept death, Antony is so drained of life that he seems to be dead. Later, he has a vision of a beam of light he asks the vision 'Where were you? Why didn't you come in the beginning to stop my distresses?' The answer comes 'I was here, Antony, but I waited to watch your struggle. And now since you have persevered and were not defeated I will be your helper for ever'.[8]

The language of wrestling and struggle, of death and of visions of new life had become familiar in the lives of the martyrs and is now applied to the life of the monk. Martyrdom had already come to mean the endurance of hardship and acceptance of suffering. Clement of Alexandria had written that 'we call martyrdom perfection, not because a man has reached the end of his life … but because he has displayed the perfect mark of love.' Later Pachomius was asked by one of his monks to pray that he might become a martyr and die for Christ. Pachomius firmly corrected him and told him that if he endured monastic life he would be 'a companion of the martyrs in heaven'.[9] The choice by the monk to remove himself from the world by renouncing all it contained was seen as equivalent to God removing the martyr from the world by death. Later it would be called 'white' martyrdom and succeed to the 'red' martyrdom of those who died for their faith.

Antony's life of ascetic struggle brought him to a new fullness of life. He became a perfect man. After the twenty solitary years in the fort, friends break down the door and Antony comes out. He has become a teacher and a healer. Athanasius describes the change in him.

> As though from some shrine, having been led into divine mysteries, and inspired by God. (His friends) were amazed to see that his body had maintained its former condition, neither fat from lack of exercise, nor emaciated from fasting and combat with demons …. The state of his soul was one of purity. For it was not constricted by grief, nor relaxed by pleasure, nor affected by either laughter or dejection.

When he saw the crowd, he was not annoyed any more than he was elated at being embraced by so many people. He maintained utter equilibrium, like one guided by reason and steadfast in that which accords with nature.[10]

Even at his death at the age of 105, Antony was more energetic than those who look after themselves with varied foods and bathing, and had all his teeth, albeit worn down to the gums. So ascetic life renews body as well as spirit, and restores the original life enjoyed by Adam at creation.[11]

Later readers recognized that there was something new in this life as understood and recounted by the bishop. This led directly to the next stage of what we have come to know as monasticism. The development happened both through the life which Antony led and also by the carefully constructed account of it in Athanasius's *Life*. It was the life as described in the book which led to the formation of monasticism. It is recognized as the paradigm of the genre of literature we call hagiography. A reasonable claim can be made that this life is the most copied and so most widely distributed book in the history of Christianity after the Bible. In the west, as well as the east, Antony became the father of monks. In his autobiographical *Confessions*, Augustine describes how an imperial official called Ponticianus introduced him to the Latin translation of a book about Anthony the Egyptian monk. Augustine had not heard about this new monastic movement in Egypt and the discovery led to his walk in the garden, his conversion and then his retirement from teaching and later formation of a monastic community.[12] '(Anthony) remained truly the Father of all monks and so in all milieus and in every period of the western Middle Ages monks considered themselves truly his sons.'[13]

Antony's hagiographer, Athanasius, was the bishop. His diocese of Alexandria was a centre of Christianity, and its bishop was an influential leader. Athanasius was at the Council of Nicaea where he opposed the heresy of Arius (325). In the *Life of Antony*, the only recorded visit of the ascetic was to Alexandria to preach against the heresy of Arius, which he did by affirming the position of Athanasius.[14] Later monks would come to ecumenical councils, sometimes with unruly and violent bands of followers, to support their orthodox faith.

Monks in Egypt, as in other places, were often asked to carry out leadership roles in the church. When one monk, Dracontius, took refuge in his monastery from the call to be consecrated, Bishop Athanasius wrote to him reminding him of seven other monks who had been bishops including Serapion of Thmuis, a disciple of Antony. Dracontius must have been persuaded because we later hear of him being arrested and exiled in 356.[15] Some monks resisted this call successfully. Ammonius, a scholar as well as a monk who was one of four monks known as the Tall Brothers who were leaders of the Origenist group, was asked to become a bishop and forcibly brought to be consecrated to this post. He took a knife and cut off his ear, telling them that a mutilated man was not permitted to be a bishop. This did not deter the townsfolk who told him this was an outdated Judaistic regulation. It was not until he threatened to cut off his tongue as well that he was allowed to return to his monastery, still in the lay state.[16]

The question of whether monks should also be bishops and the relationship of the monastery to the church continued to be debated and we will return to it later.[17] At the root of the debate is the relationship between two forms of power and authority – the institutional authority of the bishop and the charismatic power of the holy man or woman. The model of interaction is shown by a story of the occasion when Pachomius's successor Theodore visited Athanasius in 363. Athanasius says that the true father is the monk, in whom Athanasius says that he sees the presence of Christ, to which Theodore quickly replies, 'when we look at you it is as though we looked upon Christ.'[18] This exchange of courtesies shows the interaction of two forms of authority, both contributing to the well-being of the church.

The life of Antony is a programme of Christian living, in which solitude and withdrawal, struggle with demons and experience of divine grace are encountered and experienced in a form of life which becomes accessible to those who make the journey to become disciples of the holy man. The *Life of Antony* as written by Athanasius is carefully constructed. It has three parts of more or less equal length, woven into the periods of Antony's life. In the first Antony struggles against the devils, as his ascetic discipline. In the second he comes out of his place of struggle and gives a long sermon about the victory of Christ over the devils. In the third he performs a series of healings, signs and acts of power.[19] The carefully constructed life of Antony is not really a biography, but rather a description of a way of life and a theological statement of its inner meaning.

Athanasius's *Life of Antony* is an early example of a long tradition of theological genre of hagiography. The Lives of the saints, or hagiography, ensured that the lives of monastic founders remained as sources of teaching and inspiration in the lives of the monasteries. They were often written by those who knew them and were read in the monastery at occasions such as the anniversary of the death of the saint. There are repeated patterns of behaviour or events, referred to as *topoi*, which build a recognized and traditional picture of the nature of monastic holiness. This style of writing blends the historical individuality of the saint's life with a stylized pattern to hold before the listener or reader an image of holiness. As a picture in words to be held, meditated on and put into practice, it has the function of an icon.

Desert Fathers and Mothers

Another pioneer of Egyptian monastic life was Amoun. He was born in 295 and lived in the north of Egypt in the region of the Nile Delta. He was an orphan and at the age of twenty-two was forced by his uncle to marry. He went unwillingly through the ceremony but then read passages of the Bible to his illiterate new wife instructing her about the importance of chastity. She had little option but to accept his preferred way of living but wanted at least to live in the same house. Amoun worked growing balsam, ate and prayed with his wife, then retired at night to a different room. This went on for eighteen years after which his wife suggested they live separately. Amoun then happily moved to the nearby mountain of Nitria, when he was thirty-five years old. Here he built two rounded cells and lived there for another twenty-two years. He knew Antony and on one visit questioned him, asking 'since my rule is stricter than yours how is it that your name is better known amongst men than mine is?' Abba Antony answered 'it is because I love God more than you do.' These words are hardly in the spirit of the desert and come from a text written some time after the deaths of the two monks. They show that they both were early pioneers and knew each other. They firmly assert the priority of Antony.[20]

Amoun's chosen place of seclusion was the mountain of Nitria. This mountain is at the edge of the western desert of Egypt and is a strip of land which protrudes into the cultivated delta region, to the north of Cairo. It is near the Greek city of Hermopolis Parva, later named Damanhur and now known as el-Barnugi. The mountain of Nitria fell within the diocese of Damanhur whose bishop presided over the loose and expanding monastic settlement. To the northwest is the Lake Mareotis and beyond that is Alexandria. Not far away, a further settlement of monks later grew up. Their settlement was called Cellia or the cells. The whole area is rich in natron deposits. Natron is a salt collected from dried lakes or river beds and had many uses in ancient Egypt including use as soap or antiseptic for cleansing, for drying the body in mummification and, when mixed with oil, it can be used as fuel. This desert where Amoun and others settled was close to habitation, visited by traders and natron collectors and had a place in the local diocese. It lay on the margins between desert and cultivated land.

Another early monastic settlement was Scetis, which was about miles to the south of Nitria. Scetis is – confusingly – now called the wadi el-Natrun, but this should be distinguished from the mountain of Nitria. Although the settlements are close they were separated from each other. Nitria is not approached from Cellia in the north but from Terenuthis which is about 20 miles to the east of Nile. Cellia is a piece of barren land along the valley where monks settled. It remains a centre of monastic life today with four major monasteries built in a twelve-mile stretch of desert landscape.

The monks who settled in these settlements of the monastic north of Egypt taught by word and example rather than through written texts. The oral traditions of the desert took shape as a disciple came to ask advice and guidance from an ascetic who had become known for the quality of his life. Later the sayings and anecdotes of this early period of desert monastic life were collected and written down. These are the *Apophthegmata Patrum* or *Sayings of the Desert Fathers*.

The sayings convey a vibrant and engaging style of monastic spirituality. Many of the stories show the importance of humility and obedience as the ways to overcome self-will and to resist the attacks of devils. Macarius came home one day and found a thief robbing his cell, so he helped him load the camel making sure that every last item was included, but then the camel lay down and would not move until it was unloaded again.[21] Another monk also called Macarius swatted a gnat which was biting him. Shocked by this outburst of anger, he sat naked in a marsh for six months and was bitten so badly by the mosquitoes that on his return to the monastery he was so swollen that the monks could only recognize him by his voice. Paul the Simple was an early companion of Antony. He arrived at the cell of the old man when he was sixty years old and Antony thought he was too old to be a monk. He set Paul the task of weaving a cloak, then he undid the cloak and made him do it again. Paul's obedience made him perfect and he was able to cast out demons. John the Dwarf was asked by his abba to plant his staff in the ground and water it. The source of water was so far away that it took all night to fetch and then after three years the staff burst into life and produced fruit. The old man collected the fruit and took it to the brothers. He said: 'Take and eat of the fruit of obedience.'[22]

A command often repeated is the injunction to stay in the cell. One visitor asked Abba Moses for a word. The old man advised him, 'Go, sit in your cell and your cell will teach you everything.'[23] This message can be multiplied in the advice of many of the monks. At the heart of this way of life is a simple pattern of life. All the monks do is settle down, eat enough but not too much, sleep a little as needed, work and pray. It's an achievable, simple but demanding way of life.

Almost all the monks in the *Sayings of the Desert Fathers* were the abbas or fathers. There were also some ammas or mothers, such as Theodora and Syncletica, whose wisdom is included in the *Sayings*. Another female figure who appears in several texts is the nun who is so emaciated by her asceticism that she is thought to be a man. An example of this figure is Mary of Egypt. Mary is a prostitute from Alexandria, who travels to Jerusalem by boat paying for her passage by offering herself in her usual profession. On arrival she finds herself prevented from entering the sepulchre until she repents of her way of life. She then sets out into the desert, taking with her a little bread and some coins given to her by a pilgrim. Here she lives for forty-seven years until she is discovered by the priest Zossima, who is amazed to meet her and to find that this ascetic figure is in fact a woman. He gives her communion and then returns a year later to find that she has died. A lion helps him dig a grave and bury her.[24]

Anthologies of this material were remembered and collected, forming a body of monastic wisdom which captures the immediacy and simplicity of Egyptian ascetic life. There are several forms of these collections which were written in Greek or Coptic, and were then translated into Syriac, Armenian and Latin and then other languages.[25] The written collections of the *Sayings of the Desert Fathers* were probably compiled in Palestine, since they included material from both Sinai and Palestine, perhaps by monks who had left Egypt and wanted to capture and remember the teachings which had inspired their journeys.[26] Collections of sayings became a style of ascetic writing which was regularly used. Often there took the form of *Centuries*, or sets of a hundred texts on a theme collected together. Many of the books included much later in the *Philokalia* are collections of this kind.[27] The oral form of this material precedes the writing. It preserves the style of learning with teaching given as response to questions and so builds a body of oral teaching which is transmitted mainly by word of mouth. This oral character gave to monastic spirituality its universal appeal and its adaptability to different circumstances. The monks, like the rest of us, loved stories and remembered short and simple sentences of advice. Later, the oral character of the tradition would enable it to survive and flourish both in rural societies with low rates of literacy and in times of persecution when it was difficult to print and circulate written literature.

The first communities

At this early stage there were various forms of living arrangements. Each monk was free to follow his choice of ascetic lifestyle. Some lived in caves, like the hundred-year-old Elias visited by the authors of the *Historia Monachorum* who lived alone in a cave near Antinoe at the end of a narrow path. 'No description' they write 'can do justice to that rugged desert in the mountain where he had his hermitage'.[28]

John of Lycopolis lived in a two-room cell and was used to meeting and talking to visitors. Some visitors from Palestine recount how they spent three days with him and report his edifying conversation at length.[29] The huts were built from whatever materials could be found. Sometimes settlements of monks grew to become large. Abba Or is described as the father of the hermitages of a thousand brothers, probably intended as a general description rather than a precise calculation. He planted shrubs to provide wood for construction, laid out a marsh for water supply and ensured herbs for food. When a new brother arrived, the others would build a cell for him, which was a task that could be accomplished in a single day.[30]

As numbers grew and communities became more settled, monasteries followed a more disciplined and structured way of life. In Nitria, huts were arranged in clusters of various sizes, some with just a few huts together but others consisting of one or even two hundred cells. At the centre was the church. There was a guest house, seven bakeries, kitchen, workshops for rope and linen making. Doctors and pastry cooks had set up shops. Elias had some money and was concerned for the virgins living around him. He built a large monastery and gathered 300 women ascetics together, providing gardens, household utensils and everything they needed. Unfortunately, we are told 'they quarrelled continuously' and Elias left the monastery until three angels removed all feelings of lust from him, sent him back and from then on he lived in a small room and limited his contact with the virgins to the giving of advice.[31] Chronius lived alone and prayed that he would never have to return to an inhabited place. But after a few years his way of life attracted two hundred brothers who had settled with him. He accepted ordination as a priest in order to serve them and stayed in the same place, baking his own bread and drawing his own water from the well which he had dug.[32]

The accounts of the lives of the holy men show a gradual formation of communities, as disciples were attracted and the desert became crowded with many monasteries. These communities were informal and spontaneous. They were built up as disciples grouped themselves around the teacher. In the north, around the Nile Delta, monastic settlements took various forms. It was in the south, in Upper Egypt, that a different, more structured form of monastic living was established. The founder of these communal monasteries or *coenobia* was a former soldier, the third of the pioneers mentioned at the start of this chapter, Pachomius.

Pachomius

Pachomius (292–348) was born in the town of Latopolis in Upper Egypt. The town had gained its name from the *latos*, a kind of fish to which the townspeople offered sacrifices. The *Life of Pachomius* narrates how the saint as a child went with his parents to sacrifice to the *latos*. But the fish swam away from him and the priest conducting the sacrifice ejected the young Pachomius because the flight of the fish demonstrated that he was a threat to this traditional form of faith.[33] When he was twenty years old, Pachomius enlisted in the army and later was imprisoned along with his fellow conscripts. The young soldier was surprised when local Christians heard what had happened to him and to his companions and brought them food. They do 'all manner of good to everyone and treat us with love for the sake of the God of heaven'.[34] This experience had a profound effect on Pachomius and remained in his mind. The generosity of these anonymous Christians gave him an example which continued to motivate him throughout his life and which he enshrined as one of the guiding principles behind the life of his future foundations. 'Loving all men, I will be their servant' he promised. After his discharge from the army he was catechized and baptized. On the night of his baptism he dreamt that dew from heaven descended on him, then condensed to become honey in his right hand from where it flowed on to the ground around him and then over the whole earth. 'Understand this, Pachomius' the accompanying voice announced 'for it will happen to you in a short time'.[35]

From this beginning in the Christian life, Pachomius made steady progress both in the leading of an ascetic life and in the attracting of followers. He first settled in the village of Seneset for about three years, following the example of those Christians who had brought him food in prison by living a life of service. He then met a formidable ascetic called Palamon who practised fasting, vigils and prayers. The young disciple overcame Palamon's warnings that he would find the life too hard and persuaded the older man to receive him as a monk. They lived together for a while, until one day Pachomius was wandering through the thorny undergrowth of the desert and, as his feet became lacerated, he recalled the thorns which afflicted his saviour. He came to a deserted village called Tabennesis, and here an inner voice told him to build a little house, or *mone*, because many would come to join him there. Palamon helped him to do this and then went back to his own place. The two men maintained their common life even when living in different places and regularly visited each other.[36]

Pachomius's next companion was his brother John, who joined him in his life of ascetic struggle and practical charity. But the two quarrelled when Pachomius wanted to increase the size of their settlement to allow others to join, an intention which John suspected came from a desire rooted in pride and ambition. Pachomius however was strengthened in his resolve by that inner voice, which reassured him that it was 'the will of God' that he should 'minister to the race of men in order to reconcile them to himself'.[37] The tension between the brothers was resolved by the death of John after which Pachomius began to receive disciples.

From then on, the communal way of life which Pachomius felt himself called to lead grew rapidly. Three disciples came. Then they were followed by another group including a boy of fourteen called Theodore. Theodore was pursued by his mother, who, armed with letters from his bishop, demanded the return of her son. Theodore did not want to see her and instead of bringing back her son, the mother remained and enrolled in the group of women ascetics who lived nearby under the guidance of Pachomius's sister.[38] The number of monks grew to a hundred. Now the increased membership needed a second monastery which was set up at another deserted village called Phbow. Then two more monasteries nearby asked to become associated with the new foundation. More followed, mainly for men, but with communities for women as well. By the time that Pachomius died of plague in May 346, there was a network of nine main monasteries grouped along a sixty-mile stretch of the river Nile following the way of life pioneered by the saint.

It has been said that the monasteries of Pachomius did not need a rule because Pachomius himself was the rule.[39] His memory of the Christians of Luxor bringing him food in his time in prison did not leave him. The early accounts of Pachomius's life depict him as a servant to all in the monastery. He prepared the table for the monks at mealtimes; he sowed the vegetables and watered them; he answered the door when anybody knocked; and if anyone was sick he took care of him and ministered to him at night.[40] At times of special need he extended this care to those living in the villages and was criticized for this. The service of others remained a guiding principle and led to a self-effacing model of leadership. One story describes how Pachomius felt the need to discipline an offending monk and expelled him from the community. At this, one of the other monks confessed that he was a sinner too and would join the offending monk accepting expulsion with him. At this point all the other monks decided that they too

Figure 4 Pachomius, a younger contemporary of Anthony, was a founder of coenobitic monastic life.

would leave in a solidarity of sin. Pachomius apologized and all returned. Shared love and humility prevailed.[41] There were also endearing touches of gentleness which enter into the demanding ascetic rule. A practice in the monasteries was the preparation of a special mixture of sweetened fruits, called *korsenilion*, which was distributed to the monks at the end of meals.[42] Pachomius wanted his communities to be built on the principles of mutual respect and mutual support.

The study of the Bible guided Pachomius's monasteries. Pachomius himself was not educated as a boy but later learned to read and write. Morning worship in the monastery consisted of readings from the Bible, interspersed with communal recitations of the Our Father and with silence to think about what had been read. This would be repeated through the day, both at work and at more informal teaching sessions called *catachesis*. The usual time for *catachesis* was the evening, after the meal had been eaten. Visitors described Theodore, the successor of Pachomius, sitting under a palm tree with six hundred monks, discussing Scripture and allocating specific texts for meditation to different monks. When the communities grew too big for Pachomius to give his instruction personally, he devised a secret language based on letters of the Coptic alphabet, which he used to communicate with his monks by writing letters.[43] It is unclear how this worked, but it indicates the importance given to maintaining the tradition of personally directed instruction. The pattern of worship in the Pachomian monasteries encouraged a process of personal discovery of the message of the Scriptures carried out through a simple process of directed reading and meditation. The life was a planned strategy of discovering what it meant to live out the words of the Bible.[44]

The monastery was encircled by a wall. Each monastery was subdivided into houses, with each house accommodating about twenty monks. Each monk had a small house to himself, until the community grew to such an extent that three monks occupied each cell. Their space was private and others did not enter, so that the silence and solitude would be preserved. The doors were kept open so that availability to others and the principle of a common life was also affirmed. There was a guest house, kitchen and refectory inside the walls. At the centre was a place for communal prayer. This was called a meeting hall or *sunaxis*, and not a church.[45] Derwas Chitty suggests that Pachomius modelled this arrangement on the military camps he had lived in while he was a soldier. He valued simplicity. A story from one of the later traditions describes him building a beautiful church in one of the monasteries, then deciding it was too elegant and pulling the pillars with ropes until they were crooked and distorted.[46]

Each house was cared for by housemaster, who was assisted by a second. The house had a defined place in the economy of the community. Some houses would be assigned to carry out a specific specialized task. Others would go out into the fields. Others again would carry out crafts such as basket-making or weaving. Palladius describes the occupations which he discovered being carried out in the monastery. His list includes tailors, metal-workers, fuller, shoemakers, carpenters, camel drivers and bakers. Tasks in the monastery were carried out in rotation. At the start of the day the work was planned, tools distributed, and the monks lined up to be marched off to whatever job had been assigned. Again Pachomius's military background seems to have influenced the organization.

The setting up of monasteries assisted in the economic regeneration of the region. At the first place where Pachomius lived, Seneset, people from the area around left their homes and settled near Pachomius because 'of his way of encouraging them'.[47] The same movement of people happened in other places too and this contributed to the rapid growth of the monasteries. A peasant who joined the community would be given a livelihood, a job and a house. These opportunities attracted peasants who came to live near the monasteries and they often chose to join the communities. The monks seem to have welcomed those who were not Christian but were attracted to the monastery by the offer of work and food. This openness to the people of the area led to the practice of training catachumens and taking them to the monastery of Phbow each year during Lent for a communal baptism.[48] The harshness of the life, with its hard work in the fields, shortage of sleep, and regular prayers, seems not to have been a disincentive to new recruits.

Far from being a remote and exotic way of life, the monasteries were located in villages. Many of the inhabitants of the villages became monks. The spectacular growth rate happened because the way of life was compatible with peasant society and provided an attractive option for hardworking peasants. It gave them a greater measure of security than they would find if they struggled to build up their own farms. The life would not have been very different from the life on the farm. The diet would have been similar; the clothing was the simple tunic of the peasant; and the monks carried on the familiar tasks of working in the fields.[49] It was an easy adjustment for a farmer struggling to grow enough food to live on, first to move near to a monastery with its successful and varied economic activity and then to become associated with it and eventually to become a member. It offered a similar lifestyle but with more stability and security than if he was living on his own. The economic success of the monastery was assisted by gifts of pious well-wishers, the military style organization of the houses, the hard work of the monks and the scale of operations. A further attraction of the monastery may have been the opportunity for an education as well as the quality of religious instruction.

Although the sources which describe a settled life were written after Pachomius's death, there was a fixed pattern of life from an early date. Pachomius's teacher Palamon clothed his new recruit in a monk's habit or *schema*, so the practice of monastic renunciation seems to have been familiar before Pachomius founded his monasteries. The communities were called monasteries, a word derived from *mone*, meaning a lodge or house. The cell was called a *kellion*, which was the simple hut in which a poor man both slept and worked. The vocabulary of monasticism is drawn from the everyday life of the village. The arrangements of living are practical and down to earth. The way of life is built around 'proper measure in clothing, equality in food and decent sleeping arrangements'.[50] The early monasteries as conceived and built by Pachomius were groups of people living together, in much the same conditions as they would have lived outside the monastery, and who work to sustain their life together, to care for each other and to model their lives on the teachings of the Bible.

The rules were passed on by word of mouth during Pachomius's lifetime. The way of life was governed and directed by the instructions given by Pachomius. For example, he instructed the monks of Phbow 'in writing as a form of memorial that no-one should hurt his neighbour but each should keep to his rule of conduct'.[51] There was also a form of rule given to the women's monasteries and a reference to 'laws and traditions'.[52] This need not imply a written rule but rather a personal and immediate guidance by Pachomius of the communities as they built up a shared way of life. After he died, the words and advice of the founder were no longer available and so his monks recorded the tradition to ensure that it was preserved. As well as the Lives and Rules, the reports of visitors, especially Amoun and Palladius, were also written after the death of Pachomius. The accounts of life in the monasteries describe the arrangement and discipline of the monasteries after a process of evolution, when the communities had been founded and emerged out of experiment, disappointment and renewal. The written Rule was a development which took place after the death of the founder.

Shenoute and the Coptic tradition

Just a short distance from the monasteries of Pachomius, there was another network of coenobitic monasteries. These were on the opposite bank of the Nile, 60 miles downstream from Pachomius's largest monastery at Phbow. They have become associated with the name of the third superior, Shenoute, although they were founded by his uncle and teacher, Pjol. They had a huge influence on the monastic life of Egypt but are often overlooked by those outside Egypt. Shenoute of Atripe, and his White Monastery, is not mentioned by the main contemporary writers, John Cassian, the *Lausiac History* of Palladius nor the *Historia Monachorum*. This was probably because these visitors came from a Greek background and wrote in Greek for a Greek-speaking readership, while Shenoute's monastery was Coptic speaking. Coptic was derived from older Egyptian languages and used a script developed from Greek in the second century. It has two main forms. Sahidic is the version of Upper Egypt and Bohairic was spoken in the Nile Delta region and was used in the church. Coptic was used in translations of the Bible, but Shenoute produced a large collection of letters, sermons and monastic rules, written in a rich and colourful style, which provided a library of Coptic literature which was preserved and passed on by his monasteries. It is a record of a strand of monastic tradition which flourished outside the Greek Byzantine cultural world. The monasteries were the guardians and transmitters of a Coptic culture. The monasteries of Shenoute and Pachomius were later destroyed and rebuilt at various times, and the sites are still occupied today.

Shenoute has been judged unfavourably by historians. One scholar refers to the consensus of opinion that Shenoute was 'authoritarian, harsh, violent, and whose spirituality (was) lacking any mystical dimension' and he was described as 'christ-less'. He was like 'an erupting volcano, an impressive sight although not necessarily a pretty one … In monastic tradition the disconcerting figure of the great Shenoute constitutes a tragic phenomenon that compels us to consider seriously some pitfalls inherent in the monastic institution itself.'[53]

There are many tales of his violence. One day, Shenoute led a band of monks to the house of a leading pagan. They broke into his house, stole the objects of pagan worship, posted a written accusation on the house and hurled pots of urine against the door posts. So it is perhaps not surprising that Patriarch Cyril of Alexandria decided to take Shenoute and some of his monks with him to the Council of Ephesus as effective supporters of his cause. When the Council met, a chair was placed in the middle of the church and the book of the gospels was placed on it. Nestorius, the patriarch of Consantinople, came in, removed the book and sat on the chair. At this, Shenoute rushed forwards, picked up the book and struck Nestorius on the chest. Cyril saluted this righteous anger and placed his own stole around Shenoute's neck and appointed him archimandrite.[54]

The story of this turbulent and controversial monastic leader begins around 350 when two parents gave their new-born son the name Shenoute, which means 'son of God'. He was a pious, determined and uncompromising child. When he was seven, he was sent to look after a neighbour's sheep. His father became concerned because the boy did not return in the evenings. He went to complain that the shepherd did not allow the boy to come home to sleep. This complaint puzzled the shepherd who followed the boy when the day finished and found that he went to a water cistern under a sycamore tree and descended into the water. There he remained all night in prayer and he noticed that his fingers were like ten flaming lamps. The shepherd was over-awed and sent him home to his father.[55] Soon after this event, Shenoute, now aged nine, entered the monastery of his uncle who was an ascetic named Pjol. When he was about thirty years old, he became the third abbot of the monastery and remained in this position until he died in 466 at the age of 115.

The monastery which he joined was part of a federation of monastic communities which had already been formed by his predecessors. Pjol had been a monk in Pachomius's monastery and had moved across the river where he founded a coenobium with a way of life which was similar to that of Pachomius. A solitary ascetic, named Pschoi, lived nearby and had attracted a group of disciples, which had become a monastic community. The two ascetics decided to link their monasteries, which were less than an hour's walk apart. The Monastery of Pjol had white-coloured stone walls, and was known as the White Monastery, then later as Deir Anba Shenouda; while the Monastery of Pschoi had red-coloured walls and so became the Red Monastery. Later a women's monastery joined the federation. This was 2 miles to the south, at a village called Atripe.[56] There were also many hermits, who lived in the surrounding desert and these also became associated with the monasteries. The three houses were called *sunagogoi*.[57]

The three monasteries were spread over a large area, so that it is estimated that the land in which they stood was around 10 sq km, with their agricultural land reaching over a further 50 sq km. When Shenoute was abbot there were 2,200 monks and 1,800 nuns. The size of these communities is shown by the archaeological researches of the Yale Monastic Archeology Project which indicate a large and self-sufficient community, with workshops for the processing of olive oil and dyes, kitchens with twelve bread ovens and a huge well with a water distribution system. The fifth-century church at the White Monastery is still standing and its monumental size is a further testimony of the size of the monastery.[58]

The monasteries were large agricultural enterprises, which also encouraged many trades. The monks made ropes and baskets, wove linen, made shoes and pots, copied and bound books and cultivated flax. The nuns also made clothes. The monasteries provided food, security and livelihood for the peasants of the region. In times of insecurity, the monastery was an escape from poverty and need. Many came to seek admission out of a desire for a better life. They wanted to join the monastery and feared expulsion from it.

Shenoute was leader of this large economic and religious enterprise for over eighty years, from around 380 to 466. He lived at first in the monastery, but moved outside the walls and lived as a hermit for most of his time as abbot. He had been shocked by the way that his predecessor Ebonh had managed the community. He objected to Ebonh's use of resources for building projects and also for the lax treatment of a monk who was a notorious sinner. This distance from the monastery allowed him to develop a new role. He entrusted the management of the monasteries to others and himself provided the spiritual direction and formation of the monks and nuns. He was known for his scriptural learning, his power as a speaker and his claims to be sent by God. He became the spiritual head of the federation of monasteries.

He modelled his teaching on the study of the Bible. The great heroes of Scripture were his brothers and sisters. Shenoute used to meet and talk to Jesus, and we read of Jeremiah, Ezekiel and all twelve minor prophets visiting members of the community to talk to them.[59] Shenoute taught that the monastery was a community bound together as a single body, in which all were equal, in which self-assertion and pride were overcome by discipline and obedience, and in which the monks lived in familiar intimacy with their biblical forbears and examples. There is little emphasis on the forgiveness and redemption brought by Christ and the progress of spiritual growth towards theosis is absent. The pathway to heaven was travelled together in a rigidly disciplined common life.

This communal identity lay at the heart of Shenoute's vision of monastic life. It was a single community of faith. The men and the women were two monastic bodies who were bound together by the shared sense of sin and the discipline needed to overcome it. The managing of the free will, the need for obedience and the determination to ensure the purity of the community lie behind the rules and the discipline of Shenoute's monasteries. Sin and disobedience were diseases which damaged the body and which had to be removed and cut out or they would spread and infect others. The urgent determination to expel all sin and disorder from the body indicates why the system of discipline was so important to Shenoute and why this became such an important part of his leadership.

Those who entered the monastery had to affirm their readiness to live under this discipline. They were admitted only after a thorough selection process. This ensured that there was a boundary set up between the monastery and the surrounding countryside. With the monastery covering such a large area, it was important to make clear the difference between monastery and village. Anyone who wanted to join the community went through a period of testing for up to three months when they lived in 'the gate-houses of the community of the Lord'. If they managed to survive this period of testing they had to renounce all their possessions, and then make a solemn vow called a *diatheke* or covenant. The covenant was made before the altar and went like this:

I vow before God in his holy place, the word which I have spoken with my mouth being my witness, I will not defile my body in any way, I will not steal, I will not bear false witness, I will not lie, I will not do anything deceitful secretly. If I transgress what I have vowed, I will see the kingdom of heaven but will not enter it. God, before whom I made this covenant, will destroy my soul and body in the fiery Gehenna because I transgressed the covenant I made.[60]

Once admitted, the monks lived together as a community. Shenoute insisted on equality throughout his community. The monks and nuns were to 'have altogether the same in all things'.[61] They wore the same clothes, ate the same food, which was cooked in the central monastery building and sent out to the various smaller houses, and worked under the same discipline. Cells were shared, food was limited to one meal a day of bread, water and sometimes vegetables. Women were treated the same as men.

Order had to be maintained. Among his tasks was the administration of discipline, and he expected all lapses to be brought to him for adjudication and the allocation of the appropriate punishment.[62] The monks could be unruly, with sexual desires or occasional violence. Sometimes there was stealing and absconding. Transgression against the rules was firmly punished. These punishments have been often described and have contributed to the reputation of Shenoute as harsh and autocratic. There were three main punishments for transgressions. The offender might be degraded in the order of monastery, losing status to revert to being a novice again. Or she or he might receive corporal punishment. This took the form of a beating on the soles of the feet. The offender sat on the ground and was held down by some monks while others held the feet up for the beating. The most extreme penalty was expulsion from the community. The actions which led to these penalties are described in Shenoute's correspondence. For 'being imperfect in intelligence and propriety – fifteen blows; for going to the village with carnal desires – fifteen blows; for stealing – thirty strokes; for hitting a brother or a superior in the face – twenty blows; and for the combination of acting on carnal desires and lying about thefts – forty blows'. There is an instance of a monk dying in the course of a punishment, but there was also some clemency, when the penalty being moderated or pardoned because the monk was weak. One nun was let off her punishment because 'she is very fat and round and could not tolerate the beatings well.'[63]

Shenoute was not an ignorant peasant. He was familiar with Greek, and quotations from Aristophanes and Aristotle have been identified in his writing.[64] He had also read the books of Athanasius, Pachomius and Evagrius, and showed some measure of familiarity with their works in his own letters. He himself protests that he is unlearned and has no time for scholarship, but he is a passionate and prolific writer of letters and sermons. He quotes constantly from Scripture showing that he had an impressive memory and had learned with large parts of Scripture by heart. These qualities were expressed in his literary heritage and gave identity not only to Coptic monastic life but also to the Coptic Church as it struggled to maintain its life through later centuries of Islamic rule.

Shenoute's monasteries provided economic security for the peasants of the region. There was a structured and egalitarian style of life; a simple and accessible approach to the Christian faith; and the confidence of living a life pleasing to God in conformity with biblical models.

Communicating monasticism

Monks contributed to the well-being of society. Their prayers protected those who came to them. Visitors from Palestine realized how the monks supported the life of the community.

> There is no town or village in Egypt and the Thebaid which is not surrounded by hermitages as if by walls. And the people depend on the prayers of these monks as if on God himself ... it is clear to all who dwell there that through them the world is kept in being and that through them too human life is preserved and honoured by God.[65]

The movement had grown fast. Antony left his fort after his titanic struggles in 303. Pachomius founded his first community around 320. Amoun left his wife and moved to his mountain in 320. The new community of the Cells, Cellia, was founded in 338. Pachomius died in 346 and Antony in 356. The monastic movement in Egypt was fully established in the course of the fourth century, with the most rapid growth in the period between 320 and 360.

Visitors were amazed at the large numbers of men and women choosing to live the ascetic life. An early visitor, Rufinus, said that there were 3,000 monks when he visited in 373.[66] Palladius discovered 5,000 monks in Nitria, where there is a large church served by eight priests. Elias built a monastery for 300 virgins and Chronius' monastery had 200 monks. Numbers given in the *Lives of the Desert Fathers* or *Historia Monachorum* are even larger. The holy man Or has a thousand monks, Ammon has three thousand and in the town of Oxyrhynchus there are ten thousand monks and twenty thousand nuns. In Upper Egypt, Palladius says that there were three thousand monks in the monasteries of Pachomious by the time he died and this number had grown to seven thousand when Palladius visited. He gives the number of monks at the main monastery of Faou as 1,300 with 200 to 300 hundred at the smaller monasteries.[67]

The editor of this text notes that if we take these figures literally the number of monks could have exceeded the total population of Egypt. But we should not be too hasty to dismiss these large figures as wild exaggeration. The numbers given could include all who have been members of the monastery including those who have died, and of course the numbers given are suspiciously approximate, usually given in precise multiples of a thousand.[68] Archaeological research confirms the large size of the communities. This shows that, at this time, Cellia covered an area of 49 square miles and contained around 1,500 cells. These varied in size from small cells for one or two monks to larger settlement with twenty-five rooms which would have accommodated small communities. The settlement at Nitria was a similar size.[69] Even allowing for different methods of counting and some exaggeration, it is clear that huge numbers of Egyptian citizens were choosing to follow this hard way of ascetic life as set out by Athanasius and practised by ascetics living on the edges of all major towns in Egypt.

The fame of the monks spread. Visitors came from a wide distance to see for themselves and learn from the fathers. Some stayed and became monks. Many of the earliest accounts of the monks are travel narratives by visitors who were eager to tell friends at home the extraordinary things that they had witnessed. Palladius was from Galatia, was born in 363/4 and became a monk at the age of twenty-three. He spent twelve years living in Egypt, between 388 and 400. He then returned to Galatia and became a bishop. He described his experiences and encounters with holy men in a vivid narrative which has become known as the *Lausiac History*, after its dedication to the royal chamberlain, Lausus. Many of his accounts come from the mountain of Nitria and nearby Cellia where he spent nine years. Another early account came from a group of monks from Palestine who travelled through the country from 394 to 395. They described their experiences in a work which has come to us in a Latin version known as the *Historia Monachorum*.[70] Other visitors followed. John Cassian (*c.* 360–435) was a monk at Bethlehem and then came to Egypt. Here he visited the monks of the desert, listened to their stories and learned about monastic life. Later we hear of him in Constantinople from where he was sent by John Chrysostom on an embassy to Pope Innocent I in Rome. He stayed in the west and founded two monasteries near Marseilles. He wrote two books, the *Institutes* and the *Conferences*, which handed on the teachings of the monks of Egypt and were used by Benedict as a source for his own Rule. Later John Moschus, from Cilicia, was also, for ten years, a monk in Palestine. In 604, conditions became unstable and, accompanied by his friend Sophronius who later became patriarch of Jerusalem, he set off on a prolonged wandering, to Jordan, Antioch, Egypt, Cyprus and Rome, where he died in 634. He recorded the teaching of the many monks he met in his book, the *Spiritual Meadow*.[71] The attraction of the men and women who settled on the desert margins along the Nile attracted others to come to see them and to report what they experienced. Through their writings the life of the desert was transmitted across the Christian world.

The tradition of ascetic life which was taken by these travellers to their homelands and from there across the Christian world was conveyed through several forms of writing which conveyed the freshness and immediacy of monastic living. These forms of writing gave a shape and identity to the monastic life which could be shared and communicated through a tradition which was first oral and then written. There were four distinct strands of this tradition which showed how monastic life was lived. First, the practical guidance given by the holy man to the disciple was remembered in the short form of the *Apophthegmata* or *Sayings of the Desert Fathers*. This directness was continued in the various collections of sayings which were preserved in the monasteries. The form reached a definitive expression in the comprehensive anthology of the Philokalia. Then, second, the lives of the monks were recorded and became examples to be imitated. They were often read in monasteries which they founded on the anniversaries of their death. The popularity of the *Life of Antony* helped to provide a model of hagiographical writing which was followed by disciples of later monastic founders. The third strand of the monastic tradition was the rules of life which laid down the discipline to be observed in the monasteries. The beginnings of the rules were formulated by the founder and were ordered into a more systematic form after the death of the founder which led to the need to remember and write down the teaching. Then the fourth was the reports of visitors and pilgrims, the travellers' tales. These spread monastic ideals over a wide area. These forms of literature began in Egypt, were followed in other areas and became the way that the oral tradition of monasticism was communicated and shared.

Conclusion

In the fourth century the church was entering a period of greater freedom, the ascetic life style was an accepted form of religious expression and economic pressures were leading peasants to seek a more secure way of life. Many were attracted to follow the local holy man. Within this mass movement there was a mixture of living arrangements and forms of community. Antony in Lower Egypt lived a life of solitary struggle, leading to a fulfilled and perfect human life, and his community consisted of those who followed a similar style living as his disciples. The *Life of Shenoute*, like that of Pachomius, which were both written by the monks of their monasteries in Upper Egypt, describes a community life, with its rigidly disciplined pattern of life. So there were two kinds of monastic life. The eremitical or hermit life can be distinguished from the coenobitic or common life.

It was recognized that both forms were lived alongside each other and both were complementary aspects of ascetic living. Communities of disciples formed around the solitary ascetic, who sometimes tried to find ways of escaping this intrusive attention. Coenobitic communities made provision for some of its members to live alone and the abbot often guided the monastery from a hermitage at a convenient distance from the monastery itself. Later, especially in Palestine, as we will see, the two forms were carried out together in the laurite life which balanced the eremitical and coenobitic life. These two ways of life were lived within the life of the church. This way of ascetic life, based on the personal and solitary struggle of a life of prayer, fasting and battle against demons, carried out with others as part of a community, within the church governed by the bishop, took shape in Egypt and gave to the church that distinctive form which developed into the lifestyle which came to be called monastic.

So the way of life of the early monks spread across the Christian world. Within Egypt itself, as in other parts of the Christian world, the monasteries were the places from which the church was led, where ways of praying and believing were lived out and preserved, where literature was copied and kept, where people could find refuge in times of persecution. All the monasteries of these early days were destroyed and rebuilt many times. Some, including the coenobia of Pachomius, disappeared. Others continued to thrive. The monastery of Antony had a leading place in the life of the Coptic Church. Soon after the death of Anthony a monastery was built at the foot of the mountain where he had lived and where his cave is still visited by pilgrims. From the twelfth century, it was customary for a monk of Antony's monastery to be chosen to become the archbishop or abuna of Ethiopia. After 1700 the monastery's leadership was especially important. Twelve monks of the monastery were patriarchs in this period. In the desert of Scetis, monastic life continued in several centres. The monasteries of the Romans or al-Baramus, of the Syrians or al-Suriani, of Anba Bishoi and of Macarius or Abu Maqar have continued their life into the present day. Today these monasteries are growing as part of the monastic revival in the Coptic Church and former sites are re-occupied by monks. Among those being re-established are the coenobia of Pachomius and Shenoute. The witness of those ascetics who went out into the desert in the fourth century continues today.[72]

Notes

1 *Greek Life of Pachomius* 136.
2 These events are described in Derwas Chitty, *The Desert a City* (Oxford, 1966), pp. 1–2. For Athanasius playing see Rufinus, *Ecclesiastical History* 1.14; for Antony, *Life of Antony*, p. 49; for Pachomius, *Greek Life* 5.
3 Ibid., 2.
4 The details of demonic assault are described especially in ibid., 9.
5 Ibid., 3; 14.
6 These seven letters are in trans. Derwas Chitty, *The Letters of Saint Antony the Great* (Oxford, 1975).
7 *Life of Antony* 91.
8 Ibid., 10; 46.
9 This passage is in E. A. Wallis Budge, *The Paradise or Garden of the Holy Fathers*, vol. 1 (London, 1907), p. 301. This and other similar passages are in E. E. Malone, 'The Monk and the Martyr', *Studia Anselmiana* 38 (1956), pp. 201–28.
10 *Life of Antony* 15.
11 Ibid., 93.
12 This is recounted in Augustine, *Confessions* 8, trans. R. Pine-Coffin (New York, 1961), pp. 157–79.
13 Jean Leclercq, *The Love of Learning and the Desire for God* (New York, 1974), p. 125.
14 *Life of Antony* 69–70.
15 Athanasius's letter is in PG XXV, 523–34.
16 *Lausiac History* 11.
17 See below, pp. 75–7.
18 *Greek Life of Pachomius* 1.144.
19 The sections are as follows. He struggles against demons, 1–15; his sermon, 16–43; his acts of power, 44–93.
20 These accounts are in Palladius, *Lausiac History* and Amoun 1, *Sayings of the Desert Fathers*, trans. Benedicta Ward (Oxford, 1975), p. 31.
21 Macarius 40, ibid., pp. 137–8.
22 John the Dwarf 1, ibid., pp. 85–6.
23 Moses 6, ibid., p. 139.
24 The various versions of her life are collected and commented on by Benedicta Ward in *Harlots of the Desert* (London, 1987), pp. 26–57.
25 The sayings are arranged in a systematic from, with sayings arranged by theme, and an alphabetical form, with the names of the monks concerned arranged alphabetically. The

Alphabetical Collection is translated into English by Benedicta Ward as *The Sayings of the Desert Fathers*.
26 The view of L. Regnault, 'Les Apophtegmes en Palestine aux Ve-Vie siècles', *Irénikon* 54 (1981), pp. 320-30.
27 The Contents page of the first volume of the English translation of the *Philokalia* includes Isaiah the Solitary's *27 texts on Guarding the Intellect*, Evagrius' *153 texts on Prayer*, Mark the Ascetic's *200 texts on the Spiritual Life*.
28 The *Historia Monachorum* is translated by Norman Russell as the *Lives of the Desert Fathers* (Oxford, 1980), with this episode at p. 7.
29 Ibid., 1.4.
30 Ibid., 2.11.
31 *Lausiac History* 29, trans. Robert Meyer, *Ancient Christian Writers* (London, 1965), pp. 88-90.
32 Ibid., 47.
33 The Life of Pachomius is told in a Greek and a Coptic, or Bohairic, version, in trans. Armand Veilleux, Pachomian Koinonia, *The Life of St Pachomius and His Disciples vol. 1* (Kalamazoo, MI, 1980). This is in the *Greek Life of Pachomius* 3, p. 299, and Bohairic version 4, p. 25.
34 Philip Rousseau, *Pachomius* (Berkeley, CA, 1985), p. 58, citing Bo 7.
35 These are in *Greek Life* 5, and *Bohairic Life* 8.
36 *Greek Life* 6-13.
37 *Greek Life* 23.
38 Ibid., 37; *Bohairic Life* 37-9.
39 Rousseau, *Pachomius*, p. 106.
40 *Greek Life* 1, 24.
41 This anecdote is found attached to a manuscript of Palladius's *Lausiac History* and is known as Draguet 1 after the scholar who discovered it.
42 *Greek Life* 111.
43 Ibid., 99.
44 The modern Focolare Movement, founded in Italy by Chiara Lubich perhaps conveys this aspect of the life of the Pachomian communities. The spirituality is based on the shared commitment to study one text of scripture each month and to work at how to live this word out. The movement includes those living in small community houses, and those who live outside but follow the practice, and is open to non-Catholics and even non-Christians sharing in the life of the community.
45 Except by the visitor Ammon in *Ammon, Letter* 10, 14, 22, PO 10.6.
46 This may have been a fabrication to explain an inadequate design or poor building techniques. The story is in *Paralapomina* 13, in Chitty, *The Desert a City*, p. 22.
47 *Bohairic Life* 8.
48 Ibid., 81.
49 Evelyne Patleagean has discussed the similarities between the life of the poor and the life of the monk. 'Derrière les commentaires spirituels se dessinent les faits économiques, la multiplication se petits artisans libres, disperses et sans famille, rattachés cependant à d'autres hommes seuls par des solidarités religieuses, à un marché par la necessité des échanges'. *Pauvreté Economique et pauvreté sociale à Byzance* (Paris, 1977), p. 316.
50 *Greek Life* 1, 25.
51 *Greek Life* 54.
52 *Bohairic Life* 27, 104.

53 See Armand Veilleux in *Besa, Life of Shenoute*, trans. David Bell (Kalamazoo, MI, 1983), p. v. quoting J. Leipoldt.
54 *Life of Shenoute* 128, p. 78.
55 Ibid., 4, pp. 42–3.
56 See Susannah Elm, *Virgins of God, the Making of Asceticism in Late Antiquity* (Oxford, 1994), p. 299; *Life of Shenoute*, p. 74.
57 Bentley Layton, *The Canons of Our Fathers, Monastic Rules of Shenoute* (Oxford, 2014), pp. 11–21.
58 These figures are taken from the Arabic Life of Shenute, see Bell, *Life of Shenute*, p. 5. For the archaeological research, see Stephen J. Davis, *Monasticism* (Oxford, 2018), pp. 89–90.
59 *Life of Shenoute* 25, 70, 94, 96.
60 J. Leipoldt, *Shenute von Atripe und die Entstehung des National Aegyptishcen Christentums* (Leipzig, 1903), pp. 195–6.
61 *Life of Shenoute* 71, 77.
62 Layton, *Canons*, p. 24.
63 Elm, *Virgins of God*, p. 305; Layton, *Canons*, p. 49.
64 The comedian Aristophanes is a surprising author for the austere monastic leader to have known – perhaps he saw a play while he was at the Council of Ephesus, a suggestion of Adolf Eman in 'Shenute und Aristophanes', *Zeitschrift für aegyptische sprache* 32 (1894), pp. 325–8. *Life of Shenoute* 34, p. 52.
65 *Lives of the Desert Fathers* Prologue.
66 Rufinus, *Ecclesiastical History* II.3.
67 Palladius's visit is recounted in *Lausiac History* 7, 32.
68 This assessment is in Benedicta Ward, *Lives of the Desert Fathers* (Oxford, 1980), p. 20.
69 The Yale Monastic Archeology Project, under the direction of Stephen Davis, has been surveying these sites since 2006.
70 This is translated into English as *Lives of the Desert Fathers*, see above note 95.
71 See John Binns, *Ascetics and Ambassadors of Christ* (Oxford, 1994), pp. 49–53. The *Spiritual Meadow* is translated by John Wortley (Kalamazoo, MI, 1992).
72 The later history is presented in Otto F. A. Meinardus, *Monks and Monasteries of the Egyptian Deserts* (Cairo, 1989).

3

Asceticism and Society: The Holy Men of Syria

Syrian ascetic traditions

Syria is the area which lies at the eastern end of the Mediterranean Sea. It stretches from the Mediterranean coast in the west, with the city of Antioch, the modern Antakya, a few miles inland, to the Mesopotamian area between the rivers Tigris and Euphrates to the east. It has been populated since at least 10,000 BC and there are neolithic sites which date back to that period. The cities of Damascus and Aleppo are among the oldest continually inhabited cities of the world. The name Syria is derived from the older name Assyria in Mesopotamia.

Syriac Christianity had a strongly ascetic character from the beginning. Marcion (85–160) was the son of a bishop in the region of Pontus and went to Rome in 140. Here he taught that there was a distinction between the inferior creator God of the Old Testament and the true God of love as preached in the gospels and by Paul. Tatian (120–80) also travelled to Rome but separated from the church there in 172 and returned to his native Syria where he gained a following with his teaching on celibacy. This was expressed in the *Diatessaron*, a harmony of the gospels in which Tatian presented gospel texts which emphasized the celibacy of Jesus and taught the importance of renunciation. Then there was Mani (216–76), whose brand of dualistic faith has been described as the only independent universal religion to have derived directly from the Christian tradition, who grew up in a Christian community at Ctesiphon on the Tigris. When he was twelve years old, he experienced a series of visions. These showed him his true self, or soul, which he called his Twin, which spoke to him of the state before it entered the body. His religious teaching was a process by which the light hidden within the body of believers, and in the world around, could be released and brought back to their true home of light. He taught his followers to look up to the Sun to see a door into the kingdom of light swing open and to smell the perfume arising for the incense bushes of Iraq and so to become aware of the love of the Sun bringing the souls of the righteous back home.[1] After his martyrdom at the hands of the Persians, his disciples spread this evocative and vivid picture of a world of light entrapped but escaping from the surrounding darkness. It became popular in cities around the Mediterranean. Manichaeism is an example of the poetic, evocative spirituality of Syria which spread across the Christian world and would not be constrained by the disciplines of a church beginning to establish an organizational structure.

The ascetic tradition of Syriac Christianity is personified in the figure of Judas Thomas, an early apostle to the Syrian Christians. His story is told in the *Acts of Thomas*, which was written between 200 and 250 in Edessa. Here Thomas, who is the brother of Jesus rather than the apostle, goes to India as the slave of a merchant. He impresses the King Gundaphor who gives him gold and silver. But instead of building a palace, Thomas 'goes about the towns and villages, and if he has anything he gives it all to the poor and teaches a new God'. He is imprisoned, but later the king releases him and is baptized. Thomas then carries on his wandering apostolate, singing hymns, healing the sick, exorcising demons and preaching celibacy. Eventually he baptizes the wife and son of another king, Masdai, for which crime he is executed. It is a story which shows how Syrian Christians understood and responded to the teaching of Jesus. Jesus is homeless, poor, wandering and celibate. Thomas says; 'I boast of poverty, love of wisdom, humility, fasting, prayer, and the community of the Holy Spirit ... What have you come to see? A strange, poor man, one easily despised, a beggar, with neither wealth, nor possessions? But I have one possession which neither king nor rulers can take away, Jesus the Saviour of all humanity.'[2]

In these passages Thomas is the poor man or *ptochos*. This word implies that he is not only poor but destitute, huddled at the roadside in fear and emptiness, as opposed to the other kind of poor man, *penes*, who is dependent but still retains a sense of self-worth and can maintain his life. This kind of extreme poverty generates a charismatic power and leads to a close and open relationship with God, which is called *parresia* or freedom of speech. 'Perfect these things in us that we might have the freedom or *parresia* which is in you,' Thomas prays. The King Gundaphor summarizes the way people assessed and valued Thomas, and by extension the way Syrian society valued people who lived like Thomas.

> We think he a sorcerer or *magus*. But his works of compassion and the healings which he has done for free, and moreover his simplicity and kindness and his piety, show that he is righteous or an apostle of the new God who he preaches. For continually he fasts and prays, and eats only bread and salt, and his drink is water, and he wears a single garment whether in fine weather or foul, and takes nothing from anyone, and what he has he gives to others.[3]

This description could derive from any of the later monastic communities around the Christian world. Since it comes from a Syrian text probably written before 250, this shows how deeply rooted the ascetic ideals are in early popular Christianity. Here apostolic legitimacy is demonstrated by ascetic conduct.

This kind of conduct seems to have been a part of Christian living across the region of Syria. Celibacy had become recognized as a sign of holiness. Communities of virgins were found in many areas, but the Christianity of Syria especially valued celibacy and encouraged believers to accept the way of abstention. A vow of celibacy was sometimes taken at baptism or, later, by a married couple after they have brought up a family. There was a vocabulary used to describe these ascetic Christians. They might be *bthule*, virgins, or *qaddishe*, holy ones. *Qaddishe* were those who practised spiritual or continent marriage. Or they might be called *ihidaya* or single. *Ihidaya* describes

Jesus the only begotten or single Son of God, and can be extended to those who live a solitary or single life and then to those who express this through celibacy. So the *ihidaya* becomes the ascetic or a monk. These believers who follow this path of the *ihidaya* form a group within the church called *bnay* or *bnat qyama*, sons and daughters of the covenant. There is evidence for this style of life in the writing of Aphrahat, dating from around 337. The sons and daughters of the covenant were a distinct group somewhere between clergy and laity but distinct from both. At baptism they resolved to remain celibate. They lived alongside other Christians and served those in need. The life of the sons of the covenant was an example of how to live out the call of Christ in a radical form. They were valued as living examples of discipleship which were an example to others.[4]

Messalians

The Syrian deserts were mountains. This encouraged a different form of ascetic life from Egypt, where monks lived along the fertile Nile valley, where coenobitic communities were formed along the river valley and solitary ascetics lived in the dry lands beyond but remained in contact with the valley. In Syria, ascetics could roam more freely, living off the plants which grew wild in the mountainous plateaus or gleaning from the margins of cultivated land. This led to the form of ascetic life of the grazers or *boskoi*. The historian Sozomen describes these *boskoi* as living in the mountains 'continually praising God with prayers and hymns according to the law of the church. At the usual meal hours they would each take a sickle and wander in the mountains feeding off wild plants as if they were grazing.'[5] One ascetic, Macedonius, was known as the 'Barley Eater' and spent forty-five years wandering from place to place to avoid attention. This style of living has been called by the historian Peter Brown the 'Beduinisation of the ascetic life'.[6] Rather than forming themselves into agricultural communities, as in the coenobia of Pachomius or Shenoute, the Syrian monks could follow a nomadic wandering life, relying for food on nuts, asphodel roots and an edible wild thistle called mannouthia. This geography provided a backdrop for a Christian ideal following the example of the poor, homeless wandering, celibate Jesus, who brought a new kind of charismatic authority and power.

Later writers described these wandering ascetics as Messalians or people who pray, from the Syriac *msallyane*. The fathers of the Council of Ephesus of 431 disapproved, describing the Messalians, using the Greek equivalent word of Euchites, as 'the most noxious heresy in memory'. For Jerome they were the heretics of 'nearly all Syria'. There has been much debate about the Messalians. One charge made against them is the belief that baptism alone is not sufficient. This view was expressed by a leading Messalian, Adelphius, who, according to the historian Theodoret, claimed that

> there is no benefit from holy baptism for those who receive it, but only zealous prayer can drive out the indwelling demon. For each person derives an enslavement to demons along with nature. When these are driven away by assiduous prayer then the all-Holy Spirit comes giving sensible and visible signs of his own Presence. Not

only is he liberated from the agitations of the body, but he can also clearly foresee things to come, and behold the Holy Trinity with his own eye.[7]

Although these ideas were rejected by church councils, they remained influential in monastic circles.

The attractiveness of Messaliansim is shown by the popularity of the fifty *Spiritual Homilies* of Macarius. These were attributed to the Egyptian monk Macarius (c. 300– c. 390) and have been widely read. It is clear however that they came from a Syrian rather than Egyptian background, and were probably written by the Messalian Symeon of Mesopotamia. They have been valued for their emphasis on the place of the heart in the spiritual life, the action of the Holy Spirit and interior prayer. It has been suggested that a reason for the suspicion of Messalian texts within the church arose out of the difficulty of translating the poetic imagery of Syriac into the more philosophical language of Greek. 'Much of the language of Pseudo-Macarian writings are expressions in Greek of a spiritual argot characteristic of Syrian Christianity. This language sounded unusual, excessive or even dangerous when translated for a Hellenistic audience. When used repeatedly and with great freedom, this language would captivate readers by its beauty and vividness or could challenge and threaten them.'[8]

The term 'Messalianism' came to be used as a shorthand expression for this brand of ascetic lifestyle which was usual across Syria. It was anathematized at the synod of Gangra, a city in Paphlagonia. The sources provide two alternative dates for this meeting. It might have taken place sometime before 341, according to Sozomen, or sometime after 360, according to Socrates Scholasticus. The dating of this council shows that Messalian ideas were contemporary with the early days of the foundations of Antony and Pachomius. The twenty canons of the synod show why Messaliansim caused concern and how the ascetic practices of Syria were feared as subverting and undermining society. The canons of the Council describe a way of life which threatened the structure of society. The celibacy and virginity of the monks were threats to the institution of marriage. Parents and children neglect each other and break up the family when they leave to follow an ascetic life. Slaves leave their masters, again with the excuse of following asceticism. Women in these ascetic groups have left their husbands, cut their hair and wear the same clothes as men. The Messalians do not attend the regular services in the churches. They fast on Sundays rather than on Fridays. They do not recognize married priests. They were also accused of appropriating the offerings made to the church for themselves, claiming that these should be given to those who show exceptional sanctity. This relates to another charge often levelled against these groups, of *argia* or idleness. Instead of working and using income to support the poor, they devote themselves to prayer and expect the Christian community to support them.

Eustathius of Sebaste (c. 300–80) was the recognized leader and spokesman of the ascetics. He had been born in Sebaste in Armenia, then moved around to Antioch, Alexandria, to Caesarea Cappadocia, Constantinople and then to Paphlagonia.[9] In the course of these wanderings he gained supporters, so when he became bishop of Sebaste, he 'founded a society of monks in Armenia, Paphlagonia and Pontus and became the author of a monastic philosophy'.[10] His position led him to be accused of instigating the kinds of behaviour which was unsettling the bishops at Gangra who met 'for the investigation of the affair of Eustathius; and having found that many improprieties had been committed by the Eustathians, they sought to remove the evils occasioned by him'.[11] Sozomen, writing in the fifth century, thought that Eustathius's views had not been presented fairly at the synod of Gangra. It may be that the synod was opposing the extreme behaviour of some of Eustathius's followers, and that, as bishop, he was able to be a reconciler, mediating between the ascetic groups under attack and the bishops at the council. He survived the criticism of the council and continued to be a respected figure in the church, becoming bishop of Sebaste in 357. Basil of Caesarea was impressed by him and had hoped to meet him when he visited the monks of Syria.

An example of the kind of activity which the Council wanted to stamp out is shown by the career of the terrifying Archimandrite Barsawma, a name which means 'Son of Fasting'. While there is no evidence that he advocated the practices outlawed by the synod of Gangra, his ascetic life shows why he and others like him were feared and avoided. Born around 403, he lived as a youth in the hills around Samosata, following the life of a *boskos* eating wild plants. A group of disciples gathered around him and they set off on a wandering life. He travelled through Jordan and Palestine, striking terror wherever he went. At Petra, the citizens closed the gates against him but then opened them when the monks threatened to burn them down. Barsawma entered and predicted that a four-year drought would end, which happened with such dramatic force that the rain broke down the city walls. Later his band of monks was confronted by 15,000 armed Jews but these were so frightened by the iron plates he wore, presumably for penitential motives, and hair falling to the ground that they ran away. He pursued them and destroyed their synagogues. He was invited by the emperor to attend the Second Council of Ephesus, called the Latrocinium, in 448. He arrived at the head of an estimated thousand monks and took part in the brutal handling of Patriarch Flavian which led to his death. When Barsawma arrived uninvited at the Council of Chalcedon, three years later, the council turned on him and attacked him in their turn shouting 'the murderer to the lions'.[12]

The holy man

The lives of the holy men of Syria are recounted by Theodoret of Cyrrhus. Theodoret was born in 393 to a well-to-do family in Antioch. When his parents died he entered a monastery near Apamea and then in 423 became bishop of Cyrrhus, to the northeast of Antioch. Here he remained until his death in 466. When he was a bishop, he continued to follow his ascetic disciplines, avoiding the possession of property and sometimes returning for periods of withdrawal to his monastery. He is an example of a monk–bishop, carrying out a style of leadership valued in his native Syria where monks were often chosen as bishops, sometimes after resistance and flight by the unwilling monastic appointee. He was also a scholar and a writer. He was an apologist for the Antiochene two-nature Christology and a historian who wrote an *Ecclesiastical History*. Alongside that, he lovingly collected a series of portraits of the holy men he had visited and known in a *Religious History*. He wrote this history in 440 and tells the stories of twenty-nine ascetics, of whom three were women. Most came from the west of Syria, in the region of Antioch, Chalchis and Emesa, with the single exception of Julian Saba who came from Osrhoene. Julian's fame led Theodoret to include him. He lived as an ascetic for fifty years until his death in 367. A community of his disciples formed around him, from about 320, and soon numbered a hundred monks.[13] Thus the beginning of monastic community in Osrhoene took place in the same period as those of Pachomius in Egypt but following a less formalized way of life.

The monastic life of Syria was shaped not only by its ascetic traditions but also by its social background. The *Religious History* was a principal source for an important article by Peter Brown which has influenced the way that the lives of the saints are now understood. Published in 1971 and entitled the 'Rise and Function of the Holy Man in Late Antiquity', Brown shows that the holy man of Syria combined a life of extreme asceticism with a recognized place in society. He contrasts the monasteries of Egypt where the fertile river valley is sharply contrasted with the arid uninhabitable desert, where as he puts it 'to survive at all the Egyptian (monk) had to transplant in to the desert the tenacious and all-absorbing routines of the villages of the oikoumene.'[14] In Syria by contrast desert and city are interwoven, and the place of the holy man is both in the city and yet detached from it. Often the communities around the ascetic increased and diminished on a seasonal basis as monks went to work in the fields when needed for the harvest. The dwelling of the holy man is never far from the city.

Difference from the surrounding society is achieved not by physical withdrawal behind the wall of the monastic village, as in Egypt, but by constructing a distance from others by extremes of ascetic practice. Holy men found seclusion by enclosing themselves in their cell which was often so small that they could only stand in it. Palladius, for example, bricked himself up in a cell near a large and well-populated village called Imma. Marcianus's cell was not even the size of his own body and he built a further wall around that for increased protection from attention. Ascepimas remained walled in for sixty years 'neither being seen nor speaking'.[15]

Peter Brown describes the asceticism of the monks as a 'ritual of disassociation' by which the holy man becomes the stranger. Often he is an outsider, coming from a different place or leading a wandering life. This distance from society is deepened by his carefully chosen method of withdrawal. But although the holy man's lifestyle creates a distance and difference, it also roots him within the community. The dissociation arises because of the rootedness of the holy man in society.

The ascetic had a social role. It was a time when the large landed estates were breaking up and landowners were moving to the cities. Small farmers were taking their place. Agricultural work was seasonal and gangs of unemployed peasants roamed the countryside often attaching themselves to a holy man during periods of slack employment and leaving when the harvest came. 'The crowd', Brown comments, 'is the essential element of the holy man in Syria'.[16] There was instability, poverty, and a sudden absence of power and protection for the poor as the landowners left. Into this gap the holy man stepped. He took on the role of the patron, or *patronus*, offering protection and making his power available. 'To visit the holy man was to go where power was.'[17]

Theodoret's twenty-nine ascetics were protectors of the poor. Not only did they offer healings, exorcisms and the gift of children to women who were struggling to give birth, but they provided more practical assistance too. They might be asked to arbitrate in legal disputes. The holy man Abraham was called on to help when tax collectors were making exorbitant demands. He persuaded the tax collectors not to mistreat the local people, agreed to find a hundred gold pieces to pay the tax, went to a nearby city to negotiate a loan, returned with the money on the appointed payment day and paid the tax on the villagers' behalf. The consequence was that he was recognized as their patron, and was persuaded to be ordained priest and then was made a bishop for a nearby city.[18] Limnaeus lived out in the open, protected by a wall with a window through which he spoke to visitors. He was concerned at the number of blind people begging on the streets. He built houses for them around his own dwelling and required those who came to him for healing or advice to bring food to feed the beggars.[19]

The stories of Theodoret and the interpretation of Peter Brown demonstrate that the holy man – and woman – was not removed from society. Instead of their asceticism distancing them from those around it had the opposite effect. It gave them a place, a position and a power within the local community. They became important to the smooth running of social life, precisely because of their asceticism. The more extreme their ascetic practice and the more unconventional their way of life, the more effective they became in providing cohesion and compassion within the towns and villages of the region.

Stylites

The undoubted star of ascetic life in Syria was Symeon Stylites (390–439) who pioneered a form of ascetic life in which the monk lived on the top of a pillar reaching up towards heaven. He arrived at this form of asceticism by stages. Symeon was a shepherd boy who grew up on the borders of Syria and Cilicia. He could not read but was struck by hearing the Beatitudes read in church and this led him to lead an ascetic life in the monasteries of Tel'ada and then Telneshe. His life then became a search for ever more demanding forms of self-denial and mortification. His fasting was more extreme than others and the other monks found this so off-putting that he was asked to leave the monastery. He left and discovered a waterless cistern and lowered himself into that. Then he moved on to a small cottage and had the door blocked up with mud for the season of Lent. He agreed to have ten rolls of bread and a jar of water immured with him to ensure his survival but when the local people broke down the mud wall at the end of Lent, these foodstuffs were untouched and the holy man was lying almost senseless on the floor and had to be revived with a sponge dipped in water and applied to his lips. The next stage of his ongoing ascesis and desire to escape the crowds of curious visitors was to go to a mountaintop where he chained himself to a rock so he could not move away from it. It was only then, when, as one might expect, this level of ascetic practice attracted more visitors and sightseers and not less, that he began to construct the pillar on which he lived. This grew higher and higher, from six cubits, to twelve, to twenty-four and then finally to a height of thirty-six cubits, with a platform which was 6 feet square with a railing around it to stop him falling off. Sometimes the glare of the sun blinded him, sometimes ulcers went gangrenous, but he stayed on his column until he died at the age of seventy. His disciples brought him food once a week and twice a day he received visitors who climbed a ladder to his platform.[20]

Like other holy men of Syria, Symeon was an athlete and his prayer was an exercise in physical endurance as well as a mental reflection. He stood unsupported for long periods, eventually remaining standing throughout Lent. Prostration was also a part of his prayer. Theodoret tells us that he was with him when he prostrated himself 1,244 times, touching his feet with his forehead. But, as Theodoret comments, it is easier for Symeon than for others because his stomach is so reduced in size it does not get in the way.

After he died his body was carried to Antioch, 40 miles away, in a procession with seven bishops and six hundred soldiers, in a triumphal journey which took five days.

Stylitism became a popular form of ascetic living. Daniel, from Samosata in Mesopotamia, came on a pilgrimage from his monastery to Jerusalem and visited Symeon. He then went to Constantinople where he arrived in 452 at the age of forty-two. After some years in a monastery he built a pillar where he stood for the next thirty-three years until his death. He had two columns clamped together and was persuaded to allow a shelter to be constructed above his head. Sometimes monasteries were built around the stylite's pillar. At the monastery of Ar'a Rabtha at Amida, Abraham was the leading stylite. When he died another monk called Maro who had been living in a hollowed tree trunk took his place on the pillar. Then when he died the monk who had served him climbed up to take his place.[21]

Figure 5 The place of the column of St Symeon Stylites, at the centre of the ruined church at Qal'at Sima'an near Aleppo in Syria.

Holy fools

Syrian asceticism encouraged the emergence of another form of extreme asceticism, the holy fool. Symeon Salos (d. 590) came from Edessa and moved to Palestine where he became a monk in the monastery of Gerasimus, at Jericho. He did not settle in this life and the abbot agreed that he could leave. In 551 he went to Emesa.

> On a dung heap outside the city he found a dead dog. He took off the belt he wore and tied it to the dog's foot. Dragging it behind him he ran through the city gates, close to a school. The children began to shout 'the monk is mad' and ran after him, boxing his ears. The next day, which was a Sunday, Symeon took some nuts and entered the church. He threw them and extinguished the candles. When they rushed to throw him out he went up on the ambo and attacked the women with nuts.[22]

He continued to behave in a strange and unpredictable manner. He ate sausages on Good Friday. He ran into the section of the baths reserved for women. He lay on the ground shaking like an epileptic. He danced with theatre girls. But he continued to fast and pray. He performed acts of healing and power, often in order to persuade Jews or non-believers to become Christian. After his death the townspeople of Emesa recalled the wonderful things he had done and realized that he was a holy man and had simulated his madness.

He himself explained to his disciple, commenting especially on his visit to the women's baths. 'Believe me, as wood is with other pieces of wood, so I was then. I felt neither that I had a body, nor that I had entered a place where there were bodies. My whole soul was taken up with the Lord's work, and I did not desist from it.'[23]

Another fool for Christ was from Constantinople. Andrew (d. 936) was a slave of a man named Theognetus. He had a vision in which he was called to become a fool. He acted out this calling to foolishness and was sent by his master to a church known for its treatment of the mad. He was confined for four months, which he spent in prayer, and was then released since his madness could not be treated. He then went around naked, slept in the streets with the dogs and begged for food. There were a few people who recognized his ascetic path. Epiphanius, who later became patriarch of Constantinople, was his disciple. When his death approached, he prayed with Epiphanius, 'as paupers and pilgrims, in wretchedness and nakedness', then went to the edge of the city and prayed for the whole world. Then he lay down and died 'with a smile on his face', and his body was taken up to heaven.[24]

The holy fool has entered into monastic and ascetic history and is encountered in several places. It is a form of the humility of the monk who wants to take a low place. It is a virtue recognized and valued within the monastery.

The origins of monastic holy folly are found from the beginning of monasticism. When Palladius was travelling through Egypt about 420, he met a nun who pretended to be possessed by a demon. She worked in the kitchen doing the dirtiest work, eating the crumbs and scrapings from the cooking pots, wearing rags instead of the nun's robe. The other nuns beat her but she did not complain. As often happens in these accounts, it was revealed to a monk that she was more holy than the others. Then she was treated with respect. But she could not tolerate this new acceptance and she left the monastery.[25]

An ascetic lived in Edessa in the early fifth century. He was known only as the Man of God. The story, written around 470, began when he left home – the location is not stated – because his parents had arranged for him to be married. He lived as a beggar, fasting and praying. He was given a little food which he shared with others and lived outside with the other beggars. He stood through the night in prayer with his arms stretched out as a cross while they slept. The church caretaker discovered his way of life and asked him about it. The Man of God, standing among the beggars, said: 'Ask those in front of you, and from them you will learn who I am and whence I am, for I am one of them.' The Man died and was buried in the pauper's cemetery. When the caretaker went to look for the body, all he found were the rags that the Man of God had worn. The body had been taken up to heaven.[26] While the Man of God did not simulate madness, his way of obscurity had connections with the lives of the holy fools.

In commenting on this behaviour, the hagiographers of holy fools quote Paul writing to the Corinthians: 'If anyone among you thinks he is wise in this age, let him become a fool that he may become wise.'[27] The historian Evagrius wonders whether the fool has reached such a level of *apatheia*, or freedom from the passions, that he is free even from vanity. His behaviour shows that he has no concern for what others think of them which is the final stage of apatheia.[28] The hagiographer of Symeon Salos, Leontius, points out that a fool has claimed the right to behave in an unpredictable and scandalous way, and this gives him a licence to speak out without any reserve, attacking and condemning the behaviour of kings and rulers.[29]

Conclusion

The character of the Syrian landscape and social structures encouraged men and women to follow irregular and unconventional lives. They went out to live alone in the hills or in villages, or attached themselves to a holy man. This urgent longing to explore ascetic ways of life showed itself in the pathways of stylitism or holy madness or a wild wandering. This anomic and disruptive style entered into the monastic tradition and has appeared in all parts of its history, showing the uncompromising way that the Kingdom of God is not of this world.

Notes

1 This described in Mani's *Kephalaia* 65, cited in Peter Brown, *Body and Society* (New York, 1988), p. 199.
2 *Acts of Thomas*, 8, 126, 136, 139, in trans. H. J. W. Drijvers, *New Testament Apocrypha*, vol. 2 (Westminster 1992), pp. 339–411.
3 Ibid., 20; 61.
4 See Sidney Griffith, 'Asceticism in the Church of Syria: The Hermeneutics of Early Syrian Monasticism', in ed. Vincent Wimbush and Richard Valantasis, *Asceticism* (Oxford, 1995), pp. 220–45.

5 Sozomen, *Ecclesiastical History*, 6.33.2, ed. J. Bidez and trans. A-J. Festugière (Paris, 2005), p. 425.
6 Peter Brown, 'The Rise and Function of the Holy Man in Late Antiquity', *Journal of Roman Studies* 61 (1971), p. 84.
7 Theodoret, *Ecclesiastical History*, 4.11.7, ed. L. Parmentier and trans. P. Canivet (Paris 2009), pp. 225–6.
8 Columba Stewart, *Working the Earth of the Heart* (Oxford, 1991), p. 10.
9 Athanasius, *History of the Arians* 4.2; Basil, *Letters*, 244.9, 263.3. Susannah Elm, *Virgins of God, the Making of Asceticism in Late Antiquity* (Oxford, 1994), p. 107.
10 Sozomen, *Ecclesiastical History*, 3.14.31.
11 Mansi II.1106–7, see also Gilbert Dagron, 'Les Moines et la Ville', *Travaux et Mémoires* 4 (1970), pp. 229–76, at pp. 249–50.
12 The Council's acts are in Daniel Caner, *Wandering Begging Monks* (Berkeley, 2002), p. 208; and for Barsawma's life, see F Nau, 'Deux Episodes de l'Histoire Juive sous Théodose II (423 et 438) d'après la vie de Barsauma le Syrien', *Revue des études juives* 83 (1927), pp. 184–206.
13 Theodoret's *Religious History* has been translated by Richard Price as *Theodoret of Cyrrhus, History of the Monks of Syria* (Kalamazoo, MI, 1985). The Life of Julian Saba is on pp. 23–34.
14 Brown, 'Rise and Function', pp. 80–101, at p. 83.
15 These examples are in Theodoret, *History of the Monks of Syria*, pp. 69; 37–8; 114.
16 Brown, 'Rise and Function', p. 84.
17 Ibid., p. 87.
18 Theodoret, *History of the Monks of Syria*, pp. 121–4.
19 Ibid., pp. 151–2.
20 The details are taken from Theodoret, *History of the Monks of Syria*, pp. 160–76. This is the most reliable life of the saint. There are two other lives. A life by a monk called Antony describes his death but says little about his life, and a Syriac version is lengthy but has many legendary and later additions.
21 John of Ephesus, *Lives of the Eastern Saints* 4, PO 17.83–4.
22 *Life of Symeon the Fool*, in ed. John Saward, *Perfect Fools* (Oxford, 1980), p. 19.
23 Ibid., p. 20.
24 *Life of St Andrew the Fool* in ibid., pp. 20–1.
25 Palladius, *Lausiac History* 34.
26 This story is in (ed.) A. Arniaud, *Legende syriaque*, cited in Susan Ashbrook Harvey, *Asceticism and Society in Crisis* (Berekley, CA, 1990), p. 16.
27 1 Corinthians 3.18.
28 Evagrius, *Ecclesiastical History* 4.34.
29 Leontius, *Life of Symeon the Fool* 155.19–156.4.

4

An Experiment in Community Living: The Cities of Asia Minor

Basil of Caesarea and his family

Basil of Caesarea is one of the great theologians of the early church. Along with his brother, Gregory of Nyssa, and his friend, Gregory of Nazianzus, he has been known as one of the Cappadocian Fathers, a defender of the faith of Nicaea and an author of works defining the place of the Holy Spirit in Trinitarian theology. He was also the author of a monastic rule and founder of monasteries. Soon after Pachomius had begun to form his communities of peasant monks, Basil was setting up communities of the *spoudaioi* or 'zealous'. Both founders set up coenobitic communities but with distinct characters. Basil came from a different region, a different family background, had a different kind of education and a different set of responsibilities in the church. Some of his monasteries were set up in cities, rather than in villages as in Pachomius's Egypt. They were integrated into the life of the church, where Basil, as bishop, presided. They were communal and did not accept the solitary eremitical life which, Basil taught, was incompatible with the great rule of love.

Basil (330–79) was one of nine siblings, four of whom shared with him his experiments in the foundation of monastic life in Asia Minor. He was born in Pontus on the Black Sea coast and came from a Christian family, who remembered with affection and reverence their grandmother who had died a martyr for her faith in the persecutions of the third century. His elder sister, Macrina, encouraged the members of the family in their Christian zeal and was the subject of a glowing funeral oration by their brother Gregory, who had become bishop of Nyssa. Also within this group was a friend of Basil, another Gregory, known by the name of the town of Nazianzus, where he was bishop as well as being briefly patriarch of Constantinople (380–81).

Macrina was the first in the family to follow an ascetic community life. She was engaged to be married at the tender age of twelve and had to wait for two years before reaching the legal minimum age for marriage. During that period of waiting her husband-to-be, who at twenty-five was more than twice her age, died. Macrina considered herself to be a widow and refused a further engagement. Her life, written by her brother Gregory, described this decision, in language derived from the writings of Plato, as a choice to live a 'philosophical life'. She lived 'by herself', *eph eautes* and was both an unmarried girl and a widow.[1] Later her father died and she went with her mother Emmelia to live on one of the family estates at a beautiful rural spot called Annesi with mountains, clear streams, trees and a small village. Here she guided both her mother and her household into the life of an ascetic community. There was prayer, psalms which were said at various times of the day and night and manual work. This was a life followed by many devout households, but Macrina took this to a new and more subversive level. Macrina 'persuaded her mother to share a common life with all her maids, making them sisters and equals instead of maids and servants … with every difference of rank eliminated from their lives'. Macrina used to bake bread for her mother, which was a task of the slaves.[2] New recruits joined her, and among them were slaves as well as wealthy and educated women. They lived together as sisters, with all of whatever social class treated as equals.[3]

When her younger brother Naucratius died, Macrina remained calm and, in the period of mourning, was the leader and guide of the family. She felt responsible for her youngest brother Peter and was for him 'father, teacher, pedagogue, mother, counsellor of all which is good'. It was then that she became as a mother to her own mother, and also introduced her to the 'philosophical life', 'becoming of the same status as the many and sharing the same life as the virgins'.[4] The shift in her position in the family and the community around her was a significant moment, referred to by Susannah Elm as 'the first step towards the transformation of an ascetic household into an ascetic institution'.[5]

Macrina's lifestyle choice was a recognized Christian path, and, until her upsetting and subversive actions of accepting sisterhood with slaves, was not remarkable. Virgins had a recognized place in Christian tradition, appeared in the Bible and are encountered frequently in the narratives of early Christianity.[6] Virgins could be either women or men, who chose to follow a life of discipline, prayer and the search for wisdom. They were recognized as true philosophers.

The ascetic household would become a familiar form of Christian community in the church. Members of a family would decide to live on the family estates and follow a monastic life. The influential monasteries in later Byzantium of Stoudios and Evergetis both started as domestic family projects, independent of the bishop or emperor. The community which was set up by Macrina became a model followed by others.

Basil's formation

Her younger brother Basil, meanwhile, was receiving a thorough education following a traditional classical syllabus at Caesarea in Cappadocia, then at Constantinople and finally at Athens, where he studied between 351 and 356. His teacher at Constantinople was the pagan scholar Libanius. Later, at Athens, he met Gregory of Nazianzus who was to remain a friend and collaborator for the rest of his life. There was also another student, Julian, who became initiated into Eleusinian mystery religions and became the last pagan emperor, ruling for two years from 361 to 363. This education gave Basil the philosophical abilities which established his reputation in the society of the time. Later his brother referred to him as, at this time, 'exceedingly puffed up by his rhetorical activities and disdainful of all great reputations'.[7] After he had completed these studies, Basil the scholar returned to Caesarea in 356 and was baptized.

His education helped him to understand and value the Greek ideal of living the philosophic life. He had devoted himself to follow these disciplines during his studies at Athens and elsewhere. The aim of this form of life was for the rational part of man to rule over the irrational. This idea is evoked by the image of the mythical beast of the centaur, with an upper human section ruling over the lower part of the body which was that of a horse. The philosopher should be moderate and reasonable, avoiding the excesses of both self-indulgence on the one hand and destructive mortification on the other. This middle way cleanses the soul and brings it close to God. It avoids the passions of anger, hypocrisy and envy. Above all it is chaste, with purity of body leading to purity of soul. The follower of the philosophic life was a recognized figure in the Greek city. As a sign of avoidance of earthly pleasures, the philosopher often wore a special coat, called a *peribolaion*. This wide and simple overcoat was recognized as a mark of the search for wisdom. Later the monk, like the philosopher, would wear a distinctive garment.

To this philosophical and rhetorical education, Basil added ascetic zeal. He was influenced by Eustathius, the bishop of the nearby city of Sebaste, and he set out on a series of travels to visit the ascetics of Egypt, Syria, Palestine and Mesopotamia. Eustathius was a leader of ascetics and had aroused opposition because of the scandalous and controversial behaviour of some of the groups of ascetics who he had supported. Basil had hoped to meet the bishop on his travels, but Eustathius eluded him.

He wrote home during this visit, describing the ascetics who met on this tour:

> I admired their continence in living and their endurance in toil; I was amazed at their persistence in prayer and triumphing over sleep; subdued by no natural necessity, ever keeping their soul's purpose high and free, in hunger, in thirst, in cold, in nakedness, they never yielded to their body; they were never willing to waste attention on it, always as though living in a flesh that was not theirs, they showed in very deed what it is to sojourn for a while in this life, and what it is to have one's citizenship and home in heaven .... I prayed that I too as far as in me lay, might imitate them.[8]

He returned home with a burning desire to follow the ascetic life he had observed in his travels. His position in the educated urban society of Asia Minor and his elevation to the office of bishop enabled him to develop a distinctive form of monastic life and show how this could have a place within the life of the whole church.

Bishop of Caesarea

The young Basil had received a good education and had been exposed to many influences and become accustomed to diverse ways of life. From his family, there were examples of martyrdom to set before him the martyr's commitment of sacrifice; from his more immediate family, there was the expression of this through following an ascetic approach to the Christian life. His studies had initiated him into a search for philosophy; then his wandering around Asia and Egypt had shown him a mixture of ascetic lifestyles of varying levels of counter cultural non-conformity. Monastic life was already being lived in various forms, so Basil was not a founder of monastic life but a reformer, re-thinking and adapting the ascetic and monastic ideal for a cultured, educated, urban and ecclesiastical environment.

After his travels, Basil returned to his family estate in Pontus, and settled at Annesi in 357 or 358. He selected a site on the other side of the river from Macrina and her community of family members and others. Basil described his retreat affectionately. 'Learning that this (Pontus) was a suitable place for the study of philosophy on account of the quiet of its solitude, I passed a period of many successive years here.'[9] He came here to live the philosophical life. At this retreat, there was a place to live, servants to support the life of the household, space for study and prayer, and also there were visits from friends. Some accounts suggest that he spent several years living like this, perhaps even, as the historian Rufinus states, the full thirteen years between his arrival in 357 and his elevation to become a bishop in 370.[10] It seems more likely, however, that he spent only short periods in this retreat which were interspersed with periods of travel and with church business. A reconstruction of events suggests a first period of a year between 358 and 359 at Annisi, and then a second stay between 362 and 365. He describes this life as a time of solitude, with exercises of prayer at the beginning of the day, with simple but warm and practical clothes, a diet of vegetables and bread, and light periods of sleep. Basil's aim was to protect himself from too many external distractions and to give himself space for study and reflection.

He went to Caesarea in 365 where he was ordained priest and then became bishop five years later, in 370. He began his life as bishop at a time when food was short, after a supply crisis in 369. As he took responsibility for his diocese at this time of need, he combined his ascetic ideals with the care for the poor. This led him to establish the Basileiados, which was founded in 370. This institution was established at the edge of the town and was devoted to the care of the poor, sick and needy. Basil himself 'greeted the sick like brothers and dressed their wounds'.[11] Local people, especially those with wealth, supported it. It was a 'common treasury of the wealthy, where superfluous riches, sometimes even necessities are laid up ... there sickness is endured with equanimity, calamity is a blessing, and sympathy is put to the test'. At the centre was 'a house of prayer built in magnificent fashion' and near it was 'a residence one portion being a generous home reserved for the one in charge, and the rest subordinate quarters for the servants of God's worship'.[12] These passages describe a large and well-endowed community, planned to be a kind of new city, which was a place for both the ascetic life and also the care of all who are outcast or in distress. From the Basileiados, the diocese was administered, the ascetic life lived out and pastoral care provided in a creative blend which became a part of the life of a diocese in a large and prominent city.

Basil described this, in a letter written in 376.

> I desire you to know that we boast of having a body of men and women whose conversation is in heaven, who have crucified the body with its affections and desires, who do not concern themselves with food and clothing, but being undistracted and inconstant attendance upon the Lord, remain day and night

in prayer. They sing hymns to God unceasingly, while they work with their own hands that they may have something to share with those in need.[13]

The Basileiados demonstrated how the life of the monastery can be located in a city and within the life of the church. It was to be further developed in the monasteries of Constantinople where the patriarch and bishops became founders and benefactors of monasteries. Lying behind his writing, we can discern his settled, prosperous Christian family, the memory of the total gift of self of the martyr setting out a picture of an extra clear sign of zeal, the tradition of philosophical study reaching back into classical pagan culture, the life of a church in the new climate of toleration and acceptance. All this comes together in the city of Caesarea in the building up of communities of care and prayer.

Basil's monasticism

Basil's ascetical writings consist of two sets of rules and passages of correspondence which set out some of the principles which guide the life of his ascetic communities. The Shorter Rule is so-called because it is composed of shorter sections even though its total length is substantial. It is a collection of comments on Scripture or answers to questions, perhaps noted down by a secretary in conferences in which he answered questions put to him. The Longer Rule is a more systematic explanation of the ascetic life.

Basil does not describe himself as a founder of monasteries nor think that his way of life is different in kind from that which should be led by all Christians. He does not use the word 'monk' or any equivalent phrase, even though it was a word in regular use at the time, and he does not describe his community as a monastery. But he does recognize that this is a way of life that will not be followed by all. He encourages a zealous Christian life and accepts that there are different levels of enthusiasm, or *spoude*, and these need to be nurtured and accommodated within one church community. Ascetics were a recognized group within the church, distinct from both clergy and laity. But Basil does not think of them as a separate and regulated order of monks.

He urges his readers and listeners to be zealous or *spoudaios*. His audience in his letters and sermons is broad. He is writing for all and encouraging them to grow in faith and not restricting his message to those who were part of a formal community. His Rules evolved as he addressed the challenges of administering his diocese and saw the need to stiffen the dedication of the members of the community as the means of doing this.

He affirms the priority of love and shows how this is lived out within groups and communities of believers. To do this the Christian needs both to withdraw from the demands and attractions of a secular world and to live with others who share the same Christian longings. This leads to the need for some regulation to maintain the life of the community. Basil gives guidance as to how this living for others should be carried out. He describes the procedures about how newcomers should be admitted, about clothing to be worn (and here he suggests distinctive clothing in order that the Christian should be recognizable and so be challenged to live according to the standards expected of him) and the importance of obedience to the superior. The Rules set out some of the guiding principles which would become part of monastic spirituality.

Boundaries matter. If the Christian life follows different standards from secular society, then those who follow this way of life must show that they are committed to it. Basil realizes that the members of his community of the zealous should be distinctive, identifiable and set apart. Boundaries distinguish the zealous from those who have not yet arrived at this stage. The boundary both makes a distinction between the committed from the nominal and also provides an incentive for potential members to advance to the state of *spoudaios,* by taking that decision to cross the threshold into the new community. Some would respond to this gospel call, cross the boundary and become part of the smaller group. Here they would learn and pray together and receive teaching and advice from a more accomplished leader. This leader, teacher and guide was called by Basil *proestoos,* or the one who presides. Philip Rousseau noted the importance of the boundary. 'The sense of a frontier, however vague, between dedicated religiosity and a less energetic attachment to spiritual growth was probably the first and perhaps the most important step towards the development of independent monasticism.'[14]

Basil's achievement was to bring together divergent styles of living in a way which showed how the ascetic life could be lived in community within the structures of the city and regulated by the church. Gregory Nazianzus wrote of *migados bios* or mixed life. *Migados* describes two contrasting things being pushed together, literally 'mixed in confusion'. The two elements are the eremitical life which is governed by *philosophia* and *hesychia*, and the communal life. The mixed life is more useful and practical and provides service and care for those in need. It is active in charity and involves in the life of the church. While Basil recognizes the need for silence and withdrawal, he advocates community life and critical of the solitary life of the hermit. The solitary life, he writes, 'is plainly in conflict with the law of love. (As a solitary) whose feet, then, wilt thou wash? Whom wilt thou care for? In comparison with whom wilt thou be the last if thou livest by thyself?'[15] His way of life is led in community and with others.

In spite of the fact that Basil does not describe his communities as monasteries, others recognized the significance of what he taught and recognized him as a monastic founder. Contemporaries report how he set up new monastic communities. The historian Socrates Scholasticus described these communities as *asketeria*, places of ascetic struggle, and Sozomen called them *sunoikias to monachon pollas*, all the places where monks lived together.[16] Gregory of Nazianzus says that Basil produced 'written and unwritten legislation for monks' and 'written rules designed to encourage bodily purity and spiritual vision'.[17] A later monk, Nikon of the Black Mountain writing in the eleventh century, described 'the monastic state as that which clearly conforms to the precepts of St Basil'.[18] In the west, Benedict recommended Basil's writings in his own Rule.[19] He approved Basil's approach to community life, with the emphasis on obedience to the superior, the requirement for active work and the priority given to silence and humility. His Rule includes similar regulations for the admitting of newcomers and gives careful guidance for the place of boys in the community.

The monk–bishop

Basil did not only give a structure to communities in Caesarea and then across the empire. But he also set out a model of leadership in the church. He builds his understanding of leadership on the examples found in the Bible. In his homilies on the *Hexaemeron* he describes Moses as not only a man of God but also an example of leadership. Moses life can be divided into three periods, each of forty years.

During the first forty years of his life, Moses was instructed in the Egyptian disciplines; during the next forty years, under the pretext of tending sheep, he withdrew to deserted places and gave himself to the contemplation of realities. And then finally, having been judged worthy of the vision of God after this second period of forty years, he unwillingly left his contemplation and descended for the care of humanity so that he could show God's love for his people. Yet not even then did he remain continually in the active life but returned frequently into times of contemplation.[20] As he describes Moses's life, Basil is also reflecting on his own career, with its movement from study at Athens, to the withdrawn philosophical life at Annesi, from which he was summoned to lead the church at Caesarea. His brother, Gregory of Nyssa, also recalled this Mosaic threefold pattern of movement, and then reminded his readers that Moses was the great contemplative and so this model affirms the continuing priority of the vision of God even in the middle of administrative cares. 'Many times we perceived that he also was in the dark cloud wherein was God. For what was invisible to others, to him was the initiation into the mysteries of the Spirit made visible, so that he seemed to be within the compass of the dark cloud in which knowledge about God was concealed.'[21]

These commentaries were written as the church was adapting to its new place in society. Only a few decades before Basil was born, Christianity was persecuted and was maintaining a minority existence on the edge of mainstream political life. As late as 257 the Emperor Valerian pronounced that clergy, including bishops, could receive the death penalty. Now, after the toleration of the Christian faith, the church found itself with power, influence and money. This raised difficult questions about how this new kind of church should be managed and what kind of people should lead it. Basil evolved and described a style of leadership for this changed church. His leadership style grew out of his understanding of the Christian life. It brought together study, asceticism, teaching and administration. This mixture of roles in due course led to the tradition that only monks could become bishops. Delehaye suggests that the approach to leadership in the church went through a progression of ideas about what were the right models for the Christian leader. First there was the martyr/confessor, who was superseded by the ascetic/monk; and then later the bishop/leader combined these roles.[22]

The roots of the requirement for bishops to be monks can be seen in the evolution of the role of the bishop. From early times, virginity was praised and practised within the church. Communities of consecrated virgins were found throughout the church especially from the fourth century. It was the bishop who regulated and protected the virgins and he was better able to do this if he shared in their commitment to celibacy. Another responsibility was the management of church property which was becoming more extensive as it gained wealth and possessions grew. The bishop was required to keep his own property separate from that of the church and this was hard to enforce when the bishop had a family to provide for. Justinian legislated in the sixth century against married persons becoming bishops – a law which confirmed existing custom. A further consideration was the need for the bishop to care for his flock and his care for a family might conflict with this. Ephraim the Syrian wrote: 'Behold thy flock is thy wife, bring up her children in thy faithfulness.'[23]

Monks had been chosen to be bishops from an early date. An example of a monk-bishop is Rabbula of Edessa. He was born in Chalchis, then known as Qennesrin, near Aleppo, and became bishop of Edessa in 412, where he remained until his death in 436. He was educated in classical learning and was converted to Christianity as a young man through the example of some of the holy monks of Syria. He decided that the only place to be baptized was the Jordan river so he set out to the Holy Land. On his return, he gave away his possessions, freed his slaves and sent his mother, wife and children to various monasteries while he withdrew to the desert. Soon he was chosen for the vacant bishopric of Edessa, and, unlike some other monks, did not resist, even admitting – with disarming honesty – that he had within him a 'longing for this dignity'. As a bishop he continued his disciplines of fasting, vigils and abstinence, and retired each year for a forty-day retreat to his former monastery. His life tells us that he was motivated by three principles as a bishop – to continue his ascetic practices, to care for the poor, and to preach righteous living to all especially the clergy. He wanted his priests to be 'as similar to the heavenly angels as human nature allowed'.[24] His model of episcopal leadership is similar to that of Basil and shows how the idea of the monk-bishop grew.

Other bishops were married and remained unashamedly married. Synesius of Cyrene on becoming bishop of Ptolemais wrote 'I shall not be separated from her (my wife) nor shall I associate with her surreptitiously were, like an adulterer. I desire and pray to have virtuous children.'[25] But the obstinate tone of the passage suggests that there was an expectation that he should send her away and so he felt that he needed to show his commitment to his marriage. Gregory of Nyssa was married to a woman called Eusebia but seems to have had no children.

The Council in Trullo of 691 devotes two canons to the celibacy and continence of the episcopate. Canon 12 reaffirms that bishops should be celibate, reminding those bishops who are married that they should not cohabit with their wives. This seems to have been a problem in Africa, especially in Libya, and 'some other places', where cohabitation was permitted but abstinence was required in the relationship. There was unease about this and Canon 48 says that the practice of abstention is necessary for the good ordering of the church. The fathers of the council were embarrassingly aware that the Apostolic Legislation, Canon 5, had clearly instructed married bishops not to put away their wives under pretence of piety and if they did then they should be excluded. They would have been less embarrassed if they had been aware that this document did not derive from the Apostles teaching but was a much later composition.

The practice of celibacy in bishops had developed slowly. Athanasius of Alexandria, writing in 353, says that seven bishops had been monks, but this was out of a total of sixty-five bishops in Egypt.

The end of the iconoclast controversy proved to be a pivotal period in establishing the monastic character of episcopacy. The monks had remained faithful to the icons while the bishops had supported the iconoclasm of the emperors. The *Life of Stephen the Younger*, a monk in this period, refers to the *episkotoi*, or bishops of darkness, rather than *episkopoi*.[26] In fact the iconoclastic movement was supported by many monks but this inconvenient fact was overlooked, and monks claimed that they were the upholders of the true faith. After the victory of icons, the number of monks who became bishops grew. Between 600 and 795, four out of a total of twenty patriarchs of Constantinople had been monks, but after 800 the balance shifted. From then on until 1204, forty-five out of sixty-seven patriarchs of Constantinople were monks.

Further church councils confirmed this practice. In 879, the Council of Haghia Sophia declared that it was a universal custom that bishops should be celibate. It also required monks who were bishops to continue to wear monastic habit. In 1186, another council in Constantinople said that bishops must take monastic vows and if a bishop had a wife then she should become a nun.

There were still some exceptions. John Glykys was a layman when he was chosen to become patriarch of Constantinople in 1319. He was preparing to take monastic vows in preparation for this position when the Emperor Andronikos II dissuaded him because of his poor health. The last patriarch who was not a monk was John XXIV who occupied the post from 1334 to 1347. By 1429, Symeon of Constantinople was able to state that almost all candidates for bishoprics are monks, and then later in 1625 Metrophanes Kritopoulos wrote in his *Confession of Faith* that 'the Church always selects the bishops from the ranks of the monks'.[27]

The tradition that bishops are monks became established. This prevailed over the resistance of monks of earlier periods to office in the church. They had insisted that the vocation of the monks requires obedience and submission rather than authority and power, being taught rather than teaching. The growth of the monk–bishop, as lived by Basil and others, led to a style of leadership which produced many examples of bishops who lived ascetic lives which they taught to others and which became a model for all within the church.

Conclusion

Basil and Macrina died in the same year, 379. By this time monastic life had become well-established. Antony had died in 356, having moved to his inner mountain of Clysma in 313. Pachomius had died ten years before Antony. In Syria Julian Saba's followers had gathered around him and formed a community about 320. The synod of Gangra had been convened in 340 to respond to concerns about the socially disruptive character of the growing ascetic movement. These few decades in the mid-fourth century were seminal, with new styles of ascetic and communal life springing up independently yet also in contact with each other in many places across the empire. In the next stage of development of monastic life, attention moves to two cities where monks met and monasteries became integrated into the life of church and state. These cities were Constantinople and Jerusalem.

Notes

1. Gregory of Nyssa, *Life of Macrina* 3.40, 5.16, ed. and trans. Pierre Maraval, *Grégoire de Nysse, Vie de Sainte Macrine* (Paris, 1971).
2. Ibid., 5.30.
3. Slaves could receive a formal act of manumission – *manumissio in ecclesia* – carried out before the bishop and promoting the slave to the position of a free citizen, or manumission *inter amicos* when a slave owner simply declared his slave a friend and invited him to dine at the same table, as decreed in edicts of Constantine in 316 and 323.
4. *Life of Macrina* 6.8–10, 7.2–8.
5. Susannah Elm, *Virgins of God, the Making of Asceticism in Late Antiquity* (Oxford, 1994), p. 89.
6. For example, Matthew 25.1–13.
7. *Life of Macrina* 6.
8. Basil, *Letter* 223, vol. 3, pp. 287–313.
9. *Letter* 210.1, vol. 3, p. 197.
10. Rufinus, *Ecclesiastical History* 2.9.
11. Gregory of Nazianzus, *Oration* 43.63.
12. Basil, *Letter* 93.1, vol. 2, pp. 145–7.
13. Basil, *Letter* 207.2., vol. 3, p. 187.
14. Philip Rousseau, *Basil of Caesarea* (Berkeley, CA, 1994), p. 197.
15. Basil, *Longer Rule*, in PG 345E–347E. Translated in W. K. Lowther Clarke, *The Ascetic Works of St Basil* (London, 1925).
16. Socrates, *Ecclesiastical History* 4.26; Sozomen, *Ecclesiastical History* 6.15.4.
17. Gregory of Nazianzus, *Oration* 43.34.
18. Nikon, *Pandektos* 4.
19. *Rule of Benedict* 73.
20. Basil, *Hexaemeron*, PG 30.129A. Basil's authorship has been questioned but the work certainly comes from the circles in which he lived.
21. Gregory, *Life of Moses*, in ed. W. Jaeger, *Gregorii Nysseni Opera*, 10 vols (Leiden, 1952–90), vol. 10, pp. 129.5–9. Also in Andrea Sterk, *Renouncing the World Yet Leading the Church* (Harvard, 2004), p. 104.
22. Ibid., p. 218.
23. Carmina Nisibiensis 19.1, also in Peter l'Huillier, 'Episcopal Celibacy in the Orthodox Tradition', *St Vladimir's Theological Quarterly* 35, no. 2–3 (1991), pp. 271–300, at pp. 279–81.
24. Sterk, *Renouncing the World*, pp. 195–7.
25. Synesius, *Letter* 105, in trans. A. Fitzgerald, *The Letters of Synesius of Cyrene* (Oxford, 1926), p. 199.
26. Sterk, *Renouncing the World*, p. 221.
27. These examples are in l'Huillier, 'Episcopal Celibacy', pp. 271–300.

5

The Holy City of Jerusalem and Its Desert

A Christian city

While Constantine was changing the empire's view of the Christian faith and was building up the city of Constantinople, his mother Helena was similarly employed in Jerusalem. In 326 she set off on a journey to the Holy City. She arrived to find it depopulated and diminished and 'what was once Jerusalem desolate as a preserve for autumn fruits.'[1] She set out to search for the cross on which Jesus had died. She consulted various Jewish teachers as to where the place of crucifixion had been and she met a teacher called Kyriakos, who was a relative of Stephen the first martyr. He guided her to the place and they dug to reveal three crosses. A funeral procession was passing and they laid each of the three crosses in turn on the body of the dead man. When the third cross touched him, the corpse revived and came back to life.[2] The preservation of the memory of the place by local Christians had been assisted by the Emperor Hadrian who had built a large platform with temples to Jupiter and Venus in this prominent place. While this platform hid from view the place of Christ's crucifixion, it also marked it and Helena carried out her excavations under the Temple of Venus.[3] This discovery led to an ambitious programme of church building and research to identify the holy places where Christ had lived and died. From then on, the landscape of the city and surrounding area were transformed with, as one commentator puts it, 'holy places emerging from the ground like mushrooms'.[4] Pilgrims started to arrive and among these new arrivals were the monks.

This was the beginning of a period of three centuries when Jerusalem was a Christian city and a place which attracted pilgrims from all parts of the Christian world, many of whom stayed and became monks. Unlike Jews for whom Jerusalem, and the land of Israel, was always the homeland for which they longed, and Muslims, for whom Mecca was the place all wanted to go to as pilgrims, Christians have set their gaze on a 'new Jerusalem, coming down out of heaven from God', which has superseded the physical earthly Jerusalem.[5] But for this period of its history the earthly Jerusalem was the centre of the Christian world. The monasteries were a part of this Byzantine Jerusalem and even after the fall of the city to the Arabs, the traditions of the holy city have continued to be a well-spring of influence for churches.

The monasteries of Palestine lay at a meeting point for Christians from the regions around. The significance of Jerusalem as the place of Jesus's death and resurrection attracted visitors from many places and of many backgrounds. The result of this influx of visitors and pilgrims was a monasticism which formed by many influences and which in turn influenced the later development of monastic life across the Byzantine Empire. It was in Palestine that the life of the monasteries became part of the life of the church and then of the empire.

Gaza

While Jerusalem was beginning to attract pilgrims, monasteries had already been set up in the coastal region around Gaza. It was inevitable that a movement which was flourishing in Egypt should quickly spread to Palestine. The highway from Antioch in Syria to Alexandria along the Mediterranean coast was a busy trade route. It connected Egypt with the city of Gaza in the south of Palestine, and from there it was a journey of 50 miles to Jerusalem. There were also connections by sea from Gaza to Alexandria and other parts of the Mediterranean.

People in Palestine knew of Antony's flight to the desert. Antony was used to welcoming visitors from Jerusalem. He told his disciples to ask where new arrivals came from. If they were Egyptian, then they were to be given food, but if they came from Jerusalem a spiritual discourse was more fitting. The commentator does not say whether this was because the Palestinian monks had their minds on higher things than food and drink or were more in need of instruction.[6]

It may have been Antony's example which gave Bishop Narcissus of Jerusalem the idea of retiring to the desert when he had become wearied by the intrigues in his diocese. Here he remained for many years.[7] Another early Palestinian monk was Hilarion, whose life was written by Jerome. Hilarion (291–371) was, according to Jerome, the first monk in Gaza and, together with Antony of Egypt, he established monastic life. Hilarion came from a village near Gaza, was educated in Alexandria and visited Antony. In 308 he returned to Thavatha, near Gaza, where he lived in solitude for twenty-two years in a hut by the sea. Jerome tells us that 'there were no monasteries in Palestine nor did anyone know anything about monks in Syria before the holy Hilarion' and then 'by his example numberless monasteries were established in all of Palestine and many monks flocked to him.'[8] Jerome's life claims that Hilarion is a younger, better educated and more accomplished miracle worker than Antony and together they founded monastic life. He describes, for example, how a woman came to Gaza from Egypt to ask Hilarion to save and heal her sons, although she had already entrusted them to Antony's care.[9]

Gaza became a centre of monastic life. It was a prosperous area, with agricultural villages on the coastal plain. Although there was no desert to act as invitation to monks, it nevertheless attracted those who wanted to live the ascetic life. The sensitive political situation in modern day Gaza impedes archaeological research and so it is not possible to thoroughly research and excavate the monastic sites of the city, but various writings describe the monasteries of Gaza.[10]

While there must have been good communication between Gaza and Jerusalem, since the two cities are only fifty miles distant from each other, the sources from both places show a surprising lack of awareness of the other. Cyril of Scythopolis, when he wrote a history of the monasteries of Palestine in the mid-sixth century, does not describe the monasteries of Gaza, while the church historian Sozomen, born in 380 in the town of Bethelea, near Gaza, does not mention the monasteries of Jerusalem nor of the Judaean desert, although he does give space to the monasteries of Egypt and Syria.[11]

This surprising lack of mutual awareness could be because of the close relationship with Egypt. Egyptian monks often took refuge in Gaza when persecution or barbarian attacks took place. Soon after the death of Hilarion, in 380, Silvanus came from Scetis with a group of followers and they lived together in a monastic community. He died before 414 and was succeeded as abbot of the monastery by his disciple Zacharias and then by Zeno, who died in 451.[12] Some monks came as refugees fleeing the attacks of hostile tribes on the monasteries of Scetis which had taken place in 407 and then on further subsequent occasions. John Moschus reports words of Abba Irenaeus that 'when barbarians came to Scetis I withdrew and came to the district of Gaza, where I accepted a cell for myself in the laura'.[13] Others were driven out by divisions in the church. When Archbishop Theophilus condemned Origenist teachings, leading monks including the Four Tall Brothers arrived in Gaza before moving on to Constantinople.

The ascetic disciplines of Egypt were handed on by word of mouth, as the disciples of the monks asked for a word, revealed their thoughts and longings and lived in obedience. It was an oral tradition expressing the insights and learning coming out of monastic practice. We can assume that collections of the sayings of the fathers were remembered and written, but the departure from the monastery and settling in a new place gave a new urgency to the remembering and recording. The alphabetical and systematic collections of the *Sayings of the Desert Fathers* contain sayings from Palestine as well as Egypt, which suggests that the collections were made by monks who had come to Gaza, and so included the sayings which they knew and which had come out of the monasteries of both places.[14] From here, the virtues of the Egyptian fathers became more widely known. The monk Euthymius was among those who listened 'with joy ... when the venerable fathers who came to him at various times from Egypt recounted details of Arsenius' life'.[15]

Another collection of sayings which came out of Gaza is the *Correspondence of Barsanuphius and John*. These old men came from Egypt and settled near Gaza about 530, in a monastery where the abbot was Seridus. They lived in seclusion, giving advice and guidance through letters. There are 850 letters which have survived giving answers to a wide range of questions on all kinds of issues which were presented to them. Not only the enquirers included but also many others who sought help and discernment, including the Patriarch Peter of Jerusalem (524–52). Barsanuphius was 'the Great Old Man' and John was 'the Second Old Man'. The letters do not tell us about the lives of the two old men, but provide a vivid picture of spiritual direction in action in a Byzantine monastery.

The abbot Seridus, who was also the disciple of the old men, presided over the monastery. He was an extreme ascetic but also had great patience. Before he died he arranged for his succession. A layman called Aelianus was chosen. He was already considering becoming a monk and wondered why he had been chosen. He was told – in one of the letters – that the other monks of the monastery had been asked to become abbot but had declined because of their humility. Barsanuphius and John thought that this was a sign of divine choice rather than human reluctance, and Aelianus was ordained priest and then made abbot.[16]

Another arrival from Egypt was Zeno, who was a companion of Silvanus.[17] He instructed a visitor, 'do not live in a famous place, do not settle close to a man with a great name, and do not lay foundations for building yourself a cell.'[18] This describes his way of life. He did not settle in any one place but lived as a wanderer, without settling anywhere for long. He went to Jerusalem then back to Egypt, before entering into seclusion for the last year of his life. While in Jerusalem he met Peter the Iberian and his companion John, who became his disciples and later visited him in the monastery of Caphar She'artha near Gaza, where Zeno was then living. This encounter in Jerusalem led to a further group of refugees arriving at Gaza, and the formation of a community which to become in due course a distinct Monophysite Church, which will be discussed later.[19]

Wealthy women

Jerusalem was also becoming a city of monks as well as pilgrims. The Empress Helena was followed in her rediscovery of the holy places of Jerusalem by other wealthy women, who established monasteries and churches in Jerusalem. They were motivated by political and economic, as well as religious, motives. As tribes from northern Europe invaded the western Roman Empire, as there were more local outbursts of turmoil, as changing political fortunes excluded people from public life, so Jerusalem became an increasingly attractive destination which drew refugees of all classes and nationalities. It was a place of refuge and security for many who needed a place to retire to in times of instability and disruption.

Melania the Elder (325–410) was a rich aristocrat from Spain. When she was twenty-two she was widowed and since barbarian tribes were advancing on the western empire, she sold her estates, raising a small amount of money 'snatched from the jaws of the lion' and set out for the east accompanied by an entourage of relations and friends.[20] She went first to Egypt to visit the holy monks and stayed for several months. She then continued her journey to Jerusalem where she decided to stay. She set up a monastery for fifty virgins on the Mount of Olives, while her companion Rufinus of Aquileia established a monastery for men nearby. Here she provided hospitality and care for pilgrims and visitors, including Origenists when they were forced to flee from Egypt. She also welcomed Evagrius of Pontus who had left Constantinople after an unhappy love affair. She received him and then encouraged him to continue his journey to Egypt.[21] Her influence spread to other members of her family, including her granddaughter, also called Melania and so known as Melania the Younger. The younger Melania had already founded monasteries in North Africa and came to Jerusalem with her husband, desiring 'to worship at the holy places'. She arrived in 417, the year when her grandmother died. She then lived as a recluse for fourteen years and, when her husband died, she founded two monasteries, for men and women, in 431 or 432.[22]

Melania the Younger was a friend of another wealthy benefactor. Eudocia was the wife of the Emperor Theodosius II (401–50). She was a scholar and poet, who had come from a humble background and was chosen by the emperor because of her beauty and wisdom. Partly because of accusations of adultery made against her and also because of rivalry at the court, she went on a pilgrimage to Jerusalem and, like the Melanias, stayed. She gave gifts to monasteries, built churches and set up charitable institutions. Cyril of Scythopolis, writing in the sixth century, wrote that 'the blessed Eudocia built a huge number of churches for Christ, of monasteries, hospices and hospitals which it is not in my power to number.'[23] Her benefactions were so large that the chronicler Nikiphoros Kallistos, who wrote nearly nine hundred years later, reports that she spent 20,480 lbs gold while she was in Jerusalem. This is equivalent to 1,500,000 gold pieces, when two gold pieces was enough to keep someone alive for a year.[24] As well as a desire to live an ascetic life, Eudocia was also motivated by a determination to make her chosen place of residence a city to rival in magnificence the Constantinople from which she had been excluded.

The new monasteries built and supported by Eudocia and other noble and wealthy arrivals helped to form Jerusalem into a city of pilgrims and monks. It encouraged a growing number of visitors from all parts of the Christian world. The monks of the Jerusalem desert came as pilgrims and remained as monks. Sometimes they had already been monks before they came and had left their home in order to follow the monastic life in the place where Christ had lived. It was always the holy city which first drew them to Palestine, then led them to stay. The monastic life was the fulfilment of the pilgrim journey.

Even when monasteries were set up in the desert, they retained their relationship with the Holy City. Larger monasteries were close to Jerusalem so that monks could live within easy reach of the city. The surveys of the monastic sites show that they were connected by a network of foot paths and most were within walking distance of Jerusalem. The early founder of monasteries, Euthymius, knew the desert well since he liked to spend the forty days of Lent wandering the *paneremos* or utter desert. Yet when he set up his monastery, he chose a site within a few hundred yards of the main highway connecting Jerusalem and Jericho, at a distance of only 7 miles from the city.[25] Other monasteries were nearby. They formed an interconnected monastic suburb of Jerusalem.

The monasteries of the Judaean desert

There were a few monks in the Judaean desert, mostly living in caves at the oasis of Calamon near the Dead Sea, when a martyr from Iconium in Asia Minor called Chariton arrived. He had been awaiting his death in prison, a victim of the persecutions under Galerius (305–11) when he found himself unexpectedly released. Since he already considered himself a martyr, he decided to continue this vocation by travelling to Jerusalem, a progression in vocation which is one of the clearest indications in monastic literature of the continuity between the self-offering of martyr and monk. On the way he was captured by robbers and imprisoned in their cave. He was miraculously released and then stayed in the cave. The remainder of his life was a struggle to retain solitude in the middle of a steady and persistent arrival of disciples and by his death he had founded three monasteries, at Pharan, Douka and Souka. These events are described much later, in a *Life* written in the sixth century by a monk at one of his monasteries, presumably to affirm the position of these communities in the growing network of monastic settlements.[26]

It was not until the fifth and sixth centuries that the number of the monasteries grew so that they became numerous and influential. Archaeological and textual evidence shows the foundation dates of Palestinian monasteries.

Century	4th	early 5th	late 5th	early 6th	late 6th	7th	8th
Number of monasteries founded	3	3	13	12	10	0	1

Source: For this list see Yizhar Hirshfeld, 'List of the Byzantine Monasteries in the Judaean Desert', in ed. G. C. Bottini et al., *Christian Archeology in the Holy Land: New Discoveries* (Jerusalem, 1990), pp. 1-90, at pp. 81-2.

The lives and activities of two monks led to the golden age of Palestinian monasteries. These were Euthymius, an Armenian, who came to the desert in 405 and remained until his death in 473 and Sabas, a Cappadocian who came first to Euthymius's monastery in 456 and then founded and lived in other monasteries in the desert until his death in 532. The contrast between the lives and monastic careers of these two great founders demonstrates how monastic life grew and changed in the course of their lives. This evolution is recorded by a careful and observant monk, Cyril of Scythopolis.

Cyril had first met the great Sabas when he was six years old and the saint visited his home. Sabas embraced the young boy and claimed him as a future disciple. Later Cyril followed this call and went to live as a monk in 544. He moved between four monasteries and died some time after 559, when the last dateable section of the Lives was written. He wrote the lives of the two great monks and shorter lives of five others. Unlike some other hagiographers, he carefully observed events at which he was present, wrote about people he knew and carried out careful research to make sure that his historical and geographical information was accurate. The result is a series of lives which provide not only vivid pictures of great saints but a reliable record of a tumultuous period of history.[27]

Cyril tells us that 'all the desert was colonised by his (Euthymius's) seed'.[28] Euthymius was twenty-eight when he arrived at Jerusalem, in 405, and was already a monk. He had been ordained priest in Melitene in his native Armenia and entrusted with the leadership of the monasteries. He came to Jerusalem as a pilgrim to venerate the holy places and to find silence. After observing the life of the ascetics, he and another monk called Theoctistus set out into the more barren areas for Lent and happened to find a deep and inaccessible gorge, which they recognized as an ideal location for a monastery. Here they settled and they were soon joined by others, including a band of wandering Bedouin who settled nearby. Euthymius missed the solitary life and, as Cyril puts it with a play on words, his *euthymia*, or confidence, became *athymia*, or despondency. After further wandering he returned to the same area and settled in a beautiful spot on a plain not far from his friend Theoctistus and not far from the main Jerusalem highway.[29] Euthymius's new monastery was a community of hermits, which retained a close connection with the coenobium of Theoctistus. This turned out to be a creative partnership. A new arrival could go to the communal monastery of Theoctistus for formation in the monastic life and then might move to the monastery of Euthymius when he became more mature. These two monasteries, set in the silence of the desert but within walking distance of the city, attracted the visitors, many of whom stayed. The influence of the monasteries grew. Some of Euthymius's monks left to found their own monasteries, some were chosen to become bishops and some were attached to the staff of the archbishop and represented the region at the councils of the church. By the time of Euthymius's death, the monasteries of the Judaean desert were well-established, in contact with the wider movement in Egypt and Syria, and integrated into the church at Jerusalem.

The development of monastic life continued with the life of Sabas. He was a dominant presence in the desert for fifty years, from 478, when he founded his monastery ten years after the death of Euthymius, until his death in 532. He began his monastic career in his native Cappadocia, where he entered his local monastery at the age of eight. Ten years later he made the journey to Jerusalem seeking the solitude of the desert. He came to Euthymius who thought he was too young for the demanding hermit life and sent him to Theoctistus's coenobium. Like Euthymius before him, the young Sabas would set out to wander through the desert, especially during Lent. In the course of these wanderings a divine voice directed him to a cave in the Siloam valley, east of Bethlehem. Access to the cave could only be achieved by climbing down a rope suspended from the side of the valley and water was only available at a long distance. But a succession of divine interventions revealed water, a location for a new church and brought new recruits. The monastery of the Great Laura, later known as Mar Saba, had been founded.[30]

Sabas founded more monasteries. When he was fifty-four, he spent another Lent in the desert on the top of a hill called Castellium. There he was assaulted by demons. After a prolonged battle, he drove them away and claimed the hilltop as a monastery. He built cells and a church and settled some of his monks there.[31] More foundations followed. There was the New Laura near Thekoa, the coenobia of the Cave and of the Tower, and several hospices in the city itself. By the time he died, he had founded a network of monasteries across the desert.

Sabas was a different kind of monk from Euthymius. Cyril does not record that Sabas taught his monks, as Euthymius had; nor does he suggest that he had a close personal relationship with his disciples, as had been the pattern in the Egyptian desert; nor does he say that Sabas remained and presided over his monasteries, as Pachomius had done. He suggests that, once he had founded a monastery, he trusted the monks to govern their own lives. He was a founder and a builder and a leader. Cyril uses various terms to refer to Sabas's role. He was a founder or *polistes*, a lawgiver or *nomothetes*, a patron or *prostates,* and guide or *hodegos*. His position was recognized when he and another monk called Theodosius, who was abbot of a large coenobium near Bethlehem, were appointed archimandrites by the patriarch of Jerusalem after popular acclaim by the monastic body. Theodosius looked after the communal monasteries or coenobia, and Sabas cared for the hermits.³² The title of archimandrite, or chief shepherd, was given to the abbot of a large monastery. Here the authority of the archimandrite was extended to all the monks of the region of the city of Jerusalem. As Archimandrite Sabas represented the interests of the monastic body both in Jerusalem and in the capital of Constantinople.

Sabas took these responsibilities seriously. He frequently travelled to Jerusalem, and to other cities, such as Scythopolis where he stayed with the family of the young Cyril. On two occasions he took part in delegations to Constantinople, gaining support and financial grants from the Emperors Anastasius and Justinian. He also intervened in conflicts with groups of monks supporting the teachings of Origen, which were seen as dangerous heresies. Under his guidance, monasteries became institutions rather than scattered communities. They were connected and worked together. They became integrated into the life of the Jerusalem Church, shaping, influencing and directing its life.³³

Sabas's monastery was known as the Great Laura or lavra. It was an example of a form of monastic life which developed especially in Palestine. The word *laura* was used in secular society to describe a street of shops of a kind found in the crowded suqs of a Middle Eastern town. The laura was a lane with small houses for both working and living. This arrangement of a collection of dwellings suited the monasteries of the Judaean desert, where the monastery was often built in the deep wadis or valleys where water was most often to be found. The monks settled in the caves in the cliff face or they constructed their own huts. These were places to live, work and pray. They formed settlements of huts or cells, along the paths or in the cliff face of the wadi. Monks lived alone following a hermit life through the week and met at the church on Sundays for communal worship. It was a flexible arrangement which allowed a monk to move into more extreme solitude by setting up a cave further way or by going out into the deserts for periods of prayer especially during Lent. A laura was a community of hermits, providing a structure and pattern of life to enable a solitary lifestyle to be maintained and supported. This solution to the challenges and practical difficulties of living a solitary life was to be followed in other parts of the church. It was different from the communal monasteries or coenobia. In the coenobium, the monks followed a shared and common life, where monks lived together, often with several monks in a single cell or room, with work allocated, and spiritual growth achieved through the challenge and trials of living closely with others, with the guiding principle being obedience to the abbot. Later the term 'laura' would be extended to coenobitic monasteries as well as this style of laurite life.

Another development which took place in Palestine was the internationalization of monastic life. The Syrian holy men belonged in their villages and their followers were wandering and often unemployed labourers. The Egyptian monasteries were formed to provide a place for local peasants to live and work, and, while they attracted tourists and visitors, they maintained an Egyptian identity. But Jerusalem was an international centre, with people coming from many places. The monasteries brought together monks from different places in one monastery. Both Euthymius and Sabas came as pilgrims from outside the country. This immigration from around the Christian built an international monastic community. The diversity is shown by archaeological research carried out by A-M Schneider in the monastery of

Figure 6 The monastery of the Great Lavra, or Mar Saba is in the valley of Siloam near Jerusalem. The monks lived in caves and huts along the ravine, where the laurite form of life developed.

Choziba, a monastery in a gorge near the road to Jericho which is still active today. Schneider found 213 inscriptions on tombstones in the monastery cemetery, with the majority dating from the sixth and seventh centuries and of which seventy-three gave the place of origin of the monks. The seventy-three inscriptions show that thirty of these monks came from northern Syria and Asia Minor, including Cappadocia, Cilicia, Isauria and Antioch; seventeen came from the southwest of Palestine from Gaza and Maiuma; and smaller numbers from Greece, Cyprus, Mesopotamia, Georgia, Persia and Rome – with one reference to a monk from India, at that time a notoriously vague geographical term.[34]

In these monasteries, different languages were used. Often the liturgy was conducted in different places in different languages in one monastery. Sabas allowed the Armenian monks to recite psalms in their own language and then to join the rest of the monks for the liturgy in Greek. This arrangement led to a growing number of Armenians in his monastery.[35]

Jerusalem had a special attraction because of its unique significance and its geographical location. In this period of three centuries when it was under Christian rule, from the conversion of Constantine in 325 until the Muslim invasions in the 640s, monasteries grew and thrived. An international Christian monastic community lived in an integrated network of communities. Athanasius has used the metaphor of Antony making the desert into a city to show how he attracted ascetics to the desert life. In Palestine the desert becoming a city changed from metaphor to reality.

The Council of Chalcedon

It was inevitable that the monasteries should have been drawn into the Christological controversies which continued through the fifth and sixth centuries and which led to the decisive division between Chalcedonian and Monophysite. As the conflict wore on, successive emperors tried to find a formula to reconcile the two sides and bring harmony to the empire. Various councils were convened, among which were two of the Ecumenical Councils of Chalcedon (451) and Constantinople (553).

Juvenal the patriarch of Jerusalem went to the Council of Chalcedon. He assured the monks that he would remain firm in supporting the teaching of Cyril of Alexandria, affirming the one incarnate nature of Christ and rejecting the two-nature Christology set out in the Tome of Leo. 'The tome is Jewish' he told the monks 'and the ideas it contains are those of Simon Magus'. Euthymius expressed similar views to the monks who accompanied Juvenal. 'He told (them) to follow in every way Archbishop Cyril of Alexandria and Bishop Acacius of Melitene, as being orthodox.'[36]

At the council Juvenal changed sides. In a dramatic move, he crossed over the floor of the meeting hall to leave Patriarch Dioscorus of Alexandria and sit with Patriarch Anatolius of Constantinople, who he had previously opposed.[37] He gave his support to the Chalcedonian Definition with its teaching of two natures and one person. The monks who had gone with him hurried back. Stephen bishop of Jamnia and John bishop of the Saracens anxiously brought the Definition to Euthymius for his approval. They described the decision of the council that the teaching of Leo and Flavian of Antioch was in agreement with that of Cyril. 'Cyril and Leo taught alike' had been an acclamation proclaimed at the Council.[38] Euthymius scrutinized the definition and agreed that it was orthodox.

Other monks returned with a different assessment. Theodosius, one of the monks, attacked the council and encouraged his fellow monks to resist. Patriarch Juvenal was prevented from entering the city by this group and Theodosius was consecrated in his place as an alternative archbishop. They were supported by the majority of the monks and also the powerful Empress Eudocia.

Euthymius and those who supported the Council of Chalcedon were a minority. Euthymius withdrew to stay in the more remote desert of Rouba. Then the Empress Eudocia, who had at first supported the Monophysite group, received letters from Constantinople urging her to be reconciled with Juvenal. Faced with this dilemma, she consulted Symeon the Stylite on his pillar in Syria who suggested that she seek guidance from Euthymius. This led to her becoming reconciled with Patriarch Juvenal, and others followed her.[39] Theodosius remained in the city for twenty months from 452 to 453 and then Juvenal returned with soldiers from the emperor and ousted Theodosius and those he had appointed.

Many of the monks stayed faithful to the Monophysite teaching. Gerontius, the superior of Melania's monastery on the Mount of Olives, stated firmly about Juvenal. 'God forbid that I should see the face of Judas the traitor.'[40] He left the monastery and founded another at Bethlehem, which grew in importance so that he was eventually appointed archimandrite of the coenobites of the desert. Another monk Romanus founded a coenobium at Thekoa which became a centre of Monophysite resistance.

Many monks joined him so that it soon numbered over six hundred monks. He then founded another monastery at Eleutheropolis, on the land given to him by Eudocia, who in spite of her reconciliation with Juvenal did not remove support from other monks.[41] Several monasteries along the coast, at a safe distance from Jerusalem, provided a place of refuge for the monks who opposed the Council of Chalcedon, and here the beginnings of an anti-Chalcedonian Monophysite church took place. In the Gaza monasteries, Monophysite communities, including Peter's monastery at Maiuma, lived alongside Chalcedonian monasteries, apparently in peace and harmony.[42]

These events and Euthymius's resolute support of the Council of Chalcedon involved him in the doctrinal controversies afflicting the church and the empire. He became a supporter of the Jerusalem patriarchate and this further integrated the monasteries into the church of the capital. The monks were already active within the church and now this bond was strengthened. Monasteries were no longer separated from the church in the city. They were a part of the church, worked alongside the patriarch and participated in the life of the wider church and empire.

Mar Saba after the Arabs

The Great Laura was attacked during the Sassanian Persian invasion in 614. Most of the monks left and those who decided to stay were killed. After this devastation, some of the monks returned after two years' absence and the monastery continued its life until a further attack in 797. Over the following century, there were further attacks. Destruction is recorded as having taken place in 809 and 813 and no doubt there were further devastations, but the monks always came back. The monastery of the Great Laura, later known as Mar Saba, has maintained its life and witness in an insecure and disputed region, one of the oldest monasteries of the Christian east.

Its survival and its location near the holy places ensured that it continued its influence on the church. However, the number of monks steadily declined. In the early ninth century, the Emperor Charlemagne asked for information about the monasteries of Palestine, and his researcher found that there were 150 monks at Mar Saba.[43] In 1185, John Phokas reported that there were forty monks in 1185 and in the 1370s, the Russian pilgrim Archimandrite Agrafenii found twenty-five. Later visitors report a similar number. While the number of monks may have been smaller than in Byzantine times, the influence on the wider church remained important. Among its membership were some of the greatest theologians and hymn writers of the Eastern church.

Andrew of Crete was born in Damascus. He was dumb and was unable to communicate until he was miraculously given the gift of speech after receiving holy communion. He entered the Mar Saba monastery when he was fourteen years old, around 666, and later became archdeacon at Jerusalem and then a bishop in Crete for thirty years. He developed the liturgical form of the canon, verses of poetry inserted between verses of Scripture during Mattins. His Great Canon consists of 250 strophes, guiding the worshipper through the entire Bible, learning lessons of personal morality from the various characters. It is sung at various points in Lent, and the complete canon is recited on the Thursday of the Fifth Week.

Around the time that Andrew died, another future monk of Mar Saba was born in Damascus. This was John, who around 720 left his post in the government administration and became a monk in Palestine. John of Damascus lived in Mar Saba, in the cell which now contains his tomb and where he wrote his great systematic work of theology, *On the Orthodox Faith*. He also wrote three works in defence of icons, and works showing the errors of both Nestorianism and Monophysitism. In company with Cosmas, who had been adopted by John's father and had grown up with him, he wrote many hymns, including a series of canons. After ten years of this co-authorship of hymns, Cosmas became bishop of Maiuma, in the west of Palestine. John remained a monk of the monastery until his death in 749.

Further names can be added from this period of remarkable creativity. Theodore of Abu Qurrah, who had been a disciple of John of Damascus, was one of the first theologians to write in Arabic, as well as Greek, and later became bishop of Abu Qurrah, or, according to other sources, of Harran in Mesopotamia.[44] Cyprian the Sabaite and Stephen the Hagiopolite, who is reported to have been the nephew of John of Damascus, added to the corpus of hymnody produced at the monastery.

The monastery was a centre of support for icons during the iconoclast controversy in the eighth and ninth centuries. John of Damascus wrote in defence of icons, in a work which has remained a statement of Orthodox faith.[45] Another monk, Michael the Syncellus (761–846) was ordained a priest in Jerusalem and went to Constantinople with two followers, also monks of the monastery, Theodore (775–842) and Theophanes (778–845), to join those defending icons. He was imprisoned, and Theodore and Theophanes were branded on the face with verses announcing their crimes. In honour of this support of truth they have been known as the Graptoi, or branded. Michael later became a monk at the Chora monastery in Constantinople, and Theophanes became archbishop of Nicaea in 842.

This list shows the creativity of the monks of Mar Saba. Although the number of monks in the monastery was smaller than before the Persian and Arab conquests, the monastery was a centre of doctrinal scholarship and writing, the defence of Orthodoxy and the production of a large number of hymns. All these have become part of Orthodox tradition and have helped to shape the life of the church.

The monastery of Mar Saba has remained a centre of monastic life. Its position near the holy city of Jerusalem ensured that it received visitors. Many of these visitors spent time at the monastery as monks, and then returned to their homelands. Although the journey to Jerusalem had become more hazardous, pilgrims kept coming. For many, the desert monasteries were just as important as the city of Jerusalem. It has been suggested that while western pilgrims wanted to see the holy places, Byzantine pilgrims already had many relics in their churches and were more interested in visiting the monks.[46]

The life of the monk Lazarus is an example of how pilgrims came, learned the traditions of Mar Saba and then transmitted these over a wide area. He came from Asia Minor and after visiting the holy places wanted to settle at Mar Saba. He spent six years in the monastery as *canonarches* or choir leader and then left for a while because he was annoyed at not being allowed to go into the desert alone for the forty days of Lent. This absence was brief and he returned for a further six years. During this second period he was allowed to carry out the traditional Lenten fast in the desert and he tells how he visited the place where Lot's wife was turned into a pillar of salt. After one of the attacks on Jerusalem in 1009, he returned to Anatolia and settled on the holy mountain of Galesion, near Ephesus. He founded several monasteries in the region of the mountain, making sure that they did not become too large, since he wanted to retain the simple lavra traditions. His monasteries were coenobia, but he was sympathetic to those who wanted to live a more solitary life, as had been the practice in Palestine. It must also have been his Judaean desert experience which led him to prefer arid waterless places – which required the monks to carry water from the river below. He told the monks, 'If you really want to be saved, persevere on this barren mountain … the fathers of old always sought out the deserts and most uncomfortable places, not those that had springs and leafy trees.'[47] Lazarus himself lived on a series of columns, progressively moving higher up the mountain. He carried out a leadership of advice and guidance rather than administration, the task he entrusted to a neighbouring monastery which looked after the lands and administered the communities.[48]

It was claimed that the traditions which were carried by pilgrims and monks across the Byzantine Empire were the rules which had been devised by Sabas himself. The *Life of Sabas* written by Cyril of Scythopolis refers to the set of rules given to the monks by Sabas. These mostly concern the way that liturgy was to be conducted, especially the manner of reciting psalms. When a group of Armenians joined the community, they were allowed to use their own language and were told 'to perform the office of psalmody in Armenian in their own oratory on Saturdays and Sundays'.[49] Novices were sent to one of the monasteries in the network of houses founded by Sabas and stayed there 'until they had learnt the psalter and the office of psalmody and received a strict monastic formation'.[50] Later a monk called Zannus founded a monastery and was helped by Sabas who 'gave the rules of the other coenobia to this one also'.[51] The monks who came to Sabas followed a rule of life laid down by the founder and this rule was handed over by Sabas to his successor Melitus on his deathbed, 'telling him to guard inviolate the traditions handed down in the monasteries and giving them to him in writing'.[52] So by then there was a form of written rule.

According to a much later account by Symeon of Thessalonica (d. 1429), these traditions had been developed in the monasteries of the desert from the earliest times, and were passed from Chariton to Euthymius, and then on to Sabas. They were lost during one of the periods of destruction of the monastery, in 614, and then re-written by Patriarch Sophronius of Jerusalem (634–8) and by John of Damascus. Among the rules laid down by Sabas was the practice of an all-night vigil on Saturdays and Sundays. He 'decreed that there should be a vigil from eve till dawn without interval … both on Sundays and on feasts of our Lord'.[53] This vigil, or *agrypnia*, is one of the characteristics of later Sabaite typika, which marks them out from other traditions.

The liturgical typikon of Mar Saba continued to influence Byzantine liturgy. Theodore of Studium wrote to Patriarch Thomas of Jerusalem (827–1) to ask him to send monks of Mar Saba to help him introduce the Sabaite way of reciting psalms. This contributed to the liturgical traditions of Constantinople in the monasteries of Studium and Evergetis. During the Hesychast controversy, the Sabaite traditions, or *typika*, gained renewed influence, probably because of their monastic origins. As the hesychast monks became ascendant, the simpler liturgical style of the monasteries, which looked back to Jerusalem, became more popular, taking the place of the typika of the urban Constantinopolitan monasteries of Studium and Evergetis. The stage of liturgical development is often called 'neo-Sabaite'.

Later writers record the influence of the traditions of Mar Saba. Paul the Younger, living on Mount Latros in the tenth century, told his monks to observe the fasts 'as the tradition harking back to the rule of Jerusalem established from the beginning'. Later Nikon of the Black Mountain carried out reforms in the region of Antioch in the late eleventh century and commended the 'rule of our holy father Sabas'. The influence of the rule extended to Patmos. When Christodulus laid down instructions for his monastery of St John on Patmos, he instructed that 'the singing in church and the whole order of psalm singing and prayers ... be conducted according to the typikon of the lavra at Jerusalem of our holy father Sabas, the great desert teacher.'[54] When the monastery of the Mother of God Bebaia Elpis in Constantinople was founded in the fourteenth century, the founder ensured that a Palestinian model was followed.

> All doxologies to God and vigils and fasts and genuflections should be done in accordance with the typikon of Jerusalem .... The Rule should be none other than the one which came to us of old from Palestine for the benefit of our churches here, which is usually called the typikon of Jerusalem, and has been selected and preferred above all others by prudent people ... The entire church service should be celebrated by you in accordance with this rule ... including those used for nocturnal vigils.[55]

The rule of Mar Saba also influenced later liturgy. Philotheos, who had been hegumenos of the Great Lavra on Mount Athos and was patriarch of Constantinople from 1353 to 1355 and again from 1364 to 1376, composed the *diataxis tes hierodiakonias*, on the divine office, and the *diataxis tes theias leitourgias*, on the liturgy. These texts became authoritative sources for the further development of Byzantine liturgy. They were translated into Slavonic by the end of the fourteenth century and were adopted by the Trinity monastery of St Sergius of Radonezh, replacing the Studite use, in 1429. They reached Solovki in the far north by 1494. By the seventeenth century, versions of this liturgy were being printed in Venice. We can trace the liturgy of the Orthodox Church as used today back to the way of life and form of worship practised by monks who came to the Holy City and then settled in the nearby wadi Kidron. The monks of Sabas sung the psalms and celebrated the liturgy and their practice has influenced how Orthodox Christians have worshipped in centuries that followed.

Conclusion

The symphonic and harmonious interaction of monastery and city was rudely disrupted by invaders. Persians conquered Jerusalem in 614 and remained until they were ejected by the Emperor Heraclius in 631. This recovered freedom was short-lived. Arabs advanced and defeated Heraclius at the Battle of the River Yarmuk in 636 and then entered Jerusalem in 638. With the exception of the Latin Crusader kingdom of Jerusalem, which lasted from 1099 until 1187, Jerusalem was never again a Christian city. A consequence of these political and military changes was the fragmentation of the monasteries into diverging traditions of life. Yet the traditions preserved their shared forms of life and continued to share their ascetic teachings over a wide area.

Notes

1. Socrates, *Ecclesiastical History* 1.17.
2. This tradition is passed down in the Ethiopian church, with texts translated in Getatchew Haile, *The Ethiopian Orthodox Church's Tradition on the Holy Cross* (Leiden, 2018), pp. 135–61.
3. There is an account of the early history of the site in Robin Griffith-Jones, 'The Building of the Holy Sepulchre', in ed. R. Griffith-Jones and Eric Fernie, *Tomb and Temple* (Woodbridge, 2018), pp. 53–74.
4. Pierre Maraval, *Lieux saints et pélerinage d'orient* (Paris, 1985), p. 63.
5. Revelation 21.2.
6. This episode is described in Benedicta Ward, Introduction to *Lives of the Desert Fathers* (Oxford, 1980), p. 4.
7. Eusebius, *Ecclesiastical History* 6.9.8.
8. Jerome, *Life of Hilarion* 14.24 in W. A. Oldfather, *Studies in the Text Tradition of St Jerome's Vitae Patrum* (Urbana, IL, 1943), p. 317.
9. *Life of Hilarion* 32.
10. Among recent studies are Brouria Bitton-Ashkelony and Aryeh Kofsky, *The Monastic School of Gaza* (Leiden, 2006) and Cornelia Horn, *Asceticism and Christological Controversy in Fifth-Century Palestine, the Career of Peter the Iberian* (Oxford, 2006).
11. Sozomen, *Ecclesiastical History* 3.14, 3.10. Brouria-Britton Ashkelony and Aryeh Kofsky, 'Monasticism in the Holy Land', in *Christians and Christianity in the Holy Land* (Turnhout, 2006), pp. 257–91, at p. 261, suggest that Cyril was writing 'a propagandist regional history in the cause of Chalcedonian Orthodoxy and the Jerusalem Patriarchate'.
12. Sozomen, *Ecclesiastical History* 6.32–4.
13. John Moschus, *Spiritual Meadow* 55.
14. This is argued by L. Regnault, 'Les apotegmes des pères en Palestine aux Ve-Vie siécles', *Irénikon* 54 (1981), pp. 320–30.
15. *Life of Euthymius* 34.10–20.
16. This is described by Barsanuphius and John, *Letters* 571–6, in ed. and trans. F. Neyt, P. de Angelis-Noah, and l. Regnault (eds.), *Barsanuphe et Jean de Gaze, Correspondance*, Sources Chrétiennes 426–7, 450–1, 468 (Paris, 1997–2002).
17. For the life of Zeno, see trans. Benedicta Ward, *Sayings of the Desert Fathers* (Oxford, 1975), pp. 65–7. John Rufus, *Plerophoriae* 8.
18. *Sayings*, Zeno 1, p. 65.
19. See below, pp. 90–2.
20. *Life of Melania* 37, trans. D. Gorce, *Sources Chrétiennes* (Paris, 1962), p. 196.
21. See below and *Lausiac History* 46.
22. *Life of Melania* 22, 34. *Life of Peter the Iberian* 33.
23. Cyril of Scythopolis, *Life of Euthymius* 53.5–7.
24. Nicephorus Callistus, *Ecclesiastical History* 14.50, PG 146.124D.
25. *Life of Euthymius* 24.1–10, 64.20–65.5. Now known as Khan el Ahmar, the ruins of the monastery are surrounded by an industrial estate near a Jewish settlement.

26 *The Life of Chariton* 8, 13, 42, ed. G. Garitte, *Bulletin de l'Institut Historique Belge de Rome* (1941), pp. 5–50. The *Life* says that Chariton was imprisoned in the persecution of Aurelian who died in 275, and then that the church at his first monastery was dedicated by Macarius, who was bishop of Jerusalem between 314 and 333. In view of this foundation date it seems more likely that Chariton's persecutor was Galerius.
27 *Life of Sabas* 180–2.
28 *Life of Euthymius* 24.4.
29 Ibid., 15.10–20, 23.20–24.10, 25.15–25. See 21.25 for the play on words of *athymia* and *euthymia*.
30 *Life of Sabas* 97–9, 101–3.
31 Ibid., 110–1.
32 Ibid., 114–5.
33 Ibid., 139–47, 173–8.
34 A-M. Schneider, 'Das kloster der Theotokos zu Choziba im Wadi el Kelt', *Römische Quartalschrift für Christliche Altertumskunde und für Kirchengeschichte* 39 (1931), pp. 297–332.
35 *Life of Sabas* 105.5–10, 117.20.
36 *Life of Euthymius* 33.2–6; *Life of Peter the Iberian* 53.
37 Monophysite historians attribute this to ambition, but the circumstances were different from previous councils. John Binns, *Ascetics and Ambassadors of Christ* (Oxford, 1996), p. 185.
38 Ibid., p. 186.
39 *Life of Euthymius* 47.5–49.20.
40 Ibid., 49.8–10; *Life of Peter the Iberian* 35.
41 *Life of Euthymius* 49.11–12; 66.24–6; 115.12–14.
42 See *Life of Peter the Iberian* 102, 129.
43 *Commemoratorium de Casis Dei*, in Robert Schick, *Christian Communities of Palestine from Byzantine to Islamic Rule* (Princeton, New Jersey, 1995), p. 402.
44 Aristarchus Peristeris, 'Literary and Scribal Activities at the Monastery of St Sabas', in ed. Joseph Patrich, *The Sabaite Heritage in the Orthodox Church from the Fifth Century to the Present* (Leuven, 2001), pp. 171–94, at p. 174.
45 John of Damascus, *Three Treatises on the Divine Images*, trans. Andrew Louth (Crestwood, NY, 2003).
46 Alice-Mary Talbot, 'Byzantine Pilgrimage to the Holy Land from the Eighth to the Fifteenth Century', in ed. Joseph Patrich, *The Sabaite Heritage in the Orthodox Church from the Fifth Century to the Present* (Leuven, 2001), pp. 97–110, at p. 102.
47 Ibid., p. 108.
48 For the life of Lazarus, see Rosemary Morris, *Monks and Laymen in Byzantium 843–1118* (Cambridge, 1995), p. 42.
49 *Life of Sabas* 105.10.
50 Ibid., 113.8–10.
51 Ibid., 133.3–4.
52 Ibid., 182.22–23.
53 Ibid., 118.18–20.
54 See John Thomas, 'The Imprint of Sabaitic Monasticism on Byzantine Monastic Typika' in Patrich, *Sabaite Heritage*, pp. 73–83, at p. 78.
55 Ibid., p. 81.

6

The City of Constantinople: Where All Roads Meet

Moving to the city

Constantine had chosen the city of Byzantium to be the capital of his Christian empire. The city is a natural harbour strategically located at the place where the Bosphorus opens out into the Sea of Marmara, between the Mediterranean and the Black Sea, between Europe and Asia. Its foundation is associated with a mythical hero, Byzas, who was a son of the Greek sea god Neptune. It was a Greek settlement from the seventh century BC, and so an ideal location for a new capital city in the eastern part of the Roman Empire. After he had become the undisputed head of the whole empire in 325, Constantine gave his name to the city and started to build. It remained the capital of the empire and centre of church life for over a millennium.

At the heart of Christian Constantinople was the Great Church of the Immortal Wisdom of Christ or Haghia Sophia. This was consecrated in 537 and has amazed visitors ever since. An account of its construction was written in the tenth century and describes how Justinian used wood from the Ark of Noah for the doors, how an angel watched over it to see that it did not collapse and told the workers to build a triple window in honour of the Trinity.[1] It was served by a vast body of clergy. In 612 Patriarch Sergius reduced the number who served it to a modest 80 priests, 150 deacons, 40 deaconesses, 70 subdeacons, 160 readers, 25 cantors and 100 doorkeepers. While this church was not yet in existence when the monasteries were first being established, the grandeur and magnificence of the Haghia Sophia shows the prestige and wealth of the city, which quickly became a centre of church life.

People knew where to go to meet the monks. They had gone to Egypt, Jerusalem or Syria to visit the holy men and women living in remote and desert places. It might be thought that the Constantinople of the emperors was the antithesis of desert. It was the capital city, the centre of the empire, a market place of trade, a place of wealth and power. Since it was a busy metropolis, it was not suited to those seeking a life of silence. But before long its place at the centre of the empire also began to attract ascetics, and monasteries grew up. The city was the capital for a vast area which fluctuated in size as military fortunes ebbed and flowed. In spite of losses of land and the diminishing in size of the empire, its wealth, culture and prestige ensured that it remained a centre and a meeting point for monks as well as many others. The large number of monasteries and the communication with all parts of Christendom brought monks together in one place, although not necessarily in peace and harmony. It became a place of experiment and debate. By the time that Constantinople fell in 1453, a recognized form of monastic life had developed, with a shared recognition of the hesychast way of prayer and a pattern of life which had been practised in some of the monasteries, including Stoudios and Evergetis, and exported over the empire.

The first monasteries

The first monks to come to the city arrived in the middle years of the fourth century, around the time that the first monastic foundations were taking shape in Egypt. These monks were the followers of Macedonius, who was patriarch from 342 to 360, and his friend Marathonius. Marathonius was a retired civil servant who became a monk and was given the responsibility of being superintendent of the poor of the monastic communities of men and women. He later became bishop of Nicomedia. Macedonius was supported by these communities in a struggle over the succession to the patriarchate and, with their help, he prevailed and was consecrated patriarch. The two friends founded several ascetic communities. The monks in these communities wore ragged clothes, lived alongside the poor whom they served, carried out charitable work and followed strict moral codes. Their followers lived in informal communities where men and women, monks and non-monks lived alongside each other. These communities were influenced by Eustathius, who had become bishop of Sebaste in 356 and was recognized as pioneer and leader of monastic groups in Asia Minor. So, like Eustathius, the two friends were suspected of heretical Messalian tendencies. Macedonius was ejected from his position in 360 and we hear no more of his communities.[2]

The Syrian monk Isaac was another arrival, coming to the city in the late 370s. He made an immediate impression. He decided to challenge the Emperor Valens because of his support for Arianism and followed the emperor around, debating and arguing with him at every opportunity. Valens lost patience with this aged Syrian in his ragged clothes and put him in prison. He then set off on the military campaign in which he was killed at the Battle of Adrianople in 378. This unexpected event led to a dramatic vindication for Isaac. He gained the support of two imperial servants, Victor and Saturninus, and founded a monastery which was later known as the Dalmatou, which became one of the great monasteries of the city. Isaac became a familiar figure as he wandered in the streets, talking to people, blessing houses and praying for those he met. He was popular and much loved. When new patriarch, John Chrysostom, tried to enforce an earlier law expelling monks from the cities into the deserts, Isaac orchestrated a successful monastic resistance which contributed to the patriarch's removal.

Isaac was succeeded as abbot by Dalmatus, a former soldier, who gave his name to the monastery. Like Isaac, Dalmatus was a faithful and hardworking ascetic. He spent forty-eight years within the walls of the monastery, at work and prayer. He received many visitors who left gifts for the monastery. His reputation grew and with it the size of the monastery which soon was home to thirty monks. Like Isaac, he became involved in a dispute with the patriarch, in this case Nestorius, who had scandalized many of the monks with his Christological views and his preaching that Mary should not be given the title *theotokos* or the God-bearer. In a spectacular demonstration of his influence, the aged monk left his monastery after the long period within its walls and marched to the imperial palace followed by a crowd of his monks. He met with the Emperor Theodosius II and then led his supporters along the main street of the city to another part of the city where he may have joined with another monastic leader Eutyches. On his return to the monastery he wrote to the council meeting at Ephesus (431) 'in the name of the entire clergy of Constantinople'. The Council of Ephesus deposed Nestorius.

Another monastic founder was Alexander the Sleepless or *Akoimetos*. Alexander was born in an island in the Aegean Sea and went to Constantinople to study. He was a good student and seemed destined for a successful and lucrative career in the imperial civil service. This career path was disturbed when he began to study the Bible and, like Antony of Egypt before him, was struck by that verse of the gospel which had such a profound effect on both men. 'If you wish to be perfect, go sell what you have, give to the poor and come follow me.'[3] He left Constantinople and went, inevitably, to Syria. Here he spent four years in a monastery and then lived for a further twenty years by the Euphrates river. Others joined him and soon his community consisted of four hundred monks, who had come from different parts of the Christian world. He devised an unusual method of prayer, using a system of shifts of groups of fifty brothers, in order to fulfil the instruction of St Paul to 'pray without ceasing' – a verse which was a constant and disturbing challenge to the monks.[4] He followed an elaborate routine of psalmody and prostration. As a result of this programme of constant prayer, they became known as the 'Sleepless Monks'. Then Alexander set out on his wanderings – to Palmyra where he was not welcomed, then to Antioch where after a while he was expelled, and then finally in around 400 to Constantinople from where he had set out fifty years earlier. He and twenty-four monks settled on a hill near the centre of the city, and soon his community had grown to three hundred monks who came from Rome, Greece and Syria. Biblical passages still troubled him. Now he was preoccupied with the words 'take no thought for the morrow' and 'all things are possible for one who believes'.[5] In addition to his continuing discipline of prayer, he taught complete poverty. The monks owned nothing except for some scraps of parchment with Bible passages with them. We are told that they kept enough food for one day only and gave the rest away and wore only a single tunic. They lived among the poor and advocated the giving of alms by the rich.

Earlier the people of Palmyra had decided not to let the community of the Sleepless into their city. 'Who can feed all these men' they had said 'if they enter our city we will all starve'. They would have preferred the injunction of Paul, 'he who does not work, let him not eat.'[6] Now, in Constantinople, Alexander again aroused opposition and, in 428, was arrested and expelled from the city. His life says that this happened because he made enemies by criticizing prominent persons in the city and because of hostility from some of the abbots of other monasteries. The bishops accused them of idleness and refusing to work. A near-contemporary, Nilus of Ancyra, says that they 'made it a rule that young men and adults in vigorous health should not work'. Behind the conflict lay the familiar contrast between the Syrian style of wandering ascetic life and the more conventional 'philosophical' approach of other monasteries. He was accused of Messalianism, which was fresh in peoples' memory and was condemned three years later at the Council of Ephesus.

Fortunately a friendly monk, Hypatius, the abbot of the monastery of the Rouphinianoi, helped them find a new place to settle, on the Asian side of the Bosphorus. Their search for a radical poverty among the poorest of the city was maintained. One monk, John Kalybites, came from a wealthy family and joined the monastery. After a time living in the monastery, he returned to live for three years among the beggars at the gate of the mansion inside which he had lived as a young man.[7]

Although it was transplanted to a new setting at a safer distance from the city, the popularity of the Akoimetoi way of life continued. The life of the third abbot Marcellus suggests why the monastery was so attractive. The attention given to its continual liturgical singing was seen as a way of maintaining holiness within the monastery and preserving a precise and uncompromising way of life, known as *akribeia*, or living strictly according to Scripture. 'They believed they were bringing back not only the exactness of ascesis, but they were also returning a certain holiness to the houses and men devoted to God.'[8] More monks came, some from other monasteries, and numbers soon grew to over a thousand. From Constantinople their influence grew and extended. Marcellus sent some of his monks to monasteries as far away as Pontus and Edessa in response to enquiries from the abbots about the Akoimetai way of life. He also founded smaller houses or *asketeria* in the city.

The Akoimetai monasteries became caught up in the Christological controversies leading up to the Council of Chalcedon. The monasteries of the capital were divided, with the Akoimetai supporting a two-nature Christology, as taught at Antioch and Rome, while the monastery of another leading monk, Eutyches, led the Monophysite single-nature party. The Akoimetai were victorious. They built up a coalition of twenty-three out of the city's fifty abbots who publicly accused Eutyches at the Council of Ephesus in 448 and continued this opposition at the later Council of Chalcedon which finally condemned the Monophysite archimandrite. The sources do not provide an explanation of why the monks became caught up in these bitter doctrinal controversies. It has been suggested that the patronage of political groupings might have influenced the monks. But it is more likely that their allegiances arose out of personal connections. Monks came from many parts of the empire and kept in touch with their former fellow monks and friends in their home cities. With a mobile and international monastic community, it was inevitable that wider controversies would be reproduced within the monastic communities themselves.

The immigration of monks from different parts of the empire contributed to the decline of the Akoimetai, as it had to their rise. Another wave of immigrants was produced by the continuing doctrinal conflicts after the Council of Chalcedon. Monophysite refugees fleeing persecution arrived in the capital, especially in the mid-sixth century, during the reign of the Emperor Justinian and Empress Theodora. They found a welcome in the capital both from the emperor, even though it was his troops which had forced them to leave their homes, and even more from the Empress

Theodora, whose sympathies were with the new arrivals. Theodora provided refuge and a home for displaced Monophysite monks.

The first of this new wave of monastic refugees was a monk called Z'ura who arrived from Amida in 535. He was followed by an ascetic called Mar Mare. Then the exiled Monophysite patriarch of Alexandria, Theodosius, set up his home in Constantinople. Soon there were several hundred Monophysite monks in the city. Some were housed in the monastery of Sergiou in the Hormisdas palace, and others in the suburb of Sykae, which became the centres of Monophysite monastic life.

The patronage of Justinian and Theodora brought the monks from the periphery into the centre. Up till then, monasteries had been mostly confined to the space outside the Constantine walls but now they had arrived in the city itself. The Sergiou monastery was in the palace grounds in the centre of town. Another Monophysite monastery, the Sykae, was in a lively area with houses and a hippodrome and this now became a centre of monastic life. The new arrivals brought with them the Egyptian practice of supporting themselves by working on basket making and other crafts. They also devoted themselves to humanitarian and social relief work. In spite of their different doctrinal views, the Monophysite monks had good relations with Chalcedonian monasteries and this period brought renewal of monastic life. But as the conflict escalated and threatened the unity of the empire, imperial support for the Monophysites was withdrawn and the monks had left by 570.

A different kind of monastery was founded by a noble lady, Olympias. She was born in 361 into a wealthy family and set up a monastery for women which was known as the Olympiados. She was married but her husband died after only two years of marriage, and so, at the age of thirty she found herself a wealthy widow. She was then ordained deaconess in 390 by Patriarch Nectarius and formed a community of women ascetics in a house next to the Great Church of the Haghia Sophia, which was part of the family's estates. At first there were 30 members but this number increased until there were 250 nuns. Olympias knew both John Chrysostom and Gregory Nazianzus, and her community was guided by them and other patriarchs.

Another early women's monastery was set up by Matrona, who came to the capital in the early fifth century, from Perga in Pamphylia. She had arrived as a wife and mother, but set up a women's community attached to the male monastery of Bassianos. Her nuns followed a similar life to that of the men. They wore a dark leather girdle and a white robe, as the male monks did, rather than women's clothing of woollen girdles and veils. She began with eight women with her, but this number grew.[9]

This was a different strand of monastic life from those which built up around the Syrians. It was not able to prevail against the force of the alternative monastic lobby around Dalmatos in his movement against John Chrysostom. The monastery declined after two centuries of active life.[10] The Olympiados was a private house which became a monastery, remaining under the supervision of the foundress. It was a model similar to the family monastery of Macrina which was often repeated. A house, with the various family members, servants and dependants, was transformed into a monastery, remaining under the ownership and control of the family but now dedicated to the life of asceticism and charitable activity.

Stoudios

Among the great monasteries of Constantinople was the Stoudios. The story of the monastery begins in 781 when a complete family consisting of Photeinos with his wife Theoktiste, his brother Plato and his three sons – one of whom was Theodore the future abbot – and one daughter all decided to enter the monastic life. Plato had already been a monk for over twenty years and he planned this initiative with Theoktiste. They retired together to one of the family properties in nearby Bithynia and after a few years in 790 set up the monastery of Sakkoudion on the estate.

It was a success and the monastery grew fast, so that, in 798, Theodore, who was by now the abbot, and the community of one hundred monks moved to new monastery buildings at Stoudios.[11] In the next two years, the number of monks tripled to three hundred monks, then by 807 there were seven hundred, and then by 815 the community had grown so that there were over a thousand monks living in the monastery. As well as the house at Stoudios, the monastery had set up a federation of communities with a further eight monasteries in Bithynia, and several metochia, which were plots of land with a house attached. There were also connections with other monasteries further afield. These were joined together by economic and administrative links, a sense of sharing in a common lifestyle and through donations and gifts which were given to the whole network of houses.

Theodore wanted to restore the ancient traditions of the fathers. His models were the great founders of the coenobia, Pachomius, Basil, Sabas and Dorotheus of Gaza. Like them, he set up monasteries in which monks would live together in community and would express this through hard work and denial of their own will. Work was an essential part of the monk's day and there were four hours a day in winter and eight hours in summer set aside for manual or other work. Monks were reminded that 'he who is fervent in bodily tasks is also fervent in spiritual ones.' They owned nothing of their own, and this principle of non-possession was so carefully carried out that their clothes were collected in each week and others distributed so that even the garments which they wore were only used by them for a short space of time.[12]

Figure 7 The extensive ruins of the church of the Stoudios monastery in Constantinople show the size of this important community.

The community was carefully ordered. The members were the limbs in the body, well ordered, each having its own place and contributing to the well-being of the whole. The head was the *hegumenos*, or abbot. Then below him was the second in command, the *deuteron*, or vice-abbot. Below them were several administrative departments. There was the *oikonomos*, the steward or director of operations; the *epistemonarches*, or director of discipline to regulate the behaviour of monks; *hebdomarios*, or director of tutors looking after the study of monks; then the *canonarches*, or a head of worship. Each of these presided over their departments. There were altogether a total of about forty departments. This carefully planned administrative structure ensured that the community ran smoothly and gave each monk a job and position in the whole structure. So the diverse group was moulded into a harmonious integrated body.[13]

The style of life in the Stoudite monasteries is shown by the accounts of the lives of the monks which were shaped by these disciplines. Thaddaios is remembered as a Stoudite saint. He was a Scythian and was probably born in Bulgaria. He had been a slave who, on being released, joined the monastery when he was still as a teenager. He worked hard and studied, but he never managed to learn to speak Greek, and we are told that until the end of his life he 'stammered' his way through the readings in church. But he learned the psalms by heart and recited them in his life as a hermit. When the iconoclast persecutions began he was imprisoned with other monks. Some accepted iconoclasm, but Thaddaios remained firm, and died under the beatings which he received. Described by his biographer as coming from an 'ignominious, low-born and sensuous' background, he responded with enthusiasm to the Stoudite way of life and came to be recognized as a model monk and a saint.[14]

Theodore the abbot was a powerful figure. He intervened in political life when moral or religious matters were involved and this led him into a succession of confrontations. He and his monks opposed the Emperor Constantine VI (780–97) when the emperor married for a second time, which provoked the Moechian or Adultery Conflict of 795–7; then they objected to the choice of Nikiphoros for the position of patriarch in 806 since he was a layman; and then they protested again at the decision to re-instate a priest called Joseph who had officiated at the second marriage of Constantine. These controversies accustomed Theodore and the Studite monks to engage in political debate and controversy. And so, when their great challenge of the iconoclast controversy began, they were ready and prepared to stand up for their faith.

There had already been one campaign against icons, which was resolved at the second Council of Nicaea in 787, but the second attack on images was more determined and persistent. It lasted from 815 to 842. Emperor Leo V (813–20) opposed the veneration of the icons and was supported by a monk of the Sergius and Bacchus monastery, John Grammatikos. The iconodule Patriarch Nikiphoros was ejected, and replaced by John Grammatikos who became Patriarch John VII from 837 until his death in 843. Many monks joined this iconoclast movement.

Only twenty of the thousand monks of Stoudios deserted their abbot and joined the iconoclast movement. The rest stayed firm. Theodore's organizational skills once again helped to guide the community through this conflict. He formed the monks into seventy-two separate groups, each under an *archegos*, who was

Theodore's representative. He also developed a network of communication, with procedures and codes to help the dispersed groups keep in touch. So when the monks were exiled and left the capital, they were able to maintain both their common life and also their resistance to the pressures of the iconoclasts. Theodore himself wrote books setting out why icons mattered and many letters to encourage his followers. Altogether 850 letters have survived which were written in the period from the start of the controversy until his death in 826. Other leading iconodule monks, such as the hermit Ioannikios and Hilarion of the Dalmatou, also kept on the move, never settling for too long in one place and exhorting people to keep venerating the icons.

The iconoclast conflict ended in 843 when Theodora, the regent for her young son Michael III (842–67), restored the veneration of icons and the iconoclast Patriarch John VII was replaced by Methodios I. Methodios was enthroned on 11 March. It was the first Sunday in Lent and there were processions and celebrations. The Synodikon of Orthodoxy was probably compiled by the patriarch and listed the heroes who supported the icons and fought for the faith. The names remembered included patriarchs, including Germanos I (715–30), Tarasios (784–806), Nikiphoros I (806–15) and Methodios himself (843–7). But, importantly, it also included the monks – Theodore of Studium (759–806), Joannikios of Mount Olympus (*c.* 752–846), Hilarion, Dalmatus, Isaac and Symeon. So not only was the place of icons assured, but also the role of the monks as their advocates and protectors was enshrined and affirmed in the tradition. The first Sunday of Lent continues to be celebrated as the Triumph of Orthodoxy throughout the Orthodox Church.

The histories of the period describe the sufferings of the monks as martyrs who preserved true faith. But, in fact, the situation was less simple and clear cut. There were monks who had opposed icons and bishops who had supported them. But history is often written by the victors and these records were written after the event to establish the position of the monks as martyrs for the Orthodox faith. There was then a purge of iconoclast clergy. Methodios dismissed those who had opposed icons and replaced them with icon supporters, many of whom came from the iconodule monasteries. The result was a growth in influence of the monks which led to the next stage of monastic influence in the church.[15]

Theodore died in 826, before the iconoclast controversy was brought to its triumphant conclusion. He left a network of monasteries which were unified and disciplined. Before long, and possibly during Theodore's lifetime, the numerous letters and sermons of the saint had been formulated into a rule of life, the *hypotyposis*.[16] Later, monasteries over a wide area modelled their disciplines on that of Stoudios. The typikon of Studios was used by monasteries in south Italy by the ninth century; by the monastery of the Caves near Kiev in Russia in the eleventh century, in a Russian translation by its abbot Theodosius (1062–74); and then from there throughout the Balkans and Russia. Rules, such as those familiar in Western monasticism, which governed the lives of whole orders of monasteries were not known in the east. The Stoudite approach did not become a rule for others to follow but it was a source which helped to influence the direction in which eastern monasticism went.

Conclusion

The series of ecumenical councils of the church, from the first to the second Councils of Nicaea, from 325 to 787, defined and built the life of the church. Alongside doctrinal and credal statements went collections of canons which decided on disciplinary and organizational issues. The monks took part in the councils and the councils took decisions which affected the monks. Monastic life had grown across the Christian world, developing distinct characteristics in the various regions. The various styles of life met in Jerusalem, where pilgrims from across the empire were attracted and settled, and in Constantinople. The different lifestyles emerging from different societies gave a richness and flexibility to the developing monastic movement while the central place of the two cities gave a sense of shared identity and common purpose. By the time of the second Council of Nicaea, the monastic movement had established its influence and significance within the church.

Notes

1. See Judith Herrin, *Byzantium* (Harmondsworth, 2007), p. 59.
2. Socrates, *Ecclesiastical History* 2.6.96; Sozomen, *Ecclesiastical History* 4.2.141.
3. Matthew 19.21.
4. 1 Thessalonians 5.17.
5. Matthew 6.34; Mark 9.22.
6. *Life of Alexander the Sleepless* 35. The life was written in the in the late fifth or early sixth century. It is translated in Daniel Caner, *Wandering Begging Monks* (Berkeley, 2002), pp. 249–80.
7. *Life of John Kalybites* 262.29–263.25 BHG 868, in Peter Hatlie, *The Monks and Monasteries of Constantinople ca 350–850* (Cambridge, 2007), p. 85.
8. *Life of Marcellus* 13.297–8 BHG 1072 in Hatlie, *Monks*, p. 103.
9. For Matrona's monastery, see ibid., pp. 98–100.
10. Susannah Elm, *Virgins of God, the Making of Asceticism in Late Antiquity* (Oxford, 1994), pp. 181–2.
11. There are several lives of Theodore, some written by monks of his monastery. Among them are lives by Michael the Monk, PG 99.233–328; Naukratios, PG 99,1825–49; Theodore Daphnopatos, PG 99.113–232.
12. Ibid., p. 13.
13. Ibid., pp. 16–17.
14. *The Life of Thaddaios* 329.5; 331.10, 333.1–12, 335.17–337.22. The life was edited and translated by D Afinogenov in *Analecta Bollandiana* 119 (2001), pp. 327–37.
15. Rosemary Morris, *Monks and Laymen in Byzantium 843–1118* (Cambridge, 1995), pp. 9–15.
16. The hypotyposis is in PG 99.1704–20, with an English translation in John Thomas, C. Hero, and A. Constable, ed. *Byzantine Monastic Foundation Documents*, vol. 1 (Washington, 2000), pp. 84–115.

Part Three

The Forms of Monastic Tradition: After Iconoclasm

The monastic tradition, along with the church, divided. The one universal church contained within it, like the Byzantine Empire, people of different races, languages and cultures. Now this diversity within the empire led to division. Linguistic differences, doctrinal debates and political events led to the growing apart of different parts of the church. We can conveniently distinguish three broad strands into which the Christian, and so the monastic, tradition diverged. This divergence was a gradual process but divisions deepened in the period after the Councils of Ephesus and Chalcedon in the fifth century. The advance of Islam in the mid-seventh century decisively separated Syrian from Greek churches and monasteries. The church of the emperor in Constantinople was Greek speaking, accepted the doctrinal formula of the Council of Chalcedon and was within the Byzantine Empire.[1] The churches further to the east, mainly speaking Syriac or one of the other Semitic languages, separated from the church of the empire over Christological doctrines and as this happened were absorbed into the Persian and Arab Empires after the military expansion of these powers. The third strand was the tradition of faith which grew and flourished to the west of the Byzantine Empire. Here Latin was the language of the church and a two-nature Chalcedonian Christology was accepted. In these areas Germanic and other tribes expanded and occupied the regions of Western Europe. This combination of pressures led to the division of the church. Monasteries were founded within each of these traditions and shared in the tradition established in the early centuries. But historical events influenced the development of the monasteries and their place within church and society.

Note

1 The parts of the church in the Middle East which remained loyal to the emperor were known as Melkite, from the Semitic *malak* or king. This name still refers to these churches.

7

Going West: Two Benedicts

The Beginnings of Monastic Orders

Monks went west as well as east. A Western pioneer was Martin of Tours (316–97). Martin was born in the area which is now Hungary and had been a catechumen as a boy. His father had been a soldier and Martin, as was expected, followed him into the army. It was then that he divided his cloak and gave half to a beggar, after which a vision of Christ led him to be baptized. After his baptism, he refused to take further part in fighting. He lived as a hermit in the region around Poitiers and came to associate with the Bishop Hilary. Hilary was exiled from Poitiers and sent to Phrygia in Asia Minor. Meanwhile Martin continued his eremitical life. Hilary returned in 361 and Martin founded a monastery at Ligugé near Tours. From here he travelled, preaching and encouraging his listeners to become monks. He was chosen to become bishop of Tours in 371. Like many other monks when faced with this prospect of ecclesiastical promotion he tried to avoid it. He hid in a goose shed, but the geese cackled so loudly that his hiding place was easily discovered. As bishop he travelled widely in Pannonia, Italy and Illyricum, preaching and promoting the monastic life. The lives of both Hilary and Martin show how monasticism spread. Martin as a soldier left his home and went with the army to Gaul and then later travelled as a preacher. Hilary meanwhile was exiled to Phrygia, where ascetical traditions were well established. Through their travels and teaching, the monastic life which was beginning in Syria and other parts of the Eastern empire was brought to Gaul. Martin died in 397 and his life was written soon after by his friend Sulpicius Severus.[1]

Another place where monks came was the island of Lérins in the Mediterranean. An ascetic called Honoratus lived as a hermit from 410 until other joined him. Several of the monks became bishops including three successive bishops of Arles, who were Honoratus himself, then Hilarius and Cesarius.

A further source of influence on Western monasticism was the writing and teaching of the monk John Cassian. Cassian, with his friend Germanus, was a monk at Bethlehem and then Egypt. He left Egypt with Origenist monks in the expulsion of the group in 400 and went to Constantinople, possibly to intercede with the Patriarch John Chrysostom for his fellow Origenists. As a Latin speaker, he was sent on a delegation to Rome, from where he founded monasteries in the area around Marseille from around 415. He described his experiences in Egypt and the monastic traditions of the fathers in two books, the *Institutes* and the *Conferences*. These books were widely read and influenced Benedict's Rule.

By the mid-fifth century, monastic life had become established across the western parts of Europe. The lives of Martin and John Cassian show how the mobility around the empire, the preaching of bishops and the writing of books led to a system of communication which spread the example and traditions of monasticism. Ideas were taken around the empire and beyond. Thus far, the pattern of monastic life in the west follows a similar pattern to that in the east. This changed through the lives of two monks, both called Benedict, in the following centuries.

Benedict of Nursia (*c.* 480–543) was educated in Rome but left his studies to follow his call to a life of prayer. He went first to Subiaco where he lived with others and then withdrew to live in greater solitude, although he took his childhood nurse with him. He grew in his life of solitary prayer but was then asked by a group of monks who were looking for an abbot to come and live with them. Benedict hesitated because he realized that their approach was not the same as his but eventually agreed. His hesitation proved to be justified because the monks rebelled against his authority and tried to poison him. He was miraculously saved, once by the cup of poison shattering before he drank it and then by a raven flying away a loaf of poisoned bread which was intended for him. More monks came and Benedict founded twelve further monasteries in the area for them, ending with the great monastery of Monte Cassino on the top of a hill between Rome and Naples.[2] Benedict wrote a rule of life to guide his communities. So from the start, his monasteries were guided by a written rule. It drew on other rules, especially the earlier *Regula Magistri* or *Rule of the Master*. Its influence was at first limited, and the earliest copy of the Rule which has survived was made two centuries after the death of Benedict, which suggests that at that time it was not used outside his communities.

The *Rule of Benedict* later gained a new influence and soon provided a rule which was followed across the west. This popularization was the work of another Benedict. Benedict of Aniane (747–821) came from a noble family and was sent by his father, the Count of Maguelonne, to the court of the Frankish emperors, Pepin and Charlemagne. After an accident in which he was nearly drowned, Benedict promised to live as a monk. He lived for five years in a monastery near Dijon, but when the abbot died and Benedict was chosen as his successor, he left the community to seek out a more ascetic way of living at a new monastery which he founded on the family estates at Aniane in Languedoc. Thus he followed a similar path to many in the east, with his own monastery on his own lands with a way of life which he chose.[3]

Then came two developments. First, he changed his mind about the kind of life he wanted. He had previously been sceptical about the value of the Rule of the earlier Benedict because he thought it was not strict enough. But as his monastery grew, the younger Benedict recognized the value of the rule of his namesake for governing a community. He used it as the basis of the life of his own and other monasteries which he founded or worked with. He promoted its use across the Frankish empire, recognizing it as teaching a clear and simple life.

The second development was its adoption as imperial policy. Benedict of Aniane was teacher to the young prince Louis the Pious who built a new monastery for his teacher at Aachen in 814. He summoned church councils at Aachen in 816 and 817 which laid down that all monasteries in the empire should follow the rule of Benedict. This decision was enacted in the Codex Regularum and disseminated in a series of imperial capitularies.

Both the *Rule of the Master* and the *Rule of Benedict* identify four kinds of monks. There are, first, coenobitic monks, who live in community under discipline and authority. Then, second, there are hermits. These are experienced monks who undertake a life of greater asceticism and solitude. There are also two other kinds of monks, who do not live an authentic monastic life but are following their own path. There are the *gyrovagi* or wandering monks who have not settled in one place but move around. Then finally there are a group he called Sarabaites, who do not follow a rule but live as they wish. This division into classes, and the disapproval of two forms of life, diverged from practice elsewhere. In other parts of the Christian world, *xenitieia* or living as a stranger was a recognized form of ascetic life. Many ascetics lived as wanderers, denying themselves the security of a settled life. Other holy men and women set off into the desert and developed their own forms of asceticism, such as living in caves or on pillars. Benedict himself had lived as a hermit before entering a coenobium and founding monasteries. The insistence that monastic life is lived in community under a rule, and that other forms of ascetic struggle are not approved, led to the Western style of monasticism, which was lived within structured monasteries.

The *Rule of Benedict* was successful because it provided a model for a community life which was comprehensive in governing all aspects of life, with guidance for worship, work and leisure. It had a religious authority because of its association with Rome, since Benedict lived in the neighbourhood of Rome. It also had a political authority, since its use was promulgated by royal decree.

As a result of the lives of two Benedicts monastic life in the west was, firstly, regulated by the rule of Benedict and, secondly, was promoted by political and ecclesiastical authority. So monasticism became an institution within political society. It had a clear ideology which gave it a distinct identity within the church. This did not do away with diversity, protest or reform but it did establish the place of monasteries within the church and state. While in the east, the holy was uncontrolled and unpredictable, in the west the power of the holy was harnessed by the episcopal and papal hierarchy.[4]

Monasteries followed separate trajectories in the west from the east. In the west, there were separate orders and rules of life. Much later, the monastic orders of the west were to return to the countries from which monasticism began with awkward and often damaging consequences. In 1622 Pope Gregory XV founded the Congregation for the Propaganda of the Faith, which led to monastic orders setting out as missionaries to persuade Eastern monasteries, and churches, to accept the authority of the Latin Pope. These Greek Catholic Churches grew and spread across the Christian East. In the later years of the Ottoman Empire, Catholics were given the status of a recognized religious community in the millet system and shared in the fluctuation of fortunes of the Christians of the Middle East.[5]

Notes

1. Martin's life was written by his friend Sulpicius Severus, ed. J. Fontaine, *Sulpice Sevère, Vie de S. Martin* (Paris, 1967–9).
2. The *Life of Benedict of Nursia* was written by Pope Gregory the Great in Dialogues II, in *Grégoire le Grand: Dialogues*, ed. and trans. A. de Vögue and P. Antin (Paris, 1978–80).
3. The *Life of Benedict of Aniane* is translated in T. F. X. Noble and T. Head, *Soldiers of Christ Saints and Saints' Lives from Late Antiquity and the Early Middle Ages* (Philadelphia, 1995), pp. 213–54.
4. Andrew Louth, *Greek East and Latin West* (New York, 2007), p. 117.
5. See below, p. 213.

8

East to Asia and South to Africa: The Syriac Tradition

Introduction

The Syrian monks brought the Christian faith and, with it, monastic life, from the traditional heartlands of Syrian Christianity around Edessa and Nisibis to new places. They went east as far as India and China; then south into Ethiopia. In the period after Chalcedon the Syrian Churches separated from the Greek Churches of Byzantium and this separation further pushed them in new directions. West Syrians moved out of cities into the countryside to avoid the pressure of Chalcedonians in the cities. East Syrians, meanwhile, learned to live in cosmopolitan societies among people of other faiths. In Ethiopia, monks occupied the old holy places of nature religions to extend the frontiers of Christendom. These various movements took place in a turbulent history. Their history was influenced by the shared language and culture which bound Syrians together, the military campaigns which shifted boundaries and drove them into new areas and also a period of bitter doctrinal divisions which divided Syrians from other Christians.

Syriac Christianity was shaped by a shared language and culture. The Christian tradition, culture and language of Syria were formed in the area around Edessa, the modern Urfa, and Nisibis, the modern Nuseybin, in the early part of the Christian era. Syriac is a Semitic language and is closely related to Aramaic, the language spoken by Christ. Today the monks of the Tur Abdin and the area around are proudly aware that when they worship and talk in their Turoyo form of Syriac they are speaking the language used by Jesus. Syrian Christians point out that Hebrew is the language of Jews, and Greek is the language of pagans, but Syriac is the language of Christ and of Christians. While Arabic became more widely spoken after the Arab conquests, the Syriac languages continued to be used in the church and became a cultural bond linking different Syriac groups.

Then Syria was a battleground where empires clashed. There were long-running battles between Persians and Byzantines. The Sassanian dynasty ruled Persia from 224 to 641. In the third century, King Shahpur I (215–72) extended his empire over Syria as far as Antioch. Then, in the following century, he was succeeded by a namesake Shahpur II (309–79). Shahpur II became king before he was born, with a crown held over his mother's womb in a unique coronation ceremony. His long rule was a period of expansion and military victory for the Persian Empire. Under these two kings, as well as in the shorter reigns in between, the Persian armies reached Antioch in 260, before being forced back, and in 363 occupied the Christian city of Nisibis. Christians had already settled in Mesopotamia from an early date and their numbers expanded as a result of deportations and migration of Christians from the Syrian cities in the west of the region after their conquest by Persians. There were bishops in Persia, including in the capital of Seleucia-Ctesphon, by the third century. The church, now established within Persia, declared itself independent at a synod in 424 and the Catholicos, or senior bishop, established his seat in Seleucia-Ctesiphon near modern Baghdad. Meanwhile the Syrians in the west remained under Byzantine rule until Arab forces conquered most of the Middle East in the mid-seventh century.

Doctrinal debate contributed to division. The eastern and western parts of Syria took different dogmatic paths. Not only were they divided by politics as the Persian and Byzantine armies waged war across the territory, but they also developed different approaches in the debates over Christology. These debates concerned the way that the Church should understand and speak about Christ, who was both God and man, the central mystery at the heart of the Christian faith. This was the subject of a series of ecumenical councils which were concerned with whether it should be believed that Christ had one or two natures. The Council of Ephesus of 431 affirmed the single nature of Christ, having a divine nature which assumed humanity, and anathematized the two-nature Christology taught by Nestorius patriarch of Constantinople and others. The two-nature Christology was taught in the city of Antioch through the writing of theologians such as Theodore of Mopsuestia and Theodoret of Cyrrhus. It was the doctrinal position of the East Syrians.

The Church of the East at first retained its close links with Judaism and its theological traditions were rooted in the Bible and in the poetic interpretation of Aphrahat and Ephrem. Its theological School of the Persians had moved from Edessa to Nisibis, further to the east, until it was closed in 489 by the Emperor Zeno. In the fifth century, the biblical exegetical works of the Antiochene theologian, Theodore of Mopsuestia, were translated into Syriac and as a result the Persian Church accepted and remained faithful to his traditions of biblical interpretation and two-nature Christology. There were later attempts to persuade the church to accept a Monophysite Christology, especially by Henana, who became head of the school in 572, but these were not successful. The Church of the East remained loyal to the two-nature Christology of Theodore and did not accept the one-nature Christology of Ephesus. As a result, it became separated from the church in the Byzantine Empire.[1] The church has often been called Nestorian, since they accepted the teaching of Nestorius the patriarch of Constantinople who shocked many by rejecting the use of the title of Theotokos, or bearer or mother of God, to describe Mary. He preferred to say Christotokos, or bearer of Christ. Since Nestorius was condemned as a heretic at the Council of Ephesus of 431 and exiled from Constantinople, the use of the title suggests that East Syrians share heretical beliefs. So here we call the East Syrians by the more correct title of the Church of the East.[2]

The debate continued at the Council of Chalcedon of 451. Here the fathers of the church stated that Christ was to be recognized as having two natures, human and divine, but these subsisted in one person. Churches who opposed this definition by affirming one nature have been known as Monophysite, or single nature, and included churches in west Syria. These object to being called Monophysite since *monos* means single or alone, and so implies a simple and single nature. They prefer to describe themselves as Miapysite, since *mia* is the numeral one, and so the use of *mia* allows for the understanding that the 'one' nature is composite and is both fully human and fully divine. The slogan which summarizes this was the statement of Cyril of Alexandria, that Christ is 'one incarnate nature of God the Word'. The title Syrian Orthodox or West Syrian is preferable, although the title of Monophysite is widely used.

The nature of Syriac language and culture made doctrinal discussion with Greek speakers difficult and led to misunderstanding, especially when Christology was the subject of debate. Syrians had not inherited the Greek tradition of philosophical reflection and their language did not include the vocabulary to express and articulate abstract discussion about the nature of Christ. The Greek terms which were used were substance or *ousia*, nature or *hypostasis* and person or *prosopon* and these did not have equivalent concepts in Syriac languages. In Syrian theology, rooted in the Semitic culture of the Bible, a person is a single, holistic being created by God and standing before him. Theology was expressed in the poetry and hymnody of writers such as Aphrahat and Ephrem the Syrian. The philosophical concepts of spirit, soul and flesh as the abstract components of a human being did not fit with the poetry and imagery of Syriac hymnody. This made the conducting theological debate difficult and contributed to the division within the Church.

It is beyond the scope of this study to describe this long and bitter struggle. Here we need to realize why it mattered to the monks. The worship and life of the monks were a following of Christ and so the understanding and formulation of this central teaching affected their whole way of life. For the Egyptians and Syrians, it was vital that was a clear continuity of being between God the Word in eternity and God the Word in the person of Christ. In encountering Christ in word or sacrament, the believer meets God, the same Word of God, the second person of the Trinity, who has become present in the life of Jesus. This is summarized in the verse of John's gospel – 'the Word become flesh and dwelt among us.' The Chalcedonian definition expressed an alternative approach, associated especially with theologians at Antioch. For them, monks and other believers met Christ in the words, actions and events of the gospel, which told the story of the life of Jesus. They reflected on this human story in its completeness and looked towards the light of God which shone through it. For them, if you lose the fullness of humanity in Christ then you cannot recognize the radically distinct glory of God which meets us through it. For both, the way that Christ is imagined and approached is especially important as they are monks for whom prayer is a way of identifying with Christ. 'The ascetic is the point at which the human and the holy meet.'[3]

The beginnings of the Monophysite Church

The Council of Chalcedon was summoned by the Emperor Marcian (450–7) to resolve the controversy over the natures of Christ, but, far from resolving this, it exacerbated the conflict. After the news that the Council of Chalcedon had accepted a two-nature Christology reached Jerusalem, the monks were divided in their response. We saw earlier that the monasteries in the neighbourhood of the city, led by Euthymius, accepted the decisions as Orthodox. Many monks however continued in their opposition to the Council and some left the city. Several monasteries along the coast, at a safe distance from Jerusalem, provided a place of refuge for the monks who opposed the Council of Chalcedon, and here the beginnings of an anti-Chalcedonian Monophysite Church took place. In the monasteries of Gaza, Monophysite communities lived alongside Chalcedonian monasteries, apparently in peace and harmony.

The life of Peter the Iberian, who became a leader of the Monophysite monks, shows how the Monophysite movement developed. Peter was a prince from Georgia, or Iberia, born with the name Narbanugi, in 417.[4] He was taken as a hostage to the court of the emperor Theodosius II in Constantinople, where he was brought up. As a young man he and a companion, Mithradates the Eunuch, went on pilgrimage to Jerusalem where he entered a monastery and met the wandering monk from Egypt, Zeno. Narbanugi and Mithradates, now given the more appropriate monastic names of Peter and John, lived at first in the monasteries of Jerusalem, but then, on the advice of Zeno, went to Maiuma, the port of Gaza, in around 442, to escape from Archbishop Juvenal, who had wanted to ordain Peter priest. In his determination to escape ordination, Peter leapt out of the window and over the roof. However his escape was only temporary since, after he arrived at the coast, he was ordained priest and then later bishop of Maiuma.[5]

After the expulsion of Theodosius, the Monophysite patriarch, from Jerusalem, Peter was living near Gaza. His reputation allowed him to stay in Palestine, but then two years later, in 455, he decided to join the Monophysites in Egypt. Here he stayed for twenty years, living as a hermit. But he still could not escape the attention of the local church who sought his support in their struggles against the Chalcedonians. He was persuaded to share in the consecration of a Monophysite patriarch of Alexandria, since two bishops were needed to perform the consecration of a successor and Peter and another bishop, Eusebius of Pelusium, were the only Monophysite bishops available. Together they consecrated Timothy Aelurus, or Timothy the Weasel, as patriarch of Alexandria in March 457. Peter then returned to Gaza in 475, where he continued to ordain clergy to serve the Monophysite communities. The task of setting up a hierarchy for a new church was begun by Peter and those with him and would be continued by Jacob Baradeus.

Peter did not return to his former monastery at Maiuma, but first lived as a hermit in Ashkelon, where his reputation as an ascetic attracted disciples. Since he was the only Monophysite bishop in Palestine, he travelled around Palestine, and into Arabia and Phoenecia. His biographer tells how when he arrived at a village, the inhabitants joyfully came out to meet him and listened to his preaching. He remained in contact with friends and fellow monks in Egypt throughout this period.[6] He died at Jamnia in 491, surrounded by his disciples.

Peter's missionary travels extended to Phoenecia, the modern Lebanon. Among the disciples who followed him were students from the celebrated law school at Berytus. Several of these became leading members of the emerging Monophysite Church. Theodore of Ascalon became a monk and then abbot of Peter's monastery at Maiuma.

John Rufus wrote histories of the Monophysite monks, including the *Life of Peter*. Zacharias of Maiuma, who was later known as Zacharias Rhetor, decided to return to Berytus to complete his study of law, and may later have become bishop of Mitylene. The most influential was Severus of Sozopolis. Severus followed a strict ascetic life at Eleutheropolis and Maiuma, living first as a hermit and then founding a monastery. As the Chalcedonians grew in confidence and persecuted Monophysites, Severus, accompanied by the abbots of the monasteries at Maiuma and Eleutheropolis, travelled in 508 to Constantinople to gain the support of the emperor against his Chalcedonian persecutors. Severus remained in the capital and in 512 was chosen as patriarch of Antioch. He became a leader of the Monophysites.

The Monophysite monasteries of Gaza disappear from the historical record soon after Severus's consecration as patriarch of Antioch. Justin I became emperor in 518, and he was succeeded by Justinian (527–65). These emperors spoke Latin as well as Greek and were determined to retain the unity of the empire, including west as well as east. Their different perspective led to a policy which combined the implementation of the Council of Chalcedon with loyalty to the teaching of Cyril of Alexandria. The new policy strengthened the Chalcedonians and resulted in the decline of Monophysite monasteries in Gaza, and throughout Palestine. In other areas, Monophysitism remained strong. Probably there were similar numbers of Chalcedonians and Monophysities in the empire throughout this period.

The future Monophysite, Syrian Orthodox Church took shape in this seminal period at Gaza. The life of Peter describes him sharing in the ordination of an alternative episcopate and priesthood; the centres of church life were in monasteries outside the city rather than the urban churches; leaders were forced into wandering lives, to escape pursuing imperial troops and also to encourage and strengthen their supporters. It was a way of life which would later be followed by Jacob Baradeus.

John of Ephesus and Jacob Baradeus

John of Ephesus is the historian of the separation between the two sides. John was born in 507 at Amida, in Mesopotamia. All the elder brothers of the family had died in infancy, presumably because of an inherited genetic condition. As the infant John was also dying, the parents took him to the local holy man, Maro, who prescribed the remedy of feeding him as many lentils as he could eat. In spite of the scepticism of the bystanders about this cure, it worked and by the age of four John had been received into the monastery. When Maro died, John moved to the larger monastery of Mar John Urtaya in Amida. During John's time as a monk, there were attacks from the Chalcedonians and the monks were forced out of the monastery buildings into a wandering life. While on these travels, in 529, John was ordained deacon and came to Constantinople in 540. Although the Emperor Justinian was promoting the faith of Chalcedon, his wife the Empress Theodora welcomed Monophysite refugees and gave them a place to live in the Hormisdas Palace in the centre of Constantinople. Among this refugee community was the Monophysite patriarch of Alexandria Theodosius. John was welcomed and given a house in the neighbourhood of Sykae, where there was already a community of Monophysites and where he set up a monastery of which he became archimandrite. In 558 he was consecrated as the Monophysite bishop of Ephesus and when Theodosius died in 566 the Monophysites of Constantinople looked to him as their leader. In 571, the Chalcedonian John Scholastikos became patriarch of Constantinople and imprisoned John. Here John spent most of the rest of his life. A creative outcome of his confinement was that he had the opportunity for literary work and wrote an *Ecclesiastical History* and a series of *Lives of the Eastern Saints*.[7]

The *Lives of the Eastern Saints* tells the stories of twenty-seven holy men and women and gives a vivid and lively account of the lives of monks under persecution and on the move. There was a period of persecution in Amida in 532 caused by the Chalcedonian sympathies of the Emperor Justin (518–27). The monks of Mar John Urtaya left and wandered until they were able to settle at a remote monastery called Mar Mama. They stayed there for five years and then moved to a much smaller building called the monastery of the Poplars. After nearly ten years the more tolerant policies of Justinian and Theodora made it possible for them to return. They found their former buildings destroyed and in ruins. They started to rebuild but this provoked a new outburst of hostility and once again they had to leave. They went to the monastery of the Sycamores. The soldiers pursued them but when they arrived were so impressed by the sight of hundreds of ascetics standing in worship that they turned on the townspeople instead, killing their animals and eating their food. The monks left in order to save the local people further harm. And so it went on.[8]

The attacks from Chalcedonians scattered monks across a wide area. When John went to Egypt in the early 530s he encountered a community of women led by an abbess Susan. She had lived in Palestine but came from a Syrian family. At the age of eight she entered a monastery near Gaza. Then ten years later, attacks on Monophysites began. Susan decided to go to Egypt and was followed by five of the nuns. They found a place to live in a village called Mendis where there was a deserted fort. Susan went to a cave to be alone, but the nuns pleaded with her not to desert them. She divided her time between solitude in the cave and caring for the community in the fort. Her monastery became known as a place of safety for Monophysites and both women and men joined her.[9]

Another holy woman whose story is told by John was Euphemia. She and her daughter Maria lived a devout life. They devoted themselves to caring for the poor, sick, needy and distressed. John pleaded with them to extend some of the kindness they showed to others to themselves. When the persecutions started, they provided a support network for the monks and nuns who turned to them for help. The two women provided these refugees with accommodation in the city and helped them with travel arrangements if they wanted to escape. The authorities came to arrest them and demanded that they accept the Chalcedonian confession. The city was outraged and all the citizens turned out to demand their release. They were freed from prison but forced to leave the city.[10]

Amongst John's friends and colleagues was the monk who has come to be recognized as the founding father of the Church of the West Syrians, Jacob Baradeus (500–578). Jacob came from the city of Tella and was brought up in a monastery at nearby Mount Izla, on the edge of the Tur Abdin. He became known as a miracle worker and so came to the attention of the empress Theodora, who invited him to come to Constantinople to join the community of Monophysite monks which she was sheltering. So, as a young man of twenty-seven, he travelled to the capital. He did not find court life attractive and preferred to live in the Monophysite monastery of Sykae where he stayed for fifteen years. He was on hand and available when a request came from the chief of a confederation of Arab tribes, al-Harith, for a bishop who was sympathetic to Monophysitism. The Emperor Justinian approached Jacob, who prepared for this mission through consecration as bishop of Edessa by Theodosius, the Monophysite patriarch of Alexandria. Jacob went first to Alexandria. Here he consecrated two companions, Conon of Tarsus and Eugenius of Seleucia, as bishops to work with him and then he set out on his travels.

For the following thirty-five years of his life, Jacob travelled over the Middle East. The experience of living among and visiting the Syrian and other Monophysite communities convinced him of the need for a church structure and for bishops and priests to serve the Monophysites. He travelled through Syria, Asia Minor, Armenia, Egypt, Cyprus, Rhodes and also other regions. Wherever he went he taught and ordained clergy for the emerging Monophysite Church. John of Ephesus says that he 'caused the priesthood to flow like great rivers over the whole world of the Roman domains'.[11] He ordained two patriarchs, twenty-seven bishops and over a hundred thousand clergy.[12] As a result of his missionary work, the Monophysite Church of Syria, now called the Syrian Orthodox Church, was formed.

When he invited Jacob to lead a mission to the Arab tribesmen, the Emperor Justinian had hoped to incorporate the frontier region more closely into the empire. Instead he found that a new church, with its own hierarchy of bishops and priests, was taking shape and so undermining the unity of his empire. He tried to arrest Jacob and sent soldiers to pursue him. Jacob dressed in old clothes, and so gained the name Baradeus, from the Syrian *burd'ata* or horse cloth which was his clothing. Thus inconspicuously clothed, he kept on the move, travelling thirty or forty miles a day, keeping ahead of his pursuers and so building up and supporting this new church.

This new underground church grew and existed alongside the official Chalcedonian Church. Both Churches worshipped in the same place, sometimes sharing the same building. On one occasion Jacob's companion John of Hephaistos celebrated a Monophysite liturgy at which he ordained fifty priests in the gallery of the cathedral at Tralles at the same time as the Chalcedonian liturgy was taking place downstairs. This event suggests not only a less ordered style of liturgical celebration but also strong support from local people for this emerging church.

The church became known as the Jacobite Church, commemorating the pioneering efforts of Jacob. Its strength lay in rural the monasteries rather than in urban churches. A later Monophysite patriarch of Antioch, Peter of Callinicum, claimed that he had never visited the Antioch of which he was bishop. Similarly, we have no indication that John of Ephesus ever visited the city of which he was bishop and which gave him its name. Instead bishops lived in the monasteries, which became the centres of the life of the church. Monasteries were sanctuaries of refuge where many, especially clergy, withdrew to. They were also places of learning and culture. As Arabic became more widely used, the Syriac schools of learning in cities disappeared but monasteries preserved and handed on a tradition of Syriac culture and writing. The monastery of Qenneshrin on the Euphrates was known as a centre of the study of Greek writers. A tradition of ascetic literature in Syriac was guarded in many monastic centres and preserved important texts, including the writings of Evagrius of Pontus, which were rejected by Greek-speaking monasteries.

The Tur Abdin, or Mountain of the Servants, is a high plateau to the north of the city of Nisibis, modern Nuseybin. Monastic life on the plateau began with the arrival of the Egyptian monk, Awgin or Eugenius, with seventy companions. His monastery became a centre of monastic life especially for the East Syrians. The monastery of Mor Abraham which was established by Abraham of Kashkar in the sixth century became the centre of a monastic revival. Shmuyel of Eshtin and his disciple Shem'un of Qartmin founded the monastery of Qartmin, or Mor Gabriel, in 397, although it seems to have been in existence for fifty years before that. The Monastery of Mor Hananayo, or St Ananias, is known as the Saffron Monastery or Deir al-Zafaran, and was founded around 490. It was the residence of the patriarchs of the Syrian Orthodox Church from 1293 to 1924. There were over a hundred Syriac monasteries in the Tur Abdin, from which monastic life and Christian culture were preserved through a long history of triumph and tribulation and still maintains a somewhat precarious witness.[13]

The Monophysite Church settled into its rural heartland. A Monophysite historian reflected on its way of life after persecution subsided and the new hierarchy was in place.

Figure 8 Deir al-Zafaran, the Saffron Monastery, in the Tur Abdin, was the seat of Syrian Orthodox patriarchs of Antioch from 1293 to 1924.

And so the desert was at peace, and abundantly supplied with a population of believers who lived in it and fresh ones who were added to them. There grew up a commonwealth of illustrious and believing priests and a tranquil brotherhood with them and they were united in love and abounded in mutual affection.[14]

Eastwards to China

Meanwhile the Church of the East was engaged in one of the great missionary expansions of the history of the Church. Only a few memories remain of this once-glorious Church and its mission. Alone among the Churches of the east it lived and worshipped among and alongside people of many faiths. Their history shows how monasteries were able to form Christian communities in societies with different and mixed cultures. The leader of the Church of the East, the Catholicos, had his seat at Seleucia-Ctesiphon, near modern Baghdad, in the Persian Empire where Zoroastrianism was the majority religion. Among the monasteries of the East Syrian Church were Mor Abraham on Mount Izla; Mar Mari near Seleucia; Beth Abe where Isaac the Syrian lived and wrote; and the monastery of Rabban Hormuzd, to the north of Mosul, which was the seat of the Catholicos. From this starting-point, the monks and others travelled east, along the Silk Road trading routes, and established the church across Asia, in Afghanistan, Turkmenistan, India and China.

The city of Merv in modern Turkmenistan, north of Iran and Afghanistan, was one of these centres for both trade and scholarship. Its government changed several times. It was ruled by the Persian Achaemenids (500–330 BC), then the Greek Seleucids (320–60 BC), then the Persian Sassanians (250–650), then the Arabs Abbasids. There was a tradition that Alexander the Great reached it and it was called for a while Alexandria Margiana, then later Antiochia Margiana. The scholars of many faiths met in Merv. There were Zoroastrians, Buddhists, Manichaeans and Muslims, as well as Christians. The Christian presence in the city began with the monk Bar Shabba, who was bishop of Merv in 424. He arrived in the city after he had converted the wife of the Persian king Shapur II to Christianity. The king sent his wife to distant Merv to escape the influence of the monk. The plan back-fired because Bar Shabba followed her, established a church and, from here, founded many monasteries over a wide area of Central Asia in Parthia, Margiana, Bactria and Hyrcania. After his death, it is claimed that he was resurrected and continued his work for a further fifteen years. This tradition is a witness to the reputation of Bar Shabba and also the presence of a monastic church in the region of Turkmenistan as early as the fifth century. His Life was written in a Syriac manuscript, then translated into Sogdian, and preserved among the nine hundred Christian texts found at Turfan in north-east China.[15]

The Church continued on its eastward progress. The Catholicos Timothy I was consecrated around 780 and led the Church for over forty years until his death in 823. One historian described him as 'the most significant Christian spiritual leader of his day'.[16] He presided over a Church with nineteen metropolitans and eighty-five bishops. He established new metropolitan sees in Persia, Armenia, Turkestan, Tibet and Yemen.

He wrote in 780 that 'in these days the Holy Spirit has anointed a metropolitan for the Turks and we are preparing to consecrate another one for the Tibetans'.[17]

In the sixth century the Church of the East reached China. The Byzantine historian Procopius tells the story of monks who had already, in 550, lived for a long time in China, which he calls Serinda, and smuggled some silk worms into the Byzantine Empire which had important economic consequences in promoting the manufacture of the important commodity of silk.[18] A more formal mission arrived in 635 and was welcomed by the Emperor Taizong. A stela, which was erected in 781 at Sian Fu in western China in the grounds of a monastery, tells the story of Christianity in China over the previous 150 years. It tells how A-lo-pen brought the scriptures of the 'luminous religion' from Da Qin, or the Roman Empire. It proclaims the message of Christianity in language which could be grasped by the people of the region.

> The illustrious and virtuous Messiah, veiling his true dignity, appeared in the world as a man, ... he fixed the extent of the eight boundaries, thus completing the truth and freeing it from dross, he opened the gate of the three constant principles, introducing life and destroying death; he suspended the bright sun to invade the chambers of darkness, and the falsehoods of the devil were thereupon defeated; he set in motion the vessel of mercy by which to ascend to the bright mansions, whereupon rational beings were then released; having thus completed the manifestation of his power in clear day he ascended to his true station.[19]

The monks and missionaries interpreted the Christian faith in this cosmopolitan and multi-faith society. The Sian Fu stela records the name of Bishop Adam. Adam had become friends with an Indian Buddhist missionary, Prajna, who arrived in China in 782. Prajna did not know Chinese and so Bishop Adam worked with him for several years translating Buddhist texts.

The Catholicos Timothy I, meanwhile, engaged in dialogue with Muslims. He discussed faith with the caliph 'in a sweet and benevolent way'. He compared their conversations to being in a dark house at night when a precious pearl falls to the ground.

> Everyone tries to pick up the pearl, which will fall to the lot of one only. One will get hold of the pearl, another of a piece of glass, a third of a stone or a piece of earth, but everyone will be proud that he is the real possessor of the pearl. When light and day arise the one who possesses the pearl will rejoice and be happy, while those who had in hand pieces of glass and bits of stone will weep and be sad.[20]

So now all claim to have the pearl but the true pearl will not be made known in this life. It is an image of generosity and openness. It conveys the spirit of engagement and dialogue with which the monks of the Church of the East met with the variety of faiths which they encountered.

There was also close contact and mutual respect between Christians and Muslims. The prophet Muhammad had grown up in a society influenced by the Church of the East. A Muslim tradition describes a visit by the prophet as a young man to Bostra in Syria where he met a monk of the Church of the East, Bahira, who recognized the greatness of Muhammad. John of Damascus was among those who thought that Islam was a Christian heresy. In a passage which shows the shared roots of the two faiths, he wrote that 'a false prophet Muhammad has appeared in their midst. This man, after having chanced upon the Old and New Testaments and having conversed with an Arian monk devised his own heresy'.[21] Timothy I was more generous in his assessment. 'He thought that the prophet separated his people from idolatry and polytheism and attached them to the cult and knowledge of one God'.[22] Muhammad had good relations with the Christian king of Ethiopia. When his followers were forced out of Mecca in 615, the prophet arranged for eighty-two, or possibly eighty-three, of them to find refuge with the Christian king of Ethiopia 'for' he said 'the king will not tolerate injustice and it is a friendly country'. They reported that 'the Negus (king) gave us a kind reception and we safely practised our religion and worshipped God and suffered no wrong'. They debated faith with the king who declared that 'this and what Jesus brought have come from the same niche'. Later the prophet instructed his armies to 'leave the Abyssinians alone so long as they do not take the offensive'.[23]

The shared tradition is further shown in the practices of Sufi and Christian monasticism. Sufi mysticism developed within the same culture and society as Christian monasticism. Many of the ascetic disciplines of Christian monasticism are also found in Sufism. The name Sufi is derived from the Arabic word for wool and refers to the material used for the robe worn by Sufi teachers. The monks of the Church of the East, among them the bishops, also chose to wear simple woollen robes, rather than linen or silk. The fasting season of Ramadan has similar origins to the Christian fasts and both traditions practise the use of prostrations in prayer. In Sufi prayer, the *dhikr* or remembrance requires the recitation of the *shahada* or proclamation of the names of God. The prayer, '*la ilaha illa'llah*', 'there is no god but Allah' is repeated thousands of times a day and is combined with physical and breathing practices. This prayer developed especially from 1200, at about the same time as the Jesus Prayer was becoming recognized.[24] The travel writer William Dalrymple was struck by the shared traditions of Christianity and Islam when he visited Mor Gabriel monastery in the Tur Abdin. 'The Muslims appear to have derived their techniques of worship from existing Christian practice. Islam and the Eastern Christians have retained the original early Christian convention; it is the Western Christians who have broken with sacred tradition.'[25]

The Christian Church of Asia continued to flourish until the thirteenth century. As its end approached, two monks Markos and Barsauma set out on a long journey. They were probably Onggud Turks, born in China. They travelled west in 1275, visiting Christian sites as they went until they arrived in Mesopotamia.

> They arrived in Baghdad, and then went to the great church of Koke (at Seleucia-Ctesiphon) and they went to the monastery of Mar Mari the apostle and received a blessing from the sepulchres of that country ... They went to Arbela and then to Mosul, and to Sinjar, and Nisibis, and Mardin; and were blessed by the bones of Mar Awgen, the Second Christ. They were blessed by all the shrines and monasteries, and religious houses, and monks and fathers in their dioceses.[26]

From here they decided to continue to the Holy Land. In 1281 their ways parted. Markos was elected patriarch and was worried that, since he came from China, his Syriac was not good enough for this task. But his electors felt that it was more important that he communicate with their Mongol rulers than the Syriac Christians. Taking the name Yaballaha III he ruled over the thirty provinces of the church with their 250 bishoprics. He lived at Maragha near Tabriz, where he built a large monastery. Meanwhile Barsauma continued his travels and was sent by the Mongol ruler in the Middle East on a diplomatic mission to Europe in 1287, where among other places this Chinese monk from the Church of the East visited England, where he administered communion to the king.

Barsauma went to Europe as an envoy of the Mongol ruler of the Ilkhanate of the Middle East who wanted help from European kings in his struggle against Muslims. At that time Christians were influential in the Mongol court. Several tribes of Central Asia had become Christian, among them the Keraits, Ongguds and Uyghers. Genghis Khan had been protected by a Christian Kerait chief, Toghrul. He and his sons all married Christians, and his grandson Hulegu is said to have affirmed the Christian faith. Hulegu's brother was Kublai Khan, who was 'the just and wise king, lover of the Christians' according to the chronicler Gregory Bar-Hebraeus.[27] Hulegu's ruthless destruction of the cities he conquered was directed against Islam. He conquered Baghdad in 1268 and killed 800,000 inhabitants. Mosques were targeted. One of the caliph's palaces was given to the Catholicos as a new residence and a church was built in it. At this time hopes were high among Christians that Christianity would displace Islam as the faith of the Middle East and Asia. But this promise was not fulfilled. Hulegu's successor favoured Islam, and the influence – and numbers – of Christians in Asia steadily declined.

There are some traces which have survived as memorials of this golden age of Eastern monasticism. There are remains of a seventh-century monastery pagoda in Shaanxi province of China. Expeditions to Turfan, in north-west China, discovered over nine hundred manuscripts of Christian texts in a variety of languages, including Syriac, Soghdian and Uyghur. There are liturgical and biblical texts, and chronicles of church life, including a life of Bishop Bar Shabba of Merv. There were also ascetical writings, including the sayings of the Egyptian desert fathers, Macarius and Evagrius. These finds not only show the connections with Syrian church centres, but also the shared monastic heritage and culture.

The monasteries of Ethiopia

The Syrian tradition of faith evangelized Africa as well as Asia. Monks entered Ethiopia in the early sixth century and founded the monasteries from which the Christian faith evangelized the mountainous kingdom of Ethiopia.

The first monks are remembered as the Nine Syrian Saints, and their arrival is known as the Second Christianization. The First Christianization had taken place earlier, probably in 342. Two Syrian boys had been shipwrecked while travelling with their teacher to India and, while the crew of the ship were killed by the local inhabitants, the boys were spared and taken to Axum, a prosperous trading city state on the southern shores of the Red Sea. Here they obtained favour from the king and were entrusted with responsible positions in the court as they grew up. Frumentius, one of the brothers, then went to Alexandria and met the bishop Athanasius. He reported that there were Christians in Ethiopia without guidance or care, and needed a bishop to guide them. Athanasius consecrated Frumentius as bishop and he returned to Axum.[28] This had lasting consequences. The Egyptian Coptic Church retained the right to appoint the archbishops for Ethiopia. They exercised this by appointing just one bishop for the country, who was Egyptian, who often had little knowledge of the language or society and who lived with the king in his court. A forged Canon 42 was inserted into manuscripts of the Council of Nicaea around 700, which gave a spurious authority to this practice which continued until 1850 when the number of bishops was increased to four. Eventually, in 1959, an Ethiopian became patriarch. Thus the Church of Ethiopia was an episcopal church but with only one bishop, who lived in the court, and whose main purpose was to ordain clergy. As a result, the Church of Ethiopia became a Monophysite Church, dependent on Alexandria, rejecting the decisions of the Council of Chalcedon. After this first Christianization, the king became Christian and a large church was built in Axum. It was a royal, urban, state church. In other parts of Christendom, the early communities had been drawn from local people usually from poor backgrounds in cities and the kings became Christian later. This can be described as a bottom-up process of evangelization. In Ethiopia the reverse process took place. The royal house became Christian first, so it can be described a top-down process of evangelization.

The Second Christianization was carried out by monks and these brought the Christian faith into the countryside. These monks arrived in Ethiopia in the early fifth century. Tradition records the names of the 'Nine Syrian Saints', who brought monastic life. However not all came from Syria. They are also described in their lives as Romans, which means that they came from around the Mediterranean area, and their places of origin are given as Rome, Constantinople, Cilicia, Caesarea and Egypt. Various reasons for their arrival have been suggested. They might have been refugees from Syria and other Monophysite areas fleeing persecution by supporters of the Council of Chalcedon, which had taken place fifty years earlier; or they might have been part of an evangelization task force sent by the patriarch of Alexandria to strengthen the Church – and so the Byzantine Empire – on its insecure southern frontier. Both are possible reasons for this arrival. But the variety of places of origin of the Nine Saints, and the ease of travel by sea or land suggests that Ethiopia was easily within reach of monks seeking new places to settle.[29] An indication of the ease of access of Ethiopia is shown by the inclusion in the *Philokalia* of two texts by St John of Karpathos, an island in the Aegean Sea, addressed to the monks of India, which probably refers to Ethiopia.[30] The closeness of Ethiopia to Arabia and Syria beyond enabled the writings and teachings of both East and West Syrian writers to enter the church's tradition, giving it a strongly Syrian theological tradition, of which the insistence that these nine pioneers of monastic life were Syrian is an example.

As a result of these arrivals, the region along the borders of what is now Eritrea and Ethiopia was settled by the monks. The monks' desire for silence and prayer led them

124   *The T&T Clark History of Monasticism*

to found monasteries in inaccessible places usually on the tops of mountains. One of the Nine Saints was Za-Mikael, meaning 'for Michael', who was also known as Abuna Aregawi or 'our father the old man'. He had been a monk at one of the monasteries of Pachomius before he came to Ethiopia. He arrived at flat-topped mountain of Debre Damo with its precipitous rock cliffs. He was enabled to ascend this on the tail of a huge serpent which carried him to the top. Here he settled and offered advice and counsel to kings including King Kaleb in the sixth century. Since his life was written in the sixteenth century, some commentators have been sceptical about these details and indeed have questioned whether the saint even existed. But whatever the method of foundation of the monastery, access is still only possible by being pulled up by a rope up the sheer sides of the cliff and an ancient church dating back to the eighth century or earlier is still located at the top of the mountain. All are indications of the presence of monasteries at an early date.[31]

The further extension of monastic life is associated with the career of one of the great saints of Ethiopia, Tekla Haymonot, which means the 'Plant of Faith'. There are several versions of his life, which make it hard to reconstruct the events, but the sources agree on the main shape of his ministry. He was born in the Shewa region of central Ethiopia to a father who was a priest and a mother who was of noble birth. His parents were probably Christian migrants from the north. Their son was ordained priest and then travelled to various monastic sites, including the hill-top monastery of Debre

Figure 9 Monasteries in Ethiopia were often in inaccessible places. At Debre Damo access is only possible when pulled up a sheer rock face by a rope.

Figure 10 Abuna Aregawi, also known as Za-Mikael, was the founder of Debre Damo monastery. He ascended the rock face with the help of a long serpent.

Damo, where he spent time as a disciple of the monk Yohanni. Here he fell off the top of the cliff and, as he was falling to the ground, six wings were given to him to enable him to escape certain death. A group of disciples gathered around him and were sent out to found various monasteries. In about 1284 he settled in a cave at a place called Debre Asbo, which was later re-named Debre Libanos. Monks and nuns lived together in the cave, which was divided into two parts, with a place for worship and a place for living. The saint himself prayed for seven years standing on one leg until it dropped off and then he prayed for a further seven years standing on the other. He placed sharpened pieces of wood around him to prevent himself falling asleep. Here he stayed for twenty-nine years until he died in 1313. His icon is a familiar sight in Ethiopian churches, with his six wings, and one of his legs detached from the rest of his body.[32]

The life of Tekla Haymonot coincided with a period of territorial expansion. King Amda Seyon (1314–44) carried out a series of military campaigns which extended his Christian kingdom to new areas. The Egyptian archbishop at the time was Abuna Ya'eqob, who shared in this desire to evangelize the new areas being conquered and he enlisted the help of Tekla Haymonot and his monks. The life of the saint tells how he chose twelve followers and sent them out – Yohannes, Qawestos, Tadewos and Matyas went south-east; Anorewos the Younger and Marqorewos went north-east, Iyosyas went south; Gebre Krestos, Yosef and Anorewos the Elder and Adhani went west, while Filpos stayed at Debre Asbo. These settled at various places in the newly conquered territories and while the armies moved on the monks stayed. Their monasteries became centres of faith, and also of education, commerce and civilization. It has been commented that while the armies built the state, the monks created the nation.

Even when there were periods of opposition between the king and the monks, monks still continued to colonize new areas and bring Christianity to a fresh audience. A leading monk Basalota Mikael, or 'by the prayer of Michael', attacked the polygamous marriages of the kings. King Amda Seyon (1314–44) and his successor Sayfa Arad (1344–72) reacted to this criticism by beating the monks and driving them into exile. The unintended outcome was that the monks left the kingdom and settled beyond the borders, with the result that new outposts of Christianity were established in pagan areas. This prepared the way for the royal armies and so led to a further extension of the kingdom. In this extension of the kingdom, the monks came to Lake Zway, a notoriously hostile area. 'Those who lived there were Muslims and they did not know Christ. They were murderers and the king sent his enemies to them so that they might take his revenge on them.'[33] Here Tekla Haymonot's two monks arrived, persevered and founded a monastery on an island in the lake which remains a centre of faith and learning to the present day.

The life of Tekla Haymonot contains many dramatic stories. On one occasion he arrived at a place called Katata. Here there was a tree where a devil lived and which was worshipped by the local people. The saint expelled the devil, which complained bitterly that he had already been expelled from Israel by the power of Christ and now had to be on the move again. The tree was uprooted by the saint's power and flew through the air, with its trailing roots killing twenty-one people. Tekla Haymonot brought these back to life through his prayer, but at the same time his powerful prayer also summoned back to life a further 4,004 people who happened to have been buried in the area. These others described how they were enduring the pains of hell. Tekla Haymonot baptized them and then returned them to their place of rest. Meanwhile the governor of the region was infuriated at the loss of revenue from the worshippers of the tree and arrived as the tree was being cut up to become building material for the new church. At this point a large splinter broke off during the tree cutting and embedded itself in his eye. The holy man healed him and he joined in the church construction. Then Tekla Haymonot summoned monks to come to settle in the place and after three years he moved on to the next stage of his missionary journey.[34]

Stories like this are lively and make absorbing reading. But they are more than pious legends. They point to the historical process of the expansion of the monasteries and their place in the history of the region. Visits to Ethiopian churches show that they are often built in sites with significant natural features – on hill-tops, by streams of water, in caves or by groves of trees. These locations were already used as holy places in traditional pre-Christian religion and people came to worship the spirits who inhabited them. The encounter of Tekla Haymonot with the devil in the tree shows how he moved to this spiritual place, encountered the spiritual power within it and demonstrated that the power of Christ is stronger. The monks brought with them a spiritual force which established a new centre of faith. Their journeys of evangelization transformed the landscape from being the dwelling of the spirits of traditional natural religion to a Christian country of monasteries.

The monks who founded new monasteries retained their relationship with the place from which they came. Large monastic 'houses' took shape. The 'house' was the group of monasteries which shared a descent from the same founder and allegiance to a tradition of faith. The 'house' of Tekla Haymonot had colonized the southern parts of Ethiopia. In the north however, the 'house' of Ewostatewos was dominant. Ewostatewos (1273–1352) came from the north of the country, which was influenced by Semitic traditions from Palestine and Syria. It retained many practices which had been received from Judaism, such as circumcision, the dietary rules of the Old Testament and the observance of Saturday as well as Sunday as a holy day. The influence of the 'house' of Ewostatewos was especially strong in the north and opposed the Alexandrian faith of the archbishop and the court, which did not accept Sabbath observance. Eventually the northern traditions were accepted by a council at Debra Mitmaq (1450), and the Church has retained its Judaic practice. The course of this controversy which divided the Church for much of the medieval period illustrates the monastic character of the Church, with the two traditions upholding and teaching alternative Syrian and Alexandrian traditions.

There are many monasteries in Ethiopia, especially in the north where the Syrian Saints first arrived. A famous monastic settlement is at Waldebba, near the border with Sudan. It covers a large area which requires over a day's walk to cross, has four main churches and over a thousand monks. Its foundation can be dated to the period of Tekla Hymanot. Altogether there are over eight hundred monasteries in the country.[35] The Church of Ethiopia remains a large and growing church, with some projections suggesting that it will soon be the largest national Orthodox Church in the world.[36]

Conclusion

The series of Ecumenical Councils which decided on the Christological doctrine of the Church and the growing power of both Persians and Arabs led to the breakdown of relationships between the Byzantine and Syrian Churches. The Syrians were ejected from the cities of their homeland. Western Syrians withdrew into rural areas and Eastern Syrians travelled east into Asia. For both, monasteries preserved the tradition of the Church. Their life was built around a rhythm of worship and they were centres of scholarship and teaching. They did not need large buildings nor a complex administration but the ascetic life of the monks pushed them into a life of movement and wandering. A monastic church worships, teaches and is close to the people. As the Church extended across Asia into China, Christians learned to live as one faith among many, working alongside people of other faiths and building relationships within the society of the area. The monasteries of the Syrian Churches set up centres of faith across the continent. Its decline and, in some places, disappearance has diminished the church through the loss of this generous and tolerant branch of Christianity. Meanwhile the Ethiopian Church remained apart from these conflicts. Relationships with Islam were generally good and in Ethiopia a Christian emperor remained in power until 1974, apart from a short period of Muslim control in the sixteenth century. Here monasticism flourished and, as in other parts of the Syrian tradition, popular faith looked to monasteries for guidance and healing.

Notes

1. For the history of the Church in the East, see Hilarion Alfeyev, *The Spiritual World of Isaac the Syrian* (Kalamazoo, MI, 2000), pp. 18–25.
2. The full title of the church is the Apostolic Catholic Assyrian Church of the East. Its current membership is around 300,000 of which many live in the diaspora, in the United States and Europe.
3. Susan Ashbrook Harvey, *Asceticism and Society in Crisis* (Berkeley, CA, 1990), p. 14.
4. The earlier date of 407 is also suggested. See Cornelia Horn, *Asceticism and Christological Controversy in Fifth-Century Palestine* (Oxford, 2006), p. 53.
5. The life of Peter the Iberian was written by the Monophysite historian, John Rufus. It is translated by Cornelia Horn and Robert Phenix, *John Rufus, the Lives of Peter the Iberian Theodosius of Jerusalem and the Monk Romanus* (Leiden, 2008).
6. Horn and Phenix, *Life of Peter the Iberian*, pp. 126–7.
7. John describes his life at various places in the Lives of the Eastern Saints. These are conveniently summarized in Harvey, *Asceticism and Society in Crisis*, pp. 28–30.
8. The accounts of these events are in contemporary chronicles, Pseudo-Zachariah Rhetor, *Ecclesiastical History* 8.5; Michael the Syrian, *Chronicle* 9.15; John of Ephesus, *Lives of the Eastern Saints* 35 in PO 13.620.
9. *Lives of the Eastern Saints* 27, PO 8.541–554.
10. Ibid., 12, PO 17.171–186.
11. John of Ephesus, *Life of James bar-Addai*, PO 18, p. 696.
12. Ibid., PO 18, pp. 696–7; PO 19, pp. 156–8.
13. For the history of the monasteries and description of the area, see Hans Hollerweger, *Turabdin* (Linz, 1999). This contains articles by Sebastian Brock, 'Tur Abdin – A Homeland of Ancient Syro-Aramaean Culture', pp. 22–3, and Andrew Palmer, 'The 1600-Year History of the Monastery of Kartmin (Mor Gabriel)', pp. 37–46.
14. Pseudo-Zachariah Rhetor, *Ecclesiastical History* 8.5. *Syriac Chronicle* trans. F. J. Hamilton and E. W. Brooks, pp. 211–12.
15. The life of Bar Shabba is unpublished and is among the texts are the subject of a research project on the Christian Library at Turfan, directed by Dr Erica Hunter of the School of Oriental and African Studies at London University.
16. Philip Jenkins, *The Lost History of Christianity* (London, 2008), p. 6.
17. Ibid., pp. 11, 45–6.
18. Procopius, *History of the Wars*, 8.17.1–7, cited in Jenkins, *Lost History*, p. 64.
19. Ibid., p. 15.
20. Alphonse Mingana (ed.), *Timothy's Apology for Christianity*, vol. 2 (Cambridge, 1928), p. 41, cited in Ibid., p. 17.
21. John of Damascus, 'Writings', in *The Fathers of the Church*, vol. 37 (Washington, 1958), pp. 153–60.
22. Mingana, *Timothy's Apology*, p. 41. Conveniently cited in Jenkins, *Lost History*, p. 185.
23. These traditions from the Muslim chronicler ibn Hisham are described in John Binns, *The Orthodox Church of Ethiopia, a History* (London, 2017), pp. 125–6.
24. Margaret Smith, *Studies in Early Mysticism in the Near and Middle East* (Oxford, 1995), Alphonse Mingana, *The Early Spread of Christianity in India* (Manchester, 1926), p. 35.
25. William Dalrymple, *From the Holy Mountain* (London, 1998), p. 105.
26. E. A. Wallis Budge, *Monks of Kublai Khan*, cited in Jenkins, *Lost History*, p. 94.
27. Jenkins, *Lost History*, p. 121.

28 These events are described in Rufinus, *Ecclesiastical History* in PL 21, 478–80. He says he heard the story from one of the brothers, Aedesius.
29 For discussion of the reasons for their arrival see Taddesse Tamrat, *Church and State in Ethiopia* (Oxford, 1973), pp. 29–30, and Binns, *The Orthodox Church of Ethiopia*, pp. 102–5.
30 These are in trans. Geoffrey Palmer, Philip Sherrard, and Kallistos Ware, *Philokalia, the Complete Text* (London, 1979), pp. 298–326.
31 For further discussion of the reliability of these lives, and of the nature of oral tradition see Binns, *The Orthodox Church of Ethiopia*, pp. 105–9.
32 The Life of Tekla Haymonot is translated by E. A. Wallis Budge, *The Life of Tekla Haymonot* (London, 1906).
33 Carlo Conti Rossini, *Acta Sancti Basalota Mikael*, CSCO 20 (Louvain, 1905), p. 30.
34 Wallis Budge, *The Life of Tekla Haymonot*, 36–45, pp. 75–95; Binns, *Orthodox Church of Ethiopia*, pp. 112–13.
35 There is a full survey of the contemporary state of the monasteries of Ethiopia in Christine Chaillot, *The Ethiopian Orthodox Tawehedo Church Tradition* (Paris, 2002), pp. 152–90.
36. For these projections, compiled by Patrick Johnstone, see Binns, *Orthodox Church of Ethiopia*, p. 232.

9

City and Mountains: The Byzantine Tradition

After iconoclasm

That urge to discover even more inhospitable and remote places; that longing to leave the familiar and to set out on an endless journey of wandering exile; that martyr's instinct to renounce all that is familiar – all these urges had carried the tradition of monastic living east into Asia, west into Gaul and south into Africa. But Constantinople remained the centre of monastic life. It continued to be a city of monks. There were large coenobitic monasteries with hundreds of monks with powerful influence in society and also small communities of one or two monks or nuns peacefully living on a family estate. It was here that the size and scale of monasticism led to the formulation of what monasteries should be like and how they should be governed.

Monks had left the city during the iconoclast period – at least many had, although some had stayed. At the Triumph of Orthodoxy in 843 the exiles returned vindicated and victorious. Monks were appointed to positions of influence over both church and state, many new monasteries were founded and Byzantine prestige reached new heights. The growth in number and size of monasteries led to the reflection on what a monastery was and how monasteries related to wider society. Out of this period of consolidation, an answer to the question of the identity of a monastery slowly emerged.

The importance of the monasteries in the city is shown by demographic studies. Without accurate census figures, our knowledge of the size of the city is inevitably approximate. Estimates of the population size can however be attempted, based on the level of building activity, the size of the grain fleets which brought food to the city and the volume of government business. These suggest that there were 200,000 people living in the city at the time of the Council of Chalcedon and within this number there were between 10,000 and 15,000 monks. Numbers grew in the following century until the population level reached 500,000 at the time of the Emperor Justinian (527–65). Then bubonic plague swept through the empire and led to a sharp decline with the number of inhabitants falling to fifty thousand and the number of monasteries to fifty. Fluctuation continued in the centuries which followed with disease reducing and immigration increasing the number of inhabitants. Historians calculate that in the year 1000 the total population of the empire was 20 million. Within this number there were probably 150,000 monks living in seven thousand monasteries. Thus around 2 per cent of the adult population were monks, nuns and their dependents. This proliferation of monasteries is shown in legal documents of the period. The Emperor Nikiphoros Phokas (963–9) was concerned that there were 'thousands' of monasteries suffering from a shortage of labour and a successor. Basil II (976–1025), in his attempts to regulate the monasteries, said that there was a monastery in 'many villages'.[1] About a third of the cultivable land in the empire was owned by monasteries. As the city declined towards its fall to the Ottomans in 1453 the number of monasteries also decreased, but they remained a significant part of Byzantine society. When they entered the city, the Ottoman conquerors found eighteen monasteries still functioning with over five hundred monks living in them.[2] In this period after iconoclasm the growth in the number and type of monastery required them to find their place in urban as well as rural society and, more fundamentally, to come to a shared understanding of what a monastery is and how it should be managed.

Monasteries are part of society and belong within in it. Relationships with the wider world are always present and so the life of the society around affects what the monasteries became. When monks said they were abandoning the world, this did not mean that they were leaving human relationships behind, but were reshaping them in a new way and in a spiritual context. Changes in Byzantine society were reflected in the monasteries which formed a part of it. While monks wanted to leave the world behind, they built another social structure in the place to which they moved and it was not so very different from the one which they had left behind. In Byzantium, the suspicion that their way of life was subversive and undermined the structures of society diminished and now they were seen as the guardians and upholders of social values. 'Monasteries – the non-conformists par excellence in the fourth through the sixth centuries – were not only domesticated and put under the surveillance of the episcopate, but now became the primary guardians and culture.'[3]

The funding of urban building projects was deeply rooted in Greek and Roman classical culture and was valued as a sign of 'greatness of soul'. When the historian Procopius set out to praise the Emperor Justinian, he did so by writing a book which described the various buildings which the emperor had set up across the empire.[4] Both the city of Constantinople and the holy city of Jerusalem were the recipients of a vast amount of money and resources which were poured into new construction projects. The chronicler Zonaras, writing in the twelfth century, said that emperors overspent on 'their own pleasure and the construction of religious houses'.[5] This virtue was not limited to the imperial family. Those of other classes could also build.

It was easy to found a monastery, and many people did so. 'Certain people give the name of monastery to their own establishments and possessions and announce that they have been dedicated to God and inscribe themselves as masters of the things that have been consecrated'.[6] 'They say' states a novel of Basil II issued in 996, 'that it happens in many of the villages that the peasant builds a church on his land and with the permission of his fellow villagers, grants it all his property, then becomes a monk and spends the rest of his life there'.[7] The monastery of Stoudios, which grew to become the leading monastery of Constantinople, began when a family decided to venture into monastic living. The later monastery of the Theotokos Evergetis was also the private initiative of a pious nobleman called Paul.

There were numerous small communities. These consisted of a few monks or nuns, sometimes with both sexes living together in a single house. Most of these small monasteries have left no record of their existence, but some have entered into the pages of letters or chronicles. Sometimes a group of monks lived together around a shrine or altar dedicated to a local saint or martyr. In one of his letters, Gregory of Nazianzus tells us about a shrine 'at the Wooden Circus' with a few monks presided over by an archimandrite whose former profession was that of bear keeper.[8] There was a wide variety of styles of life, forms of monastery, sizes of community, doctrinal conviction and social engagement.

Monks became a familiar part of life in the capital. The city was growing in this period and, with it, the monastic population also expanded. Houses spilled over the old walls of Constantine, and a new wall was built by of Theodosius II (402–50) to include a larger area. In the space between the walls, called Regio XIV, the population was less dense and here monks settled. It became the monastic quarter, being at a sufficient distance from the city centre to allow some seclusion but near enough to remain engaged with urban life.

Monasteries were founded in all parts of the empire. A small monastery on an island in the Aegean Sea is described in a document in the archives of the Great Laura on Mount Athos. This was set up on the island of Syros in 1012. A certain official of the rank of *kouboukleisos* called John declared that his home on the island of Skyros should become a monastery with a church dedicated to Christ the Saviour. The bishop of Skyros tried to gain control but was unsuccessful and this small monastery on John's private estate retained its independence. It probably had a membership of about twenty monks. There was no episcopal authorization needed to found a monastery such as this, and no ceremony of dedication required either.[9] Like others, this monastery jealously guarded its independence.

In the eleventh century, when the monastery on Syros and many others were established, monasteries had escaped the jurisdiction of the Church as their founders took the initiative and made their own foundations. Earlier, in the fifth century, the Council of Chalcedon had met and discussed the regulation of the then new and growing institution of monasticism. There were twenty-seven canons of Chalcedon of which nine concerned monks. These canons provided a structure for the conduct of monastic life. They laid down that monasteries were to be under the jurisdiction of the bishops. Bishops were made responsible both for the foundation of monasteries and for the provision of revenue for them. Monks were required to live in monasteries and not wander around the town. Slaves were not to be admitted to monasteries and if they were then they should be removed and returned to their owners. This placed monasteries firmly within the Church. It removed their independence but ensured that they would be able to shape and influence the identity and spirituality of the Church. In the long term, it provided guidelines for the development of Eastern monasticism. In the short term, it was unable to bring order to the widespread and spontaneous popular monastic movement.

As the number of monasteries continued to grow so they became diverse and divergent. It was probably never possible to claim that monasteries should be under the jurisdiction and authority of the bishop. The tenth-century emperor Romanos

Lekapenos (920–44) wrote that there are six types of monastery. These are imperial, patriarchal, archiepiscopal, metropolitan and episcopal as well as *autodespoton* or self-governing. It is significant that this list comes in the somewhat disconnected context of a document describing the requisitioning of horses, which shows that the nature of the authority over the monastery had implications for the emperor's ability to collect taxes.[10]

The founder or benefactor decided how the monastery should be managed. He carried out this responsibility by carefully drafting a foundation charter or typikon to ensure that he retained some control over the nature and management of the community. The typikon was called by a variety of titles. It might be a *hypotyposis*, or an *apotyposis*, or a *theke* or a *thesmos*. The typikon prescribed what the monastery should be like and how it should be managed. There are around fifty examples of monastic typika surviving from the period of the ninth to the fifteenth centuries. The provisions would usually include regulation of the method of electing the abbot or *hegumenos*, the setting up of boundaries and the way that the enclosure would be preserved and the receiving of new monks into the noviciate. These defined how the monastery related to the world outside and how it would maintain its life. In addition, the typikon laid down rules for diet and fasting, clothing, discipline and the conduct of services.

The foundation typikon set the monastery in place. Among its provisions was the method for appointing a superior, or *hegumenos*. He should be a person of insight and wisdom, who could act as spiritual father to the monks. But there was a need for a different kind of leadership. The monastic founders were faced with the question of how to administer their lands and property. The founder provided lands and others might later give donations and gifts. But someone had to manage these monastic lands, to ensure that they were productive and profitable and, sometimes, to go to court for the resolution of a dispute. There was a need for good management of the internal life of the monastery. This led to a distinction made between the owner who was usually the founder, or *despotes,* and the possessor or administrator of the lands, the *kyrios*.

Often the *kyrios* would appoint a protector or lay official to manage the estates on behalf of the monks and ensure that their interests were upheld in law suits and the payment of taxes – tasks which lay outside the scope of a monastic vocation. This was especially important when the monastery owned large estates which were often at a distance from its main buildings. Legal documents of the period speak of officials who looked after the affairs of monasteries and use various titles. The steward might be called *ephoros, epitropos, antilambanomenos, pronoetes* or, as was often the case, *charistikarios*. The different titles show that there were a variety of ways of managing property. These officials ensured the administration of lands and good governance in the monastery.

The control of estates could lead to abuses. The patriarch John V Oxites of Antioch (1090–8) described – and attacked – the office known as *charistikarios*, a lay holder of power. This position was set up with the intention of benefitting the monastery. 'The emperors and patriarchs transferred monasteries and poor houses which had been destroyed or were falling into ruins into the hands of important men, not in the way of a gift, nor a worldly benefit, but in order that they should be restored and made of spiritual use.' John says that all monasteries were in the hands of *charistikarioi* 'with the exception of a very small number of them and a few more recently founded houses'.[11] Abuses are reported. The typikon of Mamas monastery says that the house has suffered 'through the insatiety and shamelessness of the *charistikarioi* who held it from time to time and who like wolves grasped ravenously upon it'.[12] The system also concerned both emperors and patriarchs because prosperous monastic holdings would be removed from the control of church and state, and used to benefit others. There were unsuccessful attempts to diminish the power of the *charistikarioi*.

As well as the need for good administration of the lands of the monastery, there was also the need to manage the personal property of the monks. There was inconsistency in practice and debate about ownership of private property. Some monks wanted to retain their property. This question is discussed in a series of questions and answers about monastic life in the Life of Lazarus of Mount Galesion. He had founded a 'traditional private religious foundation ... at the time when coenobitic institutions of this sort were undergoing severe stress'.[13] The typikon has been lost but the Life of Lazarus, the saint, written after his death in 1053, shows the process of the typikon being developed, with the record of questions about the life and work of the monastery and the responses of the founder. Among them was the problem of private property. Some monks declined to give their property to the poor or to the monastery and instead kept it for themselves. These richer monks used their money to have an easier life and gain more power in the monastery. Lazarus exhorted and even bargained with these monks to give up their wealth. In his later foundation of Pausolype, which was self-governing, monks who brought money with them did not surrender it to the community. Monks who practised various crafts sometimes retained some of the profits of their sales. Others did not take their meals with other monks but preferred to make their own eating arrangements.

A further question which faced the founder was whether the monastery should include both men and women. The principle of the exclusion of women from the men's monastery was hard to maintain. Many monasteries were private foundations, with men and women living in the monastery. These double monasteries were sometimes founded to allow all members of the family to become monks. A married couple with children might agree to become monks and so might live within the same community. The second Council of Nicaea (787) legislated against double monasteries and when legislation is needed this suggests that double monasteries were being founded and causing concern.

Debates about private property and the separation of women and men are often considered to be as a sign of collapse and decay in monastic discipline. But this could be seen not so much as decadence but as healthy debate about the form of monastic life. With the expansion of the number of monastic houses and the lack of direction, we could conclude from the tribulations of Lazarus that there was a debate among monks as to the style of life they should be leading. As well as the monks wanting to keep their property, Lazarus's questions include many requests from monks who want to pursue solitary vocations. While there might have been a relaxation away from the rigidity of coenobitic standards, this could represent a process of healthy exploration of the nature of monastic living rather than a decay in morals and discipline. The period after the Triumph of Orthodoxy was a time of growing popularity of the monastic vocation, a huge increase in the number and type of monastic houses and the evolution in the nature of a monastery.[14]

The Evergetinos and reform

One monastery among the many which were built in the area at the edge of the city started from modest beginnings and then went on to extend its influence on later foundations both within the city, in the country around, and as far as Mount Athos, the Balkans and Russia. Such was its influence that the period of change which it initiated has been described as the Byzantine Monastic Reform Movement.[15]

Reform is a constant theme of monastic history. Founders and superiors of monasteries seek to recall their monastic communities to a former purity which has been obscured and perverted in a compromised and secularized society. Since the basis of monastic living is the maximalist response to a call to live a life in conformity with the gospel and since this will inevitably be always incomplete and partial, then reform will be a constant feature of monasticism. So we find several periods described as Reform Movements.

The reform movement which scholars identify as taking place in the eleventh and twelfth centuries is associated with the monastery of the Theotokos Evergetis, which can be translated as the Beneficent Theotokos or, more simply, the Mother of God who does Good. Its way of life is well-known through a large collection of documents from the monastery which have been preserved. They include the *Hypotyposis*, or Foundation Document, which describes the life of the monastery; the *Synaxarion*, the most comprehensive set of liturgical regulations from that period; the *Katachetikon*, a series of 308 talks and instructions by Paul, an early *hegumenos*; and the *Synagoge*, a four-volume set of extracts from previous monastic literature giving advice and guidance on many problems and concerns which monks encountered. Of these, the *hypotyposis*, a rule which is contained in less than seventy pages of a modern translation, shows the principles and aims of this eleventh-century monastic reform movement.[16]

Among this voluminous set of writings there is one document missing. There would have been a *brebion*, or list of the properties and possessions of the monastery. This absence has the result that we know little about the actual monastery building, its location, its lands and its endowments. References in the typikon show that it was less than two miles outside the land walls constructed by the emperor Theodosius, and that there was a *metochion*, or dependent house, within the city. We can conclude that the Evergetis monastery was within a short journey of the capital city with connections with urban society yet it guarded its distance and isolation.

The hypotyposis tells us that the monastery came out of the dedication of a man called Paul who, in the year 1049, 'pierced by a burning love for virtue and the contemplative life immediately left this imperial capital, his own birthplace, also his parents and the rest of his relations, his friends and his associates and his wealth, and all the other things in this world that enslave a soul that loves the world'.[17] He went to one of the family estates about two miles out of the city and stayed there until his death five years later. His successor as *hegoumenos*, Timothy, developed this informal community into a monastery. He built a church and improved the living areas, and he bought icons, vestments and books. He acquired further estates to establish the monastery on a firmer financial footing. He also drafted the foundation charter, the *hypotyposis*.

The hypotyposis begins by describing the foundation of the monastery. Immediately after this, the worship in the church is described. The monks are woken before dawn and go to the church for the Orthros, and the First Hour, after which they return to their cells for further psalmody. The divine liturgy is celebrated each day with the 'pure' among the monks receiving communion three times a week, and others once a week or less, as the *hegumenos* directs. Then later in the day is the worship of the Ninth Hour, Hesperinon (evening worship) and the day finishes with a further period of worship in the church with the short office of the Apodeipnon. A large part of the day is spent either in the church or at private prayer in the cell. Each act of worship includes both regular elements of worship, or the ordinary, and the hymns, litanies of prayers of the saint to which the day is dedicated or other seasonal material. The combination of these various elements is described in much greater detail in the Synaxarion.[18]

The hypotyposis goes on to remind the monks of the importance of regular confession, which is made privately to the hegumenos. There are two periods set aside for this each day. This practice has been at the centre of monastic living from the earliest days, and has a therapeutic rather than forensic purpose. It is through the revealing of thoughts that the superior guides the monk.[19]

Then follow the regulations concerning food, since a monk has a body as well as a soul and so this needs to be properly cared for. The time of meals and the arrangement of seating are laid down. The food which is permitted in the various fasting periods is carefully described. On two days, the first Monday of Lent and Holy Saturday, there is no meal in the refectory or *trapeza*. Otherwise boiled beans and vegetables cooked in water were eaten in Lent, with a dish cooked in oil and some wine on certain days. The chapter about fasting is the longest in the Hypotyposis.[20]

The typikon goes on to describe how the monastery is governed. The main principle here is its independence. 'This monastery is to be independent, free of everyone's control and self-governing, and not subject to anyone's rights, be they imperial, ecclesiastic or of a private person, but it should be watched over, steered, governed and directed only by the Theotokos Evergetis.'[21] This became a guiding principle of the Reform movement. The influence of the *charistikarios* was rejected, as were the decisions of councils beginning with the Council of Chalcedon in 451 which tried to place monasteries under the rule of the bishop. All aspects of the life of the monastery were to be directed by the superior and leading monks. The superior, or *hegumenos*, is chosen by the monks themselves, and in turn he appoints a steward or *oikonomos*.

There were two *hegumenoi*. The usual practice was that there should be one superior only, but in some cases a second was appointed. If this was done, one would usually be a hermit. This recognizes the presence of two forms of monastic living – solitary ascetic struggle and a disciplined communal life. Monasteries found various ways of recognizing these alternative ways of life, often providing for a limited number of the more experienced monks to live an eremetical life in or near the monastery. In the

Evergetis monastery, both the ascetic life of the solitary and the practical business of the community were legislated for. It was expected that the hegumenos would be occupied in teaching through catachesis, or giving guidance and healing through *exagoreusis*. To complement this, it was prudent to appoint another hegumenos to attend to the practical demands of the monastery. This need was more urgent so that the independence of the monastery from outside control was maintained. Administration was done by the monks themselves and not left to a *charistikarios*. In spite of these practical responsibilities the hegumenos should remain within the monastery and only leave to go into the city in a few special and unusual circumstances, such as attack by an invading force.[22]

Then follow further regulations concerning property, visitors, idle talk, baths, which were taken three times a year unless the monk was sick. There are to be no servants or slaves, and all monks are to have the same food and living conditions.[23]

The provisions of the typikon are not to be changed and it is to be read in its entirety at meal times once a month.[24]

This short and simple document clearly defined several principles which became accepted by other monasteries. A monastery was an independent house, governed by the *hegumenos*, with most of the day set aside for worship and prayer, with eating carefully regulated to ensure modest consumption of food, individual guidance by the superior, and all to live equally and without private property. The monastery was a coenobium but recognized the importance of encouraging some to live an eremetical life. This pattern of living is immediately recognizable and is familiar as a way of life practised in monasteries across the Orthodox world. While it was practised in many places, it was set out with simplicity and clarity by Timothy and his successors at the Evergetis monastery and so became a model for others.

The typikon of the Evergetis monastery became a model for later foundations. Large sections of the hypotyposis are copied exactly in the typika of three monasteries, Phoberos, on the southern coast of the Bosphorus, Kosmosoteira founded by the emperor Isaac Komnenos in Thrace and the Serbian monastery of Hilendar on Mount Athos. All these were founded in the twelfth century and came under the influence of the Evergetis monastery. Many other monastic foundations have borrowed phrases and ideas from the hypotyposis, which have been identified by researchers. Among this large group is the women's monastery of Kecharitoumene founded by the empress Irene Doukaina and the monastery of St Mamas. The typikon of St Mamas was followed by further later foundations which in turn extended the influence of the Evergetis further. Two of these monasteries, Hilendar and Machariras in Cyprus, are still in existence today and so the monastic life so carefully worked out within the walls of a monastery just outside medieval Constantinople which has now disappeared from our knowledge has a continuing influence over Orthodox monastic life.[25] It comes at the end of a period when monasticism was growing and provided a model of life which was followed by others.

The Evergetis monastery was one of many monasteries in the capital. The influence of its hypotyposis shows how monastic life had developed shared ideals and practices. This process of development took place not only in the metropolis of the capital city. Monasteries also spread in more remote rural areas, among them mountains. The growth of the monasteries of the mountains and of the islands also led to a definition and development of the monastic tradition which continued alongside and in relation to the monastic life of the capital.

Moving to the mountains

In 843 the Empress Theodora joined with Patriarch Methodios to celebrate the restoration of the icons with a great procession and liturgy. The chronicler Joseph Gennesios, writing in the tenth century, records that there were monks from the mountains of Ida, Kyminas, Olympus and Athos.[26]

Their presence in the capital for this celebration shows that there was a new focus of monastic life which had become more prominent in the course of this doctrinal conflict. The mountains had been a home and refuge for the monks. When life gets difficult in cities then the remote and inhospitable terrain of the high and barren mountains provides a place of greater safety. The refuge of the mountains had made it possible for the monks to maintain their life when under pressure not only from iconoclasts in the capital but also, later, from Persians, Turks, Arabs, Normans and Petchenegs who threatened the empire at various times.

Monasteries were established in the area around Constantinople and in the margins of the empire, where military expansion was taking place. Monks became agents in the expansion of Byzantine civilization. They were on the look-out for barren and unoccupied places to live in. As they explored and settled in new places where they could continue their ascetic life, they became colonizers and builders of empire. While the military conquests by the army built the state, it was the presence of the monks with their centres of culture in the monastery that formed the nation.

An example of colonization carried out by monks is the incorporation of the island of Patmos in the Byzantine Empire. It fell into the sphere of Byzantine influence as a result of naval dominance and so became accessible to monks. The ascetic Christodulos had tried out various locations for the practice of the ascetic life. He had lived on Mount Latros, then Strobilos on the coast of Asia Minor, then the island of Kos and then he discovered Patmos. He wanted to achieve solitude and was looking for 'a place from which the laity has been completely removed; a place of hesychia for yourself and your brethren which can contribute to the work of the spirit', as it was expressed in the Hypotyposis of the monastery.[27] When he arrived on Patmos in 1088 he found the island 'inaccessible, deserted and lacking in water' and so an ideal place for ascetic endeavour. But he could not maintain his solitude. Others came to join him and as the monastery grew so did the population of the island. Within four years twelve families of settlers, or *paroikoi*, had arrived, amounting to forty-one adults and no doubt bringing children as well. Then there were more arrivals and by 1270 the population of the island had reached four hundred. The villagers were required to work five days a week for the new monastery. Gradually the monastery grew and with it the productive capacity of the island. Olive groves, vines and figs were planted by the founder and in the following century the island became an exporter of sheep and goat's cheese. Agricultural activity continued to grow as the monastery received further grants of lands on the neighbouring islands of Crete, Leipsos and Leros. On Leros the monks were granted grazing rights and, so that their solitude was maintained, the local villagers were excluded from the island and their traditional grazing rights removed. Four boats were built for transporting of grain and other products and these were exempted from the payment of taxes. The monastery became well established and remains a centre of monastic life. Its history illustrates the uneasy relationship with society around. The search for poverty went alongside the need for agricultural productivity, the maintenance of solitude was preserved alongside economic and political activity.

Mountains as well as islands were an environment which was suited to monastic life. Desert, we have noted, worked as an antithesis to city. For withdrawal from society, there needs to be both a place to withdraw to and a place to withdraw from. The advantage of the mountain is the mixture of environments. The mountain itself provided scope for ascending levels of ascetic endeavour. Ascending the mountain is a metaphor for a spiritual ascent towards God and in the mountains around Constantinople the metaphor could become a reality. There was usually agricultural or grazing land at the foot, where a coenobium could be established and maintained. Then as the ascetic ascended the land became rocky and rough. Here the solitary ascetic found a desert of seclusion. As he climbed higher so his ascetic life became more austere.

The move to the mountains developed in the ninth and tenth centuries, with literary sources describing how monks settled in these areas inland, away from the cities and the coastal strips. Their attraction increased after Arabs occupied large parts of the Middle East and mountains in Cappadocia and other less populated areas became inaccessible to monks. There were holy mountains in Bithynia, near to Constantinople in western Asia Minor – Mounts Olympus, Kyminas, Ida and Auxentius. Other monastic mountains were further south, at Latros, Mykale and Galesion.

These mountains were not only a contrast but also a complement to the city. The attraction of the city of Constantinople was its place at the centre of the life of the empire and so monks had found their way into the city, both in the outskirts where there was space for monastic establishments and also in the centre where they took part in the ecclesiastical, civic and political life of the city and empire.

Near to the city was Mount Olympus, in Bithynia, the province directly to the east of Constantinople, near the town of Brousa, or Prousa, about sixty miles distant from the capital. Coenobia were set up at the foot of the mountain, among them the monastery of Sakkoudion where Theodore the Stoudite and his uncle Plato had lived before the move to Constantinople in 798. The ascetic Joannikios also lived on this mountain. There were over fifty monasteries in the area by the end of the ninth century. Many of these are referred to as lavrai, and were located at higher altitudes. From here monks travelled to other centres, including Mount Athos. The closeness of Olympus to Constantinople made it a place where forms of monastic life could be developed and then exported to other areas.

Further south was Mount Latros. Here too a fertile valley was a propitious place for larger monasteries. The Life of Paul of Latros, written in the tenth century, describes how Paul settled in the area around 900 and found the monasteries of Karyes and Stylos at the foot of Mount Latros, which were 'large and highly populated'. There were also caves and other places nearby where solitary monks lived. Paul himself lived for a while on a pillar of rock. There were probably other monasteries in the area, since there are records of donations of money given to the group of monasteries of Latros by the emperor Romanos Lekapenos (920–44).[28] Other mountains occupied by monks were Mounts Mykale and Galesion, both near Mount Latros, and Mount Kyminas, near Olympus.

Monasteries on Athos

There was another mountain which was about the same distance from Constantinople as Latros but to the west. Like the other mountains, it had good pasture for sheep and fertile land to enable cultivation of olives, grapes and other crops. There was rich vegetation and most of the area was covered by forest. There were also high mountainous areas, reaching a height of over 2,000 metres. In addition, the mountain was on the sea coast, so could be approached by boat. Because of its location at the end of a peninsula reaching out into the sea, it was cut off on three sides from the surrounding lands. This ideal location for pursuing a life of religious seclusion and struggle has become a home for monks. Monastic life vanished many centuries ago from the most of the monastic mountains of Byzantium, with the exception of this mountain of Athos, the Holy Mountain. Here monasteries have not only remained but the peninsula has become a monastic republic, governed according to the ideals and principles of the ascetic life. Today it is an international centre, and its monastic practice influences and encourages the monastic life of many churches and has extended this to new areas and to non-Orthodox as well.

The beginnings of monastic life on the Mountain reach back over a millennium. Many monasteries claim foundation dates at the beginning of the Byzantine period. The monastery of Vatopedi preserves a tradition that it was built by the emperor Constantine (324–37), destroyed by the pagan Julian the Apostate (361–3) and then rebuilt by Theodosius (379–95). Theodosius added new buildings in gratitude to Mary the Mother of God who saved his infant son Arcadius from a shipwreck by bringing him safely to shore and leaving him in a bramble bush. This is the origin of the name Vatopedi, from *vatos* or bramble bush and *paidi* or child. A holy well can still be seen which marks the spot where this miracle happened.[29] Other monasteries preserve their own traditions which place their origins early in the history of the church.

By the ninth century, monks had discovered the mountain. Euthymius the Younger was living on Mount Olympus when he heard that Athos was a tranquil place and so he moved there in 859 and lived in a cave for three years. When he came out of his seclusion in the cave, he found that others had the same idea and he was not alone. Disciples joined him, among whom was John Kolobos who founded a monastery towards the north of the peninsula at the town of Ierissos. Another early ascetic was Peter, who is remembered as Peter the Athonite, who was a soldier in Syria, where he was captured and imprisoned by Arabs, then was made a monk by the pope in Rome, before finally settling in a cave on the mountain which he said contained 'more crawling animals than the sky has stars or the sea sand, and with them a host of demons nesting who raised up a swarm of trails against the holy man such as no tongue can recount'. He lived here with these animals as his companions for fifty years until his death in 890.[30]

The beginning of communal monastic life on the holy mountain is recognized as beginning in 963, when Athanasios founded the Great Lavra. He was born with the name Avraamios in Trebizond between 925 and 930. He moved around the empire living in a succession of different monastic places. As a young man he had had lived a private or secret ascetic life in Constantinople as 'a monastic among non-monastics'.[31] He then joined a community, referred to as a lavra, as one of a group of monks under the guidance of a spiritual father Michael Maleinos at Kyminas, another of the holy mountains of Bithynia. After four years his spiritual father gave him a blessing to live as a hermit. He then moved to Athos in search of greater solitude and chose an 'utterly deserted' part of the mountain at the southern end of the peninsula. It has puzzled later commentators why, after this long period living the solitary life, he built and governed a communal monastery, or coenobium, modelled on the style of life of the monastery of Stoudios. It is likely that he was encouraged in this by a visit to Crete where he went as spiritual guide to the future emperor Nikiphoros Phokas, and they seem to have planned this new initiative together. On his return to the mountain in 961, Athanasios began to build near his previous dwelling at the southern end of Athos. The new church was complete by 963 and other buildings followed. Meanwhile Nikiphoros returned to Constantinople where he was later crowned emperor. While this deprived Athanasios of a companion in monastic life, it provided him with a patron and protector. The new emperor made Athanasios hegumenos, gave the monks the right to appoint his successor, granted the monastery an annual payment of 244 gold nomismata and fixed the number of monks at eighty.

The way of life of this new monastery is described in a series of documents. There are two versions of the *Life of Athanasios*; the foundation charter of typikon of the monastery; and the diatyposis and hypotyposis which are texts written by Athanasios laying down

Figure 11 The mountainous peninsula of Athos has been a home for monks for more than a thousand years.

Figure 12 The Great Lavra was the founding monastery on Mount Athos.

how the monastery is to be governed and directed. He states clearly that he is following ancient traditions and quotes directly from the writings of Theodore the Stoudite. He has chosen a remote setting so that the 'angelic calling' of prayer can be followed and monks can be 'undistracted and free from external activities'. There are instructions about the prayer in church and insistence that everything should be held in common. Not even a needle, he commands, can be held as an individual possession. 'Let only those things that you call your own be your body and soul, and let even these be shared in an equality of love among all your spiritual children and brethren.'[32] The abbot or hegumenos also lives a life of simplicity but has the responsibility of directing the community. He does this through his practice of *exagoreusis logismon* or confession of thoughts. Each monk came to see Athanasios each day to confess their thoughts and receive his direction. With at least eighty monks this must have been a demanding ministry, and the *Life* records that Athanasios would see monks in the night as well as the day to do this.

He also instructed that the monastery should not keep female animals. This prohibition of women was called the *abaton* – which could be translated as the 'no-go' area. The extension of this rule to animals was probably less to do with avoiding women and more to do with the maintenance of a simple life style. The absence of female animals ensured that animal breeding could not be carried out.[33]

While this was a carefully regulated and disciplined community, it also included space for the solitary life. It kept the name of Lavra, even though the style was that of a coenobium. Athanasios allowed up to five monks to live outside the monastery, but not too far distant and still under the direction of the hegumenos. They are also expected to have a servant living with them, and so solitude was not complete. The inclusion of hermits within the community was a divergence from the Stoudite way of life.

The new foundation was a success. At first it was laid down that the maximum number of monks should be eighty. This limit was soon raised to 120, and after fifteen years the number had grown to 150. It continued to grow so that it is recorded that there were seven hundred monks by 1030 and there may have been as many as a thousand by the end of the century.[34] By the time Athanasios died – killed by falling masonry during further construction in the church – there were three thousand monks on the mountain of Athos. His biographer comments that now 'the whole mountain became a city'.[35]

It might have been the size of the buildings and the growth of the numbers that led to tension with monks of other smaller and more traditional types of monastery. They complained that Athanasios was subverting the traditional way of life and that he was allowing worldly concerns to impinge. When the emperor Nikiphoros was murdered by his nephew John Tzimiskes, the monks of Athos complained about Athanasios to the new emperor. The outcome of the controversy was the dispatch of an imperial representative, Euthymius of the Stoudite monastery, to Mount Athos and the drafting of a typikon or charter for the whole mountain.

This document is known as the *Tragos*, or goat, since it was written on a goatskin, and that original piece of goatskin is still preserved on the mountain. It sets out the regulations which order life on the mountain. It laid down that there should be three regular meetings of the whole community each year, sets down how new monks should be admitted, regulates the property and prohibits the presence of eunuchs and beardless youths.[36] A result was that the coenobium of the kind set up by Athanasios became a pattern for life on the mountain. The monasteries were recognized by the emperors and began to receive gifts of land and money in the surrounding areas. The *Tragos* was signed not only by Athanasios but also by the abbots of a further forty-six monasteries. These may have been small settlements but the number indicates that monastic life was already well established by the time of Athanasios. His innovation was not to initiate monastic life but to set up a way of living which proved to be lasting and effective.

Further monasteries followed. The monastery of Iviron was founded in 979 or 980. This was also the result of a grant by the emperor, Basil II, as a recognition of the military support given by John Tornik, a Georgian. A group of Georgian monks from the Great Lavra settled in this new monastery, built on the site of an earlier monastery of Clement. John the Iberian was appointed as hegumenos in 980, with the support of Athanasios, and the monastery gained land and money so that it became similar in size and influence to the Great Lavra. Then monks were attracted from Amalfi in Italy. They had heard of the reputation of Athanasios and were given practical help in finding a site by John the Iberian. These followed the Benedictine Rule and were helped and supported by John the Iberian to find a site near Iviron. This monastery was well endowed and was allowed to maintain a large ship to enable it to trade. It survived for three centuries in spite of the Great Schism of 1054 and the invasion of Constantinople by the Fourth Crusade in 1204, until it finally disappeared in 1287. The presence of a Latin monastery suggests both that monastic life was able to embrace a variety of forms and that the split between Rome and Constantinople was not so decisive at this time as is sometimes suggested.[37]

Throughout its history there has been a variety of ways of living, among them both coenobia and hermitages. There are hermits living alone and groups of monks living in collections of cells, which became known as sketes. The skete, a title which is probably derived from the Greek title *asketerion*, is a smaller group of monks living under the direction of a spiritual father. There are today twelve main sketes, dependent on the ruling monasteries, some of which are large.

The steep cliffs on the southern end of the peninsula have attracted hermits, who have built cells clinging to narrow ledges overlooking the sea. One settlement of hermit cells, in a narrow ravine, is Kafsokalyvia, a word meaning burnt huts. The name is

Figure 13 The hermitages at Karoulia cling to the precipitous cliff face of Mount Athos.

derived from a fourteenth-century ascetic Maximus of Kafsokalyvia. Maximus, born with the name Manuel, followed the way of life of a holy fool. He ignored conventions and behaved in an eccentric and even scandalous way. At the age of seventeen he left home and lived as a wandering ascetic. He eventually arrived on Athos, lived for a while at the Great Lavra, and then, after a vision of the Mother of God, moved out of the monastery. For ten years he wandered over the mountain, eating nuts and berries, moving from place to place, sometimes living in caves and sometimes huts, which after a while he burnt as he moved on. 'He did not possess even a needle or a spade or two garments, he had no bread, no wallet, not a single coin,' so his biographer Theophanes recounts. He died around 1370. Three hundred years later the ascetic Akakios settled in one of Maximus's caves, and soon others joined him. From then on the huts of Kafsokalyvia – no longer systematically burnt – have been a skete under the guidance of the Great Lavra.[38]

The typika

The Tragos described the way of life and the regulations which governed the mountain. It was the first typikon or founding charter of the mountain. Others followed, each drafted and promulgated to respond to changing circumstances or historical challenges faced by the monks. They show how the life on Athos survived and evolved through its long history.

The second typikon was issued in 1045, during the reign of the Emperor Constantine IX Monomachos (1042–55). It was made necessary because of the growth in number of monks. Since the number of monks was growing so fast, the administration needed to be revised. There were now over forty large monasteries as well as many hermitages and smaller lavrai. This second typikon was signed by 180 abbots. It confirmed the rules contained in the Tragos and also provided further arrangements for government. There was a General Assembly and also a Protos, or elected leader, who was appointed by the emperor and administered the mountain, which was called the Holy Mountain for the first time. It exempted the monasteries from taxation and declared them independent of both the local bishop and the ecumenical patriarch. This arrangement lasted until the fourteenth century when the power of the emperor was diminishing under the attacks of the Ottomans who would conquer Constantinople in the following century. Emperor Andronikos IV Palaiologos transferred the authority over the mountain to the patriarch, and this was confirmed in a further typikon promulgated in 1400.

The succession of typika regulated life on the mountain and responded to changing political and social circumstances. There were both foundations of new monasteries and also some closures. There are now twenty monasteries which, between them, own the land which makes up the mountain and are responsible for its government. These were founded at various times through the Byzantine period, with one, Stavronikita, set up by Patriarch Jeremiah I in 1541, after the Ottoman conquest of Constantinople.

Notes

1. For the 'Thousands of Monasteries', in a novel of Nikiphoros Phokas, in Peter Charanis, 'The Monastic Properties and the State in the Byzantine Empire', *Dumbarton Oaks Papers* 4 (1948), pp. 53–118, at pp. 56–8; 'Monasteries in Many Villages' in a novel of Basil II, cited in Rosemary Morris, *Monks and Laymen in Byzantium 843–1118* (Cambridge, 1995), p. 132.
2. For these figures see Peter Charanis, 'The Monk as an Element of Byzantine Society', *Dumbarton Oaks Papers* 24 (1971), pp. 63–84, especially p. 72, and Peter Hatlie, *The Monks and Monasteries of Constantinople ca 350–850* (Cambridge, 2007), pp. 181, 219.
3. A remark of A. P. Kazhdan, *History of Byzantine Culture 650–850* (Athens, 1999), pp. 11–12.
4. Procopius's work was entitled *On the Buildings*, for its influence Averil Cameron, *Procopius and the Sixth Century* (London, 1985), p. 89.
5. Zonaras III in ibid., p. 18.
6. Morris, *Monks*, p. 148, citing *Syntagma canonum* II.2 col 577 A-C.
7. These examples are cited in Morris, *Monks*, p. 132.
8. This is from Gregory Nazianzus, *Anthologia Palatina* 8.166.74, also in Caner, p. 234.
9. Ibid., pp. 148–9.
10. See Morris, *Monks*, p. 151.
11. Patriarch John V Oxites of Antioch, *Against the Charistike* 9, p. 109; 11, p. 113. This work is summarized in John Thomas, *Private Religious Foundations in the Byzantine Empire*, Dumbarton Oaks Studies 24 (Washington, 1987), pp. 186–92.
12. See Morris, *Monks*, p. 265 citing S Eustratiades in *Hellenika* 1 (1928), pp. 256–311, at p. 257.
13. John Thomas, 'Documentary Evidence from the Byzantine Monastic Typika for the History of the Evergetine Reform Movement', in ed. Margaret Mullett and Anthony Kirby, *The Theotokos Evergetis and Eleventh Century Monasticism* (Belfast, 1994), p. 271.
14. Ibid., pp. 249–50.
15. See Andrew Louth, *Greek East and Latin West* (New York, 2007), pp. 281–7; and John Thomas, *Byzantine Monastic Foundation Documents*, vol. 2 (Washington, 2000), pp. 441–53.
16. *Hypotyposis*, pp. 147–214. There is a major British Academy research project working on this dossier of material directed by Margaret Mullett of Belfast University. This has published several studies, including ed. R. H. Jordan and Rosemary Morris, The *Hypotyposis of the Monastery of the Theotokos Evergetis, Constantinople (11th–12th Centuries)* (Ashgate, 2012) and a set of conference proceedings ed. Margaret Mullett and Anthony Kirby, *The Theotokos Evergetis and Eleventh Century Monasticism* (Belfast, 1994).
17. *Hypotyposis* 2, in Jordan and Morris, *Hypotyposis*, p. 149.
18. *Hypotyposis* 4–6, pp. 152–9.
19. Ibid., 7, pp. 160–3.
20. Ibid., 9–10, pp. 164–74.
21. Ibid., 12, p. 175.
22. Ibid., 13, pp. 177–9.
23. Ibid., 19–25, pp. 189–94.
24. Ibid. 43, pp. 210–11.
25. Ibid., pp. 29–32.

26 Graham Speake, *Mount Athos, Renewal in Paradise* (New Haven, CT, and London, 2002), p. 38.
27 Morris, *Monks*, p. 48, citing the *Hypotyposis* of Christodoulos.
28 See Morris, *Monks*, pp. 32–43. *The Life of Paul the Younger* 6, 7, 17. In 'Vita S. Pauli Junioris in Monte Latro', in ed. H. Delehaye, *Analecta Bollandiana*, vol. 11 (1892), pp. 19–74, 136–81.
29 Speake, *Mount Athos*, p. 27.
30 Kisopp Lake, *Early Days of Monasticism on Mount Athos* (Oxford, 1909), pp. 26–7.
31 *Life of Athanasius*, 14.17, ed. P. Lemerle, *La vie ancienne de saint Athanase l'Athonite composée au début di XIe siècle par Athanase de Lavra*, vol. 1 (Chevtogne, 1963), pp. 59–100.
32 Ibid., 140.1–2, 155.8.
33 Speake, *Mount Athos*, pp. 25–7.
34 Morris, *Monks*, p. 181, referring to an act of 1102 which speaks of 'a great increase in monks'.
35 See Kallistos Ware, 'St Athanasios the Athonite: Traditionalist or Innovator?' in ed. Anthony Bryer and Mary Cunningham, *Mount Athos and Byzantine Monasticism* (Aldershot, 1996), p. 3, and *Life of Anthony* 238.5. This phrase recalls Antony of Egypt who 'made the desert into a city'.
36 The regulations of the Tragos are summarized in Speake, *Mount Athos*, pp. 40–1.
37 Ibid., pp. 51–8.
38 There are four surviving lives of Maximus, edited by F. Halkin in *Analecta Bollandia* 54 (1936), pp. 38–112. For the significance of Maximus, see K. Ware, 'St Maximus of Kapsokalyvia and Fourteenth Century Athonite Hesychasm', in *Kathigitria* (London, 1988), pp. 409–30.

10

Missionaries and Kings: The Balkans

Missions to Moravia and Bulgaria

The two brothers Cyril and Methodius are revered as the apostles to the Slavs, as equal to the apostles and patron saints of Europe.[1] Their missionary labours in bringing the gospel to parts of Eastern Europe took place in the ninth century and contributed to a renaissance of translation, culture and scholarship. This was part of a renaissance of Byzantine civilization which led to a new prestige and cultural influence which went alongside political and military decline. It's a story which concerns the empire and the church and belongs in monastic history too. Cyril and Methodius were both monks, as were their followers Clement and Naum.

Cyril (826–69) was a scholar. Born with the name Constantine in Thessalonica, he went to study in Constantinople and was recognized by his teacher, Patriarch Photius, as a brilliant student. He was given the responsible position of chartophylax at the church of Haghia Sophia, overseeing the documents and records of the church, and then, about 850, became a teacher of philosophy. He was an accomplished linguist with a good knowledge of Greek, Latin, Slavonic, Hebrew, Syriac and Samaritan. He was known as Constantine the Philosopher. He ended his life in a Greek monastery in Rome, where he fell ill and became a monk taking the name Cyril.

Methodius (815–85) was his older brother. After a career as a courtier in Constantinople and as a diplomat, he became a monk at the monastery of Polikhron on Mount Olympus in Bithynia. It was here that Constantine retreated during a period of political conflict in Constantinople and joined his brother. We are told by their biographers that during this period they 'devoted themselves to books' or 'conversed with books'.[2] This shared literary endeavour must have included work on languages and so it was in the monastery on Mount Olympus that they started their work of devising an alphabet in which the sounds of Slavonic language could be accurately transliterated. This script was later called Glagolitic, from the word *glagol* meaning utterance or something spoken, and it made possible the translation of Greek liturgical and theological texts into a form and language which could be understood by those who spoke Slavonic languages.

The brothers involved others in their work. They 'took pains to impart the divine knowledge (of these letters) to the shaper-witted of their disciples'.[3] These disciples were Gorazd, Clement, Naum, Angelarius and Sava. Clement (840–916) was from Bulgaria, 'from the European Moesians, who are also known to most people as Bulgarians', and so came from a Slavonic and Greek background. He was a follower of Methodius. He 'set the great Methodius as the model for his own life … for he knew his own life as no one else did, as he had followed him from his tender youth, and saw with his own eyes all the things that his master did'.[4] He joined Methodius in his monastery on Mount Olympus, probably as a layman, and became a monk later.

Constantine, Methodius and their co-workers were then sent as missionaries to Moravia at the request of Rastislav, the prince of the land. There they spent three years, translating the Bible and various theological and liturgical texts and teaching people to use them. Then they went to Rome to arrange for their disciples to be ordained as priests so as to continue the evangelistic work. Here they lived in a Greek monastery where Constantine died.

Before he died, Cyril exhorted his brother Methodius not to return to his monastery but to continue the missionary work which they had begun. Pope Hadrian II consecrated Methodius as Archbishop of Sirmium. He then gave his approval to the Slavic version of the liturgy and sent him back to Moravia as papal legate. The Moravian mission did not succeed in establishing a church. There were many setbacks. There was rivalry and conflict with Frankish missionaries in the area; hostility from Svatopulk, the ruler of Moravia, who eventually gave his support to the Franks; lack of interest from the pope; then finally invasion by the Hungarians, with the result that the kingdom of Moravia disappeared from history. In 885 Methodius died and his disciples and collaborators were escorted out of the kingdom to the river Danube. Three of them, Clement, Naum and Angelarius, made a raft out of three lime trees and manoeuvred this across the river and so came safely to Belgrade, a frontier town, from which the military governor arranged for them to travel on to Pliska, the capital of Bulgaria.

They arrived in Bulgaria at an opportune moment. Boris, the ruler of Bulgaria, had been baptized in 864. He had wondered where to look for support and for clergy for his new church. Rather than seek help from Rome, he decided to approach Constantinople. The Bulgarians spoke a Slavonic language but the Byzantine clergy were Greek speakers and so could not communicate. Boris, we are told, 'thirsted after such men' as Clement and Naum, the new arrivals.[5] With their support and the use of Slavonic in the liturgy and in teaching he was able to build a Bulgarian Church, using the Slavonic language and within the ecclesiastical jurisdiction of the patriarch of Constantinople. The use of Slavonic made access to Byzantine culture possible but gave some protection from the Universalist claims of the emperor. The three survivors of the Moravian mission spent some months with Boris. Then Angelarius died and Clement went to Macedonia. Naum stayed at Pliska.

Clement's achievement was his teaching of many disciples. This work is described in two lives of the saint. The Long Life was written by Theophylact of Ohrid, in the eleventh century, with a Brief Life written later by Demetrios Chomatianos. These sources refer to him living at Koutmitsinitsa, and to houses in Diabolis, Ohrid and Glavinitsa, all places near Lake Ohrid in western Macedonia.[6] Clement was appointed *didaskolos* or teacher, which was a title given to a senior priest with special responsibility for education. He spent seven years in this position, from 886 to 893, moving between his three residences. He taught children to write in the new Glagolitic script and, his biographer notes, his students were amazed by his ability to 'write books', by which he means copy, at the same time as teaching. He encouraged the best students to progress to more advanced studies and many went on to be ordained as priests. A total of 3,500 students progressed to this study of the 'more profound scriptures'. A historian has described this as 'by any standards, an educational undertaking almost without parallel in the Middle Ages'.[7] As well as teaching in these three educational centres, he founded the monastery of St Panteleimon on the shores of Lake Ohrid. At some stage he had become a monk – presumably under Methodius's influence and possibly in those early days on Mount Olympus. This monastery became a centre for training clergy and for bringing the message of Christianity to the region. Clement loved the place, and eventually died there.

Meanwhile in Pliska, Boris abdicated his throne in 889 and became a monk. His son Vladimir succeeded him, revived paganism and persecuted the Christian clergy. After four years, Boris emerged from his seclusion, imprisoned and blinded Vladimir, summoned a council and selected his third son Symeon to be king. After this brief excursion back into the secular world to resolve the situation, he returned to his prayers in the monastery. Symeon, who then ruled from 893 to 927, had been educated in Byzantium and continued the work of his father in developing Slavonic language and literature. His reign has been described as the Golden Age of Bulgarian literature. He summoned Clement to the new capital of Preslav and arranged for him to be consecrated bishop of a diocese called Dragvista, or Velitsa. Here Clement continued teaching, translating and writing. His Life says that he 'skilfully devised other shapes of letters with a view to making them clearer than those which the wise Cyril invented .... and wrote down all the scriptures, panegyrics, and lives of martyrs and holy men, as well as sacred hymns'.[8] This could refer to the adaptation of Cyril's Glagolitic script into the simpler Cyrillic.

The second centre of study and learning in Bulgaria was at Preslav and was presided over by the other of Methodius's disciples, Naum. When Clement was consecrated bishop in 893, Naum was transferred to succeed Clement at Ohrid, and carried on the work of teaching. He also founded a monastery on the shores of the lake, in 905, where he died five years later.

The monks Methodius and Clement spent many years translating and teaching, using the script and language devised in Constantinople. They carried out an unsuccessful mission in Moravia, but established a Slavonic-speaking Church in Bulgaria. From this beginning Slavonic churches spread across Eastern Europe. It had been a laborious and erratic process, with failures and setbacks but was ultimately successful. It belongs within the history of monastic life, and shows how monks were scholars, teachers and missionaries as well as men of prayer.

Sava of Serbia

The Serbian kingdom was in the centre of the Balkans. The size of the kingdom varied through the medieval period. At its largest, under Stephan Dušan (1331–46), it extended into Greece and included Mount Athos. At this time, Serbia consisted of two kingdoms. Diokleia was on the Adriatic coast and looked towards both Rome and Italy, while Raška was inland and within the Byzantine sphere of influence. When Byzantium declined after the sack of the city at the Fifth Crusade in 1204, Serbia, as well as Bulgaria, gained political influence. The Church which had been established by missionaries in the ninth century, perhaps by some of Methodius's two hundred clergy expelled from Moravia, became autocephalous in 1219. The first archbishop of Serbia, Sava, is recognized as the founder of the Serbian Church. He was a prince, a monk, an archbishop, a diplomat, a patron of the arts, a writer and a teacher. Not only did he lead the Church to independence, but he also founded monasteries and established communications between the monastic life of Byzantium and the Balkan states. As a result of his achievements Serbian Christianity can be called and is known by Serbs as Svetosavlje, which can be awkwardly translated as Saint-Sava-ism.

Sava, the founder, was born Rastko and was the son of Stephan Nemanja, grand župan or ruler of Serbia.[9] He was born in 1175. When he was fifteen his father put him in charge of the region around Ragusa, now Dubrovnik. After two years in this post, in 1191, he ran away to Mount Athos where he joined the community at the Russian monastery of St Panteleimon. His father sent a search party to bring him back. One of the sources, written in the late thirteenth century, describes a chase through the monastery, with the young prince hiding from his pursuers, wearing his monastic clothing, climbing to the top of the tower. From this high place, he threw down his royal clothes, the hair which was shaved off in his tonsuring and a letter to his father, at which point the pursuers withdrew. Rastko took the name Sava, which suggests a reverence for Sabas of Palestine, and lived as a monk in the monastery of Vatopedi. Then, in 1196, Sava's father followed the example of his son and also became a monk, taking the name, Symeon. He lived first at the monastery of Studenica, which he had founded in 1190, and then travelled to Athos to join his son.

The arrival of the king, now a new and humble monk, on the Holy Mountain, made a strong impression. Symeon had brought buckets of gold and silver, horses and mules and liturgical vessels, which were distributed around the monasteries on the mountain. This benefaction followed on from earlier gifts to monasteries in Jerusalem, Constantinople and Rome. *Ktitors*, or founders, were remembered and commemorated in the monasteries, and major benefactors were included in this category of founder. This stream of donations ensured that the Serbian royal family entered into the annals of several of the monasteries.

Then father and son began to realize a longing to establish a Serbian monastery on the mountain. They chose a ruined monastery, formerly occupied by a Greek community, twelve miles from Vatopedi. It was called Chelandarion, or of the Boatman, which is transliterated into Slavonic as Hilendar. It required an imperial chrysobull, issued by the emperor Alexios III in June 1198, to negotiate its release from the jurisdiction of other monasteries. The edict declared Hilendar to be a self-governing, independent monastery, with the same privileges as other non-Greek houses. The patrons or *ktitors* were the three members of the Serbian royal family, Symeon, Sava and Symeon/Stephan's successor on the throne, also called Stephan. It has remained a Serbian foundation and is now fourth in precedence in the hierarchy of monasteries on the mountain.

Symeon moved there in 1198, and died there the following year, in February 1199. Sava wrote a description of his father's death in the monastery they had founded together. It is a moving account of the last hours of the king.

> He said 'My child. Bring me the icon of the most holy Mother of God, for I have made a vow to yield up the ghost in front of her'. (Then he said) 'Clothe me in the rason appointed for my funeral and place me in the same sacred position in which I shall lie in my coffin. Spread matting on the ground and place a stone under my head that I may lie here until the Lord comes to visit me and take me hence'. I did this and all who looked on wept bitterly. He whom all men in his country feared, and before whom all trembled, was now seen as a stranger and beggar ... asking everyone's forgiveness and blessing with love in his heart. ... I remained by his side all night. ... When morning came and the singing of matins began the blessed father's face was suddenly illumined and he looked up to heaven and said 'Praise God in his sanctuary' and when he had said this he yielded up his spirit and died in the Lord.[10]

Later that year Sava spent several months at the monastery of Evergetis in Constantinople – another monastery which had received benefactions from the Serbian royal family. Here he became familiar with the liturgical and other practices of this monastery and studied its typikon. He translated the typikon into Slavonic and brought it back with him to Hilendar, where he adapted it slightly to make it the typikon of his new Athonite monastery. Later the typikon was to become a model for other monasteries in Serbia. This process gives us an insight into how the Evergetis typikon became so influential. Visitors to Constantinople, in this case Sava, stayed at the monastery, became familiar with the lifestyle and took the example back home. Sava was also influenced by a visit to Palestine. Sava went as a pilgrim to the Holy Land in 1229, and stayed at Mar Saba, the Great Laura of Sabas. Here he learnt the Sabaite traditions for himself and also incorporated these in the monastic rules of Serbia.

Sava was now a leading monk. He was ordained deacon, then priest, by the local bishop, and then was ordained as archimandrite by three bishops at the main church of Thessalonica. This position made him the second in rank on Mount Athos. Perhaps this promotion led to tensions with the senior monk, the protos, because in 1206 or 1207 Sava returned to Serbia. He took with him his father's body which was laid in a tomb in the monastery of Studenica, where Sava became abbot.[11] In this period Sava founded many monasteries and hermitages, including Žiča, which became the seat of the archbishops. The typika of these monasteries followed the Athonite and Evergetis examples.

These activities, including new monastic foundations, gave further responsibilities to the monk Sava and he set off on another journey to visit the emperor at Nicaea in 1219. The ruler of Serbia, Stephen the First-Crowned, or *Prvovenčani*, and the new emperor, Theodore I Lascaris, were both married to sisters in the Byzantine royal family and this must have contributed to the warmth of Sava's welcome. Sava was consecrated *Archbishop of Serbia* by the Patriarch Manuel and the Church of Serbia was given autocephalous status. As a result, future archbishops were chosen from within the Serbian Church and the approval of the patriarch in Constantinople was not required. On his way home, he spent time at one of the monasteries he had given money to, Philokales, in Thessalonica, and drafted a body of canon law which would become the basis of a Serbian legal code. It has become known as Sava's nomocanon, and draws on various legal texts which were in use in this period.

Sava returned home in 1220 and settled at the monastery of Žiča. He set up eleven dioceses and appointed Serbian, Slavonic speakers to be the bishops. Some of the bishops had come with him from Hilendar and some of the dioceses were based in monasteries. The three southernmost dioceses, of Ras, Prizren and Lipljan, were already part of the archdiocese of Ohrid, which had been formed three centuries earlier by Clement. Here the Greek bishops were replaced by Serbs, and the dioceses were incorporated in the new Serbian Church. Not surprisingly the archbishop of Ohrid, Demetrios Chomatianos sent a furious letter, protesting at the removal of these dioceses from his jurisdiction and also accusing Sava of various failings. He wrote angrily, 'Enslaved by the love of country … he began to take part in banquets, to ride thoroughbred horses, richly caparisoned and fair to behold, to go about with a large retinue, to give himself airs while walking in processions, and to be accompanied by a lavishly and diversely dressed bodyguard'.[12] These allegations show hostility from Chomatianos, but also show some of the awkwardness of the life of the monk-bishop with a lifestyle in conflict with the spirit of monastic simplicity. Sava did not reply to Chomatianos's letter, and the argument was resolved by the passing of time, with the three dioceses accepted as part of the new Serbian Church.

Figure 14 The monastery of Žiča was founded by St Sava of the royal house of Serbia.

Sava made a further pilgrimage to Jerusalem, Egypt, Sinai, Antioch, Constantinople and then to Turnovo in Bulgaria. Here he died in January 1236. He was buried in the monastery of Mileševo, and his tomb attracted pilgrims and visitors. It remained there until the Ottomans conquered Serbia in 1594. They removed the body from the tomb, carried it triumphantly to Belgrade and burnt it.

Through the life of Sava, and his father Stephan/Symeon, the state and the church in Serbia became inextricably linked. Sava was both prince and archbishop. In the course of his lifetime, Serbia was ruled by his father, his brother and two of his nephews. The monasteries which he founded at Studenica and Žiča, and then the later foundation of Mileševo were the places where the Serbian nation was formed and its culture took shape. The monasteries with their communities drawn from all classes of society, their traditions of scholarship, their nurturing of the arts were a seedbed for the life and identity of the nation.

Conclusion

The new states of the Balkans and Eastern Europe grew to fill the vacuum left by declining Byzantium. The change in the balance of power is illustrated by two events. In the battle of Manzikert in 1071, at the eastern boundary of the empire at Lake Van, the new power of the Seljuk Turks defeated the Byzantine army and took Emperor Romanos IV Diogenes captive, an event which shaped future European history.[13] Then, more than a century later, the Latin warriors of the Fifth Crusade were side-tracked in their mission to re-capture the Holy Places of Jerusalem and instead occupied Constantinople in 1204. Niketas Choniates lamented: 'Constantine's fine city, the common delight and boast of all nations, was laid waste by fire and blackened by soot, taken and emptied of all wealth.'[14] This catastrophe led to unexpected renaissances. After the fall of Constantinople to the Latins smaller Byzantine enclaves remained in several places including Epirus, Trebizond and Nicaea. From here they regained the city of Constantinople.

The cultural and religious vitality of Byzantium flourished amid military and political decline. Judith Herrin noted that 'curiously, Byzantine cultural influence expanded almost in inverse proportion to its political strength'.[15] On Mount Athos, the monks followed their ways of prayer which they described and taught. This was hesychasm which was witnessed to by Gregory Palamas and supported by Church Councils in Constantinople, including a Council in 1341.[16] The recognition of the hesychast way of prayer led to a revival not only in monastic life but made sure that its influence spread through the empire and beyond. After the recognition of the teaching of Gregory, hesychast monks were appointed to the leading positions in the Church. A succession of Ecumenical Patriarchs in the fourteenth century were hesychast monks. These were Isidore I (1347–50) a monk from Athos; Kallistos I (1350–3, 1355–63) formerly abbot of Iviron; and Philotheos Kokkinos (1353–5, 1364–76) abbot of the Great Lavra. From here, hesychast traditions spread to other areas. They were brought from Mount Athos to Paroria in Bulgaria, which had been founded as a monastic centre by Gregory of Sinai in the 1330s, and to Kilifarevo near Turnovo also in Bulgaria, founded by Theodosios of Turnovo. Then they extended further north. Sergius of Radonezh was in correspondence with Patriarch Philotheos who persuaded him to constitute his monastery as a coenobium. Monasteries were founded in Wallachia by Nicodemus an Athonite monk, and on the Meteora rocks in Thessaly in Greece. So, while the Byzantine Empire was declining as a political and military power, the hesychast and monastic revival was spreading and influencing the new nations across the Balkans and north into Russia. It carried the hopes and aspirations of Byzantium to new places which preserved and nurtured them after the city itself fell in 1453.

Notes

1 Pope John Paul II gave them the title of patron saints of Europe, along with Benedict of Nursia, in 1980.
2 F. Grivec and F. Tomsic, *Constantinus and Methodius Thessalonicenses* (Zagreb, 1960), pp. 108, 154.
3 Ibid., pp. 129, 154.
4 Dmitri Obolensky, *Six Byzantine Portraits* (Oxford, 1988), p. 12.
5 *Life of Clement* 16, 47, in ibid., p. 21. There is an English translation of the life by S. Nikolov, in ed. I. Duichev, *Kiril and Methodius, Founders of Slavonic Writing* (Boulder, CO, 1985).
6 The location of his residence is discussed in the *Long Life of Clement* 17.53–4.
7 Robert Browning, *Byzantium and Bulgaria* (London, 1975), p. 155.
8 *Life of Clement* 23.68, in Obolensky, *Six Byzantine Portraits*, p. 29.
9 The sources for the lives of Symeon and Sava are two lives of Stephen Nemanja, by Sava himself and by Symeon's son Stephan; and the Lives of St Sava by monks of his monastery Domentijan and Teodosije. See also Nicholai Velimirovich, *The Life of St Sava* (New York, 1989).
10 *Life of Sava* 169–70 cited in Obolensky, *Six Byzantine Portraits*, p. 139.
11 The tomb of St Symeon remains in the monastic church of Studenica. It is opened once a year, when the sweet scent of perfume coming from the body can be smelt. So he is now St Symeon Mirotočivi or 'myrrh oozer'.
12 From Pitra, *Analecta sacra et classica*, vi.381–390, cited in Obolensky, *Six Byzantine Portraits*, p. 158.
13 I recall my interest when my history teacher at school told us that this was the most significant date in European history.
14 Nicetas Choniates, 'O City of Constantinople!', in trans. H. Magoulias, *Annales of Nicetas Choniates* (Detroit, 1984), p. 315.
15 Judith Herrin, *Byzantium* (London, 2007), p. xix.
16 See below, pp. 190–1.

11

Monasteries in the North: Russia

Arrival of Christianity

The first encounters of the Christians of Constantinople with the Russians were not encouraging. In 860, boats from Russia sailed down the Dnieper River, crossed the Black Sea into the Bosphorus and appeared before the walls of Constantinople. Patriarch Photius (810–91) tells how the people were terrified by the red hair, incomprehensible shouts and wild clothing of these invaders. But further encounters followed and in due course these wild invaders were to become a great Christian nation. Moscow became the capital city of Russia and claimed to be the third Rome, succeeding to the city of Constantinople as the centre of the Eastern Christian world.[1]

Christianity spread into these wild northern lands. There are several references to this infiltration of the Christian faith. Patriarch Photius dispatched a bishop, said to be called Michael, to make contact with the khagan or leader in the northern settlement of Gorodische, which was later to become the city of Novgorod, but we do not know what resulted from this bold missionary initiative. Discoveries of Byzantine coins in the area of Novgorod confirm these early contacts. There were also communities of Christians further south in a diocese at Tmutakaran, a city on the peninsula between the Black and Azov Seas, which was then a principality dependent on Kiev. In this period merchants travelled from Kiev to Constantinople, bringing slaves, furs, wax and honey, which they traded for silks and other luxury goods. Russians settled in Constantinople and established a place where Russian visitors could lodge. One of these trading delegations arrived in 957 and included the Russian princess, Olga, widow of Igor and mother of Svyatoslav. She was welcomed by Emperor Constantine VII (945–59) and was baptized, taking the name Helena.

These early encounters led Olga's grandson, Vladimir, to follow her example. He was baptized and in 989 married Anna, the sister of another emperor Basil II (976–1025). The colour and drama of Byzantine church life is recorded in a famous passage of the Primary Chronicle written in the eleventh century. Vladimir had sent envoys to research the various faiths of the world in order to decide which should become the faith of Russia. They were not impressed either by Judaism or by Western forms of Christianity. Then they were taken to the Haghia Sophia in Constantinople. They were amazed. 'We knew not whether we were in heaven or on earth. For on earth there is no such splendour or such beauty, and we are at a loss how to describe it. We only know that there God dwells among men.'² When she went to her new home in Kiev, Anna took with her clergy, monks and scholars from Constantinople. They brought the new Slavonic translations of the Bible and other texts made by Cyril and Methodius a century earlier, which made the Christian faith accessible. Constantinople was near enough for good relations to be maintained but far enough away for any military threat to be avoided.

The first Russian monasteries were founded as a result of this cultural meeting. Russians found their way to Mount Athos. We hear of a monastery 'tou Rhos' (of the Russians) in 1016. This was probably Xylourgou which is referred to as a Russian settlement at that period.³

One of these Russian travellers was a young man from Chernigov, just to the east of Kiev, who was called Antipas. He became a monk at the monastery of Esphigmenou and was given the name of Anthony. He returned to his homeland in 1051 and settled in a cave overlooking the river Dnieper. He was joined by others and in 1062 the monastery of Kievo-Pecherskaya, the Kiev Monastery of the Caves, was founded, 'with the blessing of and in accordance with the statutes of the Holy Mountain', as noted by the Primary Chronicle. Anthony himself stayed in his cave, which was, he himself admitted, 'dark and narrow' and, since he wanted to preserve his solitude, he arranged for others to care for the monks.⁴ The first superior was a monk called Barlaam, who was succeeded by Theodosius. Theodosius established the monastic rule. He identified a suitable space for a church and obtained a copy of the Stoudite typikon from a friend in Constantinople which he arranged to be read to the monks. Theodosius's life was later written by Nestor a monk of the monastery.

Nestor praised Theodosius's humility. As a boy he refused to wear new clothes and always wore old and patched garments; he preferred the simple work of a peasant; he devoted himself when young to making bread for the liturgy, a task which shocked his mother as being especially demeaning; he ate simple food; he slept sitting down. He was friendly with the prince Isiaslav and on one occasion went to visit him. The prince arranged for Theodosius to ride back in a carriage and, on the journey, the boy who was leading the carriage complained bitterly that this badly dressed monk should be in the carriage rather than himself. Theodosius allowed the boy to ride in the carriage until they approached the monastery when he told the boy to get out of the carriage so as not to be criticized by the monks, and then invited him to be given food and drink and then gave him some money. The boy was deeply embarrassed when he discovered the identity of the passenger who he had displaced.⁵

The monastery of the Caves was a success and became a seedbed of Byzantine Christianity in Russia. It produced a supply of bishops, scholars and icon painters. People of all classes became monks and before long there were over a hundred monks. From this beginning in the monastery of the Caves, further foundations were made. These were usually founded by rich landowners and were built in or around cities. Monks were required to contribute money or lands on joining. At this early stage, the style of early Russian monastic life was urban and aristocratic.

From the beginning, the Church of Russia was closely connected to the Church of Constantinople. Bishops were appointed by the ecumenical patriarch, Russians lived in Constantinople and correspondence passed freely. Monks and other clergy were able to travel to the monasteries of Athos, Constantinople and the Holy Land. Patriarch Philotheos, writing to the Grand Prince Dmitri in 1370, described himself as 'common father, established by the most high God, of all Christians found everywhere on earth' and in 1393 Patriarch Anthony IV commented in another letter to Russia during a controversy over whether the emperor in Constantinople should be commemorated in the liturgy, that 'it is not possible for Christians to have the church and not to have the empire ... the emperor is not as other rulers and is elected king of all Romans, that is of all Christians'.[6] The Church of Russia continued to be dependent on Constantinople until 1588 when the Metropolitan of Moscow was given the title of Patriarch and the Church of Russia became autocephalous.

Russian Spirituality

Russia followed the worship and the traditions of the Church of Constantinople. But as the Orthodox Church took root, Russian spirituality developed characteristics of its own. Northern Russia was not only distant from the Mediterranean and Middle East, where until now Orthodox Christianity had been nurtured, but it had different cultural and religious traditions. The interaction between the cultures of Constantinople and Moscow produced new perceptions of the nature of God and understandings of the spiritual life. Much has been written about this, trying to capture that elusive spirit of Russian Christianity. While conclusions can be at best provisional, they do at least point to some guidelines and directions which help us approach and appreciate the special character and emotional depth of Russian spirituality.

Faith is expressed in the feelings and sensations of those who follow it. People combine the fresh with the familiar, the new with the old. This leads to a mixture of old tradition and new faith. The term *duoverie* or duality of faith has been used to describe that mixing of traditional pagan religious instincts and Christian gospel in early Russian Christianity. Within the pre-Christian religion of Russia, there was a reverence for the earth which is personified as female. She is described as moist-mother-earth, a term which evokes fertility and motherhood. Dmitry Pospielovsky gives the example of Raskolnikov, the central character in Dostoevsky's novel *Crime and Punishment*, who kneels to kiss the earth, the source of life, as atonement for his crime of murder. Pospielovsky connects moist-mother-earth with Russian veneration of the Virgin Mary, where there is greater emphasis on the Motherhood of Mary rather than her Virginity. He goes on to suggest that this has given a distinct ethical character to Russian Christianity. 'The mother taught ... kindness and fidelity, not freedom and valour – the male virtues'.[7]

This sense of the earth as mother and the emphasis on the qualities of kindness and care suggests how some of the features of Russian spirituality took shape. Running through the Russian idea of holiness is humility, or kenoticism. Nestor, the author of the *Life of Theodosius*, wrote another work of hagiography describing the life and death of the two princes Boris and Gleb, who were killed during civil strife between 1015 and 1019. They were sons of Vladimir and their brother Sviatapolk – known as Sviatapolk the Accursed – grasped the throne and then proceeded to kill first Boris then Gleb.

The brothers were warned that he was planning their deaths but chose to accept their fate with patience and humility. While the historical circumstances are confused, the story of their lives presents a hagiographical model of patience and acceptance of martyrdom. They were the first Russian saints to be canonized. It was objected in Constantinople that they were not true martyrs because they did not die for their faith but were victims of war. The Russian view prevailed and those who accepted suffering are as Passion Bearers which became a prototype of saintly behaviour. Humility was to become a recurrent theme of Russian literature, and so the idea of kenoticism, or humility, can be applied to the lives of many of the saints.

Later Sergius of Radonezh chose to live in the inaccessible forest rather than the town. His life contains narratives which show his kenotic humility. One section tells how he worked all day to improve the cell of a fellow monk and received only a few pieces of mouldy bread as payment; another describes a visitor who came to meet the famous monk who he found working in the garden wearing in old clothes so the visitor did not believe that this is Sergius and complained that he has been shown an indigent beggar. One outcome of the self-effacement is that we know little of many of the monastic saints. They chose obscurity rather than fame; quietness rather than activity and did not write about themselves or allow others to do so.

The response of Vladimir's messengers to the beauty of the liturgy of Constantinople points to another characteristic. The northern monasteries of Trinity-Sergius and Kirillov contain large libraries. There were three hundred manuscripts at Trinity and 212 at Kirillov. These libraries included a large collection of Byzantine ascetical writings by John of the Ladder, Isaac of Nineveh, Dorotheos, Symeon the New Theologian and many more. But there was no theology. The standard patristic works of the Cappadocian Fathers, Cyril of Alexandria and the theological works of Maximus the Confessor are absent. In 1516 the grand prince Basil III of Moscow asked for a Greek monk to be sent to Russia to help people read the Greek manuscripts and to translate them into Slavonic, since these were so little known. The mission was entrusted to a monk of Mount Athos named Maximus, known as Maksim Grek in Russian. He had formerly been a Dominican friar and had studied at Florence and Venice before becoming a monk at Vatopedi. He found the task entrusted to him to be a sensitive and difficult commission and he ended up imprisoned for twenty-three years.

There seems to have been little interest in philosophical theology and instead Russians were sensitive to the beauty of liturgy, music and painting. The divine was expressed in light, image and form. The icon painter Andrei Rublev painted his icon of the Trinity for the new wooden church built to contain the relics of St Sergius in 1422. David Miller in his account evokes the sense of the wonder of 'the two dozen monks and their visitors who gathered in the small stuffy church and wondered at the icon illuminated with candles occupying a space to the right of the holy doors …. with the three figures bathed in the uncreated light of God', and in this image art critics have noted that 'the inclination of the bodies and heads of the three figures formed the arc of a circle uniting them in an ideally perfect form'.[8] The short sentence of Dostoevsky is often quoted, that 'beauty will save the world'.[9]

These qualities of gentleness, humility and sensitivity to beauty made the Russian monks receptive to the new movement of hesychasm which was arriving from

Constantinople. The acceptance of the hesychast teachings of Gregory Palamas led to a new emphasis on prayer and the inner life. It gave encouragement to the monks and provided a framework for their lives of silence and obscurity. This form of prayer gave the body as well as the mind a place in prayer and taught how divine light can shine through the physical. 'The hesychasts restored the notion of body as a God-created vessel of the spirit and taught that human spirituality can be achieved only in a harmony between the spirit and the body, controlling the latter by the spirit but not mortifying the body. The highest mystical experience is the vision of the uncreated light of God achieved through prayer, spiritual concentration and asceticism.'[10]

Sergius of Radonezh

The monasteries grew in number, size and influence. It is estimated that by the early thirteenth century There were twelve monasteries in Kiev, twenty in Novgorod and more in the surrounding area, amounting to a total of seventy throughout the country.[11] Then the Mongols invaded. Vladimir was sacked in 1238 and, after that, Kiev was seized. Many people died from hunger or disease and southern Russia was depopulated as people fled north. While it was a tragedy for Russia, the churches escaped the worst of the impact. In 1279 Metropolitan Cyril III negotiated with the Mongols for the Church to be given a *jarlik* or imperial decree which guaranteed the privileges of the Church and granted further benefits; forbade any confiscation of church property; exempted it from taxation; and also freed clergy from the burden of compulsory state service. The growth of the Church was able to continue through the Mongol period.

The beginnings of a distinctively Russian form of monastic life came with the life and witness of Sergius of Radonezh (1314–92).[12] Bartholomew, or Varfolomei, was born to devout parents, from Rostov who moved to Radonezh nearer Moscow following the loss of their fortune in their home town. His early life follows a pattern familiar from saints' lives. While in the womb he leapt for joy at the mention of the Holy Trinity, then as a boy he was given a miraculous gift of learning when a passing monk prayed and so bestowed on him the ability of being able to read the psalms and other parts of the service. After the death of his parents, Bartholomew and his brother Stephen went to a place by a stream in the centre of the forest and there built themselves a hut and a chapel. Stephen found the life too hard and went to live in the Bogoyavlensky Monastery in Moscow where he eventually became abbot. Bartholomew meanwhile remained living as a hermit for two years. He made friends with a bear with whom he shared his meals of bread, sometimes denying himself even that modest food so that the bear did not go short. He became a monk and took the name Sergius, and as his fame spread others joined him so that there were twelve companions. In 1354 he was ordained priest and formed his group of monks into a monastic community. Life was hard in the forests. There were occasions when food ran out but on one occasion an unexpected gift of fresh warm bread arrived at the monastery gate when the situation was desperate. Sometimes there was no wine to celebrate the liturgy and in place of candles there was a single wooden torch. His monastery was dedicated to the Holy

Trinity and remained a centre of prayer and pilgrimage. After a life of prayer and struggle the saint died in 1392.

One night Sergius had a vision of flocks of birds flying in the air with a voice from heaven telling him that 'as many birds as you see, by so many will your flock of disciples increase, and after your time they will not decrease if they follow in your footsteps'. He quickly called another monk called Simon from a nearby cell who saw the bright light as it declined. This prophetic vision was fulfilled as further monasteries were founded either by Sergius or by his disciples or by those inspired by him. The recent biographer of many of these saints has seen the forests of northern Russia as a Northern Thebaid, corresponding to the name given to early monastic settlements in Egypt.[13]

Some of these monasteries were established by Sergius himself. On one occasion, some monks grumbled about Sergius. He immediately left the monastery and made his way to a place called Makhra and here he founded a monastery which was dedicated to the Annunciation. The disaffected monks regretted their remarks and begged him to return. After the new monastery church was consecrated and an abbot chosen, Sergius returned.[14] The chronicles tell of a further eight monasteries which he founded.

One of Sergius's disciples was Cyril of White Lake or Beloozerski. He came from Moscow and became a monk at the Simonov monastery where the nephew of Sergius was abbot. He worked in the bakery, and when Sergius visited his nephew he used to seek out the young Cyril and spend time with him. After some years Cyril left to seek a more remote place and, guided by Sergius, settled on the shores of the White Lake. He built a hut and a church dedicated to the Dormition of the Mother of God. His Kirillov-Beloozerski monastery became a centre of hesychastic prayer, known for its remote location and ascetic discipline. It became the second largest monastery in Russia, after Sergius's Trinity monastery. From White Lake the monks went even further north. Nothing is known of the background of the monk Sabbatius of Cyril's monastery until he set out from the monastery in 1429 and made his way to the White Sea in the far north. Here he was told about the islands of Solovki, which were uninhabited and could only be reached by boat in calm weather after two days sailing. This remoteness was an invitation for the ascetic and so Sabbatius and a companion Germanus made the journey to the island and lived there for six years. Sabbatius died on the island in 1435 and then in the following year Germanus returned with another monk called Zossima and together they established a monastery.

The settlement at Solovki opened up new possibilities for colonizing this remote area. It became a centre of trading and commerce and a strategically important base in the far north. By the seventeenth century there were 350 monks and also 700 servants and peasants. Later, in Soviet times, it gained a new and regrettable notoriety as a prison camp in which many monks and other faithful ended their lives.

Although Sergius lived in the forest and followed a simple life style, he was also involved in ecclesiastical and political life. As the reputation of the monastery grew, it became known to the Church in Constantinople. Visitors brought a letter from Patriarch Philotheos in which he said that he had heard about the monastery and advised Sergius to establish it as a coenobium. This change in the nature of the monastery took place in 1374 and turned out to be a pivotal moment in the history of Russian monasticism, as it led to further growth and to the monastery becoming the centre of popular church life. Three years later Metropolitan Alexei died and both he, before his death, and the prince, after it, tried to persuade Sergius to become Metropolitan of Moscow. He refused. The eventual appointee, Cyprian, wrote to Sergius and to his nephew Theodore, who was abbot of the Simonov monastery in Moscow, to gain their help in negotiating with Lithuania and Moscow who were competing for power. So Sergius became an advisor in political as well as ecclesiastical affairs.

Sergius of Radonezh has come to be recognized as the protector and patron saint of the Russian nation. His fame had spread quickly. A monk of his monastery, Epiphanius the Wise, wrote the life of the saint and expanded it with a growing number of accounts of miracles and stories in the succession of editions. This work was then taken further by Pachomius the Serb, another monk at the monastery, who added a list of posthumous miracles by the saint after his death. These hagiographers described the saint's role in the battle of Kulikovo Field in 1380. This is one of the events which grew in significance through these successive versions of the *Life*. The later versions describe how Mamai, a determined Muslim fundamentalist Mongol, set out to attack Russia. The prince Dmitri came to the monastery to ask Sergius what he should do. Sergius told him that, since he had the responsibility to care for his people, he should go to protect them against the enemy. When he arrived and saw the superior numbers of the enemy, he lost heart, at which point a messenger arrived from Sergius giving encouragement and blessing. Dmitri prevailed, and the blessing of Sergius on the army was recognized as giving divine protection and success to the army.

Sergius's successor as abbot, Nikon, built a new church in 1422. He adorned it with Rublev's famous icon of the Trinity and transferred Sergius's body to the church and found, when the grave was opened, that the body of the saint was uncorrupted and exuded a sweet perfume. Pachomius included in his life the vision in which the Mother of God appeared to Sergius and another monk to show herself as the protector of the monastery. Sergius's cult spread and he became revered as the patron saint of Russia.

The monasteries of Russia continued to grow steadily in both size and number. Figures show that 150 new monasteries were set up in the fourteenth century, 250 in the fifteenth century and 320 in the sixteenth century. Not all survived and so it is estimated that there were over five hundred monasteries in Russia by the end of the sixteenth century. In addition, there were a large number of hermitages and sketes. Monasteries were growing not only in number but also in size, wealth and influence in the community. Especially in frontier and marginal areas, monasteries were centres of economic and cultural life, providing a market place for trade, opportunities for education and care in times of need. In times of famine the larger monasteries arranged huge feeding programmes. The St Cyril or Kirillov monastery at the White Lake fed seven hundred people a day and the Paphnutiev monastery fed a thousand. Not surprisingly, peasants moved to live near the monasteries hoping for a better life. Wealthy landowners made donations of money and even of whole villages, so that monasteries became wealthy landowners. And it was this that led to trouble.

Figure 15 In Russia the monastery of St Sergius to the north east of Moscow has remained a centre of church life. The relics of the saint attract many pilgrims.

Figure 16 The blessing of the troops of Dmitri Donskoi as they set out to battle against the Tartars by St Sergius contributed to his recognition as patron saint of Russia.

Possessors and Non-Possessors

There were two styles of and approaches to monastic life in medieval Russia. Both wanted to return to the roots of monastic and ascetic struggle but they took different routes, which corresponded to the two kinds of monastic life which had been practised from the beginning. Each of the two strands of reform was associated with a leading theologian, each was associated with a different area and, while in other parts of the Christian world these two approaches were able to co-exist and support each other, in Russia they diverged and clashed. Eventually one prevailed and the other became marginalized but not removed. This was the conflict between the Possessors and Non-Possessors.

The Non-Possessors were the monks who followed the example of Sergius in moving to remote and lonely places in the northern forests. Many settled in the areas to the north of the Volga River and so were also known as the trans-Volga elders. Their approach to monastic life was set out in the teaching of Nilus of Sora. Nilus (1433–1508) came from a noble family called Maikov and became a monk at the Kirillov monastery at White Lake. He became frustrated by the life there, writing to a friend 'I did not see the preservation of the way of life according to God's law and the traditions of the Fathers but rather a life according to one's own will and human ideas, and many there were also who, acting in such a corrupt way, imagined that they were living a virtuous life'.[15] And so, like Anthony of Kiev and others, he went to Mount Athos where there was a Russian community at Xylourgou and then on to Constantinople, where he lived for several years. Here he read the classics of the ascetic life which included not only the accounts of the fathers of the desert by John of the Ladder and John Cassian, but also the writings of the Hesychasts, Gregory Palamas and Gregory of Sinai. He also discovered the skete life, where a few monks lived near each other combining the solitary life of the hermit with times of communal prayer. He returned to Russia in 1478 bringing these ideas with him and went back to White Lake. He settled in a desolate marshy area by the river Sora about ten miles from the White Lake monastery. Here he built a hut and dug a well. Later when others joined him he built two wooden churches and a mill. He preferred obscurity to fame and so we know little of his life. At his death, he left a will and testament.

> I pray you, cast away my body in the desert, to be devoured by the beasts and birds, for that body has greatly sinned before God and is unworthy of burial. If you will not do this, then dig a pit on the grounds where we live and bury me in it with every kind of dishonour ... I beg all to pray for my sinful soul and I beg forgiveness for everyone and may there be forgiveness also from me, may God forgive us all.[16]

Nilus wrote a rule and direction for the monks. It consists of eleven sections which describe inner prayer and presents the teachings he had soaked himself in on the holy mountain. It begins with an analysis of demonic temptation and inner struggle, describing a four-stage process by which evil becomes rooted in the soul, beginning with the soul being faced with thoughts of evil and progressing to these becoming ingrained passions. He also discusses the eight main temptations, as earlier described by Evagrius and John Cassian.¹⁷ A large part of this short work is devoted to the Jesus Prayer, as the way to counter the attacks of the demons. His advice covers posture and breathing as well as the words to be used in prayer, and also suggests that the recitation be balanced with singing psalms and reading. He describes a state beyond prayer, which is a spiritual union, for which no one knows the name. It is illumination with uncreated light, infusion with joy, paralysis of the tongue and 'he thinks that this is indeed the kingdom of God and can be nothing else'.¹⁸

This is the purpose of monastic life. There is little about ordering the monastery, beyond the need for simplicity. There should be no possessions or property, which would detract from the concentration on inner prayer. A passage warns the monks against the practice of giving alms. 'As for giving alms or lending this is not expected of a monk.' The reason for this advice is not hardness of heart or ungenerosity but simply that the monk should not have anything which can be disposed of, so this virtue is not applicable. He wrote that 'a true monk is dispensed from alms giving since they can honestly say "we have given up all things to follow thee" … the monk's alms are a helpful word spoken to a brother or spiritual advice with which he gives comfort'.¹⁹ And in writing this he would have had in mind the alternative method of monastic reform in which the possession of goods by the monastery was a good to be desired.

The Possessors looked to the example of Joseph, or Iosif, of Volokolamsk (1439 or 1440–1515). Joseph was born to a poor family in the town of Volokolamsk around 120 km northwest of Moscow. In contrast to Nilus, who was reticent about his personal life, Joseph's monks have left us a full record of his life with three hagiographers writing his life.²⁰ He became a monk at the monastery of Paphnutiev, which had been founded by a follower of Sergius. When Abbot Paphnutius died, Joseph was chosen to succeed him, but controversy soon arose, perhaps because of his plan to follow a coenobitic rule and ensure that all property was held in common. So Joseph left and went to the Kirillov monastery, where Nilus had also spent a while, and then returned briefly to Paphnutiev. In 1479 he found a spot where two rivers met near his home town of Volokolamsk. He was, so his life tells us, guided to the place by a fisherman who was carried to it by a whirlwind and then lightning struck on a clear sunny day and church bells were heard. Within a week of his arrival he had started work on the construction of a wooden church which was completed in just seven weeks. Then he built the refectory, bakery and cells. A stone church followed in 1484 and over the next twenty years further stone buildings extended the monastery. The support of local people made this rapid growth possible. The prince gave Joseph a village and some hamlets and then ten more villages were given and the monastery became a wealthy landowner.

Joseph recognized that the monastery had an important place in the community and especially had a responsibility to care for the poor. He exhorted landlords to be gentle and just; he built an orphanage for children left at the monastery gates; and also a second monastery to be an infirmary. He instructed the monks to buy enough food so that no one who came in need should be sent away hungry. Sometimes he used all the food on feeding those in need, so that the monks had nothing to eat and complained. His response was to tell them to pray, at which point carts arrived with gifts of grain and so the stocks were replenished.²¹ In times of famine the monastery fed seven hundred people a day.

Joseph wrote two rules. One was shorter, and was written around 1504, when the monastery was well established, and then he followed this with an expanded version ten years later, shortly before he died. The rules consist of a series of chapters on different topics. First there are regulations governing the prayer in church, then the food in the refectory, silence, clothing and then sections on further aspects of community life. The main part of each section is a series of extracts from the fathers, followed by some practical instruction about how these should be applied. Some of the instructions, especially in the extended later rule, are very specific. In the chapter on food, there are directions on how many dishes should be provided and on which days; when fish can be eaten; and which monks should eat two dishes and which monks are allowed to have three. This precise regulation of life has resulted in Joseph being judged as harsh and disciplinarian. However, while life in the monastery was certainly austere, the rules give insight into the methods of an abbot who is determined to put into practice the way of monastic life as practised by the fathers of the church and applies these to specific circumstances.[22]

The Rules also show how his attitude to property developed. For Nilus, it was easy. The monk lived a simple life. He only had what he needed. But Joseph's communities were larger and required money, property and resources to carry out their lives of service and to continue their worship and study. He was clear that the monk should not own personal possessions. 'He who desires to be worthy of divine grace ... must have perfected non-possession and Christ-like poverty'. So in the monastery, clothes and food are regulated and issued by the abbot. In the Longer Rule he allowed the use of coins, books and handicraft materials and money.[23] On the institutional level, he recognized the need for possessions and income. This enabled the monastery to arrange dignified liturgy, carry out scholarship and provide charitable support for those in need. Within the monastery the principle governing the life is not poverty, but obedience.

He also realized that there should be some flexibility. He prescribed three orders, or levels, of monastic rigour. This allowed for some monks to aspire to a more ascetic discipline, but others to live a more relaxed life with a change of clothes and a little more food.

Both Joseph and Nilus were reformers in the tradition of Sergius. Joseph's monastery and those which followed his example were communal monasteries or coenobia, teaching obedience, caring for the poor and acting as centres for charitable work. In contrast, Nilus and the trans-Volga elders lived in small groups and followed lives of inner prayer. For Joseph, 'externally ascetic deeds and a wide activity take that place which Nilus devotes to prayer of the mind'.[24] For a while the two monastic leaders seem to have worked together. When faced with a Judaizing heresy, they collaborated on a book attacking these beliefs, called the *Enlightener*, with, some historians suggest, Nilus being the author of the opening section.[25] So these two ways of living both emerge out of St Sergius monasteries and both follow traditional but alternative paths of monastic living.

Conflict arose out of their responses to a set of historical circumstances. In 1487 the new archbishop of Novgorod, Gennadii, was troubled by an outburst of heresy. Gennadii's account tells how a Jew named Skharia or Zechariah and two merchant companions argued with some of the clergy of Novgorod. They persuaded the clergy that the New Testament teaching of the divinity of Christ contradicted the Old Testament message of the unity of God. This led them to reject the Trinity, the divinity of Christ who they considered to be a prophet in the Old Testament style, as well as icons, crosses, monasticism and some other teachings of the Church. This Judaizing teaching spread. Judaizing priests were appointed to two Kremlin cathedrals in Moscow and the prince Ivan's chief diplomat Theodore Kuritsyn promoted these ideas in the court. Then in 1490, Zossima, a Judaizer, was appointed Metropolitan of Moscow. To call this Judaistic may be inaccurate since it does not seem to have been connected with the Jewish communities in Ukraine and other areas, but was more likely to have been an anti-clerical social movement. It was reacting against the medieval autocratic church and affirming the kind of rationalistic intellectual ideas which were popular in Moscow but aroused strong opposition from the more traditional church community in Novgorod. It may have been connected with early Protestant movements in the West.[26]

Joseph responded to the Judaizers with a series of writings which asserted the doctrines of the Trinity and Incarnation, the value of ritual including iconography and the tradition of the fathers. His main work, the *Enlightener*, has been recognized as the first book of theology to come out of Russia. In addition to writing against the heresy, he and Metropolitan Gennadii led a series of actions against the heretics, with synods at Moscow in 1490 and 1504 trying and convicting Judaizing heretics. One of their supporters in Novgorod was a Croat Dominican friar called Benjamin who had been invited by Metropolitan Gennadii to assist with a Slavonic version of the Bible. Benjamin had been in Spain and was able to share information about the methods being followed by the Inquisition. Throughout the trials, Joseph demanded severe penalties. At the Moscow Synod of 1504, several of the accused were sentenced to death although only six were actually executed. Others were imprisoned in monasteries. Joseph objected to the use of monasteries as places of imprisonment, in case those incarcerated spread their heretical teachings among the monks. He wanted them to be sent to prisons instead. He also argued against forgiveness for those who repented. Vassian Patrikeev, a disciple of Nilus, had a different approach. He protested against the death penalty and wanted a compassionate and merciful approach. He followed the teaching approach of Nilus who preferred that a heretic should be re-educated, sent away while he re-considered and then welcomed back like the prodigal son.

The second cause of conflict was monastic landowning. This is also reported to have been debated at the 1504 synod. When the prince Ivan III invaded and occupied Novgorod, he confiscated Church and monastic lands in order to give them as reward to his supporters. This sequestration was approved by the trans-Volga elders, the Non-Possessors, who opposed the acquisition of villages by monasteries, but Joseph, and probably also Serapion abbot of the Trinity-Sergius monastery, wrote in defence of monastic land. They said that property should not be taken from the monasteries since lands were needed to carry out the charitable work of the monasteries. They also pointed out that the possession of villages was necessary to attract noble and well-born monastic recruits who were necessary for the well-being of the monastery and of society more generally.

Political changes brought a resolution. Ivan III supported the Non-Possessors but was succeeded by his son Basil III who supported the Possessors. Nilus died in 1508 and Vassian Patrikeev was tried for heresy in 1531. The Possessors had won and the Non-Possessors retired to their sketes beyond the Volga. The trans-Volga elders quietly carried on a life of withdrawal in sketes and hermitages in the forests of the north. Meanwhile, the coenobia of the Possessors had the support of government and kept their villages, serfs and property. They provided charitable care and support to many in need and they remained close to the government in combating heresy and dissent. The eremitical and coenobitic strands of monastic life diverged.

Church and state

The success of the Possessors had a lasting effect. It allowed and encouraged the growth of large monasteries, with extensive lands and wealth and an active part in social and educational activities. Good relations with the state and those with power benefitted the monasteries which received generous benefactions from them. But the greater the benefits, the more vulnerable the monasteries became. Land ownership led to a mutual dependency, which could lead either to co-operation or to conflict. Compromise and threat to the well-being of the monasteries was the result. Some would claim that this placed the church in a destructive dependency on the state with disastrous consequences in centuries to come. While we should not trace the origins of the Communist atheist programme back to the Possessor conflict, this onslaught came at the end of a history of a tension between the monasteries and the governing powers.

Joseph taught that religious and secular, church and state, archbishop and king were ordained by God and were called to work together to build a godly society. This follows earlier teaching in the Byzantine Empire. Nicholas Cabasilas, writing in the fourteenth century, had pointed out that both priest and king are anointed with holy oil and so both offices 'have the same intent and the same power'.[27] Following this understanding of government, Joseph held that the state was the representative of God and was put in place to carry out the divine will within society. Joseph expected the government to punish heretics and to support the monasteries, but he was aware that this was a dangerous doctrine and so he addressed the question of what happens if the state does not support the church. He wondered about the situation of a tsar who was not God-fearing and respectful to the church. 'Should a tsar fall prey to ugly passions and sins .... and even worse want of faith and slander – such a tsar is not God's but the devil's servant ... thou shouldst not fulfil such a tsar's orders'.[28] This led to an ambiguity in Joseph's position – and a danger. The active involvement of the church in society, as lived out by the Possessors, required them to engage with the political life of the nation. This meant a partnership of the 'two swords', the spiritual and the secular. 'But', as Pospielovsky puts it, 'the physical sword would sooner or later vanquish over the spiritual sword, and this would eventually deprive the Church as institution of any sword'.[29]

This tension quickly showed itself and relations with the prince soon became difficult. Metropolitan Varlaam (1511–21) condemned Basil III for killing his rival princes and he was then dispatched by Basil to retirement in a monastery. Daniel, Joseph's successor as abbot of Volokolamsk and so a Possessor monk, was the next Metropolitan. He gave his support to the prince. When Basil III, in a further high-handed action, placed his allegedly barren wife Solomonia in a convent and married again in order to gain an heir, Metropolitan Daniel accepted this while the ecumenical patriarch, the monks of Athos and other Russian bishops condemned the action. Metropolitan Daniel remained loyal.

Conclusion

The controversy between Possessors and Non-Possessors is an indication of the richness and variety of monastic life in Russia. Monasteries spread over a wide area of this huge country. They were present in the cities of Moscow, Kiev and elsewhere; they flourished in the far north; they also helped to extend the Christian faith eastward into Asia and eventually to Alaska and so into the United States. After the great cities of the Middle East were conquered by Arabs and then Constantinople fell to the Ottoman Turks, Russia became an increasingly important centre of Church, and so monastic, life.

Notes

1. Judith Herrin, *Byzantium* (London, 2007), p. 137.
2. A passage which is often quoted, for example, in John Meyendorff, *Byzantium and the Rise of Russia* (New York, 1989), p. 5, and more fully in trans. S. H. Cross and O. P. Sherbowitz-Wetzor, *The Russian Primary Chronicle* (Cambridge, MA, 1953), p. 111.
3. See Nicholas Fennell, *Russians on Athos* (Bern, 1901), pp. 51–5.
4. For the 'dark and narrow' cave see G. P. Fedotov, *A Treasury of Russian Spirituality* (London, 1910), p. 21.
5. Ibid., p. 34.
6. Meyendorff, *Byzantium and the Rise of Russia*, pp. 103, 116.
7. Dmitry Pospielovsky, *The Orthodox Church in the History of Russia* (New York, 1998), p. 24.
8. David Miller, *Saint Sergius of Radonezh* (de Kalb, IL, 2010), pp. 44–5.
9. Dostoevsky places these words in the mouth of the naïve and innocent prince Myshkin in his novel *The Idiot*.
10. Pospielovsky, *Orthodox Church*, p. 42.
11. These figures are in Sergius Bolshakoff, *Russian Mystics* (Kalamazoo, MI, and London, 1977), p. 9.
12. The Lives of Sergius were written by monks of his monastery, Epifanii the Wise and Pakhomii. There is an abbreviated version in G. P. Fedotov, *Treasury of Russian Spirituality* (London, 1950), pp. 55–84, and a fuller version in Michael Klimenko, *The 'Vita' of St Sergii of Radonezh* (Houston, TX, 1980).
13. The title of a modern hagiography by Ivan Kontzevich, *The Northern Thebaid, Monastic Saints of the Russian North* (Platina, CA, 1973). For the episode with the birds see Fedotov, *Treasury*, p. 73.

14 Ibid., pp. 74–5.
15 See Kontzevich, *Northern Thebaid*, p. 85.
16 Fedotov, *Treasury*, p. 89.
17 See below, p. 141.
18 Ibid., p. 104.
19 Ibid., p. 92.
20 For Joseph's life, see David Goldfrank, *The Monastic Rule of Iosif Volotsky* (Kalamazoo, MI, 1983), pp. 22–49.
21 Pospielovsky, *Orthodox Church*, p. 60.
22 The rules are translated in Goldfrank, *Monastic Rule*.
23 Joseph of Volokolamsk, *Discourse* III.18, III.21, in Goldfrank, p. 192.
24 See Pospielovsky, *Orthodox Church*, p. 59.
25 Ibid., p. 57.
26 For the bias of the sources, see Goldfrank, *Monastic Rule*, p. 33.
27 Nicholas Cabasilas, *Life in Christ* 3.1, trans. Carmino de Cantanzaro (New York, 1974), p. 103.
28 Pospielosvsky, *Orthodox Church*, p. 61.
29 Ibid., p. 62.

Part Four

The Meaning and Purpose of Monastic Life

12

Hesychasm from Origen to Gregory Palamas

Introduction

Arsenius was a monk at Scetis. He had been born in about 360 to a respectable senatorial family in Rome, received a good education and was appointed by the Emperor Theodosius I as tutor to the princes, Arcadius and Honorius. After taking the decision to become a monk he left Rome secretly and came to Egypt, where he adopted the simplest of lifestyles. A visitor met him and was surprised by this and asked him why he with such education in Greek and Latin culture asked advice of an elderly Egyptian peasant monk. 'I have indeed been taught Latin and Greek' Arsenius replied 'but I do not know even the alphabet of this peasant'.[1]

Monasteries were places of ascetic struggle and were populated by women and men who lived by different standards and had a different set of values from those of the city. They were suspicious of education and learning, which they associated with the world which they had left behind. They recognized the need to read and understand the Bible and other books but wanted to distinguish this form of knowledge from secular education.

One way of addressing the problem was to attribute the ability to read and write, and the knowledge this gave, to a special divine grace rather than a discipline of study. Abba Or, according to Sozomen, had the gift of memory so that 'everything he received in his mind was never afterwards forgotten' and when Cyril of Alexandria was studying the Bible as a monk 'it was enough for him to read a book once for him to know it by heart, until at the end of his stay in the desert he knew all the canonical books by memory'.[2]

Monks could not, however, rely on divine grace alone to grasp the teachings of the Bible. They needed to read the Bible. The daily routine of the monasteries of Pachomius included study of the Bible. The housemasters were required to give three lessons a week to the monks, on Saturdays and Sundays, and the second was to give a further two, on the fast days. The *Life of Pachomius* gives an engaging picture of the monks sitting under a tree at the end of the day's work discussing the meaning of passages of Scripture.[3]

Monks were encouraged to study Scripture, but their study developed in other directions too. As they lived and prayed, they were discovering a new way of living the Christian faith and forming a tradition of knowledge. Monks needed to understand what they were doing and why. So from the beginning they discussed, thought out and passed on an oral body of reflection and learning, which showed the nature and purpose of the ascetic and monastic life.

Monastic life was carried out in obedience to the spiritual father. Its aim is a personal knowledge of God in prayer. The ceaseless questions addressed to the fathers of the desert and the recalling of the teaching in a growing body of remembered, and then written, material show us the monks' thinking and learning what they should be doing and how they should be doing it. As they did this, they shared in forming a theological and anthropological tradition. It was marked by an acute psychological perception of how the human personality can thrive and manage its instincts and compulsions. It was also marked by an immediate and experiential experience of prayer. Lying behind this was a vision of God which invites the participation of the monk in the divine.

Origen

The two writers who, more than others, thought out and articulated the theory of monastic life were both anathematized as heretics. As a result, their influence was overlooked by later generations. Origen and Evagrius had described the aim and method of the monastic vocation, which for them could not be disentangled from the Christian vocation. All are called to live according to Christ and to come to knowledge of God.

Origen lived at the time before monastic life was taking shape as a distinctive form of living. He died soon after 250, about thirty-five years before Antony set out into the desert. As he preached, mostly in Caesarea in Palestine, he set out a vision of an ascetic lifestyle, which, as one commentator has summarized it, 'united the practices of (fasting and sexual abstinence) with a radical poverty and Scriptural meditation, to locate them within a single interpretative frame and in a single lifestyle'.[4] This approach to Christian living has had a huge influence. His writing was studied by Basil of Caesarea (330–79) who, in collaboration with his friend Gregory of Nazianzus (c. 329–90), studied the works of Origen and made a collection of extracts in the Philokalia.[5] Origen's approach also influenced Evagrius of Pontus and John Cassian, who transmitted it to the East and West, respectively.

Origen was born into a Christian family in Alexandria around 184. He was a brilliant scholar who was educated according to classical principles and also was a devout Christian. When he was 17, a period of persecution took place under the Emperor Septimius Severus (193–211). Origen encouraged his father to become a martyr and not worry about his wife and family. He wanted to follow his father, but his mother hid his clothes so he could not leave the house. Frustrated in this longing for martyrdom, instead he followed an ascetic lifestyle. He was 'careful to sleep never on a couch but on the floor'.[6] In 204, he became head of the catechetical school at Alexandria, at the young age of 19. He then gave up classical secular learning, sold his philosophical books and decided to set up a more advanced school. He has become celebrated for his voluntary castration, which was carried out when he was 20.[7] He did this both in order to follow the commendation in Matthew's gospel of those who 'made themselves eunuchs for the sake of the kingdom of heaven' and to avoid any suspicion of improper behaviour with the women who enrolled at this school.[8] We should not see this as a gory act of self-mutilation. The eunuch had a recognized place in society and we can assume that the operation was carried out by an experienced surgeon.

Origen was now famous and in demand as a teacher. He went to Rome, to Constantinople, to Caesarea and became involved in doctrinal debate and discussion, 'a one-man academic task force in various theological rows across the eastern Mediterranean'.[9] In Caesarea, people wanted him to preach to them and, since this was not permitted to a layman, he was ordained as a priest in 230. It was probably this ordination which led to his expulsion from the Church of Alexandria by the bishop Demetrios since a eunuch, seen as an incomplete and damaged human being, should not be a priest. Origen spent the rest of his life teaching in Caesarea, where he finally achieved the death of a martyr in the persecutions of Decius in 250. He was imprisoned, tortured and died soon after.

To grasp the motivation for Origen's thinking and why he aroused such controversy, provoking both admiration and emulation, and also opposition and hostility, we need to recognize the passion and enthusiasm of his approach. He was formed and educated in a world which was interpreted by a mixture of Platonist and Stoic philosophical ways of thinking. One of his teachers was probably Ammonius Saccas, a Platonist who also taught Plotinus. From these, the philosophy known as Neo-Platonism developed, which taught how to move beyond sceptical and dualist speculation and to reach out to the ultimate reality of God, who exists absolutely, apart from any notion of time or space.

He taught and lived as a faithful member of the church. 'O Church', he says in a sermon on the book of Joshua, 'If I who seem to be your right hand, bearing the name of priest and preaching the word of God, should ever offend against your canon and your rule of faith thus giving scandal, let then the Universal Church in unanimous accord cut off me, her right hand, and cast me away from her'.[10]

He taught that Christ, the Logos and Word of God, formed the world and fills it. Christ is everywhere but is especially encountered throughout Scripture. Because Christ is there in every part of the Bible, then the reader can search and explore each text to discover Christ, sacramentally present in it, moving from the literal historical meaning, to the moral guidance to faith and life, and then on to a deeper encounter with and knowledge of the living Christ. So Origen made a meticulous and detailed study of the Bible, collecting the various versions known to him in his massive six-columned version called the Hexapla. This included the text in Hebrew, with a Greek transliteration alongside it, then the Septuagint and three other versions known to him. It probably filled around forty manuscript books when complete, although only some parts have survived. This textual work went alongside his prayer, as he searched the texts which he researched and commented on to discover more of God's love in Christ which was contained with these pages of Scripture.

At the heart of his thinking is our need for transformation. The idea which lay behind his teaching on the spiritual life is the possibility of personal transformation, the call to it and the purpose of it. His understanding of the world and our place in it is set out in the *De Principiis*, or *On First Principles*, which survives only in the Latin translation of Rufinus. He struggled to make sense of the vision of the perfect unity of God and its contrast with the diversity, differences and divisions of the world of experience. He concluded that if we have fallen away from God, then it is because we made the choice to do so. The consequence of this is that we can also return to God if we choose to do so. Every spirit that was made was originally caught up in contemplation of the wonder and wisdom of God. Each being, whether angels, humans or demons, can only come from God. At first, they must have been united to God but, as free beings, chose what they became. Through a succession of freely made decisions these spiritual beings fell away from their origin. They became cold and more distant from the heat and light and life of God. Those who fell away a little are the angels, those who diverged more seriously are the demons, while those whose failure was less extreme became humans with souls and bodies. He explained that the Greek word for soul *psyche* is related to the word for becoming cool *psychesthai*. In his summary of Origen's thought Peter Brown writes:

> Compared with the fiery spirit that flickered upward, always straining to sink back into the primal fire of God, the conscious self was a dull thing, numbed by the cold absence of love. The baffling diversity of the present universe, marked on earth by an apparently infinite variety of human destinies was the end product of countless particular choices, by which each spirit had freely chosen to be what it was.[11]

The body then, in Origen's world view, has both a negative and positive character. The bodies which we inhabit have a double purpose. They are punishments for falling away, and so are prisons in which the spirit which had fallen from God has come to rest, marking the distance from God which those choices had finally taken it to. But they are also the location in which the spirit can learn, choose and return back to the God from whom it has fallen, and so are the opportunity for growth and transformation. And so 'a vast impatience', another of Peter Brown's phrases, runs through the universe.

Within this scheme there is one spiritual being which did not fall away, and that being became united with the soul of Christ, who is able to show us the way and lead us back to the union from which we originally fell. The final destination of this great journey is a restoration in which all beings will be re-united with God who made them.

For Origen the Christian life is a movement towards knowledge of God and union with him. In the sermons and commentaries, several ideas are presented. The sense of movement and progress makes the Christian life into a journey, which is the philosopher's search for truth and also the pilgrimage of the children of Israel into the Promised Land. It is a process of growth towards maturity in which we are nourished by the word of God brought by Christ, who provides milk for babes, vegetables for the weak and solid food for the mature, here using the categories referred to by Paul as he writes to the Corinthians.[12] It is also struggle and warfare, as the Christian obstinately persists in faith. Struggle was a feature of the lives of the martyrs and extends into all Christian life as well.

Origen's philosophy was controversial, and this led his condemnation as a heretic. As a result he is overlooked and has been censured out of the official narrative of the Church's doctrine. Yet his ideas and approach have influenced all who came after him, and the monastic life as it took shape cannot be understood without reference to the thinking of this great teacher. The later writer Cassiodorus used the image of seasoning of food. 'Certain men have said that (Origen) ought to be compared to aniseed for, though he seasons the food of sacred letters, he himself is thrown away when he has been boiled down and the juice extracted.'[13]

Evagrius

Origen's thinking was taken a stage further by Evagrius (345–99), who lived in the Egyptian desert monasteries of Nitria for two years and then in the more remote and solitary communities at Cellia for a further fourteen years. He came from Pontus in Asia Minor where his father was a landowner and also a *chorepiscop*, or assistant bishop.[14] He knew Basil and Gregory of Nazianzus, who also came from Pontus, and so would have been familiar with their work of collecting extracts from the writings of Origen and collating these into an anthology which they entitled the *Philokalia*.[15] He moved to Constantinople and energetically embraced the excitement and stimulation of life in the capital. He was ordained a deacon and preached. He was known to be 'hot headed in speeches against every heresy'.[16] He also enjoyed other aspects of life in the capital. He was well dressed and we are told that he changed his clothes twice a day and had such an extensive wardrobe that it took him a full day to pack, when he left the city, which he did rather hurriedly following a liaison with the wife of a nobleman.[17] He went to Jerusalem where he was welcomed by Melania, who was living in the monastery she had founded on the Mount of Olives. She welcomed men and women alike and formed it into a centre of hospitality and study. Palladius tells us that she was assiduous in study including working her way through three million lines of Origen's writings.[18] She received Evagrius who arrived in turmoil of mind and spirit following his tumultuous time at Constantinople. He fell ill, and Melania helped him back to fullness of health, making him promise to remain true to monastic life. He went to Egypt – this time with just a change of clothing given to him by Melania.

Here he remained. He was a disciple of the two monks both named Macarius, that is Macarius the Egyptian and Macarius the Alexandrian. In due course monks gathered around him too. He ate once a day, making a pound of bread and pint of oil last for three months, and slept just a few hours a night, walking around his compound to keep himself awake. When he received letters from family and friends he burned them without reading them. He avoided bathing, not least because he was concerned to avoid demonic temptation, 'for the demons frequently light on well-watered places'.[19] The Archbishop of Alexandria tried to persuade him to be bishop of Thmuis, but he ran away. The severity of his ascetic struggles may have contributed to his death at the young age of 55.

Evagrius became the centre of a group of monks who met and discussed with him. This is described in a passage in the Coptic life.

> The brothers would gather round him on Saturday and Sunday discussing their thoughts with him throughout the night, listening to his words of encouragement

until sunrise …. He encouraged them saying to them, My brothers, if one of you has either a profound or a troubled thought let him be silent until the brothers depart and let him reflect on it alone with me. Let us not make him speak in front of the brothers lest a little one perish on account of his thoughts and grief swallow him at a gulp.[20]

Their debates must have been lively and open and they would have encouraged each other in a speculative and creative approach to the ascetic and Christian life. The talk through the night hours gives an insight into how the practice of confession of thoughts could lead to daring and dangerous speculation which had to be handled with discretion and care. The teacher needed to regulate and care for the group protecting them from unsettling or psychologically disturbing ideas.

The work and contribution of Evagrius to spirituality East and West and to the life of the Church has been re-assessed in a process of discovery which was described in one study as a 'romance of modern scholarship'.[21] Since the Fifth Ecumenical Council at Constantinople in 553 decided that Evagrius, as well as Origen, was a dangerous heretic his works were largely destroyed, suppressed or lost in the years that followed. Some of the practical works continued to be read, such as the set of writings known as *Praktikos*, but otherwise his voluminous writings were thought to have disappeared. But in the course of the last century many have been rediscovered. Some had been preserved in Armenian and Syriac versions which were published in the early years of the twentieth century; some had been attributed to other authors but careful analysis shows them to be in fact written by Evagrius. The most important discovery was the Syriac text of the *Kephalia Gnostica*, or *Gnostic Chapters*, by Antoine Guillaumont. This enables us to assess the contribution of Evagrius and see how much he has influenced the practice of the monastic life. A shadowy figure known mainly by reputation as a dangerous heretic is now recognized as a creator of the Christian spiritual and mystical tradition.[22]

His ideas and approach are demonstrated most vividly in his series of 'chapters'. These are sets of short statements, grouped together in themes. They arise out of the practice of the desert, where a visitor would seek out a monk and ask for a piece of practical advice, or a word, as was reported in the *Sayings of the Desert Fathers*. Chapters were, by convention, grouped in sets of a hundred but this could vary. There are 153 sections of Evagrius's *Chapters on Prayer*, and he devotes a section to explaining the mathematical significance of this number, as well as it being the number of fish caught at the Resurrection appearance of Jesus by the lake. Among later writers who used the chapter form are Maximus the Confessor and Symeon the New Theologian, both of whom have sets of chapters in the *Philokalia* which are in the form of centuries.

The thinking of Evagrius is set out clearly in the three sets of chapters, the *Praktikos* dealing mainly with ascetic struggle; the *Gnostikos*, on knowledge of the world around and the *Kephalia Gnostica*, on higher forms of contemplation; and also in his 153 *Chapters on Prayer*.

His aim is to help the monk approach God. God, for Evagrius who had been educated according to a classical syllabus, is beyond time and space, is perfect unity and reality, is that from which all things have come. So, if the monk seeks to approach

God, then he has to leave all concepts, representations and thoughts behind and reach out to that God which is beyond. As well as rejecting these thoughts, however uplifting, because they are not God, he goes on to say they must be recognized as coming from demons. He counsels caution if a monk is afflicted by evil thoughts and then is consoled by peaceful and tranquil comforts, because this process of tribulation and consolation are both the result of demonic assault. Passages of the *Praktikos* analyse the subtle workings of these demons and have given Evagrius his reputation for acute psychological analysis. He identifies eight categories of thoughts, which are obstacles to achieving the stillness and peace which leads to God.[23]

These eight categories were adapted and reduced in number in the West to become the Seven Deadly Sins and became examples of actions or states of mind which would lead to condemnation. But for Evagrius, it was not so much an act of sin but rather a set of processes or psychological states which the monk had to address and to negotiate on the path to unity with God. Evagrius's thinking is shown in sections of the *Institutes* by Evagrius's disciple John Cassian.[24] The eight passions work in different ways. Gluttony arises out of the proper need of the body for nourishment and is an excessive response to this need; and lust is also a misuse of a natural instinct for procreation. Avarice is not a natural instinctive function of the body and is a demonic influence. Anger leads to spiritual blindness and lack of discrimination. Dejection and listlessness or *accidie* are an occupational hazard of the monk and come out of the ascetic struggles when the monk becomes discouraged and exhausted. Self esteem also can affect the monk and can arise out of satisfaction with ascetic achievement just as much as with worldly or material success. Pride pollutes everything. This analysis shows how the ascetic struggle is carried out, and the way that the teacher guides the soul.

The final end of the life of prayer is described as *apatheia*. The equivalent word of apathy is not a good translation because it suggests an absence of feeling and passion, whereas Evagrius's *apatheia* is an uprooting of passions which is spiritual freedom. The equivalent Latin word used by John Cassian means purity of heart. It engages all the personality, thoughts, emotions and physical disciplines. Feelings are a way towards it and Evagrius emphasizes the importance of tears in prayer, the sense of joy which prayer brings and the longing of the heart reaching towards God. There are three strands of this movement and ways to progress. There are, first, the practical disciplines of the ascetic life, of fasting, work, avoidance of sleep and moral virtue. Then there is the intellectual search for understanding of the true nature of the world around. Finally, there comes the resting and unity with God in contemplation or apatheia. The most quoted sentence in the history of Eastern spirituality is a summary of what lies behind Evagrius's thinking. 'If you are a theologian you will pray truly and if you pray truly you are a theologian.'[25]

Many of his ideas were followed by later writers and have shaped the Christian path of spirituality. As well as his ideas about the eight demonic thoughts; there are the need for loving not thinking; and the three ways of practical, intellectual and unitive progress.

Evagrius died in 399, and so avoided the outburst of controversy which arose in the following year.

Controversy

Controversy over the teaching of Origen and Evagrius arose soon after the death of Evagrius and continued intermittently for the following 150 years, ending in the anathematization of both at the Council of Constantinople in 553. If the approach to the ascetic life which Evagrius taught was so widely followed, it seems odd that he should have been such a controversial figure.

The hostility to Evagrius arose because of the metaphysical speculation which accompanied the ascetical teaching. A young monk who later became the writer of lives of the saints, Cyril of Scythopolis, tells how he visited Cyriacus, a monk in the Palestinian desert, and consulted him about this controversial figure. Surely it cannot be harmful to ask about these things, he says. Cyriacus replies:

> The doctrines of pre-existence and restoration are not indifferent and without danger, but dangerous harmful, and blasphemous. ... They deny that Christ is one of the Trinity, they say that our resurrection bodies pass to total destruction, and Christ's first of all; they say that the Holy Trinity did not create the world; and that at the resurrection all rational beings even demons will be able to create aeons; they say that our bodies will be raised etherial and spherical at the resurrection; and they assert that even the body of the Lord was raised in this form; they say that we shall be equal to Christ in the resurrection.[26]

Barsanuphius and John agreed that this kind of speculation was without profit. The questioner has come across these ideas and is puzzled because he has not found them in the Bible. Barsanuphius is clear that these teachings are harmful to the monk and must be avoided. John adds the qualification that some of Evagrius's work can be read with profit.[27]

It is difficult to know what views can be properly attributed to Origen and Evagrius. As far as Evagrius is concerned, the bolder speculations are contained in the *Kephalia Gnostica*. This work has been preserved in two different Syriac versions. The bolder speculations, to which Cyriacus objects, are only one of these versions. These passages may have been written by Evagrius and then removed by his followers to preserve his reputation, or they might have been added later by these disciples.[28]

The monks who opposed the Origenist/Evagrian style of spirituality were the 'anthropomorphites'. They found that the intellectual approach of the Origenists was too far removed from the language of the Bible with its emphasis on the Incarnation and a personal understanding of God, which included reference to God's face, hands and words. John Cassian records how one monk Serapion was persuaded that the Church accepted Origen's teachings then sadly said 'ah wretch that I am. They have taken away my God, and I have none I can hold now, and know not whom to adore or whom to address myself to'.[29] A saying which shows the importance of physical language and experience is reported by a visitor to the monks. 'You must prostrate yourselves before brothers who come to visit you, for it is not them but God who you venerate, have you seen your brother, says Scripture, you have seen the Lord your God.'[30]

This sense of unease that the language of Origenists was diverging from biblical witness left a potential conflict which was a seedbed in which open conflict could emerge when stimulated by other disagreements.

After the death of Evagrius at Epiphany 399, the patriarch of Alexandria, Theophilus, wrote his Paschal Letter attacking anthropomorphism and supporting Origenism. This provoked an immediate reaction. Three out of the four congregations at Scetis refused to read the letter and a group of monks went to Alexandria. Theophilus welcomed them, saying 'so I have seen you, as the face of God' and they replied 'if you say truthfully that the face of God is like ours, then anathematise the books of Origen'.[31]

Theophilus changed his mind and instead of condemning anthropomorphism, acted against the leading Origenists instead. Theophilus was probably motivated by personal reasons and felt let down by his former favourites. He had wanted Evagrius to become bishop of Thmuis, but Evagrius had not accepted this post. Euthymius and Eusebius, other Origenist monks, had left their administrative posts in Alexandria and returned to the desert. Isidore had been in Rome and had returned to Alexandria to give evidence in a law suit against a priest of Alexandria called Peter, and then had spent money from a legacy on the poor without telling Theophilus. These were the leading Origenist monks, called the Four Tall Brothers – Euthymius, Eusebius, Isidore and Ammonius – and these, along with three hundred others, left the Egyptian desert and went to Palestine. Some went on to Constantinople where, two years later in 402, they were reconciled with Theophilus.

The next stage of the controversy over Origenism took place in the monasteries of Palestine, and led up to the anathematization of Origen, as well as Evagrius and Didymus the Blind at the Fifth Ecumenical Council of Constantinople. The events are described by Cyril of Scythopolis.

The problem arose, Cyril tells us, as a result of poor leadership. The superior of the New Laura, one of Sabas's foundations, was the 'simple' Paul who admitted a monk called Nonnus, Leontius of Byzantium and two others who 'secretly held the doctrines of Origen'. They were expelled but then re-admitted after the death of Sabas. They then started looking for support in other monasteries and circulating their ideas. They found receptive audiences in the monasteries of Firminus and Martyrius both suffering from weak leadership after the death of previous abbots. They also gained the support of 'all the more intellectual monks of the New Laura' and also managed to gain some support in the Great Laura.

The group extended its activities. Nonnus settled in Jerusalem while Leontius went to Constantinople. Leontius gained the confidence of the emperor and other figures at court. He used this influence to secure the appointment of Origenists to leading positions. Theodore Askidas of the New Laura became Metropolitan of Caesarea in Cappadocia and Domitian a monk of Martyrius's monastery became Metropolitan of Ancyra. The high point of their influence came with the appointment of an Origenist as superior of the Great Laura. At this point both Nonnus and Leontius died – Leontius in 543 and Nonnus in 547. The influence of the Origenist party declined. The group split into moderate and extreme groups. Origen and his followers Evagrius and Didymus the Blind were anathematized at the Fifth Council of Constantinople.[32]

Cyril of Scythopolis was a monk at the monastery during these events and watched them taking place. He shows the potential for conflict between groups within the monasteries – especially in Palestine with its monastic population composed of diverse nationalities and backgrounds. He also explains how doctrine becomes tangled with power as different groups use the accusation of heresy to challenge and overcome their opponents.

Influence from Syria

Two writers made a special contribution to the tradition of prayer, both of whom were read, used and quoted by later writers. Both came from monasteries and the areas to the east of the Byzantine Empire and represented a Semitic tradition of spirituality. This Syriac strand of tradition entered monastic life and developed alongside the more intellectual approach of Origen and Evagrius. The different traditions came together and led to the development of the hesychastic life.

Macarius wrote fifty homilies and some letters. It was thought that the writer of these letters was Macarius the Egyptian, a monk who lived in the Egyptian desert for sixty years and died in 390. He is mentioned in the writing of both Palladius and Rufinus. This pedigree is a reason for his writing being so highly valued. During the last century research has shown that the homilies have a Syrian background, since they contain phrases, images and illustrations reflecting a Syrian landscape and culture. In addition to this internal evidence, several ancient manuscripts state that the author was Symeon of Mesopotamia, who was a prominent member of the heretical Messalian sect. The Messalians were condemned by the Council of Gangra in 340, but in spite of this association the fifty homilies have continued to be used as much-loved and often-quoted texts. It is now usual to refer to the author as Pseudo-Macarius.[33]

Some time later, in the seventh century, a monk named Isaac was born in Qatar on the Persian Gulf and became a monk probably in Khuzistan, also on the Persian Gulf but further to the north in what is now Iran. In 676 he became bishop of Nineveh, the modern Mosul, in the Church of the East. As Bishop his seat was in the monastery of Beth Abe in northern Iraq. He stayed in this position of five months and then left 'for a reason which God knows', as his biographer demurely states.[34] He then lived as a hermit and died around 700 in the monastery of Rabban Shapur. His writing comes from his time as a hermit towards the end of his life and was collected into two anthologies or 'parts'. The first and longer part has 82 chapters, and was translated into Greek at the monastery of Mar Saba in the eighth century and was widely read. The second part disappeared until it was recently re-discovered in a manuscript in the Bodleian Library in Oxford by the Syriac scholar Sebastian Brock.

The reputation of these two writers shows the vitality and creativity of the monasteries of Syria. The Semitic background gives their writings a poetic and life-affirming character. In his edition of Pseudo-Macarius, Fr George Maloney describes the Greek tradition of Evagrius and others as light, with its sense of a reality which is beyond this physical world and which the monk enters into through prayer, attaining a new vision of God who is experienced as light. The Semitic view is referred to as life. It has a holistic view of human nature in which the heart is the centre of the human person. Growth is holistic, dynamic and leads to the existential transformation of the whole person – body, soul and spirit – through the indwelling of the Spirit. Pseudo-Macarius emphasizes the place of the 'heart', which governs and directs all other organs.

Isaac wrote passionately about God's love. 'Among all God's actions there is none which is not entirely a matter of mercy, love and compassion. This constitutes the beginning and end of his dealings with us.'[35] An extract from a sermon preached by Isaac gives a sense of the quality and style of this 'heart' approach and its sensitivity to the limitless extent of love.

> What is a charitable heart? It is a heart which is burning with charity for the whole of creation – for men, for the birds, for the beasts, for the demons – for all creatures. He who has such a heart cannot see or call to mind a creature without his heart becoming filled with tears by reason of the immense compassion which seizes his heart; a heart which is softened and can no longer bear to see or learn from others of any suffering, even the smallest pain, being inflicted on a creature. That is why such a man never ceases to pray also for the animals, for the enemies of truth, and for those who do him evil, that they may be preserved and purified. He will pray even for the reptiles, moved by the infinite pity which reigns in the hearts of those who are being united with God.[36]

Isaac's holistic view of the human person extends also to the body. He instructs his hearers about the importance of posture, saying the 'God very much wants outward postures, specific kinds of honour, and visible forms of prayer.'[37] He is speaking here of the need to stand upright and to perform prostrations, but the recognition of the part which the body plays in prayer leads to other physical practices especially in the saying of the Jesus Prayer. Prayer especially in the Syrian tradition has a physical dimension. The frequent prostrations in even local parish worship in a Syrian church make worship a physically demanding and exhausting process.

John of the Ladder

Mount Sinai was a centre of monastic life from an early date. Hermits had come to the mountain, and a monastery was founded in the reign of the Emperor Justinian (527–65). The monastery has been known by several names. It was the Monastery of the Bush, since a tree within the monastery walls is revered as the bush of the revelation of God's nature to Moses; it was the monastery of the Transfiguration, since Christ's glory was revealed on another mountain and there is a sixth-century mosaic of the transfiguration in the apse of the monastery church; and, now, the Monastery of St Catherine, since the body of the fourth-century martyr Catherine from Alexandria was transported to the top of the mountain and was discovered, incorrupt, by the monks in 850. It remains a place of monastic life and is now an autocephalous church in its own right, with the abbot having the status of archbishop.

During the seventh century, there was an abbot called John. Little is known of his life. An account was written by Daniel of Rhaithou, but Daniel does not seem well informed. There are further details in the *Narrations* of Anastasius of Sinai, but these sections may refer to another monk also called John.[38] He was born, probably, in 579 and died in 649, although alternative dates have been suggested, as early as 525 for his birth and as late as 680 for his death. He arrived at Sinai when he was sixteen years old and attached himself to a monk called Martyrius, who became his spiritual father. After several years Martyrius climbed with him to the top of the mountain and there made the young disciple a monk. On their way down they met Anastasius, the abbot, who had not met John but told Martyrius that he had just tonsured the man who would later become the abbot of the monastery. John lived for forty years as a hermit at a place called Tholas, near the mountain, and then was elected abbot in fulfilment of Anastasius's prophecy. As he was being installed, John saw a Jew in a white robe going around and giving instructions to cooks and others, and then was nowhere to be seen. He realized that this was Moses, and he had appeared as a sign that John was to be the new Moses.

Towards the end of his life the abbot of the nearby monastery of Rhaithou asked for advice. 'Tell us in our ignorance what like Moses of old you have seen in your divine vision upon the mountain, write it in a book and send it to us.' John did as asked and wrote a summary of his understanding and teaching about the monastic life which he arranged in thirty sections. These thirty sections were described as rungs of a ladder, reaching from earth to heaven with one rung for each year of Christ's life, guiding the reader on a process of spiritual and ascetic ascent. The book is *the Ladder of Divine Ascent*, and John is known as John of the Ladder, or John Climakos. It has been used ever since as a basic and authoritative statement of monastic life, and in many monasteries is read each Lent, so that some monks will have heard it read fifty or more times.

The steps of John's Ladder guide the reader through the methods and virtues of the ascetic life. Like other writers, he teaches the need for obedience. This leads to repentance, which shows itself in tears. He does not discuss the church, and there is no reference to bishops or clergy. Instead knowledge of God comes from the oral teaching of the spiritual father. The themes which had been taught by others are collected and presented in a systematic and rigorous form.

Symeon the New Theologian

The guidance of the spiritual father and the priority of direct personal experience were two foundations of monastic life. In the writings of Symeon the New Theologian, these are sharply and uncompromisingly presented. They led Symeon to a vivid experience of God as light, an experience which he communicated in a series of sermons.

Symeon was born in 949 in Paphlagonia, to the east of Constantinople and on the Black Sea coast. He was sent to the capital at the age of eleven to be educated, after which he was appointed to various positions in the court. His success and prosperity left him unsatisfied and he searched for a spiritual father to give him guidance in his aspirations to lead a life of prayer. He discovered his guide in the person of another Symeon, usually called Symeon the Pious or Symeon the Stoudite, a monk at the Stoudite monastery.

For several years he managed to combine a dissolute secular life, as he himself claims, with regular visits to his spiritual father.[39] He entered the monastery of Stoudios at the age of twenty-seven and spent a year as a novice. He then left the monastery as the result of a controversy. The reason for this is not clear but might have been because of his excessive allegiance to his spiritual father, Symeon, which conflicted with his obedience to the abbot. He then moved to the monastery of St Mamas, where he became a monk and then, three years later, abbot. He found the monastery in a weak situation. He worked to improve the buildings and church worship and also developed the spiritual level of the monks. He remained in his position of abbot until 1005 when he resigned and retired to a more silent way of life in the monastery. But controversy followed him and he was further criticized and so he left St Mamas and went to live in Chrysopolis near Chalcedon, a few miles from Constantinople. Here he founded a small monastery in 1009. The hostility to him subsided and he was asked to return but he stayed in Chrysopolis until his death in 1022, regularly visited by his disciples and working on a body of writing including letters and hymns.

He was a passionate and popular preacher and teacher who attracted both supporters and detractors. His early encounters with monastic life were influenced by his meeting with Symeon the Pious. Spiritual fatherhood was encouraged at Stoudios. It had been a centre of opposition to the iconoclast movement which had been supported by the patriarch and bishops. So, in that uncertain period and at a time when the bishops were seen as hostile and opposing the orthodox faith, the charismatic authority of the spiritual father was followed in order to encourage steadfastness under pressure from the church authorities. The monastery was a centre of study. The Hypotyposis instructed all monks to borrow a book from the library on days when there was no other work and read it until the evening office when it was to be returned. This document also describes how the abbot withdrew to a quiet part of the church during matins, 'at the beginning of the fourth ode of the canon', where the monks came to him in turn to confess their thoughts. This confession of thoughts was the responsibility of the abbot and could only be done to another monk in exceptional circumstances.[40]

Symeon the Pious was sixty when the younger Symeon first knew him. He was recognized as an elder and as a teacher. Symeon recalls:

> I was the novice … and it happened one day we were going into the city in which he lived to visit his spiritual children. We spent the whole day among them, for there were many whom he helped even by his presence alone. At evening we came back to our cell hungry and thirsty from much labour and the heat, because even though the day was hot, he was not accustomed to take the slightest nap.[41]

This gives a glimpse of the spiritual father at work among his spiritual children. His care extended to those outside the monastery and was valued by many. In many monasteries, the elder had a wide popular appeal and this enabled the monasteries to become rooted in the local community and to extend their teaching widely. Symeon had a close relationship with his spiritual father and his practice of venerating Symeon's memory led to his clashes with the church authorities.

Symeon was ready to share and write about his experiences. He prayed intensely and at length. One night

> he (he means I) was standing and reciting uttering with his mind rather than his mouth, suddenly an abundance of divine radiance appeared from above and filled all the place. He saw only light all around him ... He was wholly united to the immaterial light and thought that he himself became light; having forgotten all the world, he became filled with tears and with ineffable joy and with gladness.[42]

These visions of light were repeated on many occasions. They were accompanied by tears. He expected that tears would be given especially when receiving Holy Communion, which he expected monks would receive daily. 'Brother', he said, 'never take communion without tears'.[43]

Symeon's writings are a vivid personal account of his spiritual life. He shows the importance of personal experience and explains how this can be achieved. He lived and taught his life of prayer with a strong and passionate intensity which gained him both followers and opponents. The title of the New Theologian might have been used first as an insult by opponents since theology was expected to be traditional rather than novel, old rather than new; or it may have been used by his friends to assert his continuity with the others called Theologian – John the Evangelist and Gregory of Nazianzus.

The Jesus Prayer

One form of prayer was becoming practised more and was becoming preferred to others. This was the Jesus Prayer. The practice brings together several themes of Christian prayer in a simple formula and procedure. The name of a person was seen as summarizing, encapsulating and communicating all that a person is and does. So in the Bible, God reveals his name to Moses as the beginning of his mission of salvation of the Israelites and when the apostles start their mission they carry out signs and healings in the 'name' of 'Jesus'. The use of the name helped monks to make sense of the demanding verse of St Paul's letter exhorting the reader to 'pray without ceasing' which had led to much reflection.[44] The practice of using the repetition of a simple formula grew up, in order to develop a way of constant prayer through faith in the name of Jesus Christ. There were various prayers used, but eventually a short single-sentence prayer became the standard. 'Lord Jesus Christ, Son of the living God, have mercy on me a sinner.' This can be referred back to the prayer of the tax collector in the Gospel of Luke. 'God be merciful to me a sinner.'[45] Later commentators reflected that this short phrase contains a whole message of salvation, with the invocation to the human Jesus, recognized as Lord through the resurrection, a person of the Holy Trinity, incarnated to bring forgiveness and mercy which is directed to each of us personally.

Diadochus of Photike, writing in the fifth century, discussed the prayer telling his readers to '(cling) to the remembrance of the holy and glorious name of the Lord Jesus and (use) it as a weapon against Satan's deception'.[46] Some time later, Hesychios the Priest advises anyone troubled by distraction in prayer simply to invoke the name of Jesus.[47] Neither of these uses the fully developed form of the Jesus Prayer. We find the full prayer in Nikiphoros the Monk's texts *On Watchfulness*. 'You know that everyone's discursive faculty is centred on his breast; for when our lips are silent we speak and deliberate and formulate prayers, psalms and other things in our breast. Banish then all thoughts from this faculty and in their place put the prayer, "Lord Jesus Christ, Son of God, have mercy on me" and compel it to repeat this prayer ceaselessly.'[48] Since the prayer is discovered and placed within the heart, its practice involves more than the saying of words with the lips, or thinking with the mind, but engages the whole personality and this includes the postures and use of the body and the inhalation and exhalation of breathing. This involvement of the whole person in prayer is taught by Gregory of Sinai in the fourteenth century. It brings 'warmth and joy to the intellect, and (sets) the heart on fire with an ineffable love for God and man'.[49] The heart is enabled 'to contain within it the uncontainable God'.[50]

The Prayer became the usual way of prayer for the monks who became known as Hesychasts, from the Greek *hesychia* or silence.

Gregory Palamas

Two monks, both called Gregory and both living in the fourteenth century, explained why the Jesus Prayer was important and how it worked. Gregory of Sinai (1265–1346) was a monk on Cyprus, Mount Sinai, Mount Athos and then at Paroria in Bulgaria. Unlike the other Gregory Palamas, he avoided controversy but his writings contain a similar teaching and he refers to the divine and uncreated light of Tabor. While they did not work together, the two Gregories are representatives of the practice of the Jesus Prayer and the experiences of the hesychasts of participating in divine light.

Gregory Palamas gave a clear theological understanding of the nature of God and his relationship with the created order, a vision of the purpose of the monastic life and guidance as to the way to practise this. He developed and explained his theology in a period of uncertainty and conflict. His teaching was endorsed by church councils and this led to a period of cultural and religious renewal in both church and state.

Gregory was born in Constantinople in 1296 to a wealthy and devout family. His father, Constantine, ensured that the boy was guided by monks in spiritual matters, as well as receiving an academic education. When his father died, after being tonsured as a monk on his deathbed, the emperor took responsibility for the boy's education and provided him with an opening to live and work in the court. Then Gregory, now aged twenty, persuaded all his family to enter the monastic life and he went with two of his brothers to Mount Athos. He lived in hermitages and at the Great Lavra until 1225 when there was a period of attacks on the mountain by Turks and Gregory withdrew to Thessalonica. Here he was ordained priest, and then, at the age of thirty, retired once more to live as a hermit this time on Mount Beroea. He spent five days each week in solitude following the hesychast way of uninterrupted prayer. Once again attacks by hostile forces made him leave this refuge and he returned to Mount Athos. In 1335 or

1336 he was elected abbot of the monastery of Esphigmenou. Here he was drawn into the theological debates on the procession of the Holy Spirit and on the nature of prayer.

A later stage of Palamas's life saw him involved in the political and religious life of the empire. The Emperor Andronikos III Palaiologos died in 1341, leaving two claimants to the throne. His young son was crowned at the age of nine as John V. John, supported by his mother the empress Anne of Savoy and the Patriarch John Calecas, was opposed by John VI Kantakuzenos, a powerful courtier who had the title of *domestikos*. He had the support of many noble families and also many of the monks. As civil strife spread, there was a popular revolt in Thessalonica by a party who became known as the Zealots, who were motivated by opposition to Kantakuzenos and his aristocratic supporters. The conflict was resolved in 1347 when John VI Kantakuzenos was crowned as emperor and shared his position with John V. Kantakuzenos later became a monk as Ioasaph and devoted himself to literary works including a four-volume history of the empire. Gregory Palamas supported Kantakuzenos. His participation in this political struggle led to an eventful period of his life when he was imprisoned, excommunicated, released, consecrated archbishop of Thessalonica, prevented from entering the city by the Zealots, eventually admitted, later entrusted with a diplomatic mission, when he was imprisoned by the Turks. Gregory died in 1358 and ten years later was recognized as a saint.

Gregory's theological work was carried out in dialogue with a monk Barlaam of Calabria (1290–1348). Barlaam, born Bernardo Massari, was a monk and scholar from Italy who moved to Constantinople in 1320 and became abbot of a monastery. He first encountered Gregory when both became involved in negotiations between Western and Eastern churches, writing against the filioque addition to the creed. This debate about the nature of God showed the differences in their approach. For Barlaam, God was unknowable and so doctrinal statements, such as definitions concerning the procession of the Holy Spirit from the Father, were a rational and philosophical process of discerning conceptual truths based on scriptural texts, and so a dialectical process. For Gregory, knowledge of God is experiential. Theological reflection on the Trinity could have an 'apodictic' character, and so was able to express absolute truth. For Barlaam, theology was a philosophical enquiry, for Gregory it was an exploration through prayer.

The dialogue then moved on to prayer itself, especially the hesychastic prayer of the heart. Barlaam was shocked by the teaching of hesychasm that the human body, as well as the mind or soul, could participate in the divine life and become transfigured by the uncreated light. He was also scornful at the methods of hesychastic prayer with its physical disciplines of breathing and concentration on the heart. He called the monks *omphalopsychoi* or those with their souls in their navels, since one of the practices was to lower the eyes towards the centre of the body as a way of allowing the spirit to enter into the whole body. However this and other more derogatory phrases occur only in Barlaam's early works. The debate was carried out in conversations on prayer with Gregory, at first face to face on Mount Athos, then through written treatises and with growing hostility. It needs to be remembered that Barlaam's ideas are known only through the hostile works of his opponents, since his own writing was destroyed after church councils decided against him, and so we are not able to read his ideas in his own words.

Gregory's teaching was set out in the *Triads*, written at various times from 1336 onward. These are three sets of three treatises, from which the name comes. He also wrote other books, and left many sermons, but the *Triads* contain a clear expression of his approach. He affirmed the utter transcendence of God, who is beyond our capacity of knowing and also beyond unknowing as well. But while we cannot know God, God does come to us. We find ourselves in God's presence. We are invited to 'a change of heart and mind enabling us to attain to the contemplation of the reality which reveals itself to us as it raises us to God'.[51] So, Gregory makes a distinction between God's essence, which is always beyond us and unknowable to us, and God's energies, which make him known in the world and which we can experience. The energies are God's will, God's beauty and other divine attributes. These energies are uncreated and are made known as light, which is the uncreated light of God which shone in Christ on the mount of Transfiguration. Through prayer, souls and bodies are transformed and can encounter God's energies and God's light. The vision of this light is also participation in the divine nature and is properly described as *theosis* or deification. We can know and participate in God through prayer. Gregory's work brings together the thinking and teaching of those who had gone before him and presents their ideas in a clear and rigorous theological framework. 'Palamas combines integration of the terminology of Evagrius, theological assimilation of the mysticism of St Symeon the New Theologian, and a justification of thirteenth century methods of prayer in an approach which can be called a Christian materialism.'[52]

A church council in Constantinople met on 10 June 1341 and spent just one day in listening to the statements of both Gregory and Barlaam. The views of those present quickly became clear and Barlaam confessed his errors, was pardoned and not long after left for Italy where he was received into the Roman Church at Avignon and ended his life as Bishop of Gerace in southern Italy. This did not end the controversy and other councils met to further consider Gregory's writing, especially his views on the uncreated energies of God. A further council which met in 1351 declared Gregory to be orthodox and his teaching in conformity with the fathers of the Church.

The Councils which affirmed Gregory's teaching on hesychasm brought the long period of ascetic living and teaching to a fulfilment. The hesychastic life continued to be followed not only in the monasteries but also in hermitages and sketes on the holy mountain of Athos and throughout the Eastern Christian world. The texts of hesychasm would, in due course, be collated in the *Philokalia* and would continue to be taught and lived. They would be the continuing source of revival and renewal.

Notes

1 Arsenius 6, trans. Benedicta Ward, *Sayings of the Desert Fathers* (London, 1975), p. 10.
2 Sozomen, *Ecclesiastical History* 6.28, GCS 277.7; Severus of Ashmunein, *History of the Patriarchs of the Coptic Church of Alexandria*, PO 1 427–8, both cited in John Binns, *Ascetics and Ambassadors of Christ* (Oxford, 1994), p. 204.
3 Philip Rousseau, *Pachomius* (Berkeley, 1995), pp. 85–6.
4 Richard Finn, *Asceticism in the Graeco-Roman World* (Cambridge, 2009), p. 104.

5   Socrates, *Ecclesiastical History* 4.26.
6   This and other information about Origen's life come from Eusebius, *Ecclesiastical History* VI, and also the Funeral Oration by Gregory Thaumaturgus.
7   Eusebius, *Ecclesiastical History* 6.8.2–3.
8   Matthew 19.12.
9   The description of Diarmaid MacCulloch, *History of Christianity* (London, 2009), p. 149.
10 *Homily in Joshua* 7.6.
11 Peter Brown, *The Body and Society* (New York, 1988), p. 163.
12 1 Corinthians 3.2–4; Hebrews 5.12–14; Romans 14.2.
13 Cassiodorus Senator, *An Introduction to Divine and Human Readings*, cited in Rowan Greer, *Origen* (London, 1979), p. xv.
14 Chorepiscop means literally a 'field bishop', who exercised episcopal functions supporting the metropolitan bishop whose seat was in the city.
15 This *Philokalia* is not to be confused with a later collection of ascetic texts also called the *Philokalia*, made by Nikodimos and Macarius.
16 Palladius, *Lausiac History* 38.2.
17 This is in Palladius who does not give details of the relationship beyond that it was mutual *Lausiac History* 38.3.
18 Ibid., 55.3.
19 These details are in *Historia Monachorum* 20.16, trans. Norman Russell, *The Lives of the Desert Fathers* (Oxford, 1980), p. 107; and John Cassian *Institutes* 5.52. Cassian says this was a 'monk from Pontus' which is likely to refer to Evagrius.
20 *Coptic Life of Evagrius* 17 cited in Augustine Casiday, *Evagrius Ponticus* (Oxford, 2006), p. 77.
21 Owen Chadwick, *John Cassian a Study in Primitive Monasticism* (Cambridge, 1950), p. 82.
22 The Chapters on Prayer were attributed to Nilus of Sinai (d. 430), see I Hausherr in 'Les versions syriaque et armenienne d'evagre le pontique', *Orientalia Christiana* 22 (1933), and his Commentary on the Psalms were attributed to Origen. See John Eudes Bamberger, *Evagrius: The Praktikos, Chapters on Prayer* (Kalamazoo, MI, 1981), p. xxiii.
23 *Praktikos* 6–14 in Ibid., pp. 16–20.
24 These are summarized in one of the selections in the *Philokalia*, in trans. Geoffrey Palmer, Philip Sherrard, and Kallistos Ware, *Philokalia*, vol. 1 (London 1979), pp. 73–94.
25 This text is in Evagrius, *153 Chapters on Prayer*, and is found in the *Philokalia*, trans. G. Palmer, vol. 1, p. 62.
26 *Life of Cyriac* 230.1–10.
27 Barsanuphius and John, *Letter* 60.
28 This is discussed by Casiday, *Evagrius*, pp. 28–35.
29 Cassian, *Conferences* 10.2–4.
30 Apollo in *Lives of the Desert Fathers* 8.55, Russell, *Lives*, p. 78. In fact it was Antony who said this.
31 Socrates, *Ecclesiastical History* 6.7 and Sozomen, *Ecclesiastical History* 8.1.
32 Cyril of Scythopolis recounts these events in *Life of Sabas* 196.20–200.5.
33 H. Dörries, *Symeon von Mesopotamien* and trans. George Maloney, *Pseudo-Macarius, The Fifty Spiritual Homilies and the Great Letter* (Mahwah, NJ, 1992), pp. 7, 29.
34 This was Isho'denah in the *Book of Chastity*, see Hilarion Alfeyev, *The Spiritual World of Isaac the Syrian* (Kalamazoo, MI, 2000), p. 25.
35 Ibid., p. 36.
36 A. J. Wensinck, *Mystic Treatises by Isaac of Syria* (Amsterdam, 1923), p. 341.

37 Sebastian Brock, *The Syriac Fathers on Prayer and the Spiritual Life* (Kalamazoo, MI, 1987), p. 276.
38 There is further discussion in Kallistos Ware, introduction to John Climacus, *Ladder of Divine Ascent* (Mahwah, NJ, 1982), pp. 2–3.
39 Hymn 24.63–83 lists the sins he committed in this period.
40 Symeon's life is in Hilarion Alfeyev, *St Symeon the New Theologian and the Orthodox Tradition* (Oxford, 2000), pp. 27–42.
41 *Catachetical Discourse* 16.8–39, trans. Carmino de Catanzaro, *Symeon the New Theologian, The Discourses* (New York, 1980), pp. 198–202.
42 Ibid., 22.88–100, pp. 245–6.
43 Symeon the Studite, *Ascetical Discourse* 24, and see Symeon the New Theologian, *Catachetical Discourse* 4.11–12, pp. 82–4.
44 Exodus 3; Acts 3.6,16; 1Thessalonians 5.17.
45 Luke 18.13.
46 Diadochus of Photike, *On Spiritual Knowledge* 31 in trans. Palmer et al., *Philokalia*, vol. 1, p. 261.
47 Hesychios the Priest, *On Watchfulness and Holiness*, Ibid., pp. 162–98.
48 See Mary Cunningham, 'The Place of the Jesus Prayer in the Philokalia', in ed. Brock Bingaman and Bradley Nassif, *The Philokalia* (Oxford, 2012), pp. 196–7; Nikiphoros in trans. Palmer et al., *Philokalia*, vol. 4, p. 206.
49 Gregory of Sinai, *On Prayer*, in ibid., p. 259.
50 Philotheos of Sinai, *Forty Texts on Watchfulness* 27, ibid., vol. 3, p. 26.
51 Vladimir Lossky, *Mystical Theology of the Eastern Church* (Cambridge, 1957), p. 43.
52 John Meyendorff, *A Study of Gregory Palamas* (New York, 1964), p. 155.

Part Five

Resistances and Renewals: After 1453

13 Part One

Varieties of Tribulation: Under Islamic Government

Introduction

By the mid-fifteenth century, the Eastern tradition had – it could be argued – reached a definitive stage. Constantinople had been a meeting point and centre for monks for more than a thousand years. Its monasteries, especially the Stoudios and Evergetis, had demonstrated what a monastery should be like and how it should be managed. Their ways of life as set out in the typika had become models for other monasteries. Mount Athos was recognized as a monastic republic and attracted monks from many parts of the Eastern Christian world. It had become the guardian of a body of both written and oral teaching which handed on a theology of the monastic life and a method of prayer which expressed it. Monastic life had spread into Eastern Europe and the Balkans and into Russia. There were monasteries not only in the regions of Byzantine influence, in Russia, Serbia, Bulgaria and the Balkans, but there was also a flourishing monastic life as far south as Ethiopia and still surviving as far east as China. The formation of the monastic movement could be seen as fulfilled. But to end here would leave the story incomplete.

On 28 May 1453 a breach was made in the hitherto impregnable walls of the great city of Constantinople. The Emperor Constantine XI (1449–53) had written some weeks before to the Sultan Mehmet II, who was leading the invading Ottoman forces. 'I turn to God and God alone. Should it be his will that the city be yours where is he that can oppose it? … reign in happiness until the All-Just, the Supreme God calls us both before his judgment seat.'[1] On that final day he went to the Great Church, prostrated himself before the holy icons, confessed his sins, embraced the clergy and received the holy mysteries. The congregation wept. By the end of the following day the flag of the Ottoman Turk invaders was flying over the city. The millennium in which Constantinople had been the capital of a great Christian Empire was over and Turkish rule or Tourokrateia had begun and would last over four hundred years. The monasteries, along with the rest of the church, were no longer under Christian rule.

While this event had a symbolic significance, life as a minority faith under a non-Christian government was already a reality of daily life for much of the Church. The Christians of the Middle East had become accustomed to life under Arab rule and this had often been welcomed. In the decade after the death of the prophet Muhammad in

632 the Arab armies had made spectacular advances. Damascus was occupied in 635, Seleucia-Ctesiphon in 637, Jerusalem in 638 and Alexandria in 642. Constantinople signed a peace treaty with the Arab forces in 678, ensuring the survival of the empire, even if much reduced in size. For Syrians, the Arabs provided a welcome end to the persecutions which they had endured from Chalcedonians. Michael the Syrian expressed their relief as he wrote: 'The God of vengeance, seeing the evilness of the Romans (Byzantines) led the sons of Ishmael (the Arabs) from the regions of the south to deliver us from the Roman hands.'[2]

Like the Arabs of the seventh century, the Ottomans of the fifteenth century were often greeted as wise and tolerant rulers. After he had occupied Constantinople, Sultan Mehmet II chose Gennadios Scholarios to be patriarch and assured him of his friendship. 'Be Patriarch', he said, 'with good fortune and be assured of our friendship, keeping all the privileges that the Patriarchs before you enjoyed'. He had pragmatic as well as pious motives. He needed the support and cooperation of Christians to manage the empire. He encouraged Christians to come to the city. The Christian population of Constantinople, or Istanbul as it came to be called, grew from 50,000 to 150,000 in the century after the Ottoman occupation of the city.[3]

Dhimmi and millet

There was continuity as well as change. Both the Byzantine and the Ottoman Empires, as well as the earlier Islamic caliphates, were multi-national, multi-ethnic empires containing many peoples, races and faiths. Each of the empires had to find a way of governing which allowed both the exercise of political authority and respect for the traditions and faiths of subject peoples. The Arab dhimmi and Ottoman millet systems had similar motives to the Byzantine practice of granting a measure of autonomy to foreign groups.[4]

The Arabs recognized subject people in their caliphate as dhimmi or 'protected person'. The dhimmi system gave a status and rights to subject religious and national groups within Islamic society. The Qur'an recognized that there would be several religious groups in their caliphate, in the statement that 'we have made you into people and tribes'.[5] The dhimmi status gave Christians a recognized but subordinate place within society, with different rights and responsibilities from Muslims. Under the dhimmi, Christians paid the *jizya*, or poll tax, while Muslims were required to give *zakat* or alms. Christians could fulfil their religious commitments and Muslims were required to carry out the *hajj* pilgrimage to Mecca and other religious requirements. Christians were allowed to possess property and had a right to earn a livelihood. They were, however, reminded of their subordinate status by not being allowed to give evidence against Muslims in law cases, not being allowed to ride a horse or a camel or carry arms, to build houses which were lower in height than those of Muslim neighbours, not to ring church bells. They were not allowed to preach to Muslims and Muslims were not allowed to become Christians.

These principles were further codified under the Ottoman Empire to become the millet system. The millet was a nation which was defined in religious rather than ethnic terms. There were three millets – Greek Orthodox, Armenian and Jewish. These general religious categories incorporated different nationalities and forms of faith. The Greek Orthodox millet, for example, included Serbs, Romanians, Albanians and Arabs as well as Greeks. The patriarch of Constantinople was required to be a political and legal as well as a religious authority for this diverse ethnic group which had the single common characteristic of a shared faith affiliation. The millet system bound the Church together as a society and gave the patriarch a social position and an involvement in the life of the community, as well as a religious leadership. The system provided protection, stability and autonomy, although with a subordinate place in society. While it discriminated in many parts of life, the millet system ensured a stable position for Christians within the Ottoman Empire. Harry Luke commented: 'In the days of the Sultans, Turkey was less like a country than a block of flats inhabited by a number of families which met only on the stairs.' Karen Barkey suggested an alternative astronomical comparison. 'The (Ottoman) Empire prospered as a solar system, with the planets encircling the central sun, pulled in and held by the centre's gravitational force. No other forces pulled at the periphery, nor did the orbits of the planets interact with one another, focussed only on the centre.' Barkey continued her metaphor going on to say that as the Ottoman Empire declined so other gravitational forces influenced the system from outside, and 'in the end, the Ottoman solar system was sufficiently weakened, and then flew apart, leaving a diminished sun'.[6]

The dhimmi and the millet social systems confronted the churches with the need to find a place in a society which was not Christian, discriminated and sometimes penalized them.

Idiorrythmia

Monasteries adjusted by adopting the idiorrythmic style of life. The phrase refers to a particular pattern or method of living, and the word in modern Greek can mean quaint or peculiar. Most of the early monks followed the idiorrythmia, since they went into the desert and lived an individual and strict ascetic life. In Constantinople many of the numerous small monasteries chose their own disciplines. The development which took place in the Turkish period was the change by many monasteries from following a coenobitic to an idiorrythmic life. On Mount Athos all of the twenty ruling monasteries had become idiorrythmic by the end of the sixteenth century.

This helped the monasteries maintain their life when money ran short and estates were confiscated. Financial pressures began under the Byzantine emperors, before Turkish rule began. In 1371 Turks conquered Macedonia and occupied much imperial territory. The monasteries now owned more land than the emperor. To finance his campaigns against the invaders, Manuel II Palaiologos (1391–1425), while he was still despot of Thessalonike, confiscated half the monastic estates and required a tax to be paid on what remained. While the monasteries retained an income, they became more reliant on individual support. A class of aristocratic monks grew who retained use of their wealth while living in the monastery. Idiorrythmia also made it easier to include more aristocratic monks in the monastery, enabling them to combine life in the community with a familiar style of life. This helped to build up a stronger and varied community. The adoption of the idiorrythmic life helped the monasteries to sustain their life through more difficult times.

Idiorrythmia also conformed to the new humanist culture which was spreading in the empire. The philosopher Gemistos Plethon (1360–1452) had a following of students in Constantinople, until he was expelled by Manuel II. In one of his books, which was burned after his death by the patriarch, he called God by the name of Zeus, said that the Trinity was a threesome of the Super-Essential Creator, the Mind of the World and the Soul of the World. These ideas came from a revised Platonism and can be traced to the intellectual standpoint of Barlaam of Calabria, the opponent of Gregory Palamas. There was a new individualism within which the obedience and common life of the coenobitic monastery seemed increasingly anachronistic.

As a result, the coenobitic life on Mount Athos, as set in place by Athanasios, was gradually replaced by an idiorrythmic form of life. A coenobium was governed by the abbot, who was a spiritual father to the monks, directed the way of life and ensured regular confession of thoughts. The authority of the abbot was an essential foundation of coenobitic life and its decline led to the disintegration of the common life. In the new circumstances of Ottoman rule, government was shifted away from the Protos and was now carried out by two elders who served for a year at a time and were assisted by a committee. Monks were allowed to keep their own property and to prepare their own meals, although property was passed to the monastery on the death or departure of the monk.

The monk Pachomius wrote a sharp attack on idiorrythmia in the sixteenth century. He argued that there were three kinds of monks – coenobitic, eremitic and idiorrythmic. He called idiorrythmic monks 'half-monks' and accused them of failing to live in poverty and obedience. Instead they had an extravagant lifestyle.[7] Others agreed and so a further typikon was solemnly issued in 1574 re-introducing a common discipline and prohibiting a series of practices such as drinking spirits, keeping female farm animals but allowing women to stay in monastery farms outside the mountain boundary. This produced a temporary restoration of traditional customs. However, by this time, all the monasteries on the mountain were idiorrythmic and this practice continued until the twentieth century.

Government control in Russia

Another form of control of the church by the state leading to change in monastic life took place in Russia. The Possessors had prevailed over Non-Possessors and, as a result, monasteries became integrated into society and were able to acquire wealth. While most monasteries were small and did not own large amounts of property, the larger monasteries had been given villages, lands and benefactions of various kinds. It is estimated that the seventeen large monasteries owned over a half of the church's serfs.[8] The state looked with interest – and acquisitiveness – at this concentration of landed wealth. In the seventeenth century, Peter the Great (1682–1725) carried out reforms of both state and the church. He did not oppose monasteries but required them to contribute to the strength and well-being of the nation. His reforms were practical but lacked sympathy or understanding of the spiritual values and purpose of the monastic life. He does not fit neatly into either of Joseph's categories of being a minister ordained by God or a servant of the devil. He was trying to rule and build up the nation and wanted monasteries to contribute to this.[9]

The Law Code of 1649 had already established the Monastery Chancellery to administer monastic estates and to restrict further expansion. In 1701, Peter the Great strengthened this by carrying out an inventory of monastery lands. Then, in 1722, he initiated his programme of reform. The patriarch was replaced by a synod as the highest level of church government. The reforms of monastic life required male candidates for monastic life to be at least thirty years old, and women to be at least forty. All monasteries had to be coenobia and have at least thirty monks, with smaller monasteries forced to combine with larger to achieve this target. Hermitages were forbidden, since they were harder to control. Peter's successors continued these policies. By 1764, 138 monasteries, from a total of 1201, had been closed.

These measures were continued under Catherine the Great (1762–96) who took monastery lands under state control. Her purpose was not only to acquire the riches of the monasteries but also to remove the responsibility for management of land away from the monks and given to the state. Monasteries received payments from the government but in return were strictly regulated. The two largest monasteries, the Trinity-Sergius and Alexander Nevsky, were called lavras and were allowed to have hundred monks each. Then there were a further 272 state-funded monasteries, 190 for men and 82 for women. These were graded into three classes with different numbers of monks and nuns permitted for each class. Then a further 192 unfunded monasteries were allowed to support themselves by their own labour. The income which the state received from monastery lands was equivalent to 1.5 million roubles and the amount paid out in state funding was 208,000 roubles. The number of monasteries was reduced from 1052 to 479. The number of monastic clergy was halved to 5,450.[10]

Both the Ottoman Empire and the Russia of Peter the Great legislated to regulate the monasteries. Not only were monasteries reduced in size, wealth and importance but these changed circumstances led them to different forms of monastic life. An idorrythmic monastery was a community of monks living a retired life with individuals given more freedom to develop their own chosen lifestyle. The monasteries of eighteenth-century Russia were expected to make a productive and useful contribution to the well-being of the state. Both understandings diluted the uncompromising character of monastic life. Within them both, however, signs of new life and reform were stirring.

Notes

1 In Michael Dukas, *Historia Byzantina*, ed. I. Bakker (Bonn, 1834), p. 245.
2 Michael the Syrian, *Chronicle* 1.4.12.
3 The name Istanbul became more commonly used. There are several possible derivations. It could be the medieval Greek, *eis ton polin*, meaning into the city; or *islam bol* meaning

the plenty of Islam; or an expansion of the central syllable of Con-*stant*- inople. In any case it shows continuity between the stages of the history of the city.

4   For similarities between the Byzantine and Ottoman systems, see Harry Luke, *The Old Turkey and the New: From Byzantium to Ankara* (London, 1955), p. 7.
5   *Qur'an*, Sura 49.13.
6   Luke, *Old Turkey*, p. 8; Karen Barkey, *Empire of Difference, The Ottomans in Comparative Perspective* (Cambridge, 2008), p. 294; Khalid Dinno, *The Syrian Orthodox Christians in the Late Ottoman Period and Beyond* (Piscataway, NJ, 2017), p. 88.
7   Graham Speake, *Mount Athos, Renewal in Paradise* (New Haven, CT, and London, 2002), p. 122.
8   Scott Kenworthy, *Heart of Russia* (Oxford, 2010), p. 14.
9   His desire for reform has been examined by Russian historians such as N. N. Lisovoi, in ibid., p. 15.
10 Ibid., pp. 17–19.

Revival and Renewal in the Eighteenth and Nineteenth Centuries

The academy and the *Philokalia*

Ottoman rule and the idiorrythmic life did not stamp out the vitality or creativity of monastic life. Some new approaches were tried out on Mount Athos. In the period between 1740 and 1790, there were three initiatives which showed the freshness of life on the mountain and the potential of monasteries to lead the Church into revival. There was an attempt to set up an Athonite Academy to be a centre for Hellenistic study, the collection of ascetic texts which formed the collection known as the *Philokalia* and then a further typikon to build up the mutual responsibility of the monasteries on the mountain. While these did not have immediate effect, these measures show that, in spite of the rule of the Turks and the practice of idiorrythmia, there was a resourcefulness in the monasteries which external difficulties did not extinguish.

The Athonite Academy was set up at the largest monastery at that time, Vatopedi. The monastery received support for this venture from the new patriarch of Constantinople, Cyril V, and the synod of the mountain agreed to the formation of a new educational venture. The Academy was built on land near the monastery and opened in 1748. The purpose was to provide education for the Greek-speaking subjects of the Ottoman Empire, succeeding to a school on the island of Patmos which had closed. A monk, Neophytos, was appointed principal but was quickly replaced by a well-known scholar. Evgenios Voulgaris (1716–1806) had been born in Greece and then studied at Padua where he had become fluent in Latin, Italian and French and taught philosophy as well as theology. He was appointed to the Academy in 1753 and made an immediate impact. The number of students grew from twenty to two hundred who came to study literature, rhetoric, philosophy and mathematics as well as theology. They were offered a complete course of classical learning. Voulgaris taught students to appreciate Plato and Aristotle and, in addition, modern philosophers including Descartes and Leibniz. His predecessor, Neophytos, stayed on to teach the more basic skills. The Academy could have become a centre for reviving Hellenistic study but the venture was short-lived. There was opposition from some of the students and also the monks of the mountain who were concerned that this modern form of study was promoting secularism and atheism and undermining traditional Orthodoxy. In 1759 Voulgaris resigned and the school declined. It continued to function until the building burned in 1809, a conflagration encouraged, some said, by conservative opponents. After this the school did not re-open.[1]

Another venture which was to have, eventually, lasting success was the collection and compilation of a definitive set of patristic texts. These texts had preserved the writings of ascetic fathers on the monastic life and on hesychastic prayer. The work of compilation was begun by a monk from the Ukraine, Paisii Velichkovskii.[2] Peter, or Pyotr, was born in 1722 in Poltava in the Ukraine. His father was the dean of the Cathedral in Poltava and Peter was expected to follow in this vocation. But he had no desire for this form of ecclesiastical profession. He wanted to be a monk. As a boy he was quiet and withdrawn but determined in following his aims. He ran away from the cathedral school in Kiev, and then lived in several monasteries in Ukraine, Moldavia and Wallachia. He entered a monastery as a novice with the name Platon in 1741, then five years later, in 1746, went to Mount Athos, like so many before him, to seek a spiritual father and experience the hesychastic life. He lived as a hermit, eating bread and water only on alternate days and keeping his cell door always open. Then he received a visit from his spiritual father from Moldavia, Basil of Poiana Mărulai, who tonsured him as a monk with the name Paisii.

Paisii's life as a monk developed in two directions.[3] The first was the responsibility of leading the community which grew up around him. Soon after the visit of Basil he was joined by another monk and then, during the next few years, others came until there was a community of eight monks. Then more came and the community had to move to the larger skete of St Elias. Paisii led the monastery through this process of growth. The second strand of his life was the rediscovery and translation of texts. He did not succeed in finding the spiritual father he was seeking and so instead he looked for guidance from the spiritual traditions in the writings of the fathers. The spiritual fathers of the past would guide him through their writings. He collected books but found that the Slavonic versions were few in number and badly translated. So he first started to learn patristic Greek and then to translate ascetic texts from Greek into Slavonic. His biographer describes his life, caring for the community and guiding the monastery by day; and then working through the night in his cell reading and translating the texts on hesychasm and prayer of the heart. He slept little, three hours a night at most, and was absorbed in his work of translation.[4]

When he was forty-two, after eighteen years on Mount Athos, he left the mountain. His community had continued to expand and had outgrown its skete of St Elias. The restrictions placed on monastic life by the Ottoman authorities made it difficult to move to a larger monastery. He received an invitation, in 1764, from Prince Gregory of Moldavia to come to rebuild monasticism in this region. The monks set sail in two boats, one for the Romanians and one for other Slavonic speakers, and left the mountain and went to Moldavia, where they settled in the monastery of Dragomirna. There numbers in the monastery continued to increase and reached 350. They moved to the larger monastery of Neamt, which allowed further expansion until there were seven hundred monks and then over a thousand. The monastery became a place of pilgrimage and received many visitors. Meanwhile the work of translation into both Slavonic and Romanian was continuing. Paisii was assisted by two monks, Macarius and Hilarion, both of whom were learned in languages. There were also two teams of translators and copyists.⁵ Through this work, the ascetic traditions of the mountain were transported to Moldavia and from there to Russia.

While Paisii was working on his texts in Moldavia, the project was being continued on Mount Athos. This was the work of a group known as the Kollyvades, who were conservative, hesychastic monks who were dedicated to the revival of the monastic life. Their name came from the *kollyva*, which is the boiled wheat which is used in the commemoration of the departed, called *mnimosyne*. The commemorative memorial services were held on Saturdays as the day when Christ was in the tomb, but in 1754 the monks of St Anne's monastery on the mountain started celebrating these on other days to help them raise funds to build a new church, since offerings were made to the monastery at these memorial services. Some of the more conservative monks objected. As well as arguing for traditional liturgical observance of the memorial services using kollyva, they also encouraged daily receiving of communion and promoted inner prayer of the heart.

The Kollyvades collected, edited and published the works of Gregory Palamas and other fathers. This, they hoped, would be a 'word coming forth from silence' to renew and revive the monasteries and the wider church.⁶ Among the circle of the Kollyvades was a monk called Nikodimos, who was born in 1749 on the island of Naxos. In 1775 he came to the monastery of Dionysiou on Mount Athos. He quickly moved on from there into a life of greater silence and spent the rest of his life living in various hermitages and cells. He was simple in his manners, ascetic in his lifestyle and had no library or assistant. Here he remained until his death in 1809. When he was twenty-eight, in the year 1777, he met a new arrival on the mountain, Makarios (1731–1805), who had been bishop of Corinth, but had left the city for safety during the Russo-Turkish war of 1768. Nikodimos was a scholar and linguist and had a phenomenal photographic memory. It's told of him that on one occasion he attended Vespers on Holy Saturday in the monastery when it was discovered that there was no service book, so Nikodimos recited the fifteen Old Testament lessons from memory.⁷ Makarios was a leader of the Kollyvades movement and assembled a collection of patristic texts from the library of Vatopedi. He shared with Nikodimos his conviction of the need for these works to be edited, published and read. This led to a fruitful collaboration. Makarios assembled and collated the texts while Nikodimos edited and prepared them for circulation and publication. Some of these were published in 1782 in Venice with the title of the *Philokalia*.

Hesychasm in Russia

The teaching of the *Philokalia* had its greatest success in Russia. Here the nineteenth century was a time of social change. The Emancipation of the Serfs in 1861 changed the situation of the huge mass of peasants working on the land, then in 1885 the poll tax was abolished. Both these measures resulted in a new freedom for Russian peasants. Alongside new legal freedoms was the increased mobility caused by the building of railways. The new railways made it possible for the peasants, now released from their bondage on the land, to move around the country. They were able to visit the monasteries, where they could meet spiritual fathers and discover the traditional teachings on prayer. The number of visits of pilgrims was not recorded but there is an indication of the growing interest in pilgrimage from the monastery of Solovki. Pilgrims had to travel to the island by boat and the monastery recorded the number of voyages. The records show that 6,000 pilgrims made the voyage in 1863, and by 1900 the number had increased to 24,000 – a fourfold increase. Some pilgrims stayed and became monks. This led to a broadening of the social background of the monks. Previously monks had been recruited from the priestly caste but now increasingly novices came from all levels of society. During the nineteenth century there was a 'peasantization' of the culture and composition of monastic communities. The number of monasteries increased by 22 per cent between 1808 and 1861, and the number of monks by 77 per cent.[8]

In the midst of these social and cultural changes there was a revival of spiritual life. This was the hesychasm as set out in the *Philokalia* and taught by holy men and spiritual guides across the country. Paisii Velichkovskii continued his work of translation of texts into both Slavonic and Romanian. His collection, which was similar in content to the Greek *Philokalia*, was published with the equivalent Russian title of the *Dobrotolubiye*. While the Greek *Philokalia* was published in Venice and then reprinted once, in 1893, the Slavonic *Dobrotolubiye* was a far greater publishing success. It was published in 1793 and went through six editions in sixty years, with a translation into modern Russian appearing in 1877.

The book quickly circulated through Russia as the disciples of Paisii travelled from Neamt to monasteries in Russia taking with them their teacher's traditions of mental prayer. Russian monks had come to Paisii's monastery at Neamt after being driven out of their monasteries as a result of the restrictions imposed by Peter and Catherine so that by 1778 there over thousand monks the majority of which were Russian. And now they came back. The monk Cleopas had been on Mount Athos and then at Dragomirna with Paisii and, on his return to Russia, became abbot of the Ostrov Vedensky monastery where he introduced an Athonite life. One of the monks who worked on the publication of the *Dobrotolubiye* refounded the monastery of Valaam in the north and then went to Sarov, taking the book with him, where it was later read by St Seraphim. Another of his disciples, Macarius (d. 1811) became abbot of the Pesnoshky monastery and it was from here that the influence for reform reached Optina, which became a centre of both the Jesus Prayer and spiritual fatherhood.[9]

The monastery of Optina had its origins in the fifteenth century and had been organized in 1800 by Feofan the Cossack (d. 1819) following the hesychast principles of Paisii Velichkovskii. Although it was located in a remote part of the Kaluga region, it received many visitors. Ivan Kireevsky, a member of the Slavophil circle, supported the publishing work of Optina, and many literary figures visited the monastery. Among them was Fyodor Dostoevsky who came to visit the monastery in 1878 after his son died, in the company of Vladimir Soloviev. Here he met the *staretz*, or elder, Amvrosy who became a model for the figure of the Staretz Zossima in his novel the *Brothers Karamazov*. Passages of the novel are clearly descriptions of the monastery.

As part of its hesychastic practice, the Optina monastery set up a *pustyn'* or desert hermitage in the woods a few hundred metres distant from the main monastery buildings. In 1825 twelve monks settled there. A former hermit, Moisei, was appointed abbot. He distributed the *Philokalia* and other writings of Paisii Velichkovskii and established a library. By 1840 the pustyn had set up a publishing house dedicated to introducing monastic spirituality more widely. By the end of the century, they had published 125 books.

Here starchestvo or eldership became recognized and established. The revival began with the arrival of Leonid Nagolkin (1768-1841) at the *pustyn'* with his disciples in 1829. He had been a spiritual director in other places and recognized the importance of this ministry in the life of the monastery. He showed that it should be distinguished from sacramental confession and can only be undertaken by experienced monks who are not necessarily ordained priests. Not only did he give this spiritual advice but he also trained successors, who were then confirmed in their position by the senior members of the monastery. He was followed by others including Makarii Ivanov (1788-1860) and Amvrosii Grenkov (1812-91) who confirmed the place of Optina in encouraging a succession of startsy.

Popularization of the *Philokalia*

The title page of the *Philokalia* states that the book is intended 'for the general benefit of the Orthodox', and the compilers hoped that it would be read by all classes of society and not just by hermits and monks. This hope was realized in Russia as the Jesus Prayer or prayer of the heart became widely practised. Its popularity is shown by the successful publication in 1881 of a little book with the title of *A Sincere Tale Told by a Wanderer to His Spiritual Father* but which is better known by the shorter title of the English translation the *Way of a Pilgrim*.[10] The book tells the story of a poor and disabled peasant, who had lost the use of an arm in a childhood accident and now wandered around the country. This wandering life is better captured by the Russian term *strannik* rather than pilgrim, since it was a form of discipline rather than a journey to a destination. This wanderer hears the exhortation of St Paul's epistle to the Thessalonians to 'pray without ceasing' and asks people he meets how he can do this.[11] Among his informants is a staretz at a monastery who instructs him in the practice of the Jesus Prayer. He teaches him to say the prayer, building up gradually until he is reciting it 12,000 times in the day and the prayer becomes part of his life and personality. The staretz encourages him to buy a copy of the *Philokalia*, which he finds in a shop in St Petersburg for two roubles. He then walks across the country to Siberia and wants to go to Jerusalem. As he travels he meets a wide variety of people who describe their experience of prayer, especially prayer of the heart.

The book was discovered on Mount Athos by a monk from a monastery in Kazan who was visiting and who copied it. The author is not named and various suggestions have been made as to its provenance. It might be a genuine autobiographical account or it might be a carefully constructed piece of literary prose, modelled on the first person narrative style used by Gogol among other authors and echoing the journeys of John Bunyan's *The Pilgrim's Progress*.[12] A possible author is the Old Believer Archimandrite Mikhail Koslov (b. 1826) who had visited Mount Athos and then carried out missions in the Kazan area between 1870 and 1890 and who owned a manuscript version of the book which was recently discovered in his papers.[13] Whatever its origin it is a striking demonstration of the extending of monastic spirituality and hesychastic prayer throughout Russian society.

A further example of this popular spirituality was another but more controversial best-selling book entitled *On the Mountains of the Causcasus*. This was a collection of meditations on the wonder of God by a monk Ilarion (b. 1845) who left the monastery of St Panteleimon on Mount Athos and travelled to the Caucasus. The book describes how he meets a monk called Desideri who has been living a solitary life for ten years and who describes his experience of the Jesus Prayer. He tells how he has entered into a deeper sense of God's presence through the recitation of the Prayer of Jesus. The name of Jesus in the prayer was so closely associated with the experience of God's presence that it led the write to discover God's presence as identical with his name. This teaching became known as Imiaslavie, or worship of the name.

This identification of the name with the person of God led to controversy and the accusation that this teaching was pantheistic. The ensuing controversy, which broke out after 1912, was known as the Name of God affair. The Ecumenical Patriarch and the Russian Synod declared the teaching to be a pantheist heresy. But it had many supporters, especially on Mount Athos, and the resulting events when the Synod took action against respected elders led to disruption in the monasteries and in the wider church. In Optina the abbot Varsonofy supported the Imiaslavie and expelled those who disagreed with him, only to be ejected himself some years later. Many of the monks in St Panteleimon monastery on Mount Athos supported the Imiaslavie and 833 monks were deported to Russia in July 1913. Three boats were sent to collect them and they had to be driven on to them by fire hoses which were turned on them. When they arrived, forty monks were imprisoned and the rest defrocked, sent home to their villages but eventually allowed to return to monasteries. The majority of these expelled monks came from peasant backgrounds. They likened their sufferings to those of the iconophiles several centuries earlier.

The actions of the synod did not stamp out the Imiaslavie. Many of the Athonite monks who had been brought back to Russia found their way back into monasteries where they became spiritual elders and teachers, with the author Ilarion himself leading a group of followers in the Caucasus. The theologian Pavel Florensky defended them, seeing their view as a protest against a philosophical individualism. Others saw the affair as an attack by the synod on the monasteries.[14]

Both the *Way of the Pilgrim* and the Imiaslavie affair show the passion and extent of a popular spirituality which was located in monasteries and attracted many followers. It could lead in unorthodox and unruly directions which led to heavy-handed discipline from the Church.

Startsy

Alongside the growth in the practice of the Jesus Prayer went the growth in the ministry of those who taught it. The practice of hesychastic prayer is passed on by spiritual fathers by word of mouth. In Russia, the spiritual father is the staretz, or if a woman, a staritsa. The tradition and the nature of starchestvo is shown in the lives of the startsy. While these figures were all elders, sought out by visitors seeking healing, forgiveness and guidance, they fulfilled this calling in different ways. Their lives show how the tradition of spiritual prayer grew and influenced the life of the church in pre-revolutionary Russia.

Seraphim of Sarov has become one of the best-loved Russian saints. Prochor Moshnin was born in Kursk in July 1759. He entered the monastery at Sarov when he was nineteen years old and took the name Seraphim. He had not been long in the monastery when he fell ill. He was confined to bed for three years. In the course of the illness, he was visited by the Mother of God who stroked his head saying, as she did so, the words 'he is one of our family'. He recovered from his illness, was accepted as a monk in 1786, now aged twenty-seven, and then was ordained priest in 1793. He was a faithful to his monastic life but wanted to seek greater solitude. So he lived in a hut in the woods for ten years and after that spent a thousand days living on a rocky pillar, as the stylites had lived. His column was a large stone. He used one rock in the day and another at night. After this he retired even more fully into silence and spent several years living in the woods without speaking, not even to the monk who brought him food. Then, in 1810, physical weakness led him to return to the monastery where he stayed in his cell. Eventually, at the age of sixty-six, he started to receive visitors. Many came to seek his advice and ask for healing. In this final period of his life, for seven years, he received and welcomed those who came to him. He also cared for the nuns of the nearby convent of Diveyevo. Seraphim of Sarov died in 1833, and was made a saint in 1903, seventy years after his death. His life – while uneventful in worldly terms – demonstrates a pattern which shows the character of starchestvo. There was first, a period as an exemplary monk; then a time of solitude as a hermit; before finally receiving visitors and carrying out a public ministry of teaching and healing.

Figure 17 Seraphim of Sarov prayed for a thousand days on a rock in the forest.

Other startsy were scholars and teachers. Among these is Theophan the Recluse. He was born as Georgy Govorov in 1815. As a student he attended the theological academy at Kiev but became a monk before he had completed his studies, taking the name Theophan. He served first at the Russian Mission in Jerusalem, then was appointed rector of the Theological Academy at St Petersburg. In 1859 he was consecrated bishop of Tambov and then was moved to Vladimir. From here, he was chosen to become abbot of the monastery at Vysha. He found himself unable to combine his administrative duties with his ascetic discipline and his studies and so, in 1872 at the age of fifty-seven, he withdrew into his cell and shut the door. From then on until his death in 1894 he communicated only by writing letters. Theophan the Recluse was a scholar and author. He made translations of Greek texts and wrote commentaries on Scripture and spiritual books. Altogether he produced five hundred books and publications. He had broad learning and his library included 150 volumes of a French Theological Encyclopaedia. He painted, carved wood, played the harmonica and kept a microscope and telescope in his cell. He did not receive visitors as Seraphim had done, but gave guidance by writing letters and in this way kept in regular contact with the monks of Optina and other monasteries. Among his labours was the production of a modern Russian version of the *Dobrotolubiye*, which he worked at between 1876 and 1890. Along with Ignaty Brianchaninov, he was one of the leading theologians of the period. A bishop and theologian, he withdrew from public life to develop a theology based on the teachings of the father and to provide a manual and encouragement for contemplative prayer.

One of the best known startsy of the late nineteenth century lived in the Zosimova hermitage, attached to Trinity-Sergius Monastery, Aleksii Soloviev was born in Moscow and was deacon at a small parish and then priest at the important Dormition Cathedral. He married and had a son, but his wife died after only five years of their marriage. When his son had completed his education, Aleksii was able to become a monk. He had already gained a reputation as a confessor and spiritual father and many from Moscow and other places came to consult him. His visitors included the grand duchess Elizabeth and writers such as Pavel Florensky and Sergei Bulgakov. The constant stream of visitors made him ill and he withdrew into seclusion. He met his visitors only at weekends and the monastery managed this situation by allocating hundred tickets each weekend to those who wanted to see him. By 1916, when he was seventy years old, his health further deteriorated, and he withdrew more fully not seeing any visitors. This caused a stir in society and was discussed in the press. The Moscow Bulletin commented that he 'had "decisively" left the world …. (who had attracted) … personalities of the first rank to the last pauper. His influence was unbounded'.[15] Later he was persuaded to leave his seclusion to take part in the Council of Monastics preparing for the Moscow Church Council in 1917. At that Council, he was chosen to pick the name of one of the three candidates short-listed to become patriarch. He picked the paper with the name of Tikhon Belavin, a choice which was to have large influence on the future of the Church.

One of those who Aleksii guided and cared for was the grand duchess Elizabeth. She was a convert from Protestantism who had become a devout Orthodox Christian. Her husband was assassinated in 1905, after which she founded an Order of Deaconesses at the Marfo-Mariinski convent in Moscow, near the present Tretiakov gallery. At first there were just seventeen women, who wore a specially designed white habit. They were given the freedom to go outside the convent teaching, visiting the sick, preparing women for baptism and supporting the poor. Later this number grew. She visited staretz Aleksii nine times in 1909, and it was noted that it took her four hours to make her confession. She was herself a staritsa, acting as patron for the nuns of another monastery, the Iversko-Alkseevskaia in Sukhumi diocese.

There could be a wild and anarchic streak to this religious revival. A staritsa lived at the Sarov convent. Many people came to see Pelagia and considered her to be the true successor of Seraphim. She was born in 1809 and was married to a merchant at the age of seventeen and had two children who died in infancy. From childhood she had shown unusual and disturbed behaviour, which her mother probably concealed so as not to prevent her marriage. After her marriage she and her husband visited Diveyevo where she was blessed by the holy Seraphim, and this contributed to her reputation as a holy fool. Her husband however did not think she was mad and so chained her to the wall and beat her constantly. She would be seen wandering through the streets, beaten and half naked. When Seraphim died, the superior of Diveyevo arranged for Pelagia to join the community where she stayed for the next forty-seven years until her death. She sometimes spent the day lying in a ditch of manure, would break windows and kill cats. But she was also recognized as a healer and clairvoyant who could foretell deaths or illness of those who came to see her. She often refused to confess or take communion but her biographer said that she communicated spiritually with the angels and saints. As with other startsy, many came to consult her and find healing and forgiveness from her.

These practitioners of starchestvo show the value and importance of the practice. Some monasteries such as Optina identified and appointed experienced monks to act as startsy. When a Synodal Commission met in 1901 to consider reform in the Church it recommended starchestvo, and that monasteries where this was not practised should appoint supervisors to carry out this role. Within this outburst of enthusiasm among the spectrum of Russian society, the staretz was able to teach and pass on the tradition. There was an immediacy of the spoken word which was given within a close family-like relationship between staretz and spiritual child. It was a powerful and effective way of engaging a wide public within monastic culture. As Irina Paert comments, it was 'a component of religious memory that facilitated the transmission of religious experience from one generation to the next'.[16]

Notes

1 This is described in P. M. Kitromilides, 'Athos and the Enlightenment', ed. Anthony Bryer and Mary Cunningham, *Mount Athos and Byzantine Monasticism* (London, 1996), pp. 257–72.
2 There is an account of Paisii's life in Chetverikov, *Starets Paisii Velichkovskii* (Belmont, MA., 1980).
3 Chetverikov, *Paisii*, pp. 99–101.

4 For Paisii's life on Athos, see ibid., pp. 111–27.
5 Ibid., pp. 131–3, 216–21.
6 Kallistos Ware, 'St. Nikodimos and the *Philiokalia*' in Bingaman and Nassif, *Philokalia*, p. 12, quoting Ignatius of Antioch, Epistle to the Magnesians 8.2.
7 Ibid., p. 14.
8 Irina Paert, *Spiritual Elders* (de Kalb, IL, 2010), p. 74.
9 Andrew Louth, 'The Influence of the *Philokalia* in the Orthodox World', in Bingaman and Nassif, the *Philokalia*, pp. 50–60, at p. 53.
10 There is an English translation by R. M. French, published as the *Way of a Pilgrim* (London, 1930).
11 1 Thessalonians 5.17.
12 For these views see Paert, *Spiritual Elders*, p. 136.
13 Ibid., p. 136.
14 Ibid., pp. 172–6.
15 Scott Kenworthy, *Heart of Russia* (Oxford, 2010), p. 252.
16 Paert, *Spiritual Elders*, p. 38.

13 Part Two

Varieties of Tribulation: Genocide and Atheism

Genocide

Persecution in the Ottoman Empire happened not because of Muslim rule but the lack of it. In the nineteenth century the millet system slowly disintegrated, and with it the structure which had protected the status of Christians. There were several developments which led to the Catastrophe which expelled Greeks from their homes in Turkey; the massacres which led to the deaths of up to three million Armenians and about half of the Syrian Orthodox of the Middle East. The term 'genocide' was first used by Raphael Lemkin in 1943 to describe the systematic programme of elimination of the Armenian peoples.

Christian communities had been weakened and divided by Western missionary initiatives. The explorations and missions of the Portuguese and Spanish from 1500 had accelerated with the formation in 1622 by Pope Gregory XV of the Congregation for the Propaganda of the Faith. Missionaries were not permitted to convert Muslims, so developed an alternative strategy of attracting Syrian and other Orthodox as a first step in a process which it was hoped would lead to a mission to Muslims. Behind the actions of both Catholic and Protestant Missions was the conviction that a renewal of faith, through the acceptance of either the authority of Rome or of the Bible, would lead in the direction of conversion. One missionary stated that 'a wise plan for the conversion of the Mohammedans of Western Asia necessarily involved, first, a mission to the Oriental Churches. It was needful that the lights of the Gospel should once more burn on those candlesticks, that everywhere there should be living examples of the religion of Jesus Christ, that Christianity should no longer be associated in the Muslim mind with all that is sordid and base.'[1]

The Ottomans encouraged Western missionaries especially after the Greek War of Independence of 1821. A Catholic millet was recognized in 1830, and new Uniate churches were set up in which Orthodox worship and traditions were continued but under the authority of Rome. This led to the churches of the Syrian traditions becoming divided and fragmented. The outcome of this process of fragmentation is illustrated by the existence of six patriarchs of Antioch, presiding respectively over the Syrian Orthodox, Greek Orthodox, Greek Catholic, Maronite, Syrian Catholic and Latin Catholic Churches (although this sixth title is no longer used). Western powers put pressure on the Ottoman government to allow improved representation of

Christian minorities in government and administration, which had the reverse effect of provoking further suspicion and resentment against Christians.

As the century continued, the Ottoman Empire lost its Balkan provinces, and whole populations were displaced. Different displaced Muslim nationalities arrived in Anatolia from the newly Christian Balkan states. There were Circassians, Albanians, Macedonians and Greek Muslims coming from the lost European provinces, bringing with them resentment against the Christians who had displaced them. There were also wars against Russia which was expanding to take advantage of the weakened Turkish Sultanate. Turks suspected Armenian Christians of supporting the invaders. The sultan Abdul Hamid II (1876–1909) was losing control. He recruited regiments of mostly Kurdish troops, the Hamadiye regiments, so exploiting deep-seated resentments and rivalries as a way of encouraging division in society.

All this prepared the way for the disasters which continued from 1895 to 1915. By October 1895 violence was breaking out in Diyabakir, with slaughter of Christians and destruction of villages. This continued intermittently until it increased during the First World War. Concentration camps, forced labour and exile led to the death of an estimated half of the Christian communities of the Middle East. The monasteries of the Syrian churches were devastated along with the rest of the Christian communities.

Communists and atheists

Another wave of persecution which set out to eliminate the Christian faith and with it monastic life took place in the other main region of Eastern Christendom, Russia. This differed from the Armenian and Syrian genocides because it was directed intentionally against the Christian Church. Marxism–Leninism can be seen as a religious movement which challenged Christianity while the genocides were rooted in nationalism and intended as ethnic cleansing.

The political philosophy of Marxism–Leninism had its roots in a Christian society. An early socialist leader was Nikolai Chernyshevsky (1822–89). He was the son of a priest who, in his youth, had read Western philosophers such as Ludwig Feuerbach (1804–72). Under their influence he became socialist and atheist. He wrote a novel called *What Is to Be Done?* about a young revolutionary who devotes his life to the service of the poor. The hero leads an ascetic life, sleeping on a hard board studded with nails. The book reads like a traditional saint's life, except that God has disappeared and heaven is won through human struggle on earth. Nicolas Zernov described Marxism as 'a Judaeo-Christian apocalyptic sect born among a people familiar with the Bible'.[2] Another writer, Sergei Bulgakov, compared the early Bolsheviks to a religious order. There was an ethical code, an eschatological vision of a perfect society and an uncompromising resolution to bring the new order into being. The new faith of Marxism–Leninism held that this old unjust society would inevitably disappear and if this did not happen naturally then force would be needed to hasten the arrival of the new society.

The attack of Marxists on the Church went through a series of stages. It began with a moment of democracy. The February Revolution of 1917, which in fact took place in

March according to the Western Gregorian calendar, overthrew the tsarist regime and replaced it with a provisional government. This gave space for a Church Council to meet in Moscow for just over a month from 15 August to 17 September. There were 564 delegates to the Council, consisting of 80 bishops, 147 priests, 9 deacons, 15 sextons and 299 laypersons. It quickly re-established the patriarchate which had been abolished by Peter the Great and set up elected parish and diocesan councils. While these decisions opened Church government to a wider membership and helped to strengthen the Church for the storms ahead, it had little influence on the situation of monasteries, which were vulnerable to local conflicts and hostility. Power was transferred to the Soviets after the October Revolution in the same year. There followed changes in the law which allowed local action which closed churches and monasteries between 1918 and 1929. There was then a period of brutal repression which led to the deaths of many thousands of Christians in 1938–9.

Statistics state that there were, in 1914, 117 million Orthodox believers in Russia. There were 48,000 parish churches; 1,105 monasteries; 51,000 clergy and 130 bishops. By the end of the Civil War in 1921, 28 bishops and several thousand priests and monks had been killed. Only 352 of the 1,105 monasteries were still open. As persecution intensified the numbers who were killed grew. It is estimated that forty thousand monks had been killed by the end of 1939.[3]

The Second World War brought a relaxation of pressure and opportunities for the Church to re-enter society. The German army attacked Russia on 22 June 1941 and reached the edge of Moscow by October. The patriarch supported the Russian war effort and this led to a closer relationship with the government and to a new freedom for the Church. Stalin summoned three metropolitans to meet him on 4 September 1943 when they arranged for a sobor, or synod, to be held in Moscow just four days later. At this council Stalin agreed that theological schools and churches could be re-opened, a journal re-established, the former German embassy to become the residence of the patriarch and even groceries to be delivered to the patriarchate at special state prices. In addition to this new situation within Russia, the German occupation gave a greater freedom which allowed the Church to open new church buildings and monasteries in the areas under German occupation. These were able to stay open after the war ended and so monasteries and nunneries continued to work in these regions throughout the rest of the Soviet period, although the monasteries in Russia were later closed.

There was a further wave of persecution after the death of Stalin in 1954. Stalin was succeeded by Nikita Krushchev who was First Secretary of the Communist Party until his death in 1964. The further attacks on the Church were delayed until Krushchev could displace the Chairman of the Council of Ministers, Georgy Malenkov (1902–88). Malenkov had been sympathetic to the Church and on his enforced retirement from politics in 1961 sang in his church choir and became a reader. After he was removed, the repression re-started with closure of churches and imprisonment of believers. The number of monasteries fell from 101 in 1945, to 90 in the 1950s and then to sixteen in 1968. Of the sixteen monasteries and nunneries open in 1968, all but Trinity-Sergius were in the western areas which had been occupied by the German army during the war.

The story of Trinity-Sergius

The progress of the attempted destruction of Christianity in Russia can be traced by following the fortunes of Trinity-Sergius monastery.

A new level of persecution was encouraged by two decrees of the Bolshevik government in 1917 and 1918. The decree on land confiscated all church land and allowed local soviets to appropriate monastic lands; then the decree on the separation of church and state removed the legal status of churches and monasteries, nationalized church property and prohibited religious instruction in schools. The process of nationalization showed itself at the local level in searches, arrests and the requisition of property by members of the Red Army. These actions were usually happened at night to increase intimidation. In the case of the Trinity-Sergius monastery, rents from monastery property were confiscated and buildings, bank accounts and investments were appropriated. This process was completed in November 1918 when a further decree nationalized the monastery so that it passed into the possession of the state. The monastery founded by St Sergius became a 'living museum'.

The body of St Sergius was at the heart of the monastery and attracted pilgrims from all parts of Russia. The government decree of March 1919 had ordered the opening and destruction of relics. The opening of the tomb of St Sergius to expose the relics was arranged for 11 April 1919, shortly before the start of Holy Week. A meeting was arranged in the hall of the Theological Academy where speeches were given to the peasants and invited guests saying how dangerous religion was. At 6 pm the monastery was closed to prevent pilgrims entering and Red Army soldiers and students were positioned at the gates. Local people realized that the exhumation of the body of Sergius was about to take place and so they gathered outside in large numbers. In the church a movie camera was put in place and crowds of officials, soldiers, students and monks assembled. A monk approached the shrine, while other monks sang hymns to the saint until the army stopped them. The monk prostrated himself, opened the tomb and removed the many rich coverings one by one. When the last cover was removed, a skeleton was found with some of the hair still on the skull. The Bolshevik official wrote in his account 'as was to be expected uncorrupt relics were not found' and the word went round the crowd outside that 'there are no relics'. The official considered the event a victory for it was clear that there were no miraculous remains and the bones of the saint had the function 'only to keep the dark masses in subjection and to exploit popular ignorance'. A theological student who was present had a different view. He was not surprised that there was a skeleton rather than an uncorrupt body, nor was his faith threatened. The tomb contained not a board or a wax figure but the true body of the saint. The next day crowds formed to see the exposed bones. There was weeping, hymn singing, arguments, but many came to venerate the saint who was now regarded as a martyr to faith in his death as well as a protector of the country in his life. The procession to see the saint continued through the day. Many closed their eyes as they approached the open tomb and, when asked why, explained that they did not want to offend 'the nakedness of the saint'.[4]

Some monks continued to live in the monastery, in spite of the confiscation of rents, lands and buildings. They continued to worship until one night in November 1919 at 3 am the Red Army arrived, removed the monks and sealed the monastery. This led to complaints and protests until, after some months, forty-three monks were permitted to return to the monastery as employees of the state, with responsibility for guarding the artistic and historic treasures. Among the treasures which remained in the monastery were the relics of St Sergius. All attempts to remove these to a Moscow museum were met with anger and protest from both the patriarch and local believers. The authorities gave up the attempt to remove them and instead made them into a centre piece of an anti-religious exhibition.

Although the monastery was closed, the monks carried on their life in different ways. Some stayed living in the area around the monastery and continued to serve in parish churches and cemetery chapels. Some senior monks were recognized as startsy and continued to attract visitors and pilgrims who came for prayer and advice. In the more remote monasteries dependent on Trinity-Sergius, the monks formed themselves into agricultural collectives and remained at their monastery. When the purges of 1937–8 took place, the NKVD (Internal Affairs Commissariat) found thirty former monks living in the area of their monasteries, arrested them and most were given ten-year prison sentences.

The monastery of St Sergius re-opened in the Holy Week of 1946 as a result of the relaxation of persecution. Archimandrite Gury was given the keys to the cathedral in the monastery and opened the door on the Wednesday of Holy Week to find it empty and covered with layers of dust. With the help of local believers, he cleaned and prepared it for the services of Good Friday. He and two other monks were the beginning of a re-formed community. Gury had been made a monk before the revolution, was arrested in 1920 and survived his sentence at the camp on the White Sea Canal. After his sentence he lived as a hermit in Tashkent and escaped the notice of the NKVD during the Terror. A few months after he returned to rebuild the monastery he was chosen to be bishop of Tashkent and sent back to the region where he had lived through the Terror. Most of the other monks who joined him in this new phase of the life of the monastery had been tonsured before the revolution. They brought with them the traditions and practices of the pre-revolutionary way of life. The relics of the saint were restored to their former place in the cathedral and the lines of pilgrims re-formed. Father Filadelf Mishin (1877–1959) had entered the monastery in 1904, been ordained a priest in 1921 and served in a parish until his arrest and imprisonment in 1931. He became known as an elder and was consulted by the pilgrims who came to the monastery. He himself thought this reverence paid to him was foolish. Through the 1950s there were up to ninety monks, and as many as fifteen thousand pilgrims came to the monastery for the great feasts.

Life in the monastery continued. It survived the further waves of repression which began in 1959 and was recognized as the 'ideological and organizational' centre of the Russian Church.[5] It remained open through the remainder of the Communist period.

Monks and startsy

The story of Trinity-Sergius shows how the life of the monastery and the church first survived and then was able to revive after seventy years of hostility with periods of unrelenting persecution. The monasteries may have closed but monastic life continued.

It is possible to suggest that little changed and that the church was able to begin again in 1990 from where it had been in 1917. At the Moscow Council of 1917, most people thought that Russia was a deeply religious nation. It was claimed that there were 117 million Orthodox believers. But, one of the delegates wondered, 'we say we have 110 million Orthodox Christians but what if we have as few as ten million?' This concern was demonstrated when it was made voluntary for soldiers to attend church and receive communion in 1917. The number of communicants fell from the mandatory 100 per cent to less than 10 per cent. Distrust of church authorities and atheism among many continued alongside a deeply rooted popular devotion based around holy places and holy people.[6]

The closure of monasteries forced monks and nuns out into the world. With the arrest and execution of bishops, the structures of church organization collapsed. Those bishops who remained affirmed their support of the Soviet government, a compromise which reduced the trust and support of believers. Local and popular religious leaders filled the gap. Monks removed their habits, lived and worked among lay people and relied on their care and support. If there was no priest, nuns conducted the monastic services. This brought a new style of monastic life, lived outside monasteries and in towns and villages. Bishop Veniamin was arrested in 1929 and wrote from his prison camp: 'Before my arrest I was cut off from daily life and could not see what people lived by, what they are interested in, what is the spirit of contemporary society.'[7]

New ideas were discussed. A priest named Valentin Sventitsky wrote a series of dialogues from his place of exile. He argued for a 'monasticism in the world'. He wrote that in the early centuries of the Church there were no monasteries because all Christians lived according to monastic ideals. When Christianity became the religion of the empire, then standards lapsed and those who were zealous withdrew into the desert. Now, under Communism, all Christians have to build invisible walls around themselves to preserve themselves from infection by a godless society.[8]

Spiritual fathers became the leaders of faith. They gathered followers around them and these often followed an intense religious life, rigorously keeping the fasts and meticulously following the rules for worship. In the Communist period many new sects formed and grew as people followed the leadership of charismatic preachers. The Ioannites believed that Father John of Kronstadt was an incarnation of the Trinity. The Innokentievtsy were followers of a Moldavian monk accused of heresy in 1913. The Fedorovtsy were followers of a peasant Fedor Rybalkin who had been a prisoner of war from 1914 to 1917 and would come to judge the unrighteous.

Church divisions became less important. There had been a long-lasting schism with the Old Ritualists, or Old Believers, which had begun as a reaction to reforms to liturgy introduced by Patriarch Nikon in 1666. Then Patriarch Tikhon had declared his support for the Soviet state which led to rigorists removing themselves from his jurisdiction. The Renovationist Church had been set up by the Soviet authorities. As conditions became harder and churches closed, these divisions did not matter so much. Believers went to any church which was open. If there was no church, wandering priests and those around them kept faith alive and active. This led to a more unified church when conditions became favourable in 1943.

Natalia Kiter, a member of the Tikhonite Church which gave at least public support to the government, looked back at the 1930s. 'Underground brotherhoods grew. Their purpose was the fulfilment of the basic Commandments: the love of God and the neighbour ... there was much selfless charity work aimed particularly at helping those persecuted by the Godless state, much running around to jails, hospitals, camps, and places of internal exile.'[9]

The popular forms of Christian faith which had grown around the monasteries and been encouraged by the startsy continued in different forms and in different places after the Communist Revolution. As so often has happened, the spiritual life was carried out not only in the monastic buildings but in the lives and witness of countless believers. The character and vitality of the spiritual life in the Communist period is shown by three examples.

Staretz Tavrion Batovsky was born in 1898 and ran away to Glinsk hermitage when he was thirteen years old. He was arrested and sent to a labour camp in 1928 where he was held for twenty-seven years. He considered that this was a time when he followed Sergius into the forests and lived an ascetic life. As he travelled across the tundra he and his companions came across a trainload of frozen corpses – probably prisoners left to die. Tavrion conducted the funeral service for each of them and after this experience he resolved to celebrate the liturgy every day, which he did right up to his death.

After his release he became the staretz at the monastery of the Transfiguration at Riga in 1968. His reputation spread and the small monastery which could only feed twenty guests grew until it became a place of pilgrimage welcoming up to two hundred people a day. The report of one of those who visited the staretz shows the influence of the holy man.

> Nowhere have I seen the liturgy celebrated with such humility and gentleness, such conviction and authority, such Paschal joy. At every liturgy there is a sermon, often two or three, which is like a torrent of life-giving wisdom, like a judgment before the judgment seat of God, baring the secrets of the conscience but bathing the heart with the great love and tenderness of the heavenly Father ... When for the first time I saw the starets preaching with his eyes closed and a Gospel in his hands I felt that such sweetness, humility and power could dwell only in a saint.[10]

The life of one nun shows how monastic life could be carried on in the world. Valeriya Mekeyeva was brought up in an atheist family. She became Christian, following the example of her grandmother. Then her mother reported her to the authorities and she was imprisoned for five years. On her release in about 1950, she became a nun at Zhitomir in the Ukraine. After ten years the convent was closed and she went to live in Moscow. She gathered a group around her and they made belts embroidered with texts from the psalms which were worn under a cassock or clothes especially by monks and nuns. These belts were sold to raise money to buy accommodation for homeless former nuns. She was arrested again in 1979 and tried for the illegal manufacture of handicrafts. She was sent to a special psychiatric hospital and given an intensive course of drug treatment which paralyzed her arm and damaged her health. Her experiences show how small groups of monks and nuns continued to live together in communities and also the risks and dangers which this led to.

Many Russians left the Soviet Union. Émigré communities formed in cities in Europe and elsewhere. Among those who fled was a young woman, Liza Skobstsova. She was born Elizaveta Pilenko in Riga, then part of the Russian Empire in 1891. The family moved to St Petersburg where she became involved in radical socialist circles, wrote poetry and was briefly married to a fellow socialist Dmitri Kuz'min-Karaev. In the next stage of her life, she became Christian and moved to Anapa on the Black Sea coast where she became deputy mayor in 1918 then mayor. When the anti-Communist White Army captured the town she was tried for being Bolshevik but her judge turned out to be a former teacher and she was acquitted. She and the judge were then married. As the Red Army advanced, the family left and fled to Paris in 1923. The family group consisted of Lisa, her husband, her three children and her mother. There her two daughters died of illnesses and this marriage also broke down. In 1932, she was given an ecclesiastical divorce by her husband and she was made a nun by the Russian bishop in Paris, Evlogy, and given the name Maria. She lived at 77 Rue de Lourmel in Paris, a large rambling house with room for family, fellow nuns and a priest and also for the many people who came to her seeking help. It was a centre for all those, especially Russian refugees, in need. She provided care, advice and food for those who came to her. She calculated that in the year 1935 the house served 22,991 meals. She welcomed all who came, went out early in the morning to beg for vegetables and food from the markets. At night, she sometimes slept with the homeless under bridges on the river bank. She smoked cigarettes in public and often failed to attend church services. Her fellow nun, Evdokia Mescherakova, was shocked by her approach to monastic life and left the Rue de Lourmel. In 1935 Mother Maria founded Orthodox Action, an organization to provide social care. When the Nazis occupied Paris, she sheltered Jews and provided them with baptism certificates to help them escape. This led to her arrest in February 1943 and imprisonment in Ravensbrück concentration camp. She was killed on the day before Easter and the day before the Red Cross arrived to begin the release of prisoners. According to some reports she took the place of another in the line awaiting the gas chamber. A fellow prisoner wrote: 'All that was left of her was skin and bone, her eyes were festering, and she exuded that nightmarish sweet smell of those infected with dysentery ... She radiated the peace of God and communicated it to us.'[11]

These lives show that the closure of monasteries did not result in the end of monastic life but, instead, a new freshness and vitality. Monasteries had been places of refuge and had preserved culture throughout the history of the Eastern churches. Whether it was Chalcedonians persecuting Monophysites, Muslims showing an outburst of violence or now with Communists planning the extinction of the Church, the monasteries which were out in the country far from the towns sheltered those fleeing. Even if the monasteries were closed, groups of monks or a staretz continued monastic life outside the monastery. Staretz Tavrion withdrew and lived as a hermit, and then made himself open and available to show God's love to those who came. Sister Valeriya carried on

Figure 18 Mother Maria Skobtsova cared for the poor in Paris and ended her life in Ravensbruck concentration camp.

a simple coenobitic life shared with others. Mother Maria accepted humiliation and hostility, as the fools for Christ had done through the centuries. These are examples of how monastic life can be lived out. There were many who followed a similar life style or found other ways of being faithful to the way of life they had chosen. The closure of monasteries enabled the nature of monastic life to be seen more starkly and sharply. It also provided the foundation for renewal when – eventually – the monasteries were able to open again.

Notes

1 Rufus Anderson writing in the History of the missions of the American Board of Commissioners for Foreign Missions to the Oriental Churches, in Khalid Dinno, *The Syrian Orthodox Christians in the Late Ottoman Period and Beyond* (Piscataway, NJ, 2017), p. 58.

2 Nicolas Zernov, *Russian Religious Renaissance of the Twentieth Century* (London, 1963), p. 328.
3 Dmitry Pospielovsky, *The Orthodox Church in the History of Russia* (New York, 1998), pp. 209, 258.
4 These accounts are taken from contemporary records, in Scott Kenworthy, *Heart of Russia* (Oxford, 2010), pp. 316–17.
5 Nikolai Mitrokhin cited in ibid., p. 371.
6 Pospielovsky, *Orthodox Church*, p. 199.
7 Paert, *Spiritual Elders* (De Kalb, IL, 2010), p. 185.
8 Ibid., p. 183.
9 Pospielovsky, *Orthodox Church*, p. 259.
10 Jane Ellis, *The Russian Orthodox Church, a Contemporary History* (London, 1990), p. 148.
11 Sergei Hackel, *A Pearl of Great Price* (London, 1982), pp. 144–8.

14 Part Two

Revival and Renewal in the Twentieth Century

Discovering a new freedom

It has been estimated that three thousand people were killed for their faith in the first three centuries of the history of the Church, most of these in the persecutions of the late third century. During the twentieth century, by comparison, there were an estimated 300,000 Christians killed in the Soviet Union under Communism, over a million Armenians and Syrians killed in the period called by Syrians the Year of the Sword and many more in other persecutions such as the death of Serbs in Ustaše concentration camps of Second World War Croatia. There were more Christians killed in the twentieth century than in any other.

It has also been a century of renewal of monastic life which has also led to a wider renewal of life within the Church. This is shown in the revival of the monasteries of Mount Athos and also in the Orthodox Church in post-Communist Russia and in many other places. The seeds of this new life came especially from the lives of monks who continued to follow their ascetic disciplines in periods when the institution of monasticism was in decline and many monasteries closed.

Mount Athos

The Holy Mountain of Athos has remained as a monastic republic with the twenty ruling monasteries managing its life. Yet again its situation was changed by political events beyond its borders. The Ottoman Empire disintegrated during the First World War and the legal status of the mountain was discussed at the Treaty of Lausanne in 1923. It was decided that the mountain should be part of the Greek state. A new charter for Mount Athos was approved by the Holy Synod in 1924 and by the Greek government in 1926. This laid down that the mountain was a self-governing part of Greece, under the ecclesiastical jurisdiction of the ecumenical patriarch and under the administrative jurisdiction of a governor appointed by the Greek state. The rights of the non-Greek residents were protected. There was to be no change in the method of administration or the number of monasteries or their order of precedence. The lands of the mountain were not to be expropriated. These provisions preserved a traditional way of life which had grown and struggled for over centuries. There was one new provision in the 1924 charter. Women were forbidden to set foot on the mountain, with a penalty of a prison sentence of up to twelve months. The prohibition of women had been a tradition since monks first arrived, but now it was law. The Greek parliament discussed the removal of this ruling in International Women's Year in 1975, and have done so again since, but kept it in place partly because of the long tradition and partly because it is included in the 1924 charter.

Now the mountain was contained within Greece, which was formed out of the former Ottoman Empire. Until this time, Athos had been part of an international empire which reached out to include a mixture of nations, languages and ethnicities. The first monks had come from different countries. Throughout its history monasteries had looked to various benefactors and communities from all parts of the empire. The Georgians had set up Iviron, the Serbs had come to Hilendar and Bulgarians to Zographou. In the nineteenth century huge numbers of Russians had come as pilgrims and as monks. By 1870 there were three large Russian houses. These were the monastery of St Panteleimon and the skites of St Andrew and the prophet Elijah. By 1900 there were 3,496 Russians and 3,276 Greeks, so the Russian monks slightly outnumbered the Greeks.[1]

The Communist revolution changed this. The monasteries in Russia were closed and monks from the Slav countries no longer arrived. The membership figures of the Russian monastery of St Panteleimon, the Serbian monastery of Hilendar and Bulgarian monastery of Zographou show the impact of this change.

Figure 19 St Panteleimon monastery was a community of over 1,900 monks by the end of the nineteenth century, when there were slightly more Russian than Greek monks on Mount Athos.

	1903	1971
St Panteleimon	1928	24
Zographou	155	11
Hilendar	385	54
Great Lavra	1187	378

The inclusion of the Greek house of the Great Lavra shows that decline was not limited to the Slavs. The number of monks across the whole mountain was falling fast as these next figures show.

1903	7,432 monks
1959	1,641
1968	1,238
1972	1,145

The end of monastic life on the mountain seemed inevitable. The writer, John Julius Norwich, wrote after a visit in 1966.

> Athos is dying – and dying fast. In nearly every monastery the writing looms, all too plainly, on the walls. We have discussed what might happen when probably within the life time of most readers the thousand-year old history of the mountain comes to an end. The disease is incurable, there is no hope .... The fundamental unanswerable fact is that Mount Athos has become an anachronism.[2]

But the expected end did not happen. In 1972 the number of monks rose from 1,145 to 1,146. This was a modest rise, to say the least, but it was the start of change. The population of the mountain has continued to increase.[3] Here is another table showing the numbers of monks recorded in the period up to 2,009.

1971	1,145
1972	1,146
1976	1,206
1986	1,285
1990	1,290
2000	1,610
2009	2,000

This revival is attributed to the rediscovery of traditional hesychast teaching. While many monasteries had become idiorrythmic and all had declined in number and all buildings had fallen into disrepair, solitary monks had continued to live, work and pray in the cells in remote parts of the peninsula, as well as in the monasteries. To give just one example, the Russian monk Silouan was a member of the community at St Panteleimon. He lived in the monastery from 1892 to 1938. His disciple Sophrony wrote about his experiences of prayer. 'In a manner passing all understanding the Lord appeared to him, and his whole being was filled with the fire of the grace of the Holy Spirit ... a divine light shone about him, and he was lifted out of this world, and in spirit transported to heaven, where he heard ineffable words.' Later he was assaulted by demonic temptations, and saw a huge devil standing in front of the icons. He prayed for humility and received a word in his heart. 'Keep thy mind in hell and despair not.' That final phrase has been often reported, and the writing of Silouan has been edited by Sophrony and translated into several languages. The discovery and then canonization of this obscure Russian, and then the wide dissemination of his writings is a demonstration of why and how the revival of Athonite hesychast spirituality has taken place.

More monasteries have been renewed through the influence of these ascetic teachers and their disciples. A pattern of change is that a teacher and some followers move and settle in one of the monasteries. The monastery then changes its status from an idiorrythmic to a coenobitic house. Then this new disciplined way of life attracts further recruits.

The elder Joseph the Hesychast, also known as the Cave Dweller, lived in the New Skete and died in 1959. His teaching on hesychast prayer drew monks to him as disciples. Six monasteries have been renewed by his spiritual children including Vatopedi, Philotheou and Dionysiou. Another monastery to undergo change was Simonopetra. The new arrivals here came from a monastery in the Meteora on mainland Greece where the life was being disrupted as a result of the number of tourists visiting the monastery. The abbot Aimilianos and all the monks moved to Simonopetra, where they have acquired a reputation for theological study, and Byzantine music. They have built an extension to the monastery buildings and there is a waiting list to join the community. Further examples of other monasteries could be added. In 1992 a group of monks were sent by the ecumenical patriarch to the monastery of Pantocrator. This monastery was the last to become a coenobium, and so the practice of idorrythmia on the mountain came to an end.

Revival in Romania

This revival has extended to other parts of the Eastern Christian world. In Romania, monasteries grew in spite of the discrimination and hostility of the Communist government. As has often happened in periods when the Church is persecuted, the monasteries became centres of resistance. When the life of the Church was restricted, the monastic and ascetic life became a way that people could affirm and live out their faith. The ascetic life itself becomes a form of resistance to state policies. The spiritual fathers of Romania, as in Russia, were the holders of a tradition of prayer and faith which thrived outside the structures of the Church. One of these elders was staretz Ioanichie Moroi. He was a monk on Mount Athos who returned to Romania before the Second World War and lived in the monastery of Sihastria. After the war, the monastery continued to be a centre of Christian life and provided many bishops who led the Church in the Communist period.

The life of the elder Cleopa, abbot of the monastery of Sihastria, shows how the life and teaching of a monastic elder sustains the faith of a wider community. Constantin, as he was in secular life, was born in 1912, and at the age of seventeen entered the monastery of Sihastria. It was then a small community of fourteen monks. When he arrived, the abbot made him wait outside the monastery gates and to beat a piece of wood. After three days the abbot asked him what the wood had said. The young Cleopa replied that the wood had said nothing. That, the abbot replied, is how you must be. He was given charge of the monastery sheep and so spent much of his time outside the monastery, using his solitude to read the *Philokalia*. In 1942 he returned to live in the monastery and was made assistant to the abbot, and then abbot from 1944 to 1949. He then moved to the nearby monastery of Slatina, accompanied by thirty monks of Sihastria, in order to build up the monastery. Soon the community had grown to eighty monks. His popularity aroused unwelcome attention from the Communist authorities. Cleopa was instructed by his spiritual father to withdraw and live in solitude away from the monastery. He did this on three occasions, for six months in 1949 and then for two years between 1952 and 1954, and then again from 1959 to 1964. During this last period, the monastery announced that he had died and his mother went into mourning for him. But he was alive and not far away. He had gone into the mountains and dug a cave to live in. Some local shepherds knew where he was and brought him food. Later he said that, in spite of shortage of food, he lived like a king. When the worst of that phase of persecution was over, he returned to his former monastery of Sihastria in 1964. Here he remained for the following thirty-four years until his death in 1998, as abbot, staretz and popular teacher. He preached in the Moldavian dialect of Romanian, using simple language and accessible stories. His teaching was based on the *Philokalia* and it was said that his listeners could not distinguish passages of Cleopa's writing from those of John of the Ladder. For sixty-nine years the elder lived in two monasteries and in various places of withdrawal, following a life of prayer and also advising and guiding those who came to him. He influenced many who came to him, including the Patriarch Daniel, who was consecrated to this post of patriarch in 2007, and many bishops. His periods of withdrawal gave him an awareness of the natural world. He taught his disciples to love and care for the world around. His influence encouraged the involvement of the Church in the ecological movement.[4]

Russia after Communism

The most spectacular growth of monastic life has been in Russia. The Communist government, as we have seen, closed the monasteries. There were 933 monasteries in Russia before the revolution. These were all closed by 1939. A display in a recent exhibition on church life in Moscow recorded the statistics of decline in the number of monasteries from the 933 before the Revolution, to zero in 1939, with some relaxation of control allowing 62 in 1952, declining again to 18 in the repression under Krushchev.[5] After the end of Communism, monasteries have re-opened. In 2015 there were over eight hundred active monasteries, with about half in Russia and half in other countries of the former Soviet Union.[6]

These have taken on a wide variety of different forms of life, all contributing in different ways to the work of the Church in re-Christianising Russia. The Sretensky Monastery is in central Moscow, near the Lubyanka, former headquarters of the KGB. It is a centre of missionary activity. Its publishing house produces over a hundred new books each year on all aspects of Christian life and maintains a widely used internet site. The monastery church attracts a large congregation and there is an extensive education programme for children and adults.

A recent traveller reports on a visit to St George's, a remote parish 300 miles northeast of Moscow. Here a small community of monks is led by Fr Mefodii Kondratiev. In 1991 a group from St Petersburg bought several small houses. This led to the monks welcoming recovering drug addicts and developing a recovery programme. Eight young men share in the life of the monastery as part of a therapeutic discipline.[7]

The Marfo-Marinsky monastery in southern Moscow founded by the grand duchess Elizabeth was returned to the Church in 1992, the year in which the foundress was canonized. The tradition of care for those in need is continued. A recent visitor reports that he found fifteen nuns, of which five wear black and keep a stricter discipline. The others wear white. These have a medical training and carry out the community's social work. As well as the nuns, there are sixty employees, all Orthodox Christians, and many lay volunteers. The monastery looks after a school for orphaned girls, a summer camp for invalid children and supports the carers with disabled people.[8]

Not far away from the Marfo-Marinsky monastery is the parish of St Nicholas Kuznetsky. Here the parish priest is Vladimir Vorobiev, who was influenced by a former priest in the parish Fr Vsevolod Schpiller who had been the centre of a group of intellectuals. After 1991, Fr Vladimir organized educational activities. These have grown dramatically until now the parish is the centre of the St Tikhon's Humanitarian University, accredited by the state and offering university degrees. The number of students varies with at least three thousand students studying a variety of courses including sociology, linguistics, mathematics and information technology. The parish is also the centre of a Sisterhood of St Dmitrii, which works in hospitals. Fr Vladimir is a married priest, but has learned from monastic spiritual fathers. In a recent lecture looking back at his experiences in the Communist period, he describes how he has been influenced by his teachers. These are mostly monks and ascetic spiritual fathers. The work of parishes such as St Nicholas Kuznetsky is a demonstration of the influence of the monks within the wider church.[9]

The *Philokalia*

The influence of modern-day elders is accompanied by the re-discovery of the text compiled over a century previously by three monks on the Holy Mountain, Paisii, Makarios and Nikodimos. The *Philokalia* had encouraged revival in Russia in the nineteenth century and it was to be effective in the twentieth century but over a wider area. After the book was published in Venice in 1793 there were no further editions in Greece until 1893, and it was not until 1957 that a new Greek edition was printed. Then in Romania, Dumitru Staniloae (1903–93) began to produce a considerably enlarged version in twelve volumes which began publication in 1946 and continued slowly until 1991. Alongside this have been translations into Western languages, usually in five volumes. The English translation, of which the first four out of five volumes have been published, was done by Geoffrey Palmer, Philip Sherrard and Metropolitan Kallistos Ware.[10] This contains the same set of texts as the 1782 Philokalia but translates from better Greek versions and adds new introductory sections. There have been further versions in several languages.

This publication history reflects the vitality of hesychastic, and so monastic, spirituality over the last two centuries and is a barometer of the progress of the modern revival in monasticism in Eastern Christendom. The *Philokalia* is a tradition rather than a book. It is the written record of a movement of patristic and hesychastic revival, carried out by different teachers, in different places, and at different times. Its rich profusion of material and its publication success have enabled it to encapsulate and convey the tradition of prayer, developed and nurtured in the monasteries, especially on Mount Athos, to a wide readership. Kallistos Ware described it as a spiritual time-bomb. Its message has been heard not only in the monasteries of Eastern Christendom but in the West too. 'It is surely astonishing,' writes Metropolitan Kallistos, 'that a collection of spiritual texts originally intended for Greeks living under Ottoman rule, should have achieved its main impact two centuries later in the secularised and post-Christian west'.[11] Its origin happened when a Ukrainian monk, Paisii, was frustrated in his attempt to find a spiritual father and so he collected material from the tradition of spiritual direction so he could learn from them at a distance of time and space. His book has helped others make the same discoveries.

The success of the English translation surprised its publishers, as the remark of Metropolitan Kallistos shows. As well as the written words, Athonite spirituality was brought to England by the monk Sophrony Sakharov (1896–1993). Fr Sophrony had spent twenty years on Mount Athos as a monk at St Panteleimon monastery and then as a hermit. He was a disciple of the Russian ascetic staretz Silouan, whose writing he later published. He came to Tolleshunt Knights in Essex in 1958 and, with six monks of different nationalities, set up the monastery of St John the Baptist, for women as well as men, with a form of worship which included communal use of the Jesus Prayer according to the traditions of the holy mountain. The monastery has become a centre for Athonite spirituality which has introduced hesychasm to many visitors.

The monastery was at first under the jurisdiction of the Russian bishop Antony Bloom. André Bloom was born to a Russian diplomatic family in 1914 and was brought up as a child in Persia. In 1920, after the Communist revolution, he moved with his mother and grandmother to Paris. He became a doctor and also served in the army. From 1931, he was guided by Afanasy Nechaev, a spiritual father who had been a monk at the Valaamo monastery in Finland before becoming priest of a parish in Paris. André became a novice monk in 1939 a few days before he was called up to serve in the army, and then in 1943 he was tonsured as a monk with the name Antony. He expected to leave his family and live as a monk, but was sent back to live with his mother and grandmother, instructed to listen to them as to monastic superiors. He lived as a monk secretly, telling no-one of his new state until he was ordained priest in 1947, an event delayed until his mother was reconciled to this change. He was sent to England first as chaplain to the ecumenical Fellowship of St Alban and St Sergius, then as parish priest to the Russian congregation and then was made bishop of Sergievo in 1957, then titular metropolitan of Sourozh in 1966. He was a popular and influential teacher, preacher and writer on prayer. His influence spread in the West and then also in Russia. He was one of three candidates to become patriarch of Moscow in 1990. Today the Metropolitan Antony of Sourozh Foundation continues to encourage and reflect on his approach to faith and has a wide following in Russia. His life shows how monastic life flourished outside the walls of a monastery, how it shapes and influences the life of the Church and how it has extended into Western as well as Eastern Christianity.[12]

A different pathway to monastic life was taken by another monk-bishop who shared with Metropolitan Antony in bringing Eastern monastic life to the West. Metropolitan Kallistos Ware has recorded how in 1952 as a seventeen-year-old he chanced to go into an Orthodox church in London and, like the Russian envoys in Constantinople in the tenth century, was deeply struck by the experience of the worship. This sparked a process of reflection and encounter which led him, six years later, to become a member of the Orthodox Church, then later a monk and then a bishop. He has been a teacher of theology at Oxford and through his teaching, lecturing and writing has introduced the spirituality of the *Philokalia* to an audience both in the UK and beyond.

The Orthodox Church is now a Western as well as an Eastern Church. It grew in the UK through the popular preaching of Metropolitan Antony, the Patristic scholarship and teaching of Metropolitan Kallistos and the Athonite monastery of Sophrony at Tolleshunt Knights. The creativity and growth of the Church can be traced to the recovery of the monastic tradition. It also shows that the monastic tradition is not confined to the monastery but belongs to a whole Christian community. This pattern of influences happened in other places. Monks, monasteries and theologians have brought Eastern monastic life across the West. Among many institutions both the Institute of St Serge in Paris and St Vladimir's near New York were founded through the guidance of Russians who came to Western Europe after the Russian Revolution.

In Egypt and Ethiopia

Renewal of monastic life in the Coptic Church of Egypt can be traced to the Sunday School movement as well as to a renewal of ascetic traditions. Here the involvement of monasteries in education and scholarship, which has been part of its life through the ages, continued. It shows the pattern which is common in modern Orthodoxy where education is the most effective method of mission. A coordinated programme of religious education was established in 1918 by the director of the Coptic Institute of Higher Theological Learning, Habib Yirgis. He had built on models used by American Presbyterian missionaries. This was followed, in 1934, by a fellowship called First Step located at Shubra and founded by Sidrak Tadrus to encourage preaching. The course of preparation was based on a strict spiritual and ascetical life and continued over a two-year period. Other schools were set up with different specializations, for example education or social services. Soon there was a network of schools in various parts of Egypt, including in Cairo, Giza and Asyut.

Among those young people who attended the school at Shubra was a sixteen-year-old called Nazir Gayyid. He was awarded a BA in English from Cairo University in 1947, then was appointed lecturer at monastic college at Helwan in 1953. The following year he became a monk, taking the name Antony, then a year later he was ordained a priest. He went to the monastery of the Syrians, or Suriani, in the Wadi el-Natrun. Here he lived as a hermit in caves in the desert near the monastery. He moved from a first cave which was at 3 km distance, to another 10 km from the monastery, seeking deeper silence. In September 1962, he was summoned by Pope Cyril VI on the excuse of a disciplinary charge and knelt down in front of the pope in penitence. Instead of a rebuke, Cyril laid hands on him and consecrated him bishop with charge of theological and educational institutions of Cairo. In Cairo, he began the practice of giving weekly sermons which he continued throughout the rest of his life, which were attended by large crowds.[13] In 1971 Cyril died. Following traditional practice, the names of five candidates were written on pieces of paper and placed on the altar. A young boy was blindfolded and chose the paper with the name of Bishop Antony. He became pope with the name Shenuda. He was patriarch for more than forty years and died in 2012.[14]

A leader of monastic revival in Egypt was Matta el-Meskeen or Matthew the Poor. He was born in 1919 and was a successful pharmacist owning two businesses, houses and cars. He left this to become a monk in 1948. For the next twenty years, he lived as a hermit in different places. Like the spiritual fathers of earlier centuries in the Egyptian desert he attracted a group of disciples who lived near him. In 1969, he was asked by Pope Cyril VI to leave his solitude and settle in the monastery of St Macarius at Scetis, where six elderly monks were living. The monks rebuilt and extended the monastery, developing publishing and agricultural activities. The monastery has grown in number and became a model for other monasteries which have grown and led to further revival in the Church.

Education has also led to new initiatives in Ethiopia. Here government by an Orthodox Christian ruler continued until 1974 when the Emperor Haile Selassie was deposed and murdered. This led to a military and then a secular government. Restrictions on the activities of Evangelical churches ended with a further change in government in 1991 and since then observers have pointed to the eye-catching growth of Pentecostal churches. In 1984 there were two million Pentecostals and Evangelicals in Ethiopia, and by 2007 this number had increased to 13.7 million. This represents an increase from 5.5 per cent to 18.5 per cent of the population. This has been seen as a sign of decline in Orthodox churches. However there has been numerical growth among Orthodox too, with an increase from 21 million to 32 million in the same period, from 1984 to 2007. The traditional forms of church-based education and the growth of the Sunday School movement have been one of the areas of growth in church life and the monasteries have continued as centres of education. An association called *Mahabere Kiddusan* or Community of the Saints is a movement formed in 1991 as a student group. It has grown into a large and influential association which has set up a variety of initiatives to support the monasteries as foci of popular faith. It has set up a well-funded project to support monasteries, establish income-generating enterprises and share good practice in developing monastic life.

In Syria

The Syrian Orthodox Church has endured a history of suffering. This came to a deadly climax during the First World War. About a half of its members were killed in the series of massacres and killings in Turkey, Iraq and Syria between 1895 and 1915 in the episode it calls the Shato d' Sayfo or the Year of the Sword. Emigration from its heartlands has further contributed to its decline in the land of its origin in the Middle East. In the Tur Abdin, the Syrian population has continued to fall, with the number of families living in the region declining from 6,930 in 1915; to 3,146 in 1966; to 2,517 in 1978; to 926 in 1987; and then down to 197 in 1997. The leadership of the Church was weak with the Patriarch Abdul Massih, who lived through the Sayfo, becoming unable to continue in his post and then his successor Abdallah spending most of his time of office travelling away from Syria.

Yet here too there has been revival. Recent patriarchs have opened seminaries and improved clergy education. Since they have lived in monasteries in rural areas, the leaders of the Church have remained close to the people. This bond between patriarch and people was a crucial factor in preserving the integrity of the Church in the face of the many historical adversities that it encountered.[15] The communities in the diaspora have held to their ancient traditions, including those of the monastic life. New Syrian monasteries were founded by Bishop Julius Yeshu Cicek (1941–2005). These include Mor St Ephrem in the Netherlands, Mor Awgen in Switzerland and Mor Ya'cob in Germany. In the Tur Abdin, the traditional Syrian heartland, four monasteries have survived in the Tur Abdin. These are Deir al-Zafaran, Deir Mor Gabriel, Deir Mor Malke and Deir Mor Ya'cob the Recluse. The largest is Mor Gabriel, where there was, a visitor reports, a community of twenty nuns. Academic study of Syriac language, literature and culture has developed in Western universities as well as within monasteries. A recent history describes this as the Second Syrian Renaissance, following on from an earlier flowering of Syrian culture and religious life in the twelfth and thirteenth centuries.[16]

The Syrian Orthodox Church has a long history of monastic life. The life of the Church in its early history in the fifth and sixth centuries began in the monasteries, from where it preached, taught and provided care for its people. The monasteries were the seats of the patriarchs, centres of scholarship and places of ascetic struggle. They have lived through periods of cultural brilliance and achievement in the thirteenth century suffered through the first example of genocidal attack on a nation and have rebuilt the church through the traditions of monastic life and cultural study. In the early twenty-first century, this life is again threatened by turmoil in Iraq and Syria. The monks of Syria continue to witness to a faith in which death is experienced but which leads to resurrection.

Notes

1   These figures are in Graham Speake, *Mount Athos, Renewal in Paradise* (New Haven, CT, and London, 2002), p. 155.
2   John Julius Norwich with R. Sitwell, *Mount Athos* (London, 1966), pp. 14, 98.

3   Speake, *Mount Athos*, p. 174.
4   Nicolas Stebbing, *Bearers of the Spirit* (Kalamazoo, MI, 2003), pp. 45–7.
5   John P. Burgess, *Holy Rus'* (New Haven, CT, 2017), p. 128.
6   Ibid., p. 38.
7   Ibid., pp. 51, 64, 79, 92–4.
8   Ibid., 101–2.
9   Ibid., 81–2.
10 For this see Kallistos Ware, 'St Nikodimos and the Philokalia', in ed. Bingaman and Nassif, *Philokalia*, pp. 9–35, at 33–4.
11 Ibid., p. 34.
12 Metropolitan Anthony's life and personality is vividly described in Gillian Crow, *This Holy Man* (London, 2005), with his monastic vocation at pp. 67–88.
13 I recall attending one of these lectures on 1993 and being welcomed on arrival. There were several hundred people present, mostly young, and I was immediately provided with an interpreter to explain to me what was being said.
14 Otto F. A. Meinardus, *Two Thousand Years of Coptic Christianity* (Cairo, 1999), p. 215.
15 Khalid Dinno, *The Syrian Orthodox Christians in the Late Ottoman Period and Beyond* (Piscataway, NJ, 2017), p. 262.
16 Ibid., pp. 257–304.

Conclusion

A saying of Seraphim of Sarov has been many times repeated. 'Achieve silence and thousands around you will find salvation.'[1] This places us firmly within the tension which has been a theme of running through this study. The monastic tradition is both withdrawal from the world and involvement in it.

The paradox of the life of the holy women and men who form the tradition is that their search for silence placed them within the activity of the community. However far the monks went away from settled society and however ingenious they were in escaping from the complexities of social living, the world followed and found them. Antony went to his inner mountain and was followed by his disciples and then was drawn into the doctrinal struggles which were preoccupying the Church. The holy men of Syria devised extreme forms of asceticism and found themselves in demand as bringers of healing and counsel, and then as patrons for the village. Russian monks were divided over the question of whether or not they should build up property. Monasteries have always embraced both the solitary and the communal vocations. They have provided space for both these necessary strands of Christian tradition and forms of ascetic life.

Monastic life flourished on two levels, an outer and an inner. Monks founded monasteries which often thrived and also extended their influence to found new houses. This was a manifestation and expression of the inner life of the monks as they searched out new ways and new places to follow their chosen path of search for God. This inner life could flourish even when the buildings and structures of the organization had been removed, as in twentieth-century Russia. Monastic life does not need monasteries. Or, perhaps we should say, the monastery can take many institutional forms and a monastery is found wherever the monk struggles in her or his vocation which is monastic since it is at heart solitary and also single minded.

This paradox is the consequence of the uncompromising following of the Christian gospel. If the church offers the message of the divine entering the human, of God becoming man and if this showed itself in a death which was also a resurrection, which is also the drawing near of the Kingdom of God, then the monk lives both in this world and also beyond it. Early monks understood themselves to be martyrs and witnesses. This led them to participate in both death and resurrection and so lead others to follow this example.

The monks chose a shared ascetic way of living as disciples and martyrs. They embraced the fullness of the life of the whole church, so that the church's history became the monks' history. Monks were bishops and theologians and priests and pastors. As the early monks guarded the villages and protected the frontiers through their prayers, so they preserved and upheld the life of the church. The inspiration and leadership of the monasteries belongs to the whole church and is a source of life and hope. The monks are the martyrs to the message of death and resurrection in which they lived. Their witness has been maintained since their foundation and continues to give life to the church. That was and remains the inner reality of the monastic tradition to which I as well as countless others are deeply indebted.

Note

1. A fuller version of Seraphim's words is reproduced in G. P. Fedotov, *A Treasury of Russian Spirituality* (London 1950), p. 259. 'Most of all (the monk) must adorn himself with silence. As Ambrose says, by silence have I seen many saved, by many words, not one. Silence is the sacrament of the world to come, words are the weapons of this world.'

Bibliography

Abbreviations

CSCO	Corpus Scriptorum Christianorum Orientalium
CSEL	Corpus Scriptorum Ecclesiasticorum Latinorum
GCS	Die greichischen christlichen Schriftsteller der ersten drei Jahrhunderte
Mansi Giovanni Mansi:	Sacrorum Conciliorum nova et amplissima collectio
PG	Patrologia Graeca
PO	Patrologia Orientalis

Primary sources

Antony the Great, *The Letters of Saint Antony the Great*, trans. Derwas Chitty (Oxford, 1975).
Athanasius, *Life of Antony*, trans. Robert C. Gregg, Classics of Western Spirituality (London, 1980).
Augustine, *Confessions*, trans. R. Pine-Coffin (New York, 1961).
Barsanuphius and John, *Questions and Answers*, ed. and trans. F. Neyt, P. de Angelis-Noah and l. Regnault, *Barsanuphe et Jean de Gaze, Correspondance*, Sources Chrétiennes 426–7, 450–1, 468 (Paris, 1997–2002).
Basil, *Long and Short Rules*, PG 31. 889–1305, trans. W. K. Lowther Clarke, *The Ascetic Works of St Basil* (London, 1925).
Basil, *Letters*, 4 vols, trans. Roy J. Defarrari, Loeb Classical Library (Cambridge, MA, 1961–2).
Basil, *Hexaemeron* in *Basil, Letters and Select Works*, trans. Philip Schaff and Nicene Henry Wace and Post Nicene Father, Second Series, vol. 8 (Peabody, MA, 1994).
Besa, Life of Shenoute, trans. David Bell (Kalamazoo, MI, 1983).
Byzantine Monastic Foundation Documents, ed. and trans. John Thomas, C. Hero and A. Constable (Washington, 2000).
Cabasilas, Nicholas, *Life in Christ*, trans. Carmino de Cantanzaro (New York, 1974).
Cassian, John, *Conferences*, trans. Colm Luibheid, Classics of Western Spirituality (London, 1985).
Cyril of Scythopolis, ed. E. Schwartz, *Kyrillos von Skythopolis* (Leipzig, 1939); trans. Richard Price, *Lives of the Monks of Palestine* (Kalamazoo, MI, 1991).
Eusebius, *Ecclesiastical History*, trans. H. J. Lawlor and J. E. L. Oulton (London, 1927).
Eusebius, *Life of Constantine*, trans. H. Wace and P. Schaff, *A Select Library of Nicene and Post-Nicene Fathers*, vol. I (Grand Rapids, MI, 1979).

Evagrius Ponticus, *The Praktikos, Chapters on Prayer*, trans. John Eudes Bamberger (Kalamazoo, MI, 1981).
Evagrius Scholasticus, *Ecclesiastical History*, ed. and trans. J. Bidez and L. Parmentier (London, 1898).
Gregory the Great, *Dialogues*, ed. and trans. A. de Vögue and P. Antin (Paris, 1978–80).
Gregory Nazianzus, *Orations*, PG 35–8.
Gregory of Nyssa, *Life of Moses*, ed. and trans. Abraham Malherbe and Everett Ferguson, Classics of Western Spirituality (New York, 1978).
Gregory of Nyssa, *Life of Macrina*, trans. Pierre Maraval, *Vie de Sainte Macrine* (Paris, 1981).
Gregory Palamas, *The Triads*, trans. Nicholas Gendle, Classics of Western Spirituality (Mahwah, NJ, 1983).
Historia Monachorum in Aegypto, trans. Norman Russell, *Lives of the Desert Fathers* (London, 1980).
Hypotyposis of the Monastery of the Theotokos Evergetis, Constantinople (11th–12th Centuries), ed. and trans. R. H. Jordan and Rosemary Morris (Ashgate, 2012).
Isaac the Syrian, *Mystic Treatises by Isaac of Syria*, ed. and trans. A. J. Wensinck (Amsterdam, 1923).
Jerome, *Life of Hilarion*, in W. A. Oldfather, *Studies in the Text Tradition of St Jerome's Vitae Patrum* (Urbana, IL, 1943).
Jerome, *Letters*, CSEL 54–6.
John Rufus, *The Lives of Peter the Iberian, Theodosius of Jerusalem and the Monk Romanus*, trans. Cornelia Horn and Robert Phenix (Leiden, 2008).
John of Damascus, *Three Treatises on the Divine Images*, trans. Andrew Louth (Crestwood, NY, 2003).
John of Ephesus, *Lives of the Eastern Saints*, trans. E. W. Brooks, PO 17–19 (Paris, 1923–5).
John of Ephesus, *Life of James bar-Addai*, trans. E. W. Brooks, PO 18 (Paris, 1923–5).
John of the Ladder, *The Ladder of Divine Ascent*, ed. and trans. Colm Luibheid and Norman Russell (New York, 1982).
John Moschus, *Spiritual Meadow*, trans. John Wortley (Kalamazoo, MI, 1992).
John Rufus, *Life of Peter the Iberian*, trans. Cornelia Horn and Robert Phenix (Leiden, 2008).
Justin Martyr, *Apology*, ed. and trans. Denis Minns and Paul Purvis, Oxford Early Christian Texts (Oxford, 2009).
Life of Alexander the Sleepless, ed. E. de Stoop, *Vie d'Alexandre l'Acémète*, PO 6.5 (Paris, 1911); trans. Daniel Caner, *Wandering Begging Monks, Spiritual Authority and the Promotion of Monasticism in Late Antiquity* (Berkeley, CA, 2002), pp. 249–80.
Life of Athanasius the Athonite, ed. and trans. P. Lemerle, *La vie ancienne de saint Athanase l'Athonite composée au début di XIe siècle par Athanase de Lavra* (Chevtogne, 1963).
Life of Benedict of Aniane, in ed. T. F. X. Noble and T. Head, *Soldiers of Christ Saints and Saints' Lives from Late Antiquity and the Early Middle Ages* (Philadelphia, PA, 1995), pp. 213–54.
Life of Chariton, ed. G. Garitte, *Bulletin de l'Institut Historique Belge de Rome* (1941), pp. 5–50.
Life of Lazarus of Mt. Galesion, an Eleventh-Century Pillar Saint, trans. Richard Greenfield, Byzantine Saints' Lives in Translation III (Washington, 1999).
Life of Martin of Tours, ed. and trans. J. Fontaine, *Sulpice Sevère, Vie de S. Martin* (Paris, 1967–9).

Life of Maximus Kafsokalyvites, ed. F. Halkin, 'Deux Vies de S. Maxime le Kausokalyve Ermite an Mont Athos (XIVe s)', *Analecta Bollandiana* 54 (1936), pp. 38–112.
Life of Melania, ed. and trans. D. Gorce (Paris, 1962).
Life of Paul the Younger, 'Vita S. Pauli Junioris in Monte Latro', trans. H. Delehaye, *Analecta Bollandiana* 11 (1892), pp. 19–74, 136–81.
Life of Symeon the Fool, ed. Lennart Ryden, *Das Leben des Heiligen Narren Symeon von Neapolis* (Uppsala, 1963).
Life of Tekla Haymonot, trans. E. A. Wallis Budge (London, 1906).
Life of Thaddaios, trans. D. Afinogenov, *Analecta Bollandiana* 119 (2001), pp. 327–37.
Lives of Theodore the Studite, by Michael the Monk, PG 99.233–328; Naukratios, PG 99, 1825–49; Theodore Daphnopatos, PG 99.113–232.
Macarius (Pseudo-Macarius), *The Fifty Spiritual Homilies and the Great Letter*, trans. George Maloney, Classics of Western Spirituality (Mahwah, NJ, 1992).
Michael Dukas, *Historia Byzantina*, ed. I. Bakker (Bonn, 1834).
Michael the Syrian, *Chronicle*. ed. J. B. Chabot, 3 vols (Paris, 1899–1905).
New Testament Apocrypha, trans. H. J. W. Drijvers (Westminster, 1992).
Nicephorus Callistus (Nikiphoros Kallistos), *Ecclesiastical History*, PG 146.
Nicetas Choniates, *Annals*, trans. H. Magoulias (Detroit, MI, 1984).
Origen, *Homilies on Luke*, ed. M. Rauer, *Die Homilien zu Lukas*, GCS (Leipzig, 1930).
Origen, *Exhortation to Martyrdom, Prayer and Selected Works*, trans. Rowan A. Greer, Classics of Western Spirituality (London, 1979).
Palladius, *Lausiac History*, trans. Robert Meyer, Ancient Christian Writers (New York, 1964).
Pachomian Koinonia, vol 1, *The Life and Saint Pachomius and His Disciples*, trans. Armand Veilleux (Kalamazoo, MI, 1980).
Philo, *The Contemplative Life*, trans. F. Daumas and P. Miquel, *De Vita Contemplativa* (Paris, 1963).
Philo, *Life of Moses*, ed. R. Arnaldez, C. Mondésert, J. Pouilleux, P. Savinel, *De Vita Mosis* (Paris, 1967).
Philokalia, The Complete Text, ed. and trans. Geoffrey Palmer, Philip Sherrard and Kallistos Ware, 4 vols (London, 1979–95).
Pliny, *Natural History*, ed. H. Rackham (Cambridge, 1969).
Rufinus, *Ecclesiastical History*, trans. P. Armidon, *The Church History of Rufinus of Aquileia, Books 10–11* (Oxford, 1997).
Rule of St Benedict, trans. Abbot Parry (Leominster, 1990).
Russian Primary Chronicle, trans. H. Cross and O. P. Sherbowitz-Wetzor (Cambridge, MA, 1953).
Sayings of the Desert Fathers, trans. Benedicta Ward (Oxford, 1975).
Shepherd of Hermas, ed. R. Joly, *Le Pasteur* (Paris, 1958).
Socrates, *Ecclesiastical History*, ed. G. C. Hansen and trans. Pierre Maraval, *Socrates, Histoire Ecclésiastique* (Paris, 2004–5).
Sozomen, *Ecclesiastical History*, ed. J. Bidez GCS (Berlin, 1960).
Symeon the New Theologian, *The Discourses*, trans. Carmino de Catanzaro, Classics of Western Spirituality (Mahwah, NJ, 1980).
Synesius of Cyrene, *Letters*, trans. A. Fitzgerald (Oxford, 1926).
Tertullian, *On Fasting*, ed. E. Rafferscheid and G. Wissowa, Corpus Christianorum Series Latina 2 (Turnhout, 1954).
Tertullian, *On Prayer*, ed. G. F. Diercks, Corpus Christianorum Series Latina 1 (Turnhout, 1954).

Theodoret, *Ecclesiastical History*, ed. L. Parmentier GCS (Berlin, 1954).
Theodoret, *Religious History*, trans. Richard Price, *History of the Monks of Syria* (Kalamazoo, MI, 1985).
Timothy's Apology for Christianity, trans. Alphonse Mingana (Cambridge, 1928).
Way of a Pilgrim, trans. R. M. French (London, 1930).
Zachariah of Mitylene (Pseudo Zachariah Rhetor), *Ecclesiastical History*, ed. and trans. E. W. Brooks, *Syriac Chronicle Known as that of Zachariah of Mitylene* (London, 1899).

Secondary sources

Alfeyev, Hilarion, *The Spiritual World of Isaac the Syrian* (Kalamazoo, MI, 2000).
Alfeyev, Hilarion, *Symeon the New Theologian and Orthodox Tradition* (Oxford, 2000).
Barkey, Karen, *Empire of Difference, the Ottomans in Comparative Perspective* (Cambridge, 2008).
Baum, Wilhelm and Dietmar Winkler, *The Church of the East* (London, 2003).
Binns, John, *Ascetics and Ambassadors of Christ* (Oxford, 1994).
Binns, John, *The Orthodox Church of Ethiopia, a History* (London, 2016).
Bingaman, Brock and Bradley Nassif (eds.), *The Philokalia* (Oxford, 2012).
Bitton-Ashkelony, Brouria and Aryeh Kofsky, *The Monastic School of Gaza* (Leiden, 2006).
Bolshakoff, Sergius, *Russian Mystics* (Kalamazoo, MI, 1977).
Britton-Ashkelony, Brouria and Aryeh Kofsky, 'Monasticism in the Holy Land' in ed. Ora Limor and Guy Stoumsa, *Christians and Christianity in the Holy Land* (Turnhout, 2006), pp. 257–91.
Brock, Sebastian, *The Syriac Fathers on Prayer and the Spiritual Life* (Kalamazoo, MI, 1987).
Brock, Sebastian, 'Tur Abdin – A Homeland of Ancient Syro-Aramaean Culture', in Hollerweger, *Turabdin* (Linz, 1999), pp. 22–3.
Brown, Peter, 'The Rise and Function of the Holy Man in Late Antiquity', *Journal of Roman Studies* 61 (1971), pp. 80–101.
Brown, Peter, *The Body and Society; Men, Women and Sexual Renunciation in Early Christianity* (New York, 1988).
Browning, Robert, *Byzantium and Bulgaria* (London, 1975).
Bryer, Anthony and Mary Cunningham (eds.), *Mount Athos and Byzantine Monasticism* (London, 1996).
Budge, E. A., Wallis, *The Paradise or Garden of the Holy Fathers* (London, 1907).
Burgess, John P., *Holy Rus', the Rebirth of Orthodoxy in the New Russia* (Yale, 2017).
Cameron, Averil, *Procopius and the Sixth Century* (London, 1985).
Caner, Daniel, *Wandering Begging Monks, Spiritual Authority and the Promotion of Monasticism in Late Antiquity* (Berkeley, CA, 2002).
Casiday, Augustine, *Evagrius Ponticus* (Oxford, 2006).
Chadwick, Owen, *John Cassian a Study in Primitive Monasticism* (Cambridge, 1950).
Chaillot, Christine, *The Ethiopian Orthodox Tawehedo Church Tradition* (Paris, 2002).
Charanis, Peter, 'The Monastic Properties and the State in the Byzantine Empire', *Dumbarton Oaks Papers* 4 (1948), pp. 53–118.
Charanis, Peter, 'The Monk as an Element of Byzantine Society', *Dumbarton Oaks Papers* 24 (1971).
Chetverikov, Sergei, *Starets Paisii Velichkovskii* (Belmont, CA, 1980).

Chitty, Derwas, *The Desert a City* (Oxford, 1966).
Clément, Olivier, *The Roots of Christian Mysticism* (London, 1993).
Conti Rossini, Carlo, *Acta Sancti Basalota Mikael*, CSCO 20 (Louvain, 1905).
Crow, Gillian, *This Holy Man* (London, 2005).
Cunningham, Mary, 'The Place of the Jesus Prayer in the Philokalia,' in ed. Brock Bingaman and Bradley Nassif, *The Philokalia* (Oxford, 2012).
Dalrymple, William, *From the Holy Mountain* (London, 1998).
Dagron, Gilbert, 'Les Moines et la Ville', *Travaux et Mémoires* 4 (1970), pp. 229–76.
Davis, Stephen J., *Monasticism, a Very Short Introduction* (Oxford, 2018).
Dinno, Khalid, *The Syrian Orthodox Christians in the Late Ottoman Period and Beyond* (Piscataway, NJ, 2017).
Douglas, Mary, *Purity and Danger* (Harmondsworth, 1970).
Duichev, I. (ed.), *Kiril and Methodius, Founders of Slavonic Writing* (Boulder, CO, 1985).
Ehrman, Bart D., *The Triumph of Christianity* (London, 2018).
Ellis, Jane, *The Russian Orthodox Church, a Contemporary History* (London, 1990).
Elm, Susannah, *Virgins of God, the Making of Asceticism in Late Antiquity* (Oxford, 1994).
Erman, Adolf, 'Shenute und Aristophanes', *Zeitschrift für Aegyptische Sprache* 32 (1894), pp. 325–8.
Evans, G. R., *The I.B.Tauris History of Monasticism, The Western Tradition* (London, 2016).
Fedotov, G. P., *A Treasury of Russian Spirituality* (London, 1910).
Fennell, Nicholas, *Russians on Athos* (Bern, 1901).
Finn, Richard, *Asceticism in the Graeco-Roman World* (Cambridge, 2009).
Goldfrank, David (ed. and trans.), *The Monastic Rule of Iosif Volotsky* (Kalamazoo, MI, 1983).
Griffith, Sidney, 'Asceticism in the Church of Syria: The Hermeneutics of Early Syrian Monasticism' in *Asceticism*, ed. Vincent Wimbush and Richard Valantasis (Oxford, 1995).
Griffith-Jones, Robin and Eric Fernie (eds.), *Tomb and Templre, Re-Imagining the Sacred Buildings of Jerusalem* (Woodbridge, 2018).
Grivec, F. and F. Tomsic, *Constantinus and Methodius Thessalonicenses* (Zagreb, 1960).
Hackel, Sergei, *A Pearl of Great Price* (London, 1982).
Haile, Getatchew, *The Ethiopian Orthodox Church's Tradition on the Holy Cross* (Leiden, 2018).
Harpham, Geoffrey, *The Ascetic Impulse in Culture and Criticism* (Chicago, IL, 1987).
Harvey, Susan Ashbrook, *Asceticism and Society in Crisis* (Berkeley, CA, 1990).
Hatlie, Peter, *The Monks and Monasteries of Constantinople ca. 350–850* (Cambridge, 2007).
Hausherr, Irinée, 'Les versions syriaque et armenienne d'evagre le pontique', *Orientalia Christiana* 22 (1933).
Herrin, Judith, *Byzantium* (London, 2007).
Hirschfeld, Yizhar, 'List of the Byzantine Monasteries in the Judaean Desert', in G. C. Bottini et al. (eds.), *Christian Archeology in the Holy Land: New Discoveries* (Jerusalem, 1990), pp. 1–90.
Hirschfeld, Yizhar, *The Judean Desert Monasteries of the Byzantine Period* (New Haven, CT, 1992).
Hock, R. and A. Malherbe, *The Cynic Epistles: A Study Edition* (Missoula, 1977).
Hollerweger, Hans, *Turabdin* (Linz, 1999).
Horn, Cornelia, *Asceticism and Christological Controversy in Fifth-Century Palestine, the Career of Peter the Iberian* (Oxford, 2006).

Jenkins, Philip, *The Lost History of Christianity* (New York, 2008).
Judge, E. A., 'The Earliest Use of the Word "Monachos" for Monk (P. Coll. Youtie 77) and the Origins of Monasticism', *Jahrbuch für Antike und Christentum* xx (1977), pp. 72–89.
Kazhdan, A. P., *History of Byzantine Culture 650–850* (Athens, 1999).
Kenworthy, Scott, *The Heart of Russia, Trinity-Sergius, Monasticism and Society after 1825* (Oxford, 2010).
Kitromilides, Paschalis M., 'Athos and the Enlightenment', in ed. Anthony Bryer and Mary Cunningham, *Mount Athos and Byzantine Monasticism* (London, 1996).
Klimenko, Michael, *The 'Vita' of St Sergii of Radonezh* (Houston, TX, 1980).
Kontzevich, Ivan, *The Northern Thebaid* (Platina, CA, 1975).
Lake, Kirsopp, *Early Days of Monasticism on Mount Athos* (Oxford, 1909).
Layton, Bentley, *The Canons of Our Fathers, Monastic Rule of Shenute* (Oxford, 2014).
Leclercq, Jean, *The Love of Learning and the Desire for God* (New York, 1974).
Leipoldt, J., *Shenute von Atripe und die Entstehung des National Aegyptishcen Christentums* (Leipzig, 1903).
l'Huillier, Peter, 'Episcopal Celibacy in the Orthodox Tradition', *St Vladimir's Theological Quarterly* 35/2-3 (1991), pp. 271–300.
Lossky, Vladimir, *Mystical Theology of the Eastern Church* (London, 1957).
Louth, Andrew, *Greek East and Latin West* (New York, 2007).
Louth, Andrew, 'The Influence of the *Philokalia* in the Orthodox World', in ed. Brock Bingaman and Bradley Nassif, the *Philokalia* (Oxford, 2012).
Luke, Harry, *The Old Turkey and the New: From Byzantium to Ankara* (London, 1955).
MacCulloch, Diarmaid, *History of Christianity* (London, 2009).
Malone, E. E., 'The Monk and the Martyr', *Studia Anselmiana* 38 (1956), pp. 201–28.
Maraval, P., *Lieux saints et pèlerinage d'orient* (Paris, 1985).
Marushchak, Vassily, *The Blessed Surgeon, the Life of Saint Luke, Archbishop of Simferopol* (Manton, CA, 2007).
McGuckin, John Anthony, 'The Making of the Philokalia, a Tale of Monks and Manuscripts', in ed. Brock Bingaman and Bradley Nassif, *The Philokalia* (Oxford, 2012).
Meinardus, Otto F. A., *The Monks and Monasteries of the Egyptian Deserts* (Cairo, 1961).
Meinardus, Otto F. A., *Two Thousand Years of Coptic Christianity* (Cairo, 1999).
Meyendorff, John, *A Study of Gregory Palamas* (New York, 1964).
Meyendorff, John, *Byzantium and the Rise of Russia* (New York, 1989).
Miller, David B., *Saint Sergius of Radonezh, His Trinity Monastery, and the Formation of the Russian Identity* (De Kalb, IL, 2010).
Mingana, Alphonse, *The Early Spread of Christianity in India* (Manchester, 1926)
Morris, Rosemary, *Monks and Laymen in Byzantium 843–1118* (Cambridge, 1995).
Mullett, Margaret and Anthony Kirby (eds.), *The Theotokos Evergetis and Eleventh Century Monasticism* (Belfast, 1994).
Murray, Robert, *Symbols of Church and Kingdom: A Study in Early Syrian Tradition* (Cambridge, 1975).
Nau, F., 'Deux Episodes de l'Histoire Juive sous Théodose II (423 et 438) d'après la vie de Barsauma le Syrien', *Revue des etudes juives* 83 (1927), pp. 184–206.
Norwich, John Julian, with R. Sitwell, *Mount Athos* (London, 1966).
Obolensky, Dmitri, *Six Byzantine Portraits* (Oxford, 1988).
O'Loughlin, Thomas, *The Didache* (London, 2010).

Osiek, Carolyn, *The Shepherd of Hermas, a Commentary* (Minneapolis, MN, 1999).
Paert, Irina, *Spiritual Elders, Charisma and Tradition in Russian Orthodoxy* (De Kalb, IL, 2010).
Palmer, Andrew, 'The 1600-Year History of the Monastery of Kartmin (Mor Gabriel)', in Hans Hollerweger, *Turabdin* (Linz, 1999), pp. 37-46.
Patlagean, Evelyne, *Pauvreté Economique et pauvreté sociale à Byzance* (Paris, 1977).
Patrich, Joseph (ed.), *The Sabaite Heritage in the Orthodox Church from the Fifth Century to the Present* (Leuven, 2001).
Penniman, John David, *Raised on Christian Milk* (Yale, 2017).
Peristeris, Aristarchus, 'Literary and Scribal Activities at the Monastery of St Sabas', in ed. Joseph Patrich, *The Sabaite Heritage in the Orthodox Church from the Fifth Century to the Present* (Leuven, 2001), pp. 171-94.
Pospielovsky, Dmitry, *The Orthodox Church in the History of Russia* (New York, 1998).
Regnault, L., 'Les Apophtegmes en Palestine aux Ve-Vie siècles', *Irénikon* 54 (1981), pp. 320-30.
Rousseau, Philip, *Basil of Caesarea* (Berkeley, CA, 1994).
Rousseau, Philip, *Pachomius* (Berkeley, CA, 1995).
Saward, John, *Perfect Fools* (Oxford, 1980).
Schick, Robert, *Christian Communities of Palestine from Byzantine to Islamic Rule* (Princeton, NJ, 1995).
Schmemann, Alexander, *Introduction to Liturgical Theology* (London, 1966).
Schneider, A-M., 'Das kloster der Theotokos zu Choziba im Wadi el Kelt', *Römische Quartalschrift für Christliche Altertumskunde und für Kirchengeschichte* 39 (1931), pp. 297-332.
Smith, Margaret, *Studies in Early Mysticism in the Near and Middle East* (Oxford, 1995).
Speake, Graham, *Mount Athos, Renewal in Paradise* (New Haven, CT, and London, 2002).
Stebbing, Nicolas, *Bearers of the Spirit* (Kalamazoo, MI, 2003).
Sterk, Andrea, *Renouncing the World Yet Leading the Church, the Monk-Bishop in Late Antiquity* (Harvard, 2004).
Stewart, Columba, *Working the Earth of the Heart* (Oxford, 1991).
Talbot, Alice-Mary, 'Byzantine Pilgrimage to the Holy Land from the Eighth to the Fifteenth Century', in ed. Joseph Patrich, *The Sabaite Heritage in the Orthodox Church from the Fifth Century to the Present* (Leuven, 2001), pp. 97-110.
Tamrat, Taddesse, *Church and State in Ethiopia* (Oxford, 1973).
Thomas, John, *Private Religious Foundations in the Byzantine Empire*, Dumbarton Oaks Studies 24 (Washington, 1987).
Thomas, John, 'Documentary Evidence from the Byzantine Monastic Typika for the History of the Evergetine Reform Movement', in ed. Margaret Mullett and Anthony Kirby, *The Theotokos Evergetis and Eleventh Century Monasticism* (Belfast, 1994).
Thomas, John, 'The Imprint of Sabaitic Monasticism on Byzantine Monastic Typika', in ed. J. Patrich, *Sabaite Heritage in the Orthodox Church from the Fifth Century to the Present* (Leuven, 2001), pp. 73-83.
Valantasis, Richard, 'Constructions of Power in Asceticism', *The Journal of the American Academy of Religions*, 63 (1995), pp. 75-821.
Velimirovich, Nicholai, *The Life of St Sava* (New York, 1989).
Ward, Benedicta, *Harlots of the Desert* (London, 1987).
Ware, Kallistos (Timothy), *The Orthodox Church* (London, 1963).

Ware, Kallistos, 'St Maximus of Kapsokalyvia and Fourteenth Century Athonite Hesychasm', in *Kathigitria* (London, 1988).
Ware, Kallistos, 'St Athanasios the Athonite: Traditionalist or Innovator?' in ed. Anthony Bryer and Mary Cunningham, *Mount Athos and Byzantine Monasticism* (Aldershot, 1996).
Ware, Kallistos, 'St. Nikodimos and the *Philiokalia*,' in ed. Brock Bingaman and Bradley Nassif, *The Philokalia* (Oxford, 2012), pp. 9–35.
Zernov, Nicolas, *Russian Religious Renaissance of the Twentieth Century* (London, 1963).

Index

abaton 143
Abdul Hamid II, Ottoman sultan 214
Abdullah, Syrian Orthodox Patriarch 232
Abdul Masih, Syrian Orthodox patriarch 232
Abraham of Kashkar 118
Abraham, stylite of Amida 64
Abraham, Syrian holy man 63
Acacius, Archbishop of Melitene 88
Academy on Mount Athos 203–4
Adam, bishop in China 120
Adelphius, Syrian holy man 59
Aelianus, abbot in Gaza 81–2
Afanasy Nechaev, Russian monk 229
Aimilianos, abbot of Simonopetra 226
Akakios, hermit of Athos 146
Akoimetoi or Sleepless monks 97–8
Aleksii Soloviev, elder of Trinity Sergius monastery 210
Alexander Nevsky Monastery 201
Alexander *Akoimetos* or Sleepless 97
Alexandria
    Antony's visit 36
    communication with Gaza 80
    Frumentius consecrated 123
    Origen and Origenists 183, 198
Alexandria 1, 14, 36, 39, 60, 79, 117, 123, 176, 185, 198
A-lo-pen, missionary to China 120
Amalfi 144
Amda Seyon, king of Ethiopia 125–6
Amida 64, 99, 116
Ammonius, Origenist monk 37, 183
Ammonius Saccas 177
Amoun, monk of Nitria 38–9, 46
Amvrosy Grenkov, elder at Optina 206–7
Anastasius, abbot on Sinai 186
Anastasius, Byzantine emperor 86
Anatolius, Patriarch of Constantinople 88
Andrei Rublev 160, 163
Andrew of Crete, hymn writer 89–90

Andrew, holy fool of Constantinople 65
Andronikos III, Byzantine emperor 190
Andronikos IV Palaiologos, Byzantine emperor 146
Angelarius, companion of Cyril and Methodius 149–50
Anna, Russian princess 157
Annesi 70, 72, 75
Anthony, founder of the monastery of the Caves 158, 165
Anthony IV, Patriarch of Constantinople 159
Antioch
    city in Syria 57, 97–8, 111–12, 117, 213
    monastic life 60–4, 82, 87
Antoninus, Egyptian deacon 1
Antony 1, 4, 16
    influence 25, 30, 33, 52, 235
    life 33–6, 60, 79
    Life of Antony 36–8, 51
    pioneer in monastic life 39, 80
Antony Bloom, Metropolitan of Sourozh 229–30
apatheia 181
Aphrahat 112, 113
apotaktikoi 1
Arabs 5, 79, 92, 112, 127, 141, 170, 197–8
Aramaic language 111
archimandrite 47, 85, 116, 153
Aregawi or Za-Mikael 124
Armenia
    monks in Palestine, 119, 180
    translations into 60, 84, 87, 91, 199, 213
Arsenius 175
Ascepimas, Syrian holy man 62
asceticism
    culture and counter-culture 23–5, 60
    ascetic disciplines 30, 36, 40, 57–9, 62–6, 98, 161
Asia Minor 15, 30, 90

Assyria 57
Athanasios of Athos 142–5, 200
Athanasius Patriarch of Alexandria 1, 16, 36–8, 49, 76, 123
Athens 70, 75
Athos
    early monastic life on the mountain 136, 139, 141–4
    hesychasm on Athos 155, 189–91, 205, 207–8
    idiorrythmia 199
    Revival 223–6
    russians 152, 165, 226
    Serbs 151, 153, 155
Augustine 37
Auxentius, mountain in Asia Minor 140
Awgen or Eugenius 118
Axum 123

Bahira 121
Barlaam, first superior of the monastery of the Caves 158
Barlaam of Calabria 190–1, 200
Barsanuphius 81–2, 182
Barsanuphius, companion of John 81–2, 182
Barsauma, Syrian monk 121–2
Barsawma, Chinese monk 61
Bar Shabba, bishop in Merv 119, 122
Basalota Mikael, Ethiopian monk 126
Basil II, Byzantine emperor 132, 144, 157
Basil III, prince of Russia 169–70
Basileiados 72–3
Basil of Caesarea 18, 61, 69–77, 100, 176, 179
Basil of Poiana Mărulai 204
Benedictine rule on Athos 108, 144
Benedict of Aniane 108–9
Benedict of Nursia 2, 74, 108–9
Benjamin 168
Beth Abe, monastery ion Persia 119, 184
Bethlehem 2, 51, 85, 88, 107
Bible and study 44, 48, 175, 179–80, 203
bishops
    monk-bishop 60–1, 72–3, 75–7
    ordaining bishops 117, 154
    role of bishops 33, 72–3, 133
    resistance to ordination 37–8
Bithynia 100, 140, 150

Bloom, Antony. *See* Antony, Metropolitan of Sourozh
Boris and Gleb 159–60
Boris, king of Bulgaria 150–1
boskoi or grazers 59, 61
boundaries 48, 74
Brianchaninov, Ignatii 210
Bulgakov, Sergei 210, 214
Bulgaria 149–51, 155, 224

Caesarea 176–7
Caesarea Cappadocia 60, 70, 71–3
Caesarius, bishop of Arles 107
Calamon, monastery in Palestine 83
Cappadocia 84, 140
Cappadocian Fathers 69
Cassian John 46, 51, 107–8, 165–6, 176, 181, 182
Castellium, monastery in Palestine 85
Catherine the Great, empress of Russia 201, 206
Caves, monastery in Kiev 158
celibacy 13, 16–20, 25, 57–60, 71, 75–6
cell 40–1, 45, 49
Cellia 39, 50, 179
Chalcedon, Ecumenical Council 61, 88–9, 98, 105, 113–15, 123, 131, 133
Chalcedonians 111, 134, 198, 220
Chariton 83–4, 91
Chernyshevsky, Nikolai 214
China 4, 111, 119–20, 197
Chora, monastery in Constantinople 90
chorepiscop 18, 179–80
Choziba, monastery in Palestine 87
Christodoulos of Patmos 92, 139
Chronius, monk of Nitria 41, 50
Chrysopolis, monastery of Symeon the New Theologian 187
Church of the East 112, 119–22
Clement of Alexandria 36
Clement of Ohrid 149–51
Cleopa, monk of Sihastria 227
Cleopas, monk of Dragomirna 206
Coenobium, common life
    coenobitic and eremitical styles 2, 43, 52, 74, 85, 86, 91, 109, 138, 140, 144, 167–9
    examples 85, 88, 109, 132, 140

organization 33, 44, 48, 85, 100–2, 136–8, 142–4
   re-establishment of coenobia 53, 156, 162, 200, 226
Conon of Tarsus, companion of Jacob Baradeus 117
Constantine, Roman emperor 18, 29–30, 33, 79, 95
Constantine XI, Byzantine emperor 197
Constantinople
   capital of empire 51, 70, 77, 83, 100, 105, 125, 142
   Council of Constantinople of (553) 88, 180, 183
   Council of Constantinople of 1341 191
   monastic life 64, 73, 96–103, 105, 107–12, 139–41, 207
   Russians in Constantinople 157–9, 160, 230
Coptic culture 46–50, 52, 179
Cosmas of Maiuma, hymn writer 90
Cynic philosophy 15
Cyprian of Mar Saba 90
Cyprian, Metropolitan of Moscow 163
Cyprus 52
Cyriacus, monk of Palestine 182
Cyril VI, Coptic Pope 231
Cyril, apostle of the Slavs 149–150, 158
Cyril of Alexandria 47, 88, 113, 115, 175
Cyril of Scythopolis 81, 84, 85, 91, 182–4
Cyril of While Lake or Beloozerski 162
Cyrillic 149–51

Dalmatou, monastery in Constantinople 96
Dalmatus 96
Daniel, abbot of Volokolamsk 170
Daniel of Rhaithou 186
Daniel the stylite 64
Debre Asbo. *See* Debre Libanos
Debre Damo, monastery in Ethiopia 124
Debre Libanos, monastery in Ethiopia 125
Debre Mitmaq 127
Decius, Roman emperor 29
Deir al-Zafaran, monastery in Tur Abdin 118, 232
Deir Mor Malke, monastery in Tur Abdin 232
Deir Mor Yacob the Recluse, monastery in Tur Abdin 232

Demetrios Chomatianos 150, 154
desert
   geography of desert 12–13
   love of desert 16
   withdrawing into desert 34–5, 139–40, 161–2, 209, 227
devils 34–6, 38, 126, 165
dhimmi 198–9
Diadochus of Photike 188–9
Didache 20
Didymus the Blind 183
Diocletian, Roman emperor (284–305) 29
Dionysiou, monastery on Athos 205, 226
Dioscorus, patriarch of Alexandria 88
Diveyevo, monastery in Russia 209
Diyabakir 214
Dmitri Donskoi, Russian prince 163
Dobrotolubiye 206, 210. *See also* Philokalia
Domitian, Metropolitan of Ancyra 183
Dorotheus of Gaza 100
Dostoevsky, Fyodor 159, 206
Douka, monastery of Palestine 84
Dracontius, a monk-bishop 37
Dragomirna 204, 206

Edessa 4, 58, 66, 98, 111
Egypt
   beginnings of monastic life 1, 4, 15, 33–53
   communication with Palestine 80–2
   renewal 230
   visitors 72, 81–2, 95, 123
Elias, monk of Egypt 41, 50
Elizabeth, grand-duchess 210, 228
Elvira, council in Spain 19
Emesa 62, 65
Emmelia, mother of Macrina 70
Enlightener 167–8
Ephesus, Councils of 431 and 448 47, 59, 61, 97, 105, 112, 116
Ephrem the Syrian 112–13
Epiphanius, patriarch of Constantinople 65
Epiphanius the Wise 163
Esphigmenou, monastery on Athos 190
Ethiopia 4, 22, 111, 122–7, 197
Eudocia, Byzantine empress 83, 88, 89

Eugenius of Cilicia, companion of Jacob Baradeus 117
Euphemia of Amida 116
Eusathius of Sebaste 60–1, 71, 96
Eusebius 29
Eusebius of Pelusium, Monophysite bishop in Egypt 114
Eusebius, Origenist monk 183
Euthymius of Palestine 83–5, 88, 91, 114
Euthymius, Origenist monk 183
Euthymius, monk of Stoudios 144
Euthymius the Younger, an early monk of Athos 141
Eutyches 97
Evagrius of Pontus 49, 82, 122, 166, 176, 179–84, 191
Evdokia Mescherakova, Russian nun 220
Evergetis monastery 70, 136–9, 153, 197
Evgenios Voulgaris 203–4
Ewostatewos, Ethiopian monk 127

fasting 19–23, 121, 137
Fellowship of St Alban and St Sergius 230
Feofan the Cossack, monk of Optina 206
Filadelf Mishnin, monk of Trinity Sergius monastery 217
Firminus, monastery in Palestine 183
Flavian, patriarch of Antioch 61
Florensky, Pavel 210
Four Tall Brothers 37, 81, 183
Frumentius, archbishop of Ethiopia 123

Galen 17, 18, 21
Galesion, mountain 91, 135, 140–1
Gangra, synod 60–1, 77, 184
Gaza 80–2, 87–9, 114–15
Gemistos Plethon 200
Genghis Khan 122
Gennadii, archbishop of Novgorod 167–8
Gennadios Scholarios 198
Genocide 213–14
Gerasimus, monastery in Palestine 65
Germanus, companion of John Cassian 107
Germanus, companion of Sabbatius 162
Gerontius, Monophysite monk 88
Glagolitic. *See* Cyrillic
Glycerius 18
Gorazd, companion of Cyril and Methodios 149

grazers. *See boskoi*
Great Laura 86–7, 89–92, 133, 142, 144, 153, 183–4, 189
Great Lavra on Mount Athos 133, 225
Gregory XV, pope 109, 213
Gregory Bar-Hebraeus 122
Gregory of Nazianzus 18, 69, 70, 74, 99, 133, 176, 179, 188
Gregory of Nyssa 69, 75, 76
Gregory of Sinai 155, 165, 189
Gregory Palamas 155, 161, 165, 189–91, 200, 205
Gundaphor, king in India 58
Gury, abbot of Trinity Sergius monastery 217
gyrovagi 2, 109

Habib Yirgis 230
Hadrian, Roman emperor 79
Haghia Sophia 95, 99, 157, 197
Helena, empress 79, 82
Henana, head of Persian School 112
Heraclius, Byzantine emperor 92
Hermas 20–1
hesychasm 5, 91, 155, 161, 165, 189–91, 206, 226
Hesychios the Priest 189
Hilarion, monk of Palestine 80–1
Hilarion, translator with Paisii 204
Hilarius, bishop of Arles 107
Hilary of Poitiers 107
Hilendar, monastery on Athos 138, 152–4, 224–5
Hippocrates 21, 46
Historia Monachorum 40, 46, 50–1
holy fools 65–6, 211, 223
Honoratus, monk of Lérins 107
Hulegu 122
Hypatius, abbot of Rouphinianoi 98
hypotyposis. See typikon

iconoclasm 77, 90, 101, 131, 139
icons 160
Ida, mountain 139–40
idiorrhythmia 23, 199–201, 202
ihidaya 1, 58
Ilarion, monk of Athos 208
Imiaslavie 208
Ioanichie Moroi, monk of Romania 227

Ioasaph, formerly emperor John V Kantakuzenos 190
Irenaeus, monk of Scetis 81
Isaac, the first monk 1
Isaac, monk of Dalmatou 96
Isaac the Syrian 119, 184–5
Isiaslav, friend of Theodosius of the Caves 158
Isidore I, patriarch of Constantinople 155
Isidore, Origenist monk 183
Iviron, monastery on Athos 144–5, 155, 224–5
Izla, mountain 116

Jacob Baradeus 116–18
James the apostle 20
Jericho 12, 65
Jerome 2, 80
Jerusalem
    doctrinal conflict 88–9, 183
    Holy City 4, 12, 40, 64, 79, 114, 132, 155
    monasteries 80–7, 102
Jesus Prayer 121, 185, 188–9, 207–8
Joannikios, hermit 102, 141
John V Oxites, patriarch of Antioch 134
John VII Grammatikos, patriarch of Constantinople 101–2
John, brother of Pachomius 42
John Calecas, patriarch of Constantinople 190
John Chrysostom 18, 99, 107
John, companion of Barsanuphius 81–2, 182
John, companion of Peter the Iberian 81, 114–15
John Glykys, patriarch of Constantinople 77
John Hephaistos, Monophysite priest 117
John Kalybites, monk of Constantinople 98
John Kolobos, an early monk on Athos 141
John Moschus 51, 81
John of Damascus 90, 91
John of Ephesus 115–18
John of Karpathos 123
John of the Ladder 165, 186, 227
John Rufus 115

John Scholasticus 116
John the Baptist 13
John the Dwarf 39
John the Iberian, abbot of Iviron 144
John Tornik 144
Joseph Gennesios, Byzantine chronicler 139
Joseph of Volokolamsk 166–70
Joseph the Hesychast 226
Josephus 13
Judaising heresy 167–8
Judas Thomas 58
Julian, Byzantine emperor 30, 70, 141
Julian Saba 24, 62, 77
Julius Yeshu Cicek, Syrian bishop 232
Justin, Byzantine emperor 115–16
Justinian, Byzantine emperor 86, 98, 115, 185
Justin Martyr 20
Juvenal, patriarch of Jerusalem 88, 114

Kafsokalyvia 145–6
Kaleb, Ethiopian king 124
Kallistos I, patriarch of Constantinople 155
Kallistos Ware, Metropolitan of Diokleia 229–30
kenoticism 160
Kiev 102, 157–8, 161, 165, 170, 204, 210
Kiter, Natalia 219
Kollyvades 205
Kondratiev, Mefodii, abbot in Russia 228
Kozlov, Mikhail, priest in Russia 207
Krushchev, Nikita 215
Kulikovo Field, battle 163
Kyminas mountain 139, 140–1, 142

Latros, mountain 92, 140–1
Lake Mareotis 14, 39
laurite
    development of use of term 52, 71, 86, 91–2, 140, 142, 201
    way of life 86
Lausiac History 46, 51
Lazarus of Mount Galesion 90, 135
Lent in the desert 83–5, 88, 90
Leonid Nagolkin, monk of Optina 207
Leontius, a married priest 18
Leontius of Byzantium 183
Leo pope 88

Lérins 107
Libanius 70
Ligugé, monastery of Martin 107

Macarius of Alexandria 39, 179
Macarius of Egypt 39, 179
Macarius, monastery in Egypt 53
Macarius, translator with Paisii 204, 206
Macedonius the Barley Eater 59
Macedonius, patriarch of Constantinople 96
Macrina 69–70, 77
Mahabere Kiddusan 231
Maiuma 87, 89, 114–5
Makarii Ivanov, monk of Optina 207
Makarios of Corinth 205, 229
Makhra, monastery of Sergius 162
Maksim Grek 160
Malenkov, Georgy 215
Mamas, monastery in Constantinople 135
Mani, Manichaeism 57
'Man of God' 66
Manuel II Palaiologos, Byzantine emperor 199
Manuel, patriarch of Constantinople 153
Mar Saba. *See* Great Laura
Marathonius 96
Marcellus, abbot of Akoimetoi monastery 98
Marcianus, holy man of Syria 62
Marcian, Byzantine emperor 113
Marcion 57
Marfo-Marinskii, convent in Russia 211, 228
Maria Skobtsova 220–1
Maria, daughter of Euphemia of Amida 116
Mar John Urtaya, monastery in Amida 115–16
Markos, monk of China. *See* Yaballaha III
Mar Mama monastery 116
Mar Mare, Syrian monk 99
Maro, holy man of Amida 115
Martin of Tours 107–8
martyrdom and persecution
    monk as martyr 36, 83–4
    persecution 29–30, 71, 75, 116, 177, 214–15
    tolerance after persecution 30

Martyrius, Origenist monastery 183
Martyrius, spiritual father of John of the Ladder 186
Marxism-Leninism 214–15
Mary of Egypt 40
Matrona 99
Matta el-Meskeen, Egyptian monk 231
Maximin, Roman emperor 36
Maximus the Confessor 180
Mecca 79, 121
Mehmet II 197–8
Melania the Elder 82, 179
Melania the Younger 82–3
Meletius, successor of Sabas 91
Merv 119
Mesopotamia 57, 60, 64, 71, 89–90, 112, 115
Messalians 59–61, 96, 98, 184
Methodios I, patriarch of Constantinople 102, 139
Methodius, apostle to the Slavs 149–51, 158
Metrophanes Kritopoulos 77
Michael Maleinos, spiritual father of Athanasios of Mount Athos 142
Michael Syncellus, monk of Mar Saba 90
Michael the Syrian 198
Mileševo 155
millet. *See* dhimmi
Monophysites 88–9, 90, 98–9, 113–19, 123
Monte Cassino 108
Mor Abraham, monastery in Tur Abdin 118–19
Mor Gabriel, monastery 118, 121, 232
Mor Hananaya. *See* Deir al Zafaran
Moscow
    autocephaly 157, 159
    Council of 1504 168
    Council of 1917 210, 215, 218
    monastic life 161–2, 219, 228
Moses 12, 40, 75, 186, 188
Mount of Olives 12, 82, 179
Muhammad 12, 121, 197
Mykale mountain 140

Narcissus of Jerusalem 80
Naucratius, brother of Basil 70
Naum 149–51
Neamt, monastery in Moldavia 204, 206
Nectarius, Patriarch of Constantinople 99

Neophytos 203
Nestor 159
Nestorianism 90
Nestorius 47, 97, 112
New Laura 85, 183
Nicaea, first Council in 325 5, 37, 90, 123, 153
   second Council in 787 201
Nicholas Cabasilas 169
Nicodemus, founder of monasteries in Wallachia 156
Nikiphoras Phokas, Byzantine emperor 132, 142, 144
Nikiphoros Kallistos 83
Nikiphoros the Monk 189
Nikiphoros, patriarch of Constantinople 101
Nikodimos of the Holy Mountain 205, 229
Nikon of the Black Mountain 74, 92
Nikon, successor of Sergius 163
Nilus of Ancyra 97
Nilus of Sora 165–70
Nine Syrian Saints of Ethiopia 123–4
Nisibis 4, 111–12, 121
Nitria 39, 41, 50, 179
Nonnus, Origenist monk 183
Non-Possessors 23, 165–70, 200

Olga, Russian princess 157
Olympias, Olympiados 99
Olympus mountain 102, 140, 149, 151
Optina 207–10
Or 41, 175
ordination 41, 114
Origen 16, 176–9
Origenism 37, 82, 107, 183, 193
Ostrov Vedensky, monastery in Russia 206

Pachomius
   life 33, 41–3
   monastic life 44–6, 52–3, 175
   significance 2, 33, 50
Pachomius the Serb 163
Paisii Velichkovskii 204–6, 229
Palamon 42, 45
Palladius 46, 50, 51, 65, 184
Palladius, holy man of Syria 62
Paphnutiev, monastery in Russia 166
Paregorius, a co-habiting priest 18
Paroria 155

Patmos 92, 139, 203
Paul, abbot of Evergetis 132, 136
Paul of Latros 140
Paul of New Laura, 183
Paul the Simple 39
Paul the Younger 92
Pelagia, Russian holy fool 211
Peter the Athonite 141
Peter of Callinicum 117
Peter the Great, Russian emperor 200–1, 206
Peter the Iberian 82, 89, 114–15
Peter, Patriarch of Alexandria 30
Pharan, monastery in Palestine 84
Phbow, monastery of Pachomius 42, 45
Philo of Alexandria 13–14
Philokales, monastery in Thessalonica 154
Philokalia 40, 51, 123, 176, 179, 191, 203, 205–6, 207, 227–30
Philotheos, Patriarch of Constantinople 92, 156, 162
Philotheou, monastery of Athos 226
Photeinos, father of Theodore the Stoudite 100
Photius, Patriarch of Constantinople 157
pilgrims 83
Pjol 46
Plato 14, 21
Platon, uncle of Thedore the Stoudite 100, 140
Pliny the elder 13
Polikhron, monastery of Constantinople 149
Poplars, monastery in Syria 116
Porphyry, neo-Platonist philosopher 21
Pospielovsky, Dimitry 159
Possessors 165–70, 200
Procopius 120
property
   ambivalence of New Testament 23
   conflict over property 134–5, 165–8, 199–200
   wealth in monasteries 82–3
prostrations 64, 97, 121, 185
Pseudo-Macarius 60, 122, 184
Pschoi, monastery of Pachomius 47

Qenneshrin, monastery in Syria 118

Rabban Hormuzd, monastery at Mosul 119
Rabban Shahpur, monastery in Persia 184
Rabbula of Edessa 76
Red Monastery 47
Remnuoth 2
Romanus Lekapenos, Byzantine emperor 133, 141
Rufinus 50, 82, 184
Rule of the Master 108–9

Sabas 84–7, 100, 152, 183
Sabbatius 162
St Anne's Monastery on Athos 205
St Catherine's Monastery on Sinai 185
St Mamas, monastery in Constantinople 187
St Panteleimon Monastery on Athos 151, 208, 224–5, 229
St Serge Institute, Paris 230
St Vladimir's Seminary, New York 230
Sakkoudion, monastery in Constantinople 100, 140
Sarabaites 2, 109
Sava 152–6
Sayfa Arad, Ethiopian king 126
Sayings of the Desert Fathers 39–40, 51, 81, 180
Scetis 39, 53
schema 3, 45
Schneider, A-M 86
Seleucia-Ctesiphon 4, 57, 111, 119, 198
Serapion, abbot of Trinity Sergius 168
Seraphim of Sarov 206, 209, 211
Serapion of Thmuis, monk-bishop 37
Sergiou, monastery in Constantinople 99
Sergius of Radonezh 92, 156, 160–5
Seridus 81
Severus of Scythopolis 115
Shaanxi pagoda 122
Shahpur I, Persian king 111
Shahpur II, Persian king 111, 119
Shem'un of Qartmin 118
Shenoute 46–50, 53, 59
Shepherd of Hermas 17, 20–21
Shmuyel of Eshtin 118
Sian Fu stela 120
Sihastria, monastery in Romania 227
Silouan 226, 229

Silvanus 81
Simonopetra, monastery on Athos 226
Simonov monastery on Russia 162
Sinai 12, 40, 155, 185, 189
sketes 145, 163
Slatina, monastery in Romania 227
Sleepless Monks. *See Akoimetoi*
Socrates Scholasticus 60, 74
Soloviev, Vladimir 206
Solovki 92, 162, 206
Sophronius, Patriarch of Jerusalem 51, 91
Sophrony Sakharov 226, 229
Souka, monastery in Palestine 84
Sozomen 59–61, 74, 81, 175
Sretensky monastery in Moscow 228
Stalin, Joseph 215
Staniloe, Dumitru 229
Stavronikita, monastery on Athos 146
Stephan Dušan, king of Serbia 151
Stephan II, king of Serbia 152–3
Stephen, brother of Sergius 161
Stephen the Hagiopolite 90
Stephen the Younger 77
Stoudios monastery 70, 91, 92, 100–2, 132, 158, 187, 197
Studenica, monastery in Serbia 152–3
stylites 63
Sufis 121
Sulpicius Severus 107
Suriani monastery in Egypt 53
Susan 116
Sventitsky, Valentin 218
Sycamores, monastery in Syria 116
Sykae, monastery on Constantinople 99, 115, 117
Symeon, king of Bulgaria 151
Symeon Nemanja 152–3
Symeon of Constantinople 77
Symeon of Mesopotamia. *See* Pseudo-Macarius
Symeon of Thessalonica 91
Symeon Salos 65–6
Symeon Stylites 63–4, 88
Symeon the New Theologian 180, 186–7, 191
Symeon the Pious 186
Syncletica 40
syneisaktism 17
Synesius of Cyrene 76

Syria
  asceticism 1, 58, 60
  in Constantinople 95–8
  culture 57–8, 111–13
  holy men 61–6
  influence 70, 76, 80, 87
  renewal 232
  spirituality 184–5
Syrian Orthodox 213–14

Tabennesis, monastery of Pachomius 42
Takla Haymonot 124–7
Tavrion Batovsky, Russian monk 219
Theoctistus 84–5
Theodora 40
Theodora, Byzantine Empress 139
Theodora, Byzantine Empress, married to Justinian 98–9, 115, 117
Theodore I Lascaris, Byzantine emperor 153
Theodore Graptos or the branded 90
Theodore of Abu Qurrah 90
Theodore of Ashkelon 114
Theodore, successor of Pachomius 42, 44
Theodore the Stoudite 100–2, 140, 143
Theodoret of Cyrrhus 24, 61, 63–4, 112
Theodosius I, Byzantine emperor 114, 176
Theodosius II, Byzantine emperor 82, 97, 114, 133
Theodosius, archimandrite in Palestine 85
Theodosius, Monophysite patriarch of Alexandria 115–17
Theodosius, Monophysite Patriarch of Jerusalem 88
Theodosius of the Caves 103, 158
Theodosius of Turnovo 155
Theoktiste, mother of Theodore 100
Theophanes Graptos or the Branded 90
Theophan the Recluse 210
Theophilus, Archbishop of Alexandria 183
Theophylact of Ohrid 150
Therapeutae 14
Tikhon Belavin, patriarch of Moscow 210
Timothy 1, catholicos 120
Trans-Volga elders 165–7
Trinity Sergius monastery 160, 168, 201, 210, 215–17
Triumph of Orthodoxy 131, 136
Tur Abdin 111, 116, 118
Turfan 122
typikon and
  examples of typika and rules 73–4, 91–2, 101–2, 108–9, 137–8, 146
  oral and written rules 43, 45–6, 91–2
  transmission of typkika and rules 91–2, 138, 142–3, 152–3
  typikon as monastic rule 134–5

Valaam, monastery in Russia 206
Valerian, Roman emperor 29, 75
Valeriya Mekeyeva, Russian nun 219
Varlaam, metropolitan of Moscow 169
Varsaanofy, abbot of Optina 208
Vassian Patrikeev 168–9
Vatopedi, monastery on Athos 160, 203, 226
virgins
  communities 17–19, 41, 50, 58, 75, 80
  subversive 18–19, 70, 80
Vladimir, Russian prince 157–61
Vorobiev, Vladimir 228

Waldebba, monastery in Ethiopia 127
Way of the Pilgrim 207
White Monastery or Deir Anba Shenouda 47
widows 69
withdrawal 16, 34–5

Xeniteia 109
xerophagy 22
Xylourgou or tou Rhos, monastery on Athos 158, 165

Yaballaha III, or Markos 121–2
Ya'eqob, Archbishop of Ethiopia 125
Yale Monastic Archeology Project 47
Yohanni, monk in Ethiopia 125

Zachariah of Mitylene 115
Zacharias, disciple of Silvanus 81
Za-Mikael. *See* Aregawi
Zannus 91
Zeno, Byzantine emperor 81–2
Zernov, Nicolas 214
Žiča, monastery in Serbia 153–4
Zographou, monastery on Athos 224–5
Zonaras 132
Zossima, companion of Mary of Egypt 40
Zossima, Metropolitan of Moscow 168
Z'ura 99

www.ingramcontent.com/pod-product-compliance
Lightning Source LLC
Chambersburg PA
CBHW070028010526
44117CB00011B/1743